Independent School Libraries

Recent Titles in Libraries Unlimited
Professional Guides in School Librarianship Series

Harriet Selverstone, Series Editor

Independent School Libraries

Perspectives on Excellence

Dorcas Hand, Editor

Libraries Unlimited Professional Guides in School Librarianship Series

Harriet Selverstone, Series Editor

LIBRARIES UNLIMITED

AN IMPRINT OF ABC-CLIO, LLC
Santa Barbara, California • Denver, Colorado • Oxford, England

Library of Congress Cataloging-in-Publication Data

Independent school libraries : perspectives on excellence / Dorcas Hand, editor.
        p. cm. — (Libraries Unlimited professional guides in school librarianship series)
    Includes bibliographical references and index.
    ISBN 978-1-59158-803-0 (pbk. : acid-free paper) — ISBN 978-1-59158-812-2 (ebook) 1. Private school libraries—United States.
I. Hand, Dorcas.
Z675.S3I35   2010
025.1'978—dc22   2010014567

14 13 12 11 10 1 2 3 4 5

ISBN 978-1-59158-803-0
EISBN 978-1-59158-812-2

This book is also available on the World Wide Web as an eBook.
Visit www.abc-clio.com for details.

Libraries Unlimited
An Imprint of ABC-CLIO, LLC

ABC-CLIO, LLC
130 Cremona Drive, P.O. Box 1911
Santa Barbara, California 93116-1911

This book is printed on acid-free paper ∞
Manufactured in the United States of America

Contents

Foreword

Pauline Anderson

"The tomorrows come and go so swiftly that it is not feasible to plan for only one tomorrow in the world of libraries; one must plan for a series of unknown tomorrows ... new technological developments, new concepts of library services, new teaching methods, new curricular developments and revised purposes and goals of our schools will affect our libraries in one of the tomorrows." In 1980 I included those words in *The Library in the Independent School*, published by the National Association of Independent Schools. Three decades of those "tomorrows" have indeed brought changes, mostly technological, which have affected school libraries in dramatic ways.

Generations of librarians have faced new tools and technologies, from early telephones through computers. My generation welcomed copy machines, fax machines, microforms and their readers, film loops, TV, videocassettes, overhead projectors, early versions of computers, and relatively unsophisticated databases. Each new device became an effective tool for helping libraries accomplish their primary mission of functioning as intellectual forces within their schools. The attention of the media to computers tends to make this tool more important than any other ever invented, but in reality the computer is but one more logical tool to take its place in our highly mechanized society.

Despite dire predictions of pessimists that neither libraries nor printed pages would survive, both survive and flourish. Traditional services and programs exist, but the methods of delivery have changed radically. New technologies have caused some services and programs to be redefined even as new ones were being created. New issues such as filtering, gaming, and maintaining intellectual integrity had to be addressed; library infrastructures remained in place but became attuned to the new technologies.

Keeping abreast of changing terminology has been almost as quirky as keeping up with new technologies. Occasionally one had freedom of choice, such as deciding to remain a librarian rather than becoming a library media specialist, or choosing to reign over a library rather than a library media center. Terms such as "AV" became obsolete, and Amazon was no longer just a romantic river. Google acquired a life of its own and is no longer associated with the Barney Google of comic strip fame. The purposes of some interesting developments are lost in what appears to be a new version of "Jabberwocky." What might Lewis Carroll have made of the Lexis-Nexis Due Diligence Dashboard? (http://corporate.lexisnexis.com/Cms_managed_files/documents/DDD_Procure.pdf). The practices of communication and library promotion have merged into "advocacy," and navigating one's way through changing terminology has become a tricky art.

Librarians in independent schools have long been a close-knit group, drawn together by the freedom to develop resources, programs, services, and facilities to meet the needs of parent institutions in the absence of a far-flung bureaucracy. Many avenues of communication—informal and formal—are available. Group sharing through informal, local organizations and one-on-one contacts is supplemented by formal groups such as the Association of Independent School Librarians (AISL) and the American Association of School Librarians (AASL). Independent school librarians have now banded together to share talents, "ways and means" of administration, views of dynamic leadership, creativity, and problem solving in this book, *Independent School Libraries: Perspectives on Excellence*.

The tomorrows will continue to come and go swiftly, and each will bring new developments: physical, academic, literary, technological, mechanical, and linguistic. Librarians will continue to adapt to new developments, new ways, and new thinking to support their mission to meet the needs of their users. As part of that process, readers can learn from the present and look into the future in the following essays by peer librarians of the independent school community. Independence of thought remains a hallmark of librarianship in the independent school world, and that independence will facilitate new paths to a traditional service ethic.

> *Pauline Anderson wrote* The Library in the Independent School *(NAIS, 1968; second edition, 1980),* Library Media Leadership in Academic Secondary Schools *(Shoestring, 1985) and* Planning School Library Facilities *(Shoestring, 1990). The retired director of the Andrew Mellon Library at the Choate Rosemary Hall in Wallingford, Connecticut, Pauline is a founding member of both the Association of Independent School Librarians (AISL) and the Independent School Section (ISS) of the American Association of School Librarians (AASL). In her retirement, she continues to mentor independent school librarians and to volunteer her expertise to libraries in her home community. We who have written for this book are honored to follow her lead, offering here the first book on independent school libraries published in more than twenty years.*

Acknowledgments

It takes a village to make a book—well, to make this book. Many independent school librarians across the country took time to answer listserv and individual requests for information. Without their support, this book would not have the breadth of experience and examples it offers readers. Our independent school library community is strong and vibrant.

In particular, we thank Dianne Langlois for her inspirational class, "Libraries in the Age of Google," offered at the Taft Education Center in summer 2006, and for her ongoing support of this book effort.

Jen Cotton and Karen MacMeekin of Colorado Academy will work to set up and maintain the accompanying Web site.

C. D. McLean (Berkeley Preparatory School, Tampa, Florida) and Betsy Ginsburg (retired, St. Francis Episcopal Day School, Houston, Texas) provided editing support—more eyes are definitely better.

Lauren Singer of Houston, Texas, provided some graphics know-how.

Harriet Selverstone and Sharon Coatney of Libraries Unlimited have patiently shepherded this book from the drawing board to completion.

And I thank my library staff and the administration of Annunciation Orthodox School (Houston, Texas), who encouraged my efforts at village leadership and writing.

Introduction

Dorcas Hand, Editor

The word "essay" comes from the French verb *essayer*, to try. In the Middle Ages, students worked out their thoughts for professors in essays. In gathering these essays together, we have tried to collect useful and discerning thoughts on independent school libraries today and looking forward into the future. We have worked to break down the overarching concept of a library program into approachable elements that would allow us to reasonably present our understandings. However, library programs are vibrant because their various elements are entirely interrelated. The resources we buy depend on the school's mission and the curriculum we support, as well as on library staff time, knowledge, and budgetary constraints. Digital resources are only as accessible as available hardware and Internet access make them. The library's efforts to advocate for its students and program demonstrate success when the facility and materials are used by students. Development and institutional advancement support the budget and funding aspects of the library, and they use the excellence of the library as a demonstration to the outside world of the standards the school upholds for programs and student achievement. Every essay in this book relies directly on several other essays, and indirectly on all of them.

A group of independent school librarians, some of them among the authors of these essays, collaborated in the winter of 2008 to write what became the National Association of Independent Schools *NAIS Guidelines of Professional Practice for Librarians* (GPP). Several essays refer to these guidelines, which are included as appendix A. NAIS is an umbrella organization for accrediting agencies for many independent schools. That the GPP was the first posted to www.NAIS.org speaks to the determination of both the librarians who wrote the document and the organization that saw them as important; the posting also speaks to the need of the community of schools and librarians for guidelines that could strengthen their campus library programs.

The writing of these essays pushed each of us to reconsider our own current practices and to seek ideas from our colleagues across the country. Action research was alive and well as we sought examples to illustrate our points. The resulting conversations demonstrated the reasons we are such a strong professional community. Independent school librarians are simultaneously independent and collaborative, looking always to both our individual school missions and the broader world of school libraries, public and independent, for fresh perspectives on similar problems. We model our stated goal of "developing lifelong learners" as we consistently work to develop new solutions to ever-changing issues. We are living in the tomorrows to which Pauline Anderson refers in her foreword, and we are looking ahead to more decades of tomorrows and their anticipated changing demands on our libraries.

We offer this book to current independent school librarians who would like to reconsider their own policies and practices; to administrators who would like to better understand excellence in library service; and to new practitioners who aspire to become leaders in the community of independent school libraries. We recognize that many of the core principles here apply equally to all school libraries, whether in public or independent schools, and we hope these essays will be of some interest to the wider community as well.

We also offer a Web site that extends the content of the book, providing direct links to schools and information referred to in the essays: **http://www.lu.com/excellence.** Looking ahead from 2010, libraries will likely maintain book collections, but they will also support digital materials; this book does the same.

The Librarian as Gardener

Liz Gray, Dana Hall School (Wellesley, MA)

> *Gardening and scholarship were not so different; both took long hours and single-mindedness, resiliency in the face of major setbacks, a gift for tedium and a flair for the marriage of the unusual. Both strained the eyes and the lower back and depended to some degree on fate, prejudice, perspective and the intuitive flash.*
>
> —Beverly Lowry, *Breaking Gentle*

A well-tended garden, no matter its shape or size, is a wonder to behold. With its clear design and unique personality, it is invariably a welcoming and sheltering space. The daughter of two accomplished English gardeners, I am cursed with a black thumb when it comes to tending anything imbued with chlorophyll. However, I do see many parallels between my role as a librarian in an independent school library and the crucial role of a gardener in making a garden grow and thrive. In the words of a librarian at an all-girls, K–12 day school in Virginia (and the wife of a landscape architect), "A good library is like a good garden: it has structure provided by a harmonious blend of evergreens (the basic print collection), perennials (those titles—both print and non-print and digital) that come back, updated and renewed, each year, and annuals (the hot new titles and trends). Plus, like a garden, a library provides solace and feeds both the soul and the mind" (Gray 2009). It is the daily care and feeding by committed librarians that cultivates a healthy library.

My mother told me that the elements of a successful garden are shape, perspective, discovery of vistas, skillful use of light and shade, and knowledge of plants (Gladstone 2009). Though futile to me as a gardener, this information serves me well as a librarian. In a library, shape means having a clear mission and a program and a facility that support it. Perspective is the knowledge of where one's library sits relative to standards, best practices, and the school community that

> "A good library is like a good garden: it has structure provided by a harmonious blend of evergreens (the basic print collection), perennials (those titles—both print and non-print and digital) that come back, updated and renewed, each year, and annuals (the hot new titles and trends). Plus, like a garden, a library provides solace and feeds both the soul and the mind."

it serves. Discovery of vistas entails taking advantage of your school, your faculty, and your librarians' unique strengths. Skillful use of light and shade can be equated with establishing the correct balance of instruction and programming and finding the time to establish a strong infrastructure to support both. And finally, the all-important plants are the resources we collect over time, which will meet the needs of our users. To create this vibrant and thriving garden, the gardener/librarian must shape, fertilize, plant, water, and prune.

Shape

Shape is the consideration of the result to be achieved and has to take into account the way the light falls and the nature and quality of the soil. In a library, this translates into establishing goals and objectives, bearing in mind the students and faculty with whom one is working and the amount of time and money available to accomplish the goals. As in a garden, shaping must be repeated with every new cycle of the seasons.

The main challenges in creating one's desired shape in an independent school library are the exponential growth of information to be evaluated and the increased number of responsibilities required of the librarian. Like a gardener, a librarian is called upon to play a multiplicity of roles. In the library itself, there are the expected ones—teacher of information literacy skills, subject specialist, readers' advisor, department head and manager (if one is fortunate enough to have librarian colleagues); the ones learned through time and experience—facility manager, mediator, budget wizard, counselor to both children and adults, and archivist and/or school historian; the ones that in other environments are considered entirely separate careers—event planner, graphic designer, writer, Web page designer; and finally, ones that even those of us with active imaginations never dreamed of, like bathroom custodian. Then there are the nonlibrary roles, which include but are not limited to dance and weekend duty chaperone; dorm parent; yearbook and club advisor; car pool, playground, and lunch room monitor; committee member; trip coordinator; student and class advisor; exam proctor; hospital driver; AP coordinator; receptionist; textbook distributor; grade dean; study hall scheduler; and bus pass administrator.

Given this multiplicity of roles, the most important skill of all is the ability to juggle many balls, whether they be Web sites or job responsibilities. There are definite benefits to being a fully involved member of a school community, particularly a residential community, and as professionals, we enjoy helping people get what they need and often step up to the plate when asked to do so.

Cultivating our library garden takes time, and its success depends on the judicious investment of our professional resources.

However, one has to be wary of allowing the nonlibrary responsibilities to overshadow the library ones. Cultivating our library garden takes time, and its success depends on the judicious investment of our professional resources.

In addition to the demands on our time delineated above, in many of our institutions we have to spend a great deal of our available time educating others about what we do and explaining how we add value to the curriculum. Our ability to do this is governed in part by our placement in the school's organizational structure. An unscientific online survey conducted in June 2009, to which 141 independent school librarians from twenty-five states, Canada, China, and Morocco responded, revealed that although 76 percent of us are considered faculty, 7 percent are staff, 5 percent are administrators, and 11 percent are not classified in any of these categories. In addition, only 65 percent of those surveyed are considered department heads. This is in spite of the fact that, of the librarians surveyed, not only do 68 percent hold a master's in library science, but 17 percent also hold an additional advanced degree (Gray 2009).

As we set goals and work to achieve them each year, we also need to remember that "despite the gardener's best intentions, Nature will improvise" (Garofalo 2008). Sometimes these improvisations sidetrack us in negative ways and slow down our progress; at other times they deliver unexpected gifts that enrich our programs. One librarian in a K–12 coed day school in Rhode Island transformed her author visit program after a chance conversation with an art teacher led her to the realization that she could have an even greater impact with an author-illustrator program. And those of us who spend hours that we don't really have learning new technologies when they are first introduced often become the ones in our school who mentor others in the acquisition of these skills. Shaping the library garden is a continuous process that requires the librarian to be flexible and adaptable.

Fertilize

In "If I Were Beginning Again," Marion Cran (1995) says "if I wanted to have a happy garden, I must ally myself with my soil; study and help it to the utmost, untiringly. . . . Always, the soil must come first." Happy soil requires the gardener to dig in as much fertilizer as possible to get the earth in good heart prior to planting. In any flourishing school library, this requires the librarian to build a strong collection, create a welcoming and pleasing environment, establish ties to faculty and their curricula, and be an involved member of the school community.

The extent to which independent school librarians become involved in the school community has been referenced above, but one area of involvement that bears expanding upon is committee membership. Much of the

> *"[I]f I wanted to have a happy garden, I must ally myself with my soil; study and help it to the utmost, untiringly. . . . Always, the soil must come first."*

forward motion in an independent school—around curriculum, technology, and interdisciplinary work—is initiated and developed in committee work, and it is essential that librarians be a part of all these conversations. Participation in these committees is usually voluntary, but the value of being a part of the process cannot be overestimated.

Although later essays describe in greater detail the guiding principles of effective collection development, facility planning, and curricular collaboration, here are some examples of the many creative and unique things that independent school librarians do to prepare their soil: lead weekly book discussion groups, teach a knitting activity to ninth graders, sponsor community service trips, tutor reading and study skills after school, teach courses as varied as world mythology and AP Spanish, serve on the Honor Society committee, advocate for and manage a redesign of the library, administer Birthday Book programs and annual book fairs that supplement the library's acquisition budget, prepare summer reading lists, sponsor author visits, and participate in schoolwide curricular initiatives.

Plant

The successful gardener/librarian plants with a view to maintaining interest in the garden throughout the year: she teaches a variety of skills tied to specific curricular projects, changes displays and modifies the Web site and/or blog regularly, and keeps ahead of the curve on technological innovations. Maintaining interest in the library garden also involves engaging in a variety of advocacy and public relations activities and asserting the library's role in issues and initiatives like intellectual freedom, diversity, and sustainability that have schoolwide impact. In the words of a librarian at a coed, boarding, day high school in Michigan, "Advocacy involves making sure the administration and faculty know what the librarians do and what our present and future role is in this age of advanced technology and the Internet—through discussions, reports and any other means possible" (Gray 2009). Essay 6 expands on this point.

Gardeners are encouraged to always bear in mind the Line of Beauty, which, according to eighteenth-century artist William Hogarth, is an S-shaped curve. Such a curve signifies liveliness and activity and excites the attention of the viewer, as contrasted with straight lines, parallel lines, or right-angled intersecting lines, which signify stasis, death, or inanimate objects. In planting our libraries, this Line of Beauty can be interpreted not only literally, in the physical design of a space, but also figuratively, in creative ways of implementing programming, instruction, and even collection development. Sometimes doing the unexpected or planting a new variety results in the rejuvenation of the garden.

Water

"Gardening requires lots of water—most of it in the form of perspiration," says gardener Lou Erickson (Garofalo 2008). After the hard work of designing, fertilizing, and planting a garden comes the need for regular irrigation, which is essential to growth; without water most plants eventually wither and die. For the gardener/ librarian, this watering process includes building the collection steadily and continuously, talking with students and faculty every day and therefore staying in touch with their needs and concerns, making improvements and additions to the physical environment and to the ways in which information is communicated, and engaging in continuous professional development.

Professional development is especially important to school librarians, the majority of whom work alone or with one or two other colleagues. We do not function within a larger library community as our public and academic library colleagues do, and the faculty members whose curriculum we work to support sometimes have to be convinced of our value as teaching partners. In an independent school, we have the added challenge of working within an institution whose very existence depends on it defining itself as different from all others. Such a challenge can be a great opportunity, but it also serves as an additional isolating factor.

Independent school librarians have responded to their need for professional growth in four major ways: by participating in workshops and attending conferences side-by-side with other teachers; by joining the same school library media associations as public school librarians; by participating in national, regional, and local independent school library associations; and by taking advantage of electronic education and networking opportunities. The sidebar lists some specific examples from the survey of recent professional development activities; more details on professional development resources can be in found in essay 4.

Recent Professional Development Activity

- Regional evaluation teams (e.g., NEASC, ISACS)
- Travel grant to Denmark to research the life of Hans Christian Andersen
- Spanish immersion program in Mexico
- Workshops on learning differences, International Baccalaureate (IB), critical thinking, library leadership, and advocacy
- Oxbridge Library and the Academy Seminar in England
- Provincetown Fine Arts Work Center writing workshops
- National Educational Computing Conference (NECC)
- Gerard Manley Hopkins Poetry Festival in Ireland
- Columbia University's Institute on the Teaching of Reading
- Simmons College's National Children's Literature Conference

---

Clearly, the choices for professional development for independent school librarians are many, and there is not enough time or money available to take advantage of them all. We owe it to ourselves and our gardens, however, to engage in as many of these opportunities as we can. In the words of Colin S. Diver, president of Reed College, "Teachers cannot educate others without constantly educating themselves"; the same holds true for school librarians. Even a modest investment in this area pays large dividends in keeping us current, improving our skills, introducing us to colleagues in librarianship and education, and helping us avoid becoming discouraged in difficult times.

> *"Teachers cannot educate others without constantly educating themselves."*

Prune

The final and, in many ways the most important, step in creating a successful garden is pruning to maintain shape and balance, so that no one element dominates or takes precedence over another and unwanted plants (also known as weeds) are eradicated. In the library, pruning means weeding of resources; it also means evaluation, the constant examination of our collections, programs, facilities, instructional practices and, yes, ourselves to confirm that we are fulfilling our mission and meeting our goals, to determine what is obsolete and how we can improve. Time and the daily grind have a way of derailing us from this essential element of the growth process; there always seem to be more important things to do, and often there is no one in our schools who is encouraging us in our endeavors.

Individual evaluation in particular is an area fraught with concern for many independent school librarians. Though we work in education, the professional training for our field is unfamiliar territory for most administrators, who are often not even sure how (or even if) to evaluate us. A librarian at a coed K–8 day school in Massachusetts expressed her frustration at the fact that "I am only evaluated on my teaching with students, which is only a portion of my job" (Gray 2009). In the survey, 88 percent of respondents indicated that they are evaluated as librarians, 65 percent as teachers, and 47 percent as department heads. However, only 42 percent are evaluated every year, and 40 percent are evaluated irregularly or not at all.

Clearly, though, evaluation matters to independent school librarians. "I would welcome more feedback on a regular basis from both the administration and from the teachers I collaborate with" (Gray 2009), says a librarian at an all-boys K–8 day school in New York City, echoing the sentiments of many of her colleagues. Overwhelmingly, respondents wished that they were evaluated not only frequently and consistently, but also for all of their professional responsibilities, not just the ones, such as classroom instruction, with which administrators feel comfortable. Sometimes this requires inviting peer librarians from other schools to be part of the evaluation process, and it also places responsibility on the librarian to communicate successes and concerns to administrators even if they haven't been solicited (see essay 7).

It is not surprising that so many independent school librarians remain at their libraries for long periods of time. Cultivating a library takes time, particularly if it was in disrepair when one started tilling the soil, and as professionals we enjoy savoring the fruits of our labors. Shaping the many and varied components of a library program over the years is immensely satisfying, especially when one's efforts are validated by comments from students such as, "I feel truly blessed to have such a wonderful library available for my use and would like to thank all the librarians for their hard work and dedication to our school and library" (Helen Temple Cooke Library 2009).

Shaping the many and varied components of a library program over the years is immensely satisfying.

Mirabel Osler (1998) was mistaken when she said, "There can be no other occupation like gardening in which, if you were to creep up behind someone at their work, you would find them smiling." As we fertilize, plant, water, and prune our library gardens, and despite our occasional complaints and concerns, independent school librarians are grinning from ear to ear.

References

Cran, Marion. 1995. "If I Were Beginning Again." In *Garden Dreams,* ed. Ferris Cook, 51. New York: Stewart, Tabori & Chang.

Diver, Colin S. 2002. "Letter to Reed College Alumni." September 20.

Garofalo, Michael P., ed. 2008. *The Spirit of Gardening*. December 31. www. gardendigest.com. Accessed May 21, 2009.

Gladstone, Caroline. 2009. E-mail to author, April 18.

Gray, Liz. 2009. "Librarian as Gardener." *SurveyMonkey* file. June 30.

Helen Temple Cooke Library, Dana Hall School. 2009. "Let's Eat Cake." *Survey Monkey* file. June 7.

Hogarth, William. 1997. *The Analysis of Beauty*. New Haven, CT: Yale University Press, 48–59.

Lowry, Beverly. 1988. *Breaking Gentle*. New York: Viking, 65.

Osler, Mirabel. 1998. *A Breath from Elsewhere: Musings on Gardens*. New York: Arcade Publishing.

Visit http://lu.com/excellence for supporting links and occasional updates to all essays in this book.

Liz Gray has attended or worked at eight independent schools in Italy, England, Switzerland, and Massachusetts. She is now Library Director at Dana Hall School (www.danahall.org) in Wellesley, Massachusetts. She has also worked in a large public library, a small academic art library, and a bookstore warehouse. Her professional interests include library space planning, memoir, documentary film, art in libraries, and international education. On the rare occasions when she is not in library land, Liz is compiling a bibliography of women's memoirs, writing her own memoir, knitting, and organizing the contents of her home.

Where We Fit In: The Library in the Life of the School

Carolyn Hilles, The Wheeler School (Providence, RI)

Maybe it's in a small set of rooms placed strategically behind glass in the main hallway of a busy suburban classroom building, with well-placed displays to attract passing middle school students and their teachers. Perhaps it's housed in an imposing brick building near the gate of a New England boarding school, scattered with students curled up with their laptops in leather chairs and bent over homework at oak tables lit with study lamps. Or it could be a sunny floor in an informal downtown Toronto day school where a librarian is reading to a circle of kindergartners, asking them questions about each picture before he turns the page. In Houston, a history teacher may be conferring with a student over a research paper draft, while a librarian across the room is showing others in the class how to navigate through the array of databases available on the school's Web site.

Libraries in independent schools are busy places, frequently referred to by school heads as the intellectual heart of the school, or as "the center of everything" by other members of the school community, including students. The library is a place for personal intellectual growth, an extension of the classroom for research and discovery, a computer center with tech-savvy staff available for help, a comfortable spot for relaxing, a study area, a place to collaborate, and an inviting space for holding events and programs. It is not only a symbolic representation of intellectual freedom at a school—a physical place where the right of individuals to read whatever they want is encouraged, promoted, and protected—but a central place to take questions about copyright law and practice and minor's rights.

Hours typically extend before and after the school day in independent school libraries, and in some cases,

Freedom to Think and Learn

particularly in boarding schools, into weekends and summers. Often libraries become a home base in a school for parent volunteers and a prized location for formal and informal tutoring. The social role libraries play in upper schools in particular cannot be ignored, along with the

Who Are We? Statistics

time-honored fact that the library can be a place to be alone to catch up on work—or not.

9

Independent school libraries come in all sorts of sizes and styles. Some are well-funded and staffed, some do as well as they can with less. The rhythm of the school day and academic year create patterns of activity and quiet unique to each library. All share the traditional mission of supporting curriculum, connecting learners with resources, and promoting the love and appreciation of reading by creating collections and service to guide readers to as many well-written books as they can. And all do much more. This book features essays that explore in depth the issues and best practices related to independent school librarianship.

A school's library accomplishes a complex set of roles within its institution, as the scope and content of this volume attest. Although an independent school's library parallels in many important respects any library in any school, the amazing variety of setting and approach represented by the independent school world means that no two of its libraries look, feel, or work the same. Each school and its librarians create a setting and program that fit the philosophy, budget, and age group served by the institution. As one leader in the field has said, "It's not hard to think outside of the box—because there is no box!"

In the same way independence characterizes independent schools, the libraries in these educational settings operate without the restrictions—or the benefits—of the state oversight, district support, and externally provided standards of their public school peers. This independence creates many challenges, but also allows for an exciting degree of freedom. Librarians in particular have been very successful at forming consortia and professional organizations at the local, regional, and national levels that help them connect with others to keep up with trends, share resources, and establish guidelines for best practices.

> **We Are Not Alone**

Independent schools are small, not-for-profit businesses that must decide for themselves what their mission is and how to fund, staff, and promote their distinctive offering to parents and students. Accreditation comes from peer review in regional organizations, is mission-based, and includes an evaluative review of how well the library serves the overall vision of the school. The library also participates in the promotion of the school, through a vibrant Web presence and other activities that support development; essay 18 offers a deeper look at this topic.

> **Navel Gazing**

On a very basic level, an independent school library is an organization within an organization, with all that entails—facility and technology to plan and maintain; hours to staff; staff to supervise and evaluate; a budget to plan for, present, and keep. Depending on the size of the school and the age group served, this organizational structure can range from a modest, colorfully decorated elementary school setting to a large boarding school library that may resemble a college facility. It's difficult to generalize about the independent school world. But whatever its size or type, each school makes a decision about how the library fits into its structure organizationally; how library staff members fit into its faculty, administrative, and staff structure and how to evaluate them; and what the library's relationship is to the technology department and media services program at the school. Libraries also carry out their own action research to determine how their facility, collection, and resources are being used and determine how to better serve the community.

> **The Bigger Picture**
> **Advocacy Through Assessment**
> **Don't Lose It All**

> **What Does It Cost?**
> **Balancing the Budget**

Any school library is, by definition, a teaching environment. This may seem obvious, but school librarians often find that they need to explain the nature of their curriculum and instruction—what it is that they "do" with the students they serve. As teachers and sometimes advisors, librarians in schools establish relationships with students that sometimes span many years, particularly in multidivisional schools. Librarians often seek purchasing recommendations from students, and constantly learn from knowing and observing them as well. And, as in any library, there is an important public service component in the mission of a school library that extends beyond building student skills, helping them research, or providing them with traditional reading materials. The school's library is a direct resource for faculty, staff, parents, and others in the school community. When an administrator needs a booklist for a Parents' Night program, or a dean wants a set of articles available for teachers to prepare for an all-faculty program, she knows to ask the librarian. When librarians promote their services well enough, they find that not only do more teachers want to work with them on behalf of student learning, but more and more members of the school community come to them for personal recommendations and research help, and they are approached with increasing frequency by administrators to give presentations and teach the adults in the community as well as the students. They are also less likely to find that their budgets suffer in times when administrators need to look for places in the school's finances to make cuts.

> **To Collaborate or Not to Collaborate**
> **Are They Ready for the Next Step?**
> **Choices, Choices**

> **The Many Faces of Advocacy**

> **What Else Can We Do?**

Events and special programs that extend beyond the basics of instruction usually punctuate and highlight the library's school year—speakers, contests, poetry slams, book groups, author readings, even art and music programs. The school's library provides leadership about the ever-changing world of information technology and how those changes need to be planned for and implemented in the library and schoolwide.

> **Faster Than a Speeding Bullet**
> **Sea Changes**
> **Looking Back to the Future**

The school's library staff members not only work with other technology leaders on campus to bring the most recent digital tools to the community, but often play a role in maintaining the school's history and creating traditions of their own. Most schools keep a collection of alumni authors in their library. Sometimes the archives are part of the library's domain. Alumni of Exeter Academy keep the Senior Bookmarks they designed—with lists of their favorite books on them—for the rest of their lives.

The library is invariably among the most attractively furnished public spaces on campus and, for this reason, frequently serves as a public "face" of the school, a natural spot for a televised interview to be set up, for example, or for a fund-raising reception event. Independent schools sometimes opt to make bold statements with their libraries by empowering an adventurous architect or integrating the information technology department with the library, creating an information commons or even installing cafes.

Some types of schools are common in the independent arena but rare in the public sector, creating the demand for libraries tailored to their chosen profile. K–12 schools provide one example. Combined elementary and middle schools, or middle and upper schools, are also common in the independent school world, and boarding schools present a set of

> **If You Build It: Library Facilities**
> **What's in a Name? Information**
> **Commons**

opportunities and qualities that set them entirely apart from the day school world. The following section discusses some of the characteristics and issues particular to different age-group library settings and devotes a subsection to the unique role of the boarding school's library in the life of its community.

The Library and the Culture of the School

Any visitor to a school will usually see congruence between the library and the culture of its school. A girls' school library will usually look and feel unmistakably different than the library in a boys' school and will have different collection emphases. A religious school's faith will typically be recognizable in the library's collection and in the symbols and framed items on the walls. A progressive school and a very traditional school will each have libraries that reflect those philosophies in decor and tone.

Libraries, like their schools, not only lead and teach children, but "meet them where they are" developmentally, intellectually, and emotionally. Libraries for different age groups have an appropriately different décor, layout, program and service style, and ambience.

> Libraries, like their schools, not only lead and teach children, but "meet them where they are" developmentally, intellectually, and emotionally.

The lower school's library is typically very integrated into the school or grades it serves. In many instances every class will have an assigned time in the library each week, especially in the earliest grades. As are music, physical education, and art in many schools, these sessions may be designated as "specials," serving to provide release preparation time for classroom teachers while engaging the children in specialized curricular program activities. A school's choice regarding fixed versus flexible scheduling has a large impact on the way the lower school library in particular operates, determining if a class comes weekly or only when some curricular or other need will be met by scheduling a class.

As a result of the relatively steady level of scheduling, lower school teacher-librarians come to know the children they serve very well, seeing them grow over grade school years from preliteracy to independent reading and the beginnings of learning about the research process. Many children start their day by stopping in the library with a parent while being dropped off at school. "I'm struck by how much a part of their day the Library is," a primary grades librarian who had moved from a public library setting notes. The "captive audience" concept is often a draw to librarians who move from working with children and young adults in public libraries.

Frequently, lower school libraries create distinct areas for the primary grades (preschool through grades 1 or 2), and a more "middle grades" approach to the higher elementary grades. These library settings, and certainly those for the middle and upper school, include more technology than the early primary grades, whose schools may choose to keep technology, with the exception of circulation, out of the area.

Lower school libraries are generally colorfully decorated, featuring story room areas, numerous bright posters and displays, and small-scale furniture. They are lively places, with storytelling and sometimes music, drama, or craft activities accompanying the textual presentations. The library may offer a rich variety of activities promoting reading, such as contests, games, and clubs. Parents often spend time in the lower school library volunteering, selecting books for younger children at home, and supplementing their lower school students' reading.

The middle school years (here defined as some configuration of grades 5 or 6 through 8 or sometimes 9) are a transitional period from elementary school into the high school years. These libraries therefore represent a blending or cross-section of elementary and upper school library environments, features, and programs.

> [Middle school] libraries . . . represent a blending or cross-section of elementary and upper school library environments, features, and programs.

Younger students, even first graders, are learning the basic elements of research. By middle school, students should have learned the basic research skills and be ready to be more independent in this area; the library program in middle school becomes progressively geared toward projects while continuing to maintain a heavy promotion of reading for the joy of it. In these grades, the children are led to more independence in choosing their reading. As in the lower school, the library often offers book groups, reading contests, and opportunities for students to share with others about their reading. One librarian who directs a blended lower-middle school library describes the transition as moving from the process of helping children learn to locate books and then finding similar ones, to moving in the middle school years "towards a lot more individual reader's advisory" to help students find what they want, similar to what they will find in upper school and beyond.

In some schools, children in these grades are able to go to the library on their own during recess, during lunch, after school, or possibly during a study hall. This transitional quality between the elementary grades and the high school means that the library serving these grades frequently has the decorative look and feel of a library for elementary school students, but with more young adult-styled furnishings and layout. These libraries, like any lower school and some upper school settings, are also rarely quiet places.

In schools that include both a middle and upper division, the decision is frequently made to serve both divisions in one library facility. Although this option allows for a less fragmented staffing plan and permits the sharing of many resources that would otherwise need to be duplicated, it offers its own challenges as well. How does the library provide an environment that is suitable to both age groups' needs? Does the library combine the various collections or break them out? Does it create a designated space for younger students or incorporate this wide developmental range throughout the library? The successful blending usually requires some compromise and accommodations on everyone's part.

One of the advantages of a blended collection is that it allows students to "find their own level" with more privacy. International students, or students whose reading level or sophistication is out of synch with their peers, appreciate being able to browse a collection and find what they want without the perceived stigma of using a collection designated for younger readers. Students who need to move themselves beyond young adult texts and approaches, however, can be enabled by this setup. In my own urban middle/ upper school library, for example, upper school students persisted in using the citation and note-taking sheets used in middle school classes, rather than making the effort to learn the upper school's approach to note taking and citation, designed to prepare them for college research. It was easier doing it that way, they were comfortable with it, and they managed to find the forms even when we hid them. Only

> One of the advantages of a blended collection is that it allows students to "find their own level" with more privacy.

the changeover to electronic citation and note taking facilitated their necessary growth and change.

Independent upper schools are usually college preparatory. Teachers and librarians acknowledge that their ninth graders are still emerging from late childhood, whereas their seniors are on the brink of the independence of university life, which means that the school's program and approach need to accommodate that growth in independence and sophistication.

In upper school libraries, this transition plays out in a curriculum of increasing complexity and expectation of independence in research learning. Independent school librarians in college preparatory schools agree that the academic demands of these years take a toll on student leisure reading. Their collections invariably support those students who will always find the time to read, but there is of necessity much less emphasis on actively promoting reading for fun than there is in the lower grades. In many upper schools, the majority of leisure reading checkouts are by faculty and staff rather than students. As someone who works in a blended middle and upper school library, it is painful to see the drop-off of reading in even the most enthusiastic young borrowers once they get past the first weeks of ninth grade.

The curriculum in academically demanding schools usually includes honors and AP courses and electives that extend into areas of study found in the first years of college, and the collection and projects supported by the library reflect those expectations. Teachers in these courses expect that there will be databases, print materials, and audiovisual resources to meet the needs of these more advanced subject areas—that the library will serve as a resource to them as well as to the students.

The atmosphere and layout in upper school libraries reflect the social and academic needs of this age group. Students usually have freedom to spend at least some of their unscheduled periods as they wish, and the library fills the need of offering a place to study alone, perhaps in study carrels similar to those found in college libraries. The increasing emphasis on collaborative work is reflected in the places made available for small groups doing assignments or for group study. Libraries balance these needs typically by designating different areas of the facility for different purposes—for example, quiet reading zones, teaching, and collaborative study areas. Study halls or proctored makeup tests are sometimes held in libraries throughout the day and in the evening, adding to the mix of academic activity.

It is difficult to overstate the social importance of libraries in school settings, particularly those with limited gathering space elsewhere. Common areas in schools, including the library, become places "to see and be seen." Groups of friends stake out favorite tables during commonly free periods. Socializing with books open on library tables is a way of life for many kids. Graduates often say that studying in the library during the school day helped them learn how to work effectively in the presence of others without being distracted, an important life skill.

For students of all ages, a library can also be a place of refuge. The relative freedom of upper school students means that students who need this kind of social alternative will often seek it in the private spaces created in libraries. In a school setting, the library is likely to be the only socially acceptable, "safe," or "okay" place to be seen alone, as independent study and reading are expected and supported there.

For students of all ages, a library can be a place of refuge.

The Library in the Life of the Boarding School— A Unique Mission and Role

The library in a boarding school goes beyond the day school's roles and serves a very different additional purpose—as the "living room of the school," in the words of an experienced boarding school library director. For students whose dormitory room is everything, the library is an additional important getaway space. As a result, these libraries invariably have more upholstered, comfortable seating areas available, and one or several spaces will have a living room feel—possibly including a working fireplace with overstuffed chairs, floor lamps, and sometimes a piano nearby. To the astonishment of those unused to boarding school life, there may even be a staff member's dog lying about to dote on! The library will also offer a variety and depth of recreational materials beyond those that a day school would likely offer, including some representing the browsing interests of the international student body. Most boarding schools also build far larger and more comprehensive collections of audiovisual materials and sound recordings than do day schools, whose students have access to family recreation rooms.

By being equally available to every student on campus, libraries support the boarding school's efforts to integrate day students successfully into the life of the school. Some libraries go further, designating a section of the library for day student use. In these areas, students can park their book bags for the day and sometimes have a carrel they can decorate and "own" as a personal home base on campus.

The library remains a place where a student can go alone in the fishbowl adolescent atmosphere without feeling stigmatized.

The library sometimes serves as the public library for the faculty and their families, especially in boarding schools set in the countryside, which is reflected in both the collection and library planning. "Many families stop by after dinner in the dining hall," one boarding school library director says, "and the new children's room I've installed has been a huge hit—the most popular thing I've done in 39 years!"

There is an evening and weekend life in a boarding school library that exists in no other school setting. The "safe place to be" aspect of a library in a school is intensified in a boarding environment, where there is no escape to home at the end of a school day, and the common rooms or the snack bar may be informally claimed by groups of which one is not a member. The library remains a place where a student can go alone in the fishbowl adolescent atmosphere without feeling stigmatized. A huge part of after-hours usage in a coeducational school's library is a direct result of the fact that it is often the most acceptable and sometimes only place for boys and girls to spend time together. When your parents ask you where you've been all evening, it's always okay to say you were at the library.

Libraries inevitably reflect the mission and culture of the schools they serve, but it is ultimately the librarians, with their varying personalities and experiences, who create the collection, program, and pervading atmosphere in an independent school library. "Without a gardener, there is no garden," I once heard, and that is no less true of independent school librarians and their libraries. The librarian is the gardener, but the structure of the library garden is complex, requiring the many kinds of expertise discussed in the remaining essays in this book.

Visit http://lu.com/excellence for supporting links and occasional updates to all essays in this book.

Carolyn Hilles was a college and university librarian for nine years before shifting her professional focus to the independent school world in 1984. As the Assistant Director for Technical Services at The Hotchkiss School in Lakeville, Connecticut, she participated in the full range of boarding school life, serving in the dormitory with her husband, coaching, and teaching English. She spent a term in 2004–2005 at St. Andrews University in Scotland, having been awarded their Schoolteacher Fellowship—the only librarian ever to receive the award. She began working at The Wheeler School (www.wheelerschool.org/), a nursery–12 day school in Providence, Rhode Island, on the day of the school's groundbreaking ceremony for its new library building in 1988. She is the Upper School Librarian and Program Head and has also taught English, served as department head, and briefly been the librarian for the middle school.

Who Are We? The Independent School Library: A Statistical Profile

Susan Williamson, retired, Albuquerque Academy (Albuquerque, NM)

For a library, Simms Library is unusually bustling. It's not overly loud, but it's always moving, especially since it is the one space shared by our entire school. Sixth-graders weave through the stacks on some sort of scavenger hunt, and term-paper-writing seniors sit in the middle of the reference stacks, totally engrossed in their reading and totally unaware that they are blocking traffic. The collection is small enough to navigate as a sixth-grader, unfamiliar with basic research methods but large enough to sustain serious research for all seven years. Even on the rare occasions when I've needed to explore other libraries in the city, the training I've received here has ensured that I can find the information I need quickly.

As I worked on historical research (which was eventually published in the Concord Review) I used our own library resources as a jumping off point, a place to begin my research and gain the background needed to go further afield. Working in this library was essential to that research.

Perhaps most importantly, the Simms Library staff makes a continual effort to teach effective online research techniques. The extensive databases make it easy to move beyond Google. Even in an age when many students rely on simple search engines, Academy students have learned to analyze online information critically. I've always been attached to the print media I can hold in my hand, and much of that appreciation comes from the hours I've spent here, researching, reading or just wandering the stacks. I'm not one of those people who think books will go away. With enough children exposed to libraries like these, print media will have the wherewithal to remain alive and well.

—Sarah Zager, Albuquerque Academy class of 2009

Introduction

As independent school librarians, we can wish that all of our students will have the kind of library experience exemplified in Sarah Zager's statement and that they will pursue research with the same rigor and success. In contrast to many of my colleagues, my career as a librarian has not always been in independent schools; because of my earlier positions, I can readily argue that Sarah, as an independent school student, has been well prepared for her future college or university experience.

I began my career as a librarian in a college library, then moved to a university setting, and expanded my experiences in libraries at Albuquerque Academy in New Mexico. What I originally knew about independent schools was very limited. Having come from a public school background in Seattle, I shared some of the stereotypes about private schools circulating in public schools; that is, that the students were from wealthy families, were likely to be elitist, and had an advantage because their education gave them a better chance of getting into the "good' colleges and universities. In my freshman year as an undergraduate student at Occidental College, I experienced my first brush with a private school student. This student became a leader in our freshman class by giving a riveting speech to the class. He was confident, articulate, and polished, able to capture the attention of his audience with ease. Word went around that he came from a prestigious private high school back east. I wondered what kind of education he had received that put him way above the average public school students I knew.

My only other experience with a private school student happened when I was considering applying for the library director's position at Albuquerque Academy. I had hired an undergraduate student who, by sheer coincidence, had graduated from the Academy. I asked her a flurry of questions, many of them about the library. She told me the school's library was the largest day school library in the country. She was proud of the library and had used it extensively. The fact that she knew enough about it to compare it to other school libraries impressed me. I later discovered that she had won the prestigious National Forensic League Championship Award in Original Oratory. Another stellar student! My interest in the relationship between what libraries in independent schools offered students and the students' excellence and achievement in academia was aroused.

When I became the new director of this large day school library, I joined the Independent School Section of AASL to become part of a network of independent school librarians and to familiarize myself with this universe. Independent schools offer choices to parents seeking excellent education for their children. Prospective families can be influenced to select one school over another through awareness of library program strengths offered to students at the various schools. A strong library program would include an adequate collection of current materials covering the curriculum, librarians who can teach students library skills and encourage lifelong learning, and up-to-date technology to facilitate that learning. How does a parent know how many resources would be typical to cover a school's curriculum? How does a school administration decide how much access to technology is appropriate, how many computers to make available, how much remote access to provide? How does a librarian discover what other schools consider adequate staffing or how many hours after school to be open? Administrators and library directors would like to compare library details with other similar schools regionally and nationally as a method of determining effective and reasonable levels of service and funding. But information needed to make these comparisons has not been easily available and is inconsistently updated.

The independent school world includes a variety of school types. Comparison is difficult because schools differ in location (e.g., all schools within a geographic region, such as the Northeast), grade level (elementary, middle school, high school, or combinations thereof), governance (elected boards versus religious boards), religious status (denominational versus secular), enrollment size, coed versus single gender, rural versus urban, gifted versus special needs, day versus boarding or combined day and boarding, etc.

School Categories

Independent schools

Independent religious schools: *Independent religious schools differ from religious schools in that their governance is controlled by an elected board rather than a religious board.*

Religious schools, including both parochial schools and schools tied to specific denominations

Military schools

Alternative schools (including Montessori, Waldorf, and other schools with specific educational philosophies)

Independent schools educate approximately 10 percent of the school-going population in the United States (USDoE/NCES 2002a). According to the most recent National Center for Education Statistics (NCES) report, there are 33,740 independent schools in the United States (USDoE/NCES 2009). Not all independent schools in the United States have libraries; some 74 percent of private schools in 2007–2008 reported having a library/media center (USDoE/NCES 2009). Those that do have libraries provide valuable services and materials to the communities they serve.

One source for this statistical profile of independent school libraries is a survey conducted during 2004–2005 by the Independent School Section (ISS) of ALA/AASL. In 2002 a group of ISS librarians recognized that there were no real benchmarks available for independent school librarians to use, no statistical way to compare their school libraries with similar libraries across the country. The only data on independent school libraries came from NCES, were out of date, and did not contain the kinds of information needed to make peer comparisons. ISS formed a Data Committee to create an online survey to reach out to membership and beyond for data that would quantify our variety and quality. The ALA Information Technology (IT) Department supported development of a survey that asked for information about the budgets, staffing, hours, collections, facilities, computer access, and Web presence of independent school libraries. The survey was disseminated through ALA and other listservs for only independent school librarians; ALA/ISS membership was not a requirement because we wanted as many responses as possible from as wide a variety of school types as possible. The survey was open from May to September 2005. The respondents' school names were later compared with the ISS membership list, revealing that roughly half of the respondents were from nonmember schools, suggesting that our outreach efforts were reasonably successful.

Historical Surveys

There have been a few earlier surveys of independent schools and libraries. The earliest published data collected on independent schools are from NCES. Intermittent surveys were conducted from 1890 through 1989, at which point NCES began conducting them on a biennial basis. These reports are based on statistically randomized samples and provide estimates of school types by school levels and orientation, school enrollments, faculty sizes, pupil/teacher ratios, distribution of students by ethnic and racial background, and high school graduation rates.

Data Categories

The school library surveys provide data in four main categories:

- the presence of libraries in the schools,
- library staffing characteristics (professional vs. volunteer staffing),
- expenditures on library materials, size of collection holdings, and
- access policies (scheduled classes vs. independent, unscheduled use of the library, and borrowing privileges).

Holton et al., *The Status of Public and Private School Library Media Centers in the United States: 1999–2000* (2004).

Since 1987–1988, NCES has also conducted a series of surveys targeting school libraries in both public and private schools (independent schools are named "private schools" in all government reports). The most recent comprehensive report is *The Status of Public and Private School Library Media Centers in the United States: 1999–2000* (USDoE/NCES 2004). Although these data are valuable for a nationwide "large picture" of differences between public and private schools and their libraries, they do not provide in-depth comparisons of other kinds of variables that contribute to the resources students may have available to them. NCES didn't ask for specific information about the number of online databases and remote access to them, remote access to the library's catalog, the number of periodical subscriptions, the size of the library facilities, computer access, etc.

A 2002 study by NCES, published in 2005, presents more detailed data on public and private school libraries; 198 of the 752 total schools responding were private schools (USDoE/NCES/IES 2005). This report focuses only on those schools with tenth-grade students. These students are to be followed every two years to allow for longitudinal comparisons of the effect of school variables on educational outcomes. This survey comes closest to replicating the variables studied in the ISS survey, because it includes data on facility size, collections, computer resources, and staffing in private school libraries. It also includes valuable data on student opinions and types of library usage, discussed below.

The ISS survey of 2004–2005 is complemented by an annual ongoing survey of public and private school libraries by AASL, which began in 2007. This survey represents a large sample of public and private schools in the United States. The sample of 2008 consists of some 5,000 public and 250 private school libraries. The AASL survey will continue to be conducted on a yearly basis, with results reported online. An interactive feature has been added to the survey allowing users to make comparisons based on their regional or state groupings, type of school, etc. The results of the AASL and NCES longitudinal surveys and the ISS survey are compared below.

The results of these surveys are reported online on the AASL Web site at www.ala.org/mgrps/divs/aasl/schlibrariesandyou/slcsurvey.cfm.

The Independent School Section Survey: General Data

Many of the results of the ISS survey have been reported in an article published online in *School Library Media Research Journal* volume 11, at www.ala.org/ala/mgrpa/divs/aaslpubsandjournals/slmrb/slmrcontents/volume11/cahoy_williamson.

The sample from the ISS survey was not collected as a statistically random or representative sample. The survey focused on the Independent School Section members and the larger community of schools not administered by the public school systems. Several of us are accredited under the National Association of Independent Schools (NAIS) umbrella, but many more are accredited by a variety of other organizations and agencies. The 420 schools responding included independent, alternative, military, religious, and independent religious schools from forty-three states and several other countries. Independent religious schools differ from religious schools in that their governance is controlled by an elected board rather than a religious board. The survey included libraries from day, boarding, and combined day and boarding schools. Because the numbers of alternative and military schools were much smaller relative to the other three categories (alternative N = 5, military N = 3), the study focused on a comparison of the three primary groups (independent N = 235, independent religious N = 45, religious N = 71). The survey was missing group category information for thirty-six schools because their librarians did not reveal their school names, and they could not be coded for school group. See table 3.1.

Data Coding

Survey respondents were coded by geographic region and city size.

Geographic regions were determined by the categories provided by the U.S. Bureau of the Center (2000).

City size was determined by using NCES locale codes:

Central city = population of 250,000 or more

Midsize city/Urban fringe/Large town = population of less than 250,000 but greater than 25,000

Rural area = population of less than 25,000 (USDoE/NCES 2002b)

The largest number of responses came from

California (11 percent),

Texas (10 percent),

Massachusetts (8 percent), and

New York (7 percent).

All other states had a response rate of 6 percent or less.

Ten international schools responded to the survey.

Table 3.1. Survey Sample	
Type of School	**Percent**
Day	80
Boarding	2
Combined	14
School Group	
Independent	67
Independent Religious	13
Religious	20
Gender	
Coed	70
Single (Boys)	9
Single (Girls)	8
Geographic Region	
Northeast	29
South	36
West	20
Midwest	14
Grade Levels	
6th–12th	53

PK–6th	26
1st–12th	19
Missing info	2
Faculty Size	
25 or fewer	15
25–50	38
50–75	19
75 or more	26

Staffing and Hours

One measure of staffing in a school library is the ratio of students to degreed (usually an MLS) library professionals or to total library staff including paraprofessionals. In this sample, a majority of respondents reported a ratio of 300–400 students per degreed library professional. The ratio of students to total library staff was most often reported as 101–200 students per library staff member.

The mean number of hours the library was reported open for use each week during the school year was 49.3, with 44 percent open 40–50 hours per week. As tables 3.2a and b indicate, boarding schools reported more hours open per week than combined schools or day schools, and their total staffing was also the highest reported.

Table 3.2a. Staffing	
Type of School	**Staff per Student**
Day	1.90
Boarding	3.60
Combined	3.00
School Group	
Independent	2.30
Independent Religious	1.01
Religious	1.73
Geographic Region	
Northeast	2.36
Midwest	1.91
West	1.86
South	1.86
City Size	
Central City	2.12
Mid-sized	1.94
Rural	1.93

Table 3.2b. Hours	
Type of School	**Open Hours per Week**
Day	41.5
Boarding	79.5
Combined	57
School Group	
Independent	47
Independent Religious	45
Religious	41
Geographic Region	
Northeast	48
Midwest	48
West	42
South	46
City Size	
Central City	41.5
Mid-sized	46
Rural	52

Library Budget

School librarians were asked to provide the approximate dollar amount spent per student on library collections and to define the library budget as a percentage of the total operating budget of the school. The latter question received a much lower response rate (81 total responses) on the survey. The mean amount spent per student on library materials was $69. The mean for the library budget as a percentage of the total school's operating budget (both without salaries) was 1.5 percent.

As table 3.3 indicates, boarding schools and rural schools spend significantly more per student for library collections. Day schools and boarding schools both devoted approximately 1.7 percent of the total school's operating budget to library expenditures, whereas combined schools allocated only 0.6 percent.

Table 3.3. Library Budget	
Type of School	**Dollars Spent per Student**
Day	$ 56
Boarding	$146
Combined	$ 85
School Group	
Independent	$ 77
Independent Religious	$ 55
Religious	$ 29
Geographic Region	
Northeast	$ 69
Midwest	$ 65
West	$ 63
South	$ 47
City Size	
Central City	$ 57
Mid-sized	$ 53
Rural	$ 74

Collections

The survey also explored the details of print and nonprint collections in independent school libraries. Collections predominantly ranged between 6,000 and 20,000 items, with the largest percentage (24 percent) housing 10,000 to 15,000 items, including books, periodicals, and audiovisual materials. More than 44 percent of libraries indicated that they house an average of 25–50 collection items per student. Nonprint items (audiovisual media, equipment, etc.) were not heavily collected by responding libraries: 29 percent reported 0–200 nonprint items in their collections. Print periodical subscriptions followed a similar pattern: 38 percent of libraries had 0–25 subscriptions. Boarding and combined schools had markedly more print periodical subscriptions than responding day schools. Only combined schools boasted a higher number of nonprint items in the collection (see tables 3.4a–d).

Information about the age of collections was not gathered. While publication date or copyright year is an important marker of collection quality, issues of quality are difficult to measure and would have required more questions than ALA allowed.

Table 3.4a. Collection: Total Items	
Type of School	**Number of Items**
Day	16,936
Boarding	34,065
Combined	26,293
School Group	
Independent	20,972
Independent Religious	16,922
Religious	14,037
Geographic Region	
Northeast	19,544
Midwest	15,938
West	16,019
South	19,918
City Size	
Central City	20,253
Mid-sized	17,493
Rural	18,567

Table 3.4b. Collection: Items per Student	
Type of School	**Number of Items**
Day	1,795
Boarding	*(data corrupt)*
Combined	3,715
School Group	
Independent	2,126
Independent Religious	1,126
Religious	2,094
Geographic Region	
Northeast	2,543
Midwest	1,712
West	1,563
South	2,112
City Size	
Central City	2,086
Mid-sized	1,286
Rural	2,717

Table 3.4c. Print Periodicals Subscriptions

Type of School	Number of Subscriptions
Day	48
Boarding	98
Combined	90
School Group	
Independent	65
Independent Religious	43
Religious	40
Geographic Region	
Northeast	62
Midwest	43
West	38
South	65
City Size	
Central City	63
Mid-sized	48
Rural	60

Table 3.4d. Nonprint Items in the Collection

Type of School	Number of Items
Day	930
Boarding	1,022
Combined	2,468
School Group	
Independent	1,284
Independent Religious	1,151
Religious	800
Geographic Region	
Northeast	1,169
Midwest	968
West	923
South	1,256
City Size	
Central City	1,098
Mid-size	994
Rural	1,309

Library Facilities

A large percentage of schools (46 percent) identified their library facility as 3,000 square feet or less in size. The highest percentage of surveyed libraries (34 percent) also averaged between 26 and 50 seats in their facilities. Schools with larger collections and more staffing were, not surprisingly, more likely to have larger facilities. Regional and geographic data comparisons did not yield significant differences. See tables 3.5a and b.

| Table 3.5a. Library Facilities: Square Footage ||
Type of School	Square Feet
Day	4,755
Boarding	17,030
Combined	11,865
School Group	
Independent	6,891
Independent Religious	5,709
Religious	3,847
Geographic Region	
Northeast	
Midwest	NA
West	NA
South	NA
City Size	
Central City	4,980
Mid-sized	6,961
Rural	7,295

Table 3.5b. Library Facilities: Seats	
Type of School	**Number of Seats**
Day	65
Boarding	107
Combined	89
School Group	
Independent	72
Independent Religious	73
Religious	67
Geographic Region	
Northeast	NA
Midwest	NA
West	NA
South	NA
City Size	
Central City	69
Mid-sized	74
Rural	70

Technology

Combined schools provided the highest number of computer workstations (either desktop or laptop), with an average of 22 computers (in 2005). Wireless access was spread evenly across all three types of school environments (average 63 percent), with 71 percent of day/boarding schools, 65 percent of day schools, and 60 percent of boarding schools providing WI-FI in the library. Combined schools were much more likely (91 percent) to provide remote (off-site) access to library subscription databases, while the mean for all schools was 79 percent.

Some 2.4 percent of libraries explicitly identified themselves as "laptop schools." Although this question was not on the survey, multiple respondents explained that because their institutions were "laptop schools" (i.e., each student had his or her own computer), the library had very few workstations or laptops. Approximately 45 percent of libraries featured ten or fewer workstations or laptops.

Some 73 percent of responding libraries had a library Web page, and 94 percent provided an automated library catalog; in addition, 52 percent of all libraries indicated that they provide remote access (off-site) to the catalog. Though online catalogs were prevalent, remote access to the catalog was more varied by type of school. Regional and geographic comparisons did not yield significant differences. See tables 3.6a–d.

Table 3.6a. Technology: Number of Computers	
Type of School	**Number of Computers**
Day	17
Boarding	11
Combined	22
School Group	
Independent	18
Independent Religious	17
Religious	15
Geographic Region	
Northeast	NA
Midwest	NA
West	NA
South	NA
City Size	
Central City	NA
Mid-sized	NA
Rural	NA

Table 3.6b. Technology: Web Pages	
Type of School	**Number That Had Web Pages**
Day	73
Boarding	70
Combined	82
School Group	
Independent	77
Independent Religious	73
Religious	74
Geographic Region	
Northeast	NA
Midwest	NA
West	NA
South	NA
City Size	
Central City	78
Mid-sized	79
Rural	69

Table 3.6c. Technology: Remote Access to Catalog

Type of School	Number That Had Access
Day	52
Boarding	70
Combined	66
School Group	
Independent	59
Independent Religious	62
Religious	39
Geographic Region	
Northeast	NA
Midwest	NA
West	NA
South	NA
City Size	
Central City	62
Mid-sized	44
Rural	54

Table 3.6d. Technology: Remote Access to Databases

Type of School	Number That Had Access
Day	77
Boarding	70
Combined	91
School Group	
Independent	78
Independent Religious	84
Religious	78
Geographic Region	
Northeast	NA
Midwest	NA
West	NA
South	NA
City Size	
Central City	78
Mid-sized	80
Rural	80

Differences between School Groups

Despite the survey date of 2004–2005, the data are very useful,
especially in combination with the other research discussed here.

The ten international schools report the largest mean number of students (643) and total number of faculty (66). They also have the second highest mean number of total library staff (3.0) and the second largest library budget per student ($67). They contain the largest mean number of items in their collection (23,810) and a large mean number of nonprint items as well (2,607). They are less likely to have large print periodical collections (mean = 32) and a large number of database subscriptions (mean = 8). Their facilities are smaller in square footage (mean = 2,780 sq. ft.) and seating capacity (mean = 59). They are highly likely to have library Web pages, and all of them have automated catalogs, most of which are remotely accessible. They are more likely than the other schools to have summer programs, but none have endowments. In the results of a survey on international independent schools, we find some similarities with our international school data. The mean number of holdings in the fifteen school libraries (three were missing this information) was over 23,000, and the mean number of electronic databases offered by them was 6.93.

Though religious schools (Catholic or Jewish in this sample) have a large mean number of students (553), as well as a large mean number of faculty (63), their library collection size in terms of total items, number of print periodical subscriptions, and number of nonprint items is considerably less than the average for the other two school types (independent and independent religious) (see tables 3.4a–d).

With respect to their total library staff FTE (full time equivalent), religious schools fall below both the independent and independent religious schools. Independent schools have a mean of 2.30 library staff, whereas religious schools have a mean of 1.7 staff. Correspondingly, the number of hours the library is open per week (41.5) is lower than either the independent school group (47.5) or the independent religious group (45). The facilities' square footage and number of seats are also the lowest of the three groups (see tables 3.5–b).

Regarding access to technology, religious schools provide fewer workstations in the library, but they are second in terms of wireless access. They are least likely to have an automated catalog. Perhaps because student enrollments at religious schools are higher on average than at independent and independent religious schools (553 versus 428 and 473 respectively), the mean library budget per student is lower ($29 versus $77 and $55). This may also be explained by differing tuition levels between religious and independent schools. Independent religious and religious schools are also less likely than independent schools to have a summer program or an endowment, both of which provide additional school funding.

Survey Analysis

The descriptive data from the ISS survey are complemented by correlation analysis, conducted by Nicole Morgan at the Penn State Survey Research Center and made possible by a grant received by Ellysa Cahoy (Cahoy and Williamson 2008). With tests of significance, the data can be analyzed for the relationship between variables. For example, can we predict a library's staffing characteristics from the number of hours the library is open or from the size of its collection? What relationships exist between budgeting and collection size, and how do these variables compare in relation to faculty and student population size?

Statistical Analysis: Correlation Coefficients

In statistical analysis, a result is called statistically significant if it is unlikely to occur by chance. In this data sample, we used two kinds of tests to determine whether there are significant differences: between variables such as student body size and library collection size (using Pearson correlation coefficients) and between groups of schools such as boarding vs. day schools or independent vs. religious schools (analysis of variance or ANOVA).

The Pearson correlation coefficient measures the correlation between two variables (X and Y). It ranges between -1 to 1. A value of 1 implies that there is a positive linear relationship between the variables, such that as X increases, so does Y. The value of -1 implies the opposite. A value of 0 indicates no relationship between the variables. Correlations with a Pearson r statistic higher than 0.05 indicate that the variables do not occur together strictly by chance; they have a statistically significant relationship.

Two types of tests for significance were used to analyze the survey data. The first test was a digital cross tabulation analysis using SPSS (*Statistical Package for the Social Sciences*) software to determine correlation coefficients for variables, for example, comparing student population size with all other variables, such as collection size or computer access. Correlations are described using the Pearson *r* statistic with two-tailed significance. Correlations found between variables on the Pearson *r* test do not necessarily indicate cause and effect relationships. What we can say is that with the Pearson coefficients, where the *r* value is higher than 0.05, there is a strong indication that the variables do not occur together strictly by chance. They are said to be positively correlated.

ANOVA (Analysis of Variance)

The ANOVA test looks at whether the means for a variable between groups are different from the means within groups. The results of the F test will indicate whether the differences found between the means for two groups, e.g. religious vs. independent schools, are significant.

"The F statistic is based on the ratio of the between-group estimate of variance to the within-group estimate of variance" (Palmisano 2001).

The larger the F statistic, the smaller the p-value (or measure of statistical significance), and the lesser probability that the null hypothesis is true" (Palmisano 2001). The null hypothesis here assumes that the means are equal.

If the variance within a group is large, the variance between groups may not be due to group differences, but to within-group differences.

The second test used ANOVA, or analysis of variance, to find significant differences between groups of schools. ANOVA uses the test statistic F to test the null hypothesis that the means of all the groups studied will be equal against the alternative hypothesis that the means are not equal. According to the *World of Sociology*, "The F statistic is based on the ratio of the between-group estimate of variance to the within-group estimate of variance." "The larger the F statistic, the smaller the p-value (or measure of statistical significance), and the lesser probability that the null hypothesis is true" (Palmisano 2001) In other words, if the variance within a group is large, the variance between groups may not be due to group differences, but to within-group differences. We tested for these within and between group differences to determine which variables were significantly different between groups in our survey sample.

Correlation Analysis

The variables in our survey that showed positive correlations at a significance level above 0.05 are indicated in table 3.7. As in other studies, there are typically many variables that are positively correlated.

The obvious indication here is that the larger the school and the larger the library and collection one has to oversee, the larger the library staff will be; the highest correlations with library staff are with total collection size and square footage. A surprising statistic in these correlations is the number of hours the library is open during the school year per week, which does not correlate with total staff FTE as highly as the other variables. One might expect that the longer the library is open, the more staffing is needed to supervise the library. A possible explanation for this is the situation of a boarding or combined school library, in which faculty members other than librarians are often asked to oversee the library during evening hours. The relationship between total hours and total staff size is still significant, however. Library staff numbers also tend to be larger as grades covered in the schools go up ($r = 0.217$).

Table 3.7. Significant Correlations (r>.05)				
Variable	**Total No. Students**	**Total No. Faculty**	**Budget $/Student**	**Staff Total FTE**
Total No. Students	I	.455	NS	.583
Total No. Faculty	.455	I	.126	.432
Budget $/Student	NS	.126	I	.303
Staff Total FTE	.583	.432	.303	I
IparHours Open/Week	.124	NS	.265	.095
Collection Total No. Items	.424	.282	.270	.674
Collection Nonprint Items	.277	.183	.286	.535
Collection Print Periodical Subscriptions	.085	.086	.101	.207
Collection Database Subscriptions	.149	.110	.190	.278
Library Facilities Square Footage	.429	.379	.429	.796
Library Facilities Number of Seats	.390	.270	.217	.521
Technology Number of Computers	.399	.239	.211	.460
Grade	.196	.164	.187	.217

Another interesting finding is that the number of nonprint items in the collection is a strong indicator of school size, library budget, and library staffing. Those schools with a large student or faculty population did not necessarily have a high correlation with number of items per student in the collection ($r = 0.044$). Only nonprint collections have a strong correlation with school size. The number of faculty correlated negatively with city size ($r = -0.083$), meaning that more faculty in this sample work in independent schools in rural areas than in central cities. Also, the higher the grade level of the school, the larger the number of faculty.

The larger the school and library, the greater the chance that the school library will have a higher number of database subscriptions, but not necessarily spend more on its budget as a percentage of its school operating budget, which shows a negative correlation ($r = -0.086$).

ANOVA Analysis

The results of the ANOVA analysis (the study of between-group variation vs. within-group variation) were highly significant. The p statistic was typically at .046 or lower, indicating that the variation was due to differences between and not within the types (day vs. boarding vs. combined schools) or the groups (independent vs. independent religious vs. religious schools).

ANOVA analysis of schools grouped by geographic regions (Northeast, South, Midwest, and West) yielded no significant differences. Analysis of schools grouped by city size (central city, mid-sized city, rural small town) yielded significant differences between groups in their total number of students ($p = .001$), the number of hours the library is open ($p = .000$), their library budget as a percentage of the school's operating budget ($p=.006$), presence of an automated catalog ($p = .046$), remote access to that catalog ($p = .025$), and existence of an endowment ($p = .041$). Perhaps the most interesting point to be gleaned from the city size variable is that the libraries in rural areas are open the longest, in mid-sized cities, less long and in central cities, the least long, perhaps due to the fact that there are more boarding schools in rural areas.

It could also be that in cities students do not stay on campus beyond the school day and use either digital access or other libraries. As table 3.8 indicates, the significant differences we found in our sample of schools between *types* of schools are greater overall than differences between *groups* of schools. More variables can be said to distinguish day, boarding, and combined schools than independent, independent religious, and religious schools. Type of governance is less important in distinguishing schools than type of venue.

Table 3.8. Significant ANOVA Results (p<.100)		
Variable	Day v. Boarding v. Combined Schools	Independent v. Independent Religious v. Religious
Budget $/Student	.000	.000
Staff Total FTE	.000	.043
Collection Total No. Items	.000	.020
Collection Nonprint Items	.000	NS
Library Facilities Square Footage	.000	NS
Library Facilities Number of Seats	.030	NS
Technology Number of Computers	.084	NS
Technology Wi Fi Access	NS	.013
Technology Remote Database Access	.042	NS
Technology Remote Catalog Access	.083	.007
Does the Library Serve a Summer Program?	.001	.037
Budget Do You Have an Endowment?	.000	.027
Hours Open/Week	NS	.031

The point these analyses make is that there is statistically significant variability between the independent school groups and types in our sample. Independent school administrators and librarians seeking benchmarks for their libraries need to be aware of these differences in order to locate their libraries in the larger universe of private schools. Although these differences are not derived from a random nationwide sample, they provide points of comparison from a reasonably large and varied sample of independent schools.

School Libraries and Student Achievement

Aside from comparing school library groups, it is important to understand how school libraries are related to student achievement. According to a summary of Scholastic's latest Research Foundation Paper from studies of nineteen states:

> A substantial body of research since 1990 shows a positive relationship between school libraries and student achievement. The research studies show that school libraries can have a positive impact on student achievement whether such achievement is measured in terms of reading scores, literacy, or learning more generally. A school library program that is adequately staffed, resourced and funded can lead to higher student achievement regardless of the socio-economic or educational levels of the community. ("19 States" 2008)

With the exception of copyright date information, which was not collected in our ISS survey, the ISS survey results indicate that the independent school libraries in our sample provide most of these "increases" by virtue of their higher figures than public school measures in these categories: more staffing, more budgeting on library materials per student, larger collection sizes, more electronic access to databases and online periodicals, as well as longer hours open. These findings are compared with public school findings below to specify these differences.

Differences: Public School Studies

Earlier studies from Arkansas, Colorado, Pennsylvania, Massachusetts, Oregon, Texas, California, and North Carolina demonstrate that student achievement tends to increase (by 8–40 percent) as

- total paid library staff increases,
- average copyright date of the school library collection increases,
- the amount spent on books and other print resources increases,
- expenditures per 100 students on electronic access to information increases,
- number of hours the school library is open increases, and
- provision of online periodicals increases.

www.lrs.org/impact.asp

The most recent 2007 and 2008 AASL surveys on both public and private school libraries reveal differences between the two types of libraries. These surveys were conducted by Keith Curry Lance's RSL Research Group and presented on the AASL Web site (AASL [2007], [2008]). The statistics provided in the 2007 survey were derived from a sample of close to 4,000 public schools (95 percent) and more than 200 independent schools (5 percent). The statistics for independent schools (the report uses "private" for this group as a whole) are averaged across different categories and not broken out into separate types such as day, boarding, or combined, or groups such as religious, independent, or alternative. Although it would be desirable to compare public school data with only day school data from our sample and the AASL private school samples, the figures for school types and groups were not provided in either of the reports (day schools are the most similar independent school cohort to traditional public schools).

Despite the disparity in sample sizes between the AASL data and the ISS data, comparisons can be made on the basis of answers to similar survey questions. For example, the average number of hours school library facilities were open per week differed between public schools (31) and independent schools (40) in the AASL 2007 survey, but the difference was even greater for the schools in the ISS survey (49.3).

According to the 2007 survey, the total number of items in each library collection differed between public schools (12,800) and independent schools (16,200). The average total number of items found for independent schools in the ISS results was 18,647. The average number of print periodical subscriptions in public school libraries was 22, whereas the average for private schools was 35. The average number for the ISS sample was 56 subscriptions. Perhaps the most significant disparity showed up in the library budgets calculated as expenditures per student. For the public schools, the average amount spent was $15 per student, and the average total budget for materials was $11,000. For the independent schools in the AASL sample, the average expenditure was more than $40 per student and close to $20,500 for the total materials budget. The average amount calculated for library budget per student in the ISS survey was considerably higher, at $69 per student. Total budgets were not requested in the ISS survey. These latter figures may very well reflect the differences in student populations between public and independent schools. Public schools typically have larger student bodies, and budgets are spread over larger populations.

With respect to access to technology, the figures presented are closer between public and independent school libraries. According to the AASL 2007 survey, the average number of computers found in both public and private school libraries was 16; the average in the ISS survey was 17. The AASL 2007 survey data for remote access to databases was somewhat closer to the ISS figures. Whereas 66 percent of the public schools offer remote access, 75 percent of the private schools do so, but in the ISS survey, 79 percent of the schools do so. The figures provided in the AASL 2008 survey indicate similar patterns of difference between public and private school library resources from the 2007 survey, although the samples for both are larger (public = 5,000, private = 250). In summary, the ISS sample represents schools that invest more heavily than the public schools in their library collections, staffing, and access to technology.

If their investment in resources is greater, can we also claim that student achievement in independent schools is greater? There are several compelling answers to this question derived from publications issued by the NAIS and from the NCES. Approximately 74 percent of the schools responding to the ISS survey are members of the NAIS, an umbrella accrediting organization for independent schools with a total membership of some 1,300 schools across the United States. Table 3.9 lists other associations to which independent schools may belong, associations that may contribute elements of their school missions and goals, accreditation self-studies, and mutual support in specialized areas. Who accredits the other 26 percent of independent schools is a difficult question to answer.

Table 3.9. Private School Associations

Association	Schools	Students	Teachers
None	7,559	736,965	75,897
Religious			
Accelerated Christian Education	1,127	53,538	6,817
American Association of Christian Schools	895	123,026	12,248
Association of Christian Schools International	3,295	627,430	57,290
Association of Christian Teachers and Schools	237	37,290	3,482
Christian Schools International	361	91,214	7,914
Council of Islamic Schools in North America	35	4,567	534
Evangelical Lutheran Education Association	222	31,144	2,573
Friends Council on Education	52	12,785	1,766
General Conference of the Seventh-Day Adventist Church	680	43,747	3,829
Islamic School League of America	30	3,179	424
Jesuit Secondary Education Association	43	38,092	2,794
National Association of Episcopal Schools	262	82,732	9,878
National Catholic Educational Association	6,857	2,109,087	145,436
National Christian School Association	172	44,689	3,690
National Society of Hebrew Day Schools	178	49,769	6,117
Oral Roberts University Educational Fellowship	96	18,552	1,764
Solomon Schechter Day Schools	62	17,597	2,492
Southern Baptist Association of Christian Schools	129	29,610	2,623
Other religious school associations	2,494	469,429	44,605
Special Emphasis			
American Montessori Society	687	60,883	7,917
Other Montessori associations	588	43,076	5,795
Association of Military Colleges and Schools	23	5,986	764
Association of Waldorf Schools of North America	101	15,237	2,231
Bilingual School Association	‡	‡	‡
Council of Bilingual Education	‡	‡	‡
Council for Exceptional Children	425	49,178	6,744
National Association of Private Special Education Centers	344	38,170	5,763
Other associations for exceptional children	295	35,603	5,407
European Council for International Schools	‡	‡	‡
National Association for the Education of Young Children	1,001	171,715	16,691
National Association of Bilingual Education	‡	‡	‡
National Association of Laboratory Schools	‡	‡	‡
National Coalition of Girls' Schools	84	34,162	4,515
Other special emphasis school associations	1,178	208,738	22,150
Other School Associations or Organizations			
Alternative School Network	49	3,932	430
Institute for Independent Education	28	3,331	516
National Association of Independent Schools	1,058	474,364	61,707
State or regional independent school association	1,749	537,651	56,691
National Coalition of Alternative Community Schools	60	5,617	716
National Independent Private School Association	255	49,445	5,334
The Association of Boarding Schools	189	61,384	9,150
Other school associations	2,933	682,598	68,741

*Total number of private schools, students, and teachers (head count), by school membership in private school associations: United States, 2003–2004

Source: Characteristics of Private Schools in the United States: Results from the 2003–2004 Private School Universe Study. U.S. Department of Education, Institute of Education Sciences, NCES 2006-319. http://nces.ed.gov/pubs2006/2006319.pdf

According to a comparison made by the National Association of Independent Schools, "the 2004 combined verbal and math SAT scores showed significantly higher scores for students that attended NAIS schools compared to those students that attended public schools, irrespective of family income" (NAIS 2005). Looking at NAIS students' verbal and math SAT scores over the past thirty years compared to the combined national public and independent school scores, it is apparent that not only do NAIS school students have consistently higher scores in both categories, but there has also been a dramatic increase in NAIS student scores while the national average scores have changed little in the past thirty years (NAIS 2008). With respect to advanced placement (AP) courses, "a total of 85 percent of NAIS member schools offer AP courses, compared with 51 percent of public schools" (NAIS 2006). According to a report from the NCES, "Private high school students typically have more demanding graduation requirements than do public high school students" (NCES 2002a).

A study by NCES of private school students' academic achievements from results of the National Assessment of Educational Progress (NAEP) assessments of their performance in reading, mathematics, science, and writing in 2000, 2002, 2003, and 2005 indicates the following:

> Students at grades 4, 8, and 12 in all categories of private schools had higher average scores in reading, mathematics, science, and writing than their counterparts in public schools. In addition, higher percentages of students in private schools performed at or above Proficient compared to those in public schools. (USDoE/NCES/IES 2002)

Another report from NCES uses different statistical measures to conclude that these differences disappear when exogenous variables (race, class, etc.) are removed (USDoE/NCES 2006). However, the differences in independent school student achievements reported above are matched by differences in aspirations and outcomes associated with attendance at independent schools. This information is provided in the Freshman Survey Trends Report, "a longitudinal study of the American higher education system that charts national normative data on the characteristics of students attending colleges and universities as first-time, full-time freshmen. The survey is conducted annually by the Higher Education Research Institute (HERI), based at the Graduate School of Education & Information Studies at the University of California, Los Angeles"(Bassett 2004). According to a comparison of key findings from this report, "NAIS graduates were three times more likely than the group as a whole to report that they spent more than 11 hours per week studying or doing homework during their final year of high school (48 percent of NAIS students, compared to 15 percent of all students)." In addition, "85 percent of NAIS students go on to attend 'high' or 'highly selective' colleges or universities" and "more than two-thirds (67 percent) of NAIS students expected to make at least a B average in college, compared to 58 percent of all students" (Bassett 2004).

"86 percent of NAIS school graduates planned to pursue a postgraduate degree, versus 74 percent of all students."—Bassett (2004)

In the fall of 2006, some 56 percent of NAIS students went on to a four-year college, compared to 35 percent of all public high school graduates. In 2007 65 percent of independent school students went on to a four-year college. The comparative figure for public school students has not yet been published. (USDoE/NCES 2008)

By all of the measures stated above, independent school students show higher levels of academic rigor and achievement than do public school students. The school experiences and environments in independent schools are important in shaping student success, including the level and quality of available library resources. John H. Pryor, director of the Cooperative Institutional Research Program's Freshman Survey (mentioned above), states that "a large part of the success that students have in college comes from accomplishments and academic habits they acquired in high school" (Pryor 2008). It is arguable that the higher levels of support given to independent school libraries in this sample, in terms of staffing, hours open, collection sizes, and access to electronic resources, provide a meaningful set of advantages in terms of outcomes for independent school students.

Comparing Studies

The ELS study (USDoE/NCES/IES 2005) differs in several ways from our ISS survey:

1. The sample of private schools is smaller by approximately half. Only 5.1 percent of the total set of schools is Catholic (N = 38) and 21.3 percent comprise the "other private" category (N = 160). The total number of private schools was 198. The ISS sample contains 420 responding schools.

2. The sample is restricted to high school level students, whereas our sample includes all grade levels.

3. The sample in this report is not as current as that in our ISS survey or the AASL surveys by Keith Curry Lance (NCES 2002a; ISS 2005; AASL 2007, 2008).

4. The NCES study includes student data on their use of libraries and their opinions about them.

5. The private school libraries in this sample had fewer resources in terms of collection size and facility size than those in our ISS sample, possibly because of the differences in the dates of the surveys or in types of private schools.

The gap in library resources may help explain the achievement gap, but it is also possible there is a difference in the way independent school students use their libraries that promotes higher achievement. The most recent NCES study published in 2005 on school library media centers contains a more detailed set of results comparing public and private school libraries than the report published in 2004 (USDoE/NCES 2004). *School Library Media Centers* (USDoE/NCES/IES 2005), mentioned earlier, compares the space, organization, collections, resources, staffing, and use of a set of 752 public and private school libraries that serve tenth graders.

This report compares public and private school libraries on dimensions similar to the ISS survey; that is, collections including books, nonprint items, periodical subscriptions, and database subscriptions; presence of an automated catalog; staffing; technology (defined as different types of equipment); and facilities and seating capacity. The most valuable results in this study concern the different ways in which tenth-grade students used their libraries.

The results shown in table 3.10 reveal significant sex differences, racial and ethnic differences, socioeconomic differences, and differences in students by composite test scores, school sector (where public, Catholic, and other private schools are compared), school urbanicity, and school region. In all of the usage categories, students in private school libraries as a whole (Catholic and other private combined) used the library more than public school students did. Furthermore, their use of the library for assignments, in-school projects, homework, research papers, and Internet access differs significantly from usage by public school students.

Table 3.10. Why Students Use the School Library

Student Characteristic	Percent of students who reported "sometimes" or "often" for use of the school library for these purposes:								
	Assignments	In-School Projects	Homework	Research Papers	Leisure Reading	To Read Magazines or Newspapers	To Read Books for Fun	Interests Outside of School	Internet Access
Total	40.8	52.7	26.9	54.1	15.6	16.7	16.6	20.8	41.1
Sex									
Male	36.0	46.2	24.5	48.2	14.9	17.4	14.5	24.1	40.0
Female	45.4	58.9	29.1	59.8	16.4	16.1	18.6	17.8	42.1
Race/ethnicity									
American Indian/Alaska native/non-Hispanic	42.0	50.8	29.6	57.3	24.1	23.6	21.0	31.7	42.3
Asian,Hawaiin/Pacific islander/non-Hispanic	42.0	55.7	31.4	51.6	17.4	20.0	19.3	20.9	41.9
Black or African American/non-Hispanic	44.4	55.0	32.7	54.9	19.4	21.6	22.2	28.9	45.1
Hispanic	36.8	49.5	30.6	50.6	17.8	18.9	21.0	25.5	38.8
Multiracial/non-Hispanic	41.2	51.8	27.1	53.1	22.8	19.8	22.2	24.0	44.0
White, non-Hispanic	40.9	52.9	24,3	55.0	13.5	14.6	13.7	17.5	40.4
Socioeconomic Status									
Lowest quartile	37.4	49.9	30.3	52.6	19.3	20.9	21.4	25.9	42.5
Middle two quartiles	40.8	52.2	25.7	54.6	15.2	16.3	16.2	20.7	40.1
Highest quartile	43.9	56.4	25.9	54.5	13.2	13.6	13.0	16.4	41.7

Student Characteristic	Percent of students who reported "sometimes" or "often" for use of the school library for these purposes:								
	Assignments	In-School Projects	Homework	Research Papers	Leisure Reading	To Read Magazines or Newspapers	To Read Books for Fun	Interests Outside of School	Internet Access
Lowest quartile	34.2	46.3	31.1	48.5	20.8	23.3	22.7	28.1	41.3
Middle two quartiles	40.8	53.2	26.6	54.7	14.9	16.3	15.3	20.5	41.6
Highest quartile	46.7	57.5	23.6	58.0	12.5	11.8	13.8	15.0	39.8
School Sector									
Public	40.3	52.4	26.1	53.9	15.8	16.7	17.0	21.0	40.5
Catholic	42.9	54.8	32.5	52.5	10.3	15.0	8.4	17.7	46.2
Other private	51.4	60.1	40.5	63.2	19.6	21.3	18.4	21.5	50.1
School Urbanicity									
Urban	38.2	50.9	27.3	49.9	15.9	17.5	17.8	21.3	37.9
Suburban	41.9	53.3	26.0	55.3	15.1	14.9	15.7	20.2	41.4
Rural	41.8	54.0	28.5	57.4	16.8	20.5	17.1	21.8	44.8
School Region									
Northeast	45.5	57.2	28.2	56.8	14.5	16.0	15.3	20.4	42.6
Midwest	44.5	56.4	30.6	59.4	17.9	19.7	17.4	22.4	47.1
South	39.0	50.0	22.9	51.7	14.5	16.0	16.5	20.5	39.3
West	35.7	49.2	27.8	50.0	15.9	15.2	17.1	20.0	36.1

Students with different test scores also used the school library for different purposes. Students with high test scores were more likely than students with lower test scores to use the library sometimes or often for assignments, in-school projects, and research papers. Students with lower test scores were more likely to use the library for homework, leisure reading of magazines or newspapers, and outside interests. Test scores were a combination of reading and math scores in the tenth grade, divided into high, middle, and low quartile scores.

Regrettably, the study does not report on the testing score differences between public and private school students, but these kinds of differences have been discussed above. (USDoE/NCES 2006) This report suggests that independent school libraries are linked not just in an abstract way to student success, but in a concrete way to their usage patterns, which indicate not only greater use overall, but a greater use for academic research, assignments, and knowledge-seeking behavior, rather than leisure reading and outside interests.

Conclusion

Independent school libraries can be found in a variety of school environments, from secular boarding schools to religious and alternative day schools to schools committed to gifted students or military training. The Independent School Section of AASL successfully gathered statistical data on a sample of the universe of independent schools with a Web-based survey that reached out to a nationwide and international population. One of the major goals of the survey was to create benchmarks for the purpose of comparison between school groups (independent, independent religious, religious, alternative, and military) and school types (day, boarding, and combined day and boarding). These comparisons can be summed up as follows: the international school libraries, though small in number, appear to be well staffed and have larger collections than many of the independent schools in the United States. Boarding schools also reflect a higher level of investment in collections, have larger staff numbers, longer open hours, and larger facilities than the other types of schools. Religious schools tend to have a significantly smaller number of resources in the form of collections, staffing, and access to computers. In the analysis of school library variables, we found the greatest number of significant differences between schools based on type (day, boarding, etc.) rather than on group category (religious, independent, etc.). In answer to the question of what is an acceptable level of staffing, hours, and technology for a school library, schools can look to the collective data from other schools aiming to be better than the statistical mean.

One of the major goals of the survey was to create benchmarks for the purpose of comparison between school groups . . . and school types.

An additional goal that emerged in this study was to examine the possible relationship between independent school libraries and student achievement. What kinds of differences in independent school education are responsible for their students' demonstrated achievements in school test scores, SAT scores, greater rates of college attendance, and higher educational aspirations? It can be argued that the point of education is to encourage students to excel, not only in academic achievement, but in posteducational environments as contributing members of society. Given the higher levels of achievement demonstrated by independent school students, we can argue that independent schools may provide models of excellence for improving the public education system in our country. As shown by the data presented in table 3.9, correlations show that independent students are more likely to use their school libraries for research, assignments, and projects in school. They also tend to use their libraries more overall than public school students. We have also shown that the independent schools in our sample provide more resources and access to technology and invest more heavily in their libraries than do schools in the public sector.

If we found no correlation or a negative correlation between high test scores in school and high numbers of resources in libraries or high usage of libraries for academic research, we might conclude that library resources are insignificant in student achievement. But this is not the case, as illustrated by the Scott and Owings study (USDoE/NCES/IES 2005), as well as in the studies conducted across nineteen states ("19 States" 2008). Using the library for information seeking has some relationship with success in academia. Although we can only make tentative inferences about the effect of the advantages in independent school libraries because we have only correlations to indicate a relationship between library resources and usage and student achievement, they warrant further causal research into these factors. As the popular press reports almost daily, the world is becoming more complex and interconnected. Thus, it is imperative that our schools prepare students with the requisite skills for

> *"[A] large part of the success that students have in college comes from accomplishments and academic habits they acquired in high school."*

making informed analyses and decisions about how to address our rapidly changing global environment. Therefore, it is important that schools, both public and private, have sound data upon which to base their decisions about using limited resources. John Pryor's (2008) comment bears repeating here, that "a large part of the success that students have in college comes from accomplishments and academic habits they acquired in high school." It would seem to be in the interest of organizations such as NAIS to undertake these types of studies or to engage qualified, independent academic researchers to examine the factors that may make for success in the pursuit of an excellent education. Understanding these data will help administrators maximize the likelihood that their students will become productive citizens in their communities.

References

American Association of School Librarians. [2007]. *School Libraries Count! A National Survey of School Library Media Programs 2007.* Available at www.ala.org/ala/mgrps/divs/aasl/school_libraries_count07.report.pdf. Accessed March 7, 2010.

———. [2008]. *School Libraries Count! The Second National Survey of School Library Media Programs 2008.* Available at www.btsb.com/brochures/SLCreport2008.pdf. Accessed March 7, 2010.

Bassett, Patrick F. 2004. *Independent Schools: Preparing Students for Achievement in College and Beyond.* NAIS. Available at www.nais.org/files/PDFs/HERI_9-1-04.pdf. Accessed September 29, 2008.

Broughman, Steven. 2009. Telephone interview with author, April 2.

Cahoy, Ellysa Stern, and Susan G. Williamson. 2008. "Studying the Independent School Library."*School Library Media Research* 11 (December). Available at www.ala.org/ala/mgrps/divs/aasl/aaslpubsandjournals/slmrb/slmrcontents/volume1 1/cahoy_williamson.cfm. Accessed November 17, 2009.

National Association of Independent Schools. 2005. *NAIS and Public Schools: How Do They Compare?* Ed. National Association of Independent Schools. NAIS. Available at www.nais.org/Files/PDFs/NAIS_Public_Schools_How_Do_They_ Compare.pdf. Accessed November 25, 2008.

———. 2006. *Understanding Students at Independent Schools: A Look Through the Eyes of College Freshmen Students.* Ed. National Association of Independent Schools. NAIS. Available only to NAIS members, at www.nais.org/ resources/article.cfm?ItemNumber=148269. Accessed November 25, 2008.

———. 2008. *2006–2007 SAT Test Scores National Schools and National Averages.* NAIS. Available only to NAIS members, at www.nais.org/resources/article.cfm? ItemNumber=1151247 This link is only available to NAIS members. Accessed November 25, 2008.

"19 States and 1 Province Can't Be Wrong." 2008. In *School Libraries Work!* 3rd ed. Research Foundation Paper. Scholastic Research & Results/Scholastic Library Publishing. Available at http://listbuilder.scholastic.com/content/stores/Library Store/pages/images/SLW3.pdf. Accessed March 23, 2010.

Palmisano, Joseph M. 2001. "Analysis of Variance." In *World of Sociology*. Detroit: Gale Group.

Pryor, John H. 2008. *Today's College Freshmen Have Family Income 60 Percent Above National Average, UCLA Study Reveals.* Los Angeles: UCLS. Available at www.gseis.ucls.edu/heri/PDFs/PR_TRENDS_40YR.pdf. Accessed September 27, 2008.

United States Bureau of the Census. 2000. *Census Regions and Divisions of the United States.* [Washington, D.C.]: Bureau of the Census. Available at www. census.gov/geo/www/us_regdiv.pdf. Accessed November 18, 2008.

United States Department of Education. National Center for Education Statistics. 2002a. *Private Schools: A Brief Portrait. Findings from "The Condition of Education, 2002."* By Martha Naomi Alt and Katherine Peter. [Washington, D.C.]: National Center for Education Statistics. Available at ncesed. gov/pubs2002/2002012pdf. Accessed May 28, 2008).

———. 2002b. *School Locale Codes: 1987–2000.* By National Center for Education Statistics. [Washington, D.C.]: National Center for Education Statistics. Available at nces.ed.gov/pubs2002/200202.pdf. Accessed September 27, 2008.

———. 2004. *The Status of Public and Private School Library Media Centers in the United States: 1999–2000.* By Barbara Holton et al. [Washington, D.C.]: National Center for Education Statistics. Available at nces.ed.gov/ Pubsearch/pubsinfo.asp?pubid=2004313. Accessed May 28, 2008.

———. 2006. *Comparing Private Schools and Public Schools Using Hierarchical Linear Modeling.* By H. Braun, F. Jenkins, and W. Grigg. [Washington, D.C.]: U.S. Government Printing Office. Available at http://nces.ed.gov/ nationsreportcard/pdf/studies/200646.pdf. Accessed August 9, 2009.

———. 2008. *Characteristics of Private Schools in the United States: Results from the 2005–2006 Private School Universe Survey.* By Steven Broughman and Nancy Swaim. [Washington, D.C.]: National Center for Education Statistics. Available at nces.ed.gov/Pubsearch/pubsinfo.asp?pubid=2006319. Accessed September 12, 2008.

———. 2009. *Characteristics of Private Schools in the United States: Results from the 2007–2008 Private School Universe Survey First Look.* By Steven Broughman, Nancy L Swaim, and Patrick W. Keaton. [Washington, D.C.]: National Center for Education Statistics. Available at nces.ed.gov/pubsearch/ pubsinfo.asp?pubid=2009313/. Accessed April 13, 2009.

United States Department of Education. National Center for Education Statistics. Institute of Education Sciences. 2004. *Schools and Staffing Survey (SASS) 1999–2000.* By National Center for Education Statistics. [Washington, D.C.]: National Center for Education Statistics. Available at nces.ed.gov/surveys/sass. Accessed September 27, 2008.

———. 2005. *School Library Media Centers: Selected Results From the Education Longitudinal Study of 2002 (ELS:2002).* By Leslie Scott and Jeffrey Owings. [Washington, D.C.]: National Center for Education Statistics. Available at http://nces.ed.gove/pubs2005/2005302.pdf. Accessed August 9, 2009.

———. 2006. *The Nation's Report Card Student Achievement in Private Schools. Results From NAEP 2000–2005.* By National Center for Education Statistics. [Washington, D.C.]: National Center for Education Statistics. Available at http://nces.ed.gov/nationsreportcard/pdf/studies/2006459.pdf. Accessed August 9, 2009.

Zager, Sarah. 2009. E-mail message to author, May 21.

Visit http://lu.com/excellence for supporting links and occasional updates to all essays in this book.

Susan Williamson's career as a librarian began in 1982 at Swarthmore College, where she worked as the Social Sciences Bibliographer and taught courses in language and culture. After seven years she became director of the Annenberg School for Communication library at the University of Pennsylvania. Ten years later she moved west to become the Director of Library Services at Albuquerque Academy in New Mexico. She has recently retired, but remains connected with independent school librarians in the United States.

The author wishes to thank the members of the American Association of School Librarians Independent Schools Section Data Committee, who contributed the questions on the survey; Ellysa Cahoy, who arranged for the analysis of the data at the Penn State Survey Research Center and wrote the first article with me; Nicole Morgan, who analyzed the data; Colin O'Rourke of the Statistics Department at the University of New Mexico, who gave me helpful advice; and John Betak, who read more copies of this essay than anyone would ever want to read and gave me invaluable assistance; and Dorcas Hand, who started it all and who is editing it all, too!

We Are Not Alone

Courtney Lewis, Wyoming Seminary (Kingston, PA)
Laura Pearle, Hackley School (Tarrytown, NY)

"No man is an island" wrote John Donne; the same can be said about independent school librarians. Sometimes it *feels* as though we're islands; often we're the only librarian in the school or the only librarian for our division (while the others are in separate facilities). There's no need to feel isolated: we can all paddle to another island and build bridges between facilities, librarians, and schools.

Although we may be islands within our individual schools, in reality we're more like Galapagos fauna, evolving in our own ways but with common ancestors and shared resources. Reaching outside our library doors to other departments within our schools and to librarians at other schools is critical to our practice and pedagogy.

Many librarians are intimidated at the thought of networking, a loaded term that conjures up visions of urbane cocktail parties in which you deftly juggle a martini and whip out (and receive) business cards while asking colleagues about their circulation statistics. Although the occasional cocktail might be present, the reality is that networking for librarians takes on many forms and takes place in many venues, all of which are designed to help us create meaningful relationships with our peers and to exchange information about our profession. Networking is not only a fabulous way of extending our commitment to librarianship but also gives us a chance to shamelessly steal (with permission) great ideas that make us look like information gods(esses) to our administration. And who has a problem with that?

Of course your time is precious, and you don't think you have time to glad-hand and go on visits to other schools to get to know people. No offense, but you've got it all wrong. Networking, in its basic form, is making yourself findable and sharing resources while receiving maximum value for your investment of time and money. As librarians, each of us feels the professional pressure to keep up with the massive amount of research and best practices and standards and resources and new tools and . . . and . . . but the thought of reading blogs, keeping up with your ever-growing pile of professional reading, or attending conferences is daunting. As independent school librarians, each of us has both the mandate and the flexibility to respond to the latest research in library science, ensuring that our school has a program that increases student achievement. You don't have to do it all, but after reading this essay, you might well find that you can do more than you think, and you'll definitely be able to weigh which activities are worth your time and energy.

Island Hopping in Minutes a Day

How big does your time investment really have to be?

20–30 mins./day	Check blogs and social network sites
2 hrs./week	Professional reading
1 day/year	State/Local/Regional Institute
2–3 days/year	State or Local conference
4–5 days/year	National or International Conference

Types of Networking Strategies

There are several strategies that librarians can employ to good effect, depending on their situation. When librarians think of networking, formal involvement in professional organizations, usually related to holding an office or working on a committee, is what first comes to mind. Often that obligation can be prohibitive in terms of time and travel. Informal networking is more cost effective and can still get you recognition within your school for your leadership and openness to new ideas. Arranging best practice visits with a nearby school (don't forget to carpool with teachers or administrators who might want to visit their equivalent departments; it's a great way to build bonds and share insights) or serving on an accreditation team for schools undergoing that delightful process can be very rewarding for a small investment of time. Delegation is also an effective technique: divide up the organizations you want to join among your library staff (or among your nearby librarians). Periodically get together and share journals or forward listserv postings about hot topics. Often you can take a nonmember guest to a conference for less than it would cost to have an annual membership in the organization, and you get to kibitz with a good friend while sharing a room.

Staying Close to Home

Does your job description include all the clerical tasks we were told (by well-meaning professors in our various library schools) that we didn't need to/should not have to do? Are you Head Librarian/Librarian/Assistant Librarian/Library Assistant and Library Volunteer all wrapped in one? Do *not* spend your time locked in your library, tempting as that may be (how else would all that work get done?). Eat breakfast or lunch with your colleagues. Attend division or department meetings. Get to know the parents' association and offer to host meetings in the library—it's a great way to show them what you're doing and subtly pitch for volunteers at the same time. Asking your colleagues for advice about collection development, constantly bringing new tools/new resources to their attention, and showing them how collaboration makes their program stronger will enhance your role in the school and give you support when you feel most alone.

If you are lucky enough to have additional librarians or an assistant, plan regular (biweekly or monthly) gatherings. These don't have to have a defined agenda, but can just be a time when you collectively share ideas and plans for the future. Occasionally plan a discussion topic that would be a logical choice for an interdepartmental meeting; for example, talk about implementing open source software with the technology department or invite the math department to explore WolframAlpha (www.wolframalpha.com/) with you. Whether just a single representative or an entire department, welcoming people into your meetings injects new ideas into your discussion while making the hard work you do visible to others. Do make sure that this is uninterrupted time! Nothing breaks a mood more than having to stop and assist someone with research (or photocopier) needs.

Join school committees. Yes, we all know about the important ones (curriculum/ academic), but sometimes it's the connections you make on the fun ones that can matter most. Is there a prom committee? What about school dances? Chaperoning gets you out of the library and into parent and student lives in a whole new way. The same holds for rooting for a team, advising a club, or helping with a bake-sale.

Ramp up your Web site, going beyond the basic lists of resources and opening times, and think about using platforms that allow faculty and students to be contributors with you. Consider using Netvibes or Pageflakes to create dynamic pages that "pull" information useful to the casual learner. LibGuides is the twenty-first-century's answer to the paper-based pathfinder. *LibraryThing* can make your collection "pop" and give the community a safe place to explore and learn about other books that might make great acquisitions. Wikis enable faculty and students to share and update resources at will.

Now that you've built bridges close to home, within your school environment, go further. (WARNING: the following contains many, many acronyms.) Networking isn't just about making connections, it's about expanding your personal learning network (PLN). The connections are important: learning about new jobs and resources available to your school, garnering support for school-based initiatives, gathering data to successfully plead for increased budgets, staffing, and updating the library space are all important. Your PLN will help you become an indispensable member of the school's academic team, because you'll be armed with great tools, resources, and ideas that you've borrowed (or recycled, to use P.D.Q. Bach's term) from other librarians.

Paddling Around (Networking with Other Independent Schools Nearby)

Most independent school librarians are lucky enough to live within the catchment area of one of the many independent school groups, such as the following:

- Metropolitan Washington Independent School Librarians Association (MWISLA)
- Georgia Independent School Librarians (GISL)
- South East Florida Independent School Librarians Consortia (SEFISLC)
- Independent Schools Saint Louis (ISSL)
- Bay Area Independent School Librarians (BAISL)

Links to these groups and more can be found at http://lu.com/excellence.

These organizations are a great way to share our strengths, find resources, and make those important connections with our independent school peers. Many have e-lists, Web sites, and sharing spaces; most have regular or semi-regular gatherings. (For example, the tristate's Hudson Valley Library Association (HVLA) celebrated its fiftieth anniversary in 2009 with a party at New York City's Society Library and a talk by James Howe.) Other initiatives include the Los Angeles area's Independent School Library Exchange's ISLE-GAP, a union catalog that facilitates interlibrary loan; the Greater Boston Cooperative Library Association (GBCLA) and Houston Area Independent Schools Library Network (HAISLN) have great shared summer reading lists.

Local groups may also mix independent and public school librarians. For example, in New York State the regional Board of Cooperative Education Services (BOCES) is mandated to provide service to all school librarians. Many groups include independent school librarians on their advisory councils, and most provide consortium pricing for databases as well as training and other resources.

It's sometimes worth it to think outside the box when pondering networking partners. Local public libraries are often great resources, particularly if they are near your school. After all, theoretically they offer good books, computer access, and a friendly librarian during times that your library may not be open. Encouraging student use makes public librarians happy (hello, increased circulation and patron statistics!) and helps our students become lifelong library users, and that's the goal, right? Even if you stay in touch with your local public librarians to alert them to the popular titles flying off your shelves (and asking how many copies they've ordered) or hear from them about author visits or movie nights, this relationship can expand the boundaries of your library program and empower a vital local resource. Think about museums or historical societies that might also possess collections or programming that fit in with projects or complement what's on your shelves.

No Passport Required (State and National Networks)

All states have a library association, and most include a school library section. Although they may be connected to the American Library Association (ALA)'s agenda and needs, these groups are a great way to take advantage of any resources made available by your state's department of education.

Nationally, there are two major groups: the Association of Independent School Librarians (AISL) and the Independent Schools Section (ISS) of the ALA's American Association of School Librarians (AASL) division. AISL has one conference a year, an e-list, and a Web site, all focused on the lives and needs of independent school librarians. ISS offers an e-list and, as part of AASL, access to all the national resources that a 10,000+ member organization can offer.

Conferences are the most natural place to do external networking. For those who are shy about being all alone at a conference, keep in mind that national conferences usually have meetings based on affiliations. Your library science graduate school might be having a reception, or your state school librarian association might have a mixer. Check their Web sites before you travel. At these conferences, keep in mind two things: 1) everyone there loves libraries, and 2) librarians are nice. These sentiments may seem obvious, but 99.9 percent of people who attend conferences are motivated, friendly professionals eager to make new connections and learn about new ideas; the "shushy," cranky, resistant-to-change ones stay at home. We've heard vendors at conferences who work with a varied customer base gush about how great the librarian attendees are—we are not about to disagree!

How do you strike up a conversation? Where should you do it? If you are sitting next to someone at a vendor breakfast or session, it's natural to give a friendly "hi" and ask where others at the table are from, but the best conversations and contacts often come from riding the bus or sharing a taxi with a stranger, or standing in the interminable line waiting to pack and mail home your free swag. Just glance at people's tags and make a comment on where they live (we advise against asking the librarian from New Jersey "what exit are you from?"). Or comment on a great free vendor tote bag and ask for the booth number. The conversation will just take off from there!

Around the World Cruise (International Network Opportunities)

An increasing number of independent school librarians belong to international organizations like the International Federation of Libraries Association (IFLA) or the International Association of School Librarianship (IASL). This may seem like an unnecessary expense, but it's worth taking a closer look at their motivation. Not only are many of our schools extremely diverse, with large international populations, but practically all independent schools have embraced the imperative of imbuing students with a sense of their role in the larger global community. Participation in these organizations gives us access to virtual communities and journals that alert us to trends in other countries. If our international students are coming from schools in a country in which there is no database access (whether due to financial or computer limitations or to government censorship), we can approach instructing these students in a different manner. Identifying a sister library that might be willing to videochat with your school's foreign language classes in exchange for its students getting a chance to practice their English shows that the librarian is consistently scouting for resources to intersect with the curriculum.

Armchair Cruising (Exploring the Virtual World)

Now that you've built a few bridges to other librarians, it's time to extend your network electronically. The explosion of networking tools started with the e-list and the Web site and has grown exponentially. Don't be afraid to try, and drop(!), some of these tools. The important thing is to find what tools work best for you, but you really need to try them all to determine if they fit your work or lifestyle.

E-Lists

- LM_NET: over 13,000 members worldwide, and can be cumbersome to follow. (It does have EL-ANNOUNCE, which highlights the Best of LM_NET as well as vendor information.)
- ISED-L: for independent school educators only, and sometimes dominated by tech or head-level discussions (always a good opportunity to share the librarian's point of view).
- Child Lit: exactly what it sounds like, a list for those interested in talking about/learning about children's literature.
- YALSA-BK: for those working with an older set of students.
- FICTION_L: run by Morton Grove (IL) Public Library, this is a great resource for readers' advisory.

The simplest virtual networking strategy is to join an e-list. There are many that cover school library-related topics, ranging from administrative to readers' advisory. Some have thousands of members; others are more focused and "exclusive." Still other lists require membership in your local, state, or national organization to join (AISL, ISS, AASL, and other groups all have e-lists with varying degrees of posting and chatter).

The next level would be to join one of the many social networking options. A *ning* is an online community of people with shared interests, which allows participants to create a personal page, participate in discussions, and share resources. Nings can spring from a professional organization (like the NAIS ning), be the brainchild of a person wanting to create a specific online community (like Demetri Orlando's Independent School Educators network), or be playful (like the Nerdfighters Made of Awesome Ning, which has a young adult literature focus). Facebook is also gaining prominence in the world of librarian social networking. Often librarians post conference notes, videos, author pictures, and great links they have discovered, so this virtual space can offer a wealth of information for people unable to attend conferences.

Blogs can be goldmines of information, but they can also take up lots of valuable time. The best (and fastest) way to keep track of them is to ruthlessly skim them in a platform like Google Reader or Bloglines and only read the entries most pertinent to your work; it's easy with these tools to bookmark or save important posts for future, further thought. For people with even less time, Twitter is a fantastic resource. Many librarians post links or breaking news and, for those of us who are shameless author stalkers, you'd be amazed how many award-winning or just extremely popular authors "twit" their publicity tour dates, latest publication news, and witty musings via this interface. For those librarians for whom keeping a blog is just too much pressure, the 140-character limit of Twitter makes it easy to post the occasional insight and feel like you're contributing to a larger community.

Pack your steamer trunks: these are a great starting toolkit for your virtual personal learning network.

Nings

- Teacher-Librarian Ning (http://teacherlibrarian.ning.com)
- Independent School Educators Ning (http://isenet.ning.com/)
- Librarians Ning (http://librarians.ning.com/)
- Library Youth and Teen Services Ning (http://libraryyouth.ning.com/)

Blogs

- Students 2.0 (http://students2oh.org)
- Information Literacy Meets Library 2.0 (http://infolitlib20.blogspot.com)
- Not So Distant Future (http://futura.edublogs.org
- The Librarian Edge (http://libedge.blogspot.com/)
- The Unquiet Librarian (http://theunquietlibrarian.wordpress.com)
- Archipelago (http://archipelagoblog.blogspot.com)
- Neverending Search (http://www.schoollibraryjournal.com/blog/1340000334.html)
- Pop Goes the Library (http://www.popgoesthelibrary.com)
- School Library Media Activities Monthly Blog (http://blog.schoollibrarymedia.com)
- Blue Skunk Blog (http://doug-johnson.squarespace.com/blue-skunk-blog)
- Heavy Medal: A Mock Newbery Blog (http://www.schoollibraryjournal.com/blog/560000656.html)

Twitterers

- @Scholastic (Scholastic Inc.)
- @AASL_ISS (AASL's Independent Schools Section)
- @YALSA
- @AASL
- @ALSC
- @ReadingRants (Jennifer Hubert Swan)
- @ypulsestais (Anastasia Goodman)

Remember, networking is about what works for you, it is not a one-size-fits-all process. However, it is important to make these connections; you never know when you'll need friends in varied places, and you never know where you're going find that next great idea.

Visit http://lu.com/excellence for supporting links and occasional updates to all essays in this book.

Courtney Lewis is the Director of Libraries at Wyoming Seminary College Preparatory School (www.wyomingseminary.org/), a pre-K through 12 school that is neither in Wyoming nor a seminary. She loves living in northeastern Pennsylvania, working with her history teacher husband every day and bringing her golden retriever, Bugsy, to work, even though he is more popular than she is. Courtney can be found regularly reflecting on her profession on her blog, The Sassy Librarian (http://thesassylibrarian.blogspot.com).

Laura Pearle began her library career with a three-year stint as a student library aide at Emma Willard School, followed by a sixteen-year hiatus while she explored the varied worlds of college, off-Broadway theater, investment banking, and executive recruiting, among others. Since returning to independent school libraries in 1996, she has focused on the evaluating accreditation process, investigating the K–20 skills curriculum and developing her personal learning network. Her writings have appeared in such journals as Independent School *and* Knowledge Quest, *as well as the* Association of Teachers in Independent School Quarterly. *Laura is currently Head Librarian at the Hackley School in Tarrytown, New York (www.hackleyschool.org/).*

Who Are We? Staffing in School Libraries

Aquita Winslow-Tyler, Crossroads School for Arts & Sciences (Santa Monica, CA)

Introduction

School libraries have gone through a major transformation in the last twenty years. Always a hub of student learning, twenty-first-century school libraries must support student learning and student life. The new library needs to be open twenty-four hours a day in a virtual world to support students who prefer a free-flowing schedule while they still support traditional modes of learning. Independent schools are accepting the challenge, embracing their libraries, and even expanding their services.

- How does the library's/school's mission statement affect staffing and service?
- Who works in your school library, and why?
- How many staff members do you need in your library to run it efficiently?
- How do you determine the best service hours for your library?
- What challenges and concerns arise for libraries based on service hours and staffing?

A good library is so in large part because the staff understand the flow of the school and the curriculum and appreciate how the library fits into both. There is no one ideal model for a school library, and no one archetype for a school librarian. There are, however, some very important standard questions to look at when staffing a library and deciding the library's hours of service, including, How does the library's/school mission statement affect staffing and service? Who works in the school library, and why? How many staff members does the library need to run it efficiently? How does one figure the best service hours for the library? What challenges and concerns arise for libraries based on service hours and staffing?

Part I—Library Staffing: Who Works in Your Library?

A note about being a librarian in an independent school. Librarians are not classroom teachers. The job descriptions are very different, but few school administrators (who may have been classroom teachers themselves) have any frame of reference for the workload, duties, and challenges of a school librarian. Plainly said, they just don't know what we do. A school will have hundreds of students, dozens of teachers, staff, and administrators, but the same school will only have one—or a very few—librarians. Librarians fall into many categories within the independent school framework. We can be administrators managing substantial budgets, supervising staff and students, and managing the physical space of the library. We are also teachers responsible for our own curricula, regularly working with students, participating in lunch duty, serving on academic counsels, and leading accreditation teams. In some schools, librarians are staff, hourly (noncontracted) full-, and part-time employees (Morris 2004, 21).

No matter how the librarian is classified, the job is always twofold. We are educators who support the educational efforts of the school, and we are a small branch of a much larger professional field, maintaining our library collections and physical spaces. This duality permeates everything we do, including who we hire for our libraries. Where a classroom teacher gives tests, we catalog. Where a classroom teacher grades, we evaluate potential sources. Where a classroom teacher reads, we . . . read, read, and read some more. Where a classroom teacher is responsible to support learning for his or her individual course load of students, librarians are responsible for supporting learning for all students in the entire school, all faculty, and even parents. It is important for school administrators to understand the dualities librarians face. Our uniqueness as a department should be a factor in selecting library staff, writing contracts, and setting library hours for service. When working with an administrator to advocate for adequate library staffing, look at who your students are. Where are they on the age spectrum, the special needs to gifted spectrum, and the socioeconomic spectrum? Look at the size of your library and the services that you offer. How many students are in your school? Do you teach? Do you offer extended hours of service? Do you manage technology integration for the classrooms? Look at how library staff members are classified when advocating for any staffing changes.

Use Your Libraries/School's Mission Statement as Your Guide

Creating a quality staff is the cornerstone to any successful library. No matter the size of the school, whether it is religious in its affiliation, college prep, traditional, progressive, day, or boarding, library staff in independent schools share similar core values and professional responsibilities. We promote reading and support classroom curriculum within a school setting. And we value principles that promote lifelong learning (Moorman 2006, 57–59). However, the constant challenge for librarians in independent schools is to find a way to successfully engage and support children and young adults with their social and educational needs, while providing teachers with structured academic support services that complement classroom learning. A great place to find a description of the school's core values is the school's mission statement.

Sample Mission Statement

"An education that challenges the mind, nurtures the heart, and celebrates human dignity."

—Sequoyah School, Pasadena, California

A mission statement is a declaration of the school's core philosophies ("Mission Statement" 2009). For example, a small independent school in Pasadena, California, has a mission statement that reads: "An education that challenges the mind, nurtures the heart and celebrates human dignity" (Sequoyah School 2008). Mission statements generally accompany the school's educational philosophy, which gives specific examples of a school's core values in action. This same school's educational philosophy discusses the school's seven habits of mind, one of which is collaboration (Sequoyah School 2008). As individual librarians look for ways to best fit the staff into the life of the school, they create programs in which the librarian and staff are actively collaborating with teachers and students, thereby modeling one of the school's core values.

When choosing library staff members and deciding on library hours of service, librarians should use the school's core values as a guide. For example, if your school's mission statement declares "Valuing Diversity" to be a core goal, the library staff should reflect the school's commitment to diversity in race, religion, gender, ethnicity, or sexuality. If your school has declared a commitment to specialized curriculum such as the arts, science, outdoor education, or religion, the library should employ people who have additional training or a keen interest in these areas to better support collaboration with the classes that teach these topics. Hiring staff members who can support the school's mission will give the library a stronger voice within the school community in addition to enhancing collection development and curricular collaboration with faculty.

Does your school library have its own mission statement? The library's mission statement is also helpful when deciding what qualities you want your library staff members to possess. Libraries hold as a core value "promoting lifelong learning." Many librarians translate this mission statement to mean creating quality collections and providing services that will teach patrons the value of using libraries throughout their lives (*Education and Continuing Learning Brochure* 2007). However, if a librarian were to use this core value as a guide in making hiring decisions, he or she could look for staff members who demonstrate a passion for lifelong learning in their own lives, and have a desire to support students to learn for the sake of learning.

Take some time to look at your own library's mission statement. What are some concrete ways your staff can exemplify the library mission every day? This list can begin to show administrators what the library could do to enhance the school mission, curriculum and image if you had enough staff to teach all the classes, budget to fund the expanding collection, and computer access points to support the increasing number of students working in the library during study periods. These direct links between library and mission statement can also open a conversation about filtering limits, the pros and cons of Internet searching, or the value of print research versus database or online research.

Although the library or school mission statement is a great source of information, it is not the only one. The librarian seeking a better understanding of the school's core values should be in constant contact with teachers, administrators, and students. These user groups will help to provide a better context for school life, which will help library staff members integrate the library into school life more effectively.

Who Works in the Library: Job Descriptions

Libraries employ in paid positions personnel with a variety of job titles and descriptions, including librarians, library clerks and assistants, catalogers, archivists, and library monitors. They also have unpaid volunteers and interns. Libraries work extensively with and rely on tech coordinators and IT support, positions that may or may not fall under the library's umbrella.

Professional Positions: Librarians

An independent school librarian may be called Director of Libraries, Head Librarian, Library Department Chair, Reference Librarian, Division Librarian, Upper School Librarian, Middle School Librarian, Lower School Librarian, or Library Specialist (*Membership Directory* 2009). The overarching job description for the department includes a wider variety of duties than classroom teachers, and includes administrative responsibilities such as budget management.

Librarian Job Description

- **Collection Development:** Actively shape the library collection based on classroom curriculum and a commitment to valuing personal as well as academic reading, which includes reviewing publishers, reading review and advanced copies of books, writing reviews, and evaluating potential sources.

- **Teaching:** Teach library skills, research, and information literacy classes to student and faculty. These classes teach patrons general to specific techniques for doing research in a school or academic library. Most librarians develop a specific curriculum over time that becomes progressively more difficult as students get older.

- **Library/Collection Maintenance:** Catalog book and other library materials. Librarians manage library serials, ordering and purchasing of books (which includes discerning appropriate vendors and prices), and processing those materials to shelf availability.

- **Technology:** Evaluate and purchase educational databases and library software, and regularly teach students to use the Internet and other online resources for research and evaluation. Troubleshoot computers.

- **Administrative Duties:** Advocate for library services and support from faculty and staff. Librarians develop library polices with school administration. Librarians manage library budgets, purchase educational databases, run book-fairs or book sales, and work with library software. Librarians create end-of-year reports and receive money for fine and book replacement costs.

- **Student Support:** Book talk interesting books, advise student clubs, create displays, and attend field trips. Generally, know the students well enough to provide individual readers' advisory and research skill support.

- **Teacher Collaboration:** Collaborate with classroom teachers on their individual curriculums, as well as the library's information literacy curriculum. Librarians participate in academic counsel, act as student advisors, and attend faculty meetings.

- **Supervision:** Supervise library staff members, volunteers, students, and the library's physical space.

No independent school is complete without a librarian. A major responsibility of the librarian is to create a cohesive service model for library service within a school setting. The librarian is the bridge between the larger library community and his or her individual school. The librarian translates the school's mission into tangible services, which are carried out by the library staff. The librarian sets a tone for the library that welcomes and supports faculty students and staff alike.

Librarians are professional faculty members. Most commonly, they have a master's degree in library science or information studies, but some effective librarians have degrees in English literature or other disciplines that require the mastery of research. Librarians may also have been classroom teachers with some state certifications or library media teachers (LMT), who hold a library media teacher credential. School librarians need an extensive knowledge of fiction and nonfiction titles suitable for children and young adults, with a particular emphasis on children's and young adult authors. We teach library skills or information literacy to students, which focus on all aspects of library service, from the Dewey Decimal system to evaluating sources for research papers. Independent school librarians find support from national organizations such as the American Library

Association (ALA), American Association of School Librarians (AASL), Independent School Section (ISS) of the American Association of School Librarians; and state and local consortiums ("Librarian" 2009; *Membership Directory* 2009; Morris 2004, 211).

Within a school setting, librarians can be many things to students: confidants, advisors, teachers, and friends. Librarians see students in all their emotional states and work to create a space in which students feel valued. The knowledge that a librarian has about individual students can be very extensive. Students will come to librarians for help with homework, research papers, literary criticism, and for reading suggestions. In turn, librarians work to make libraries a haven for students. We create collections that support student interest and hobbies, we let students use the library for clubs and other extracurricular activities, and we provide a sympathetic ear. Independent school librarians are rare and special people who help children grow into adulthood.

Librarians as Administrators

An effective librarian can institute excellent programs that affect the entire school even without the designation of administrator. All school librarians have an administrative component to their duties. All are managers of space and of staff, whether paid or volunteer. All librarians manage budgets, participate in hiring decisions, and act as advocates for staff members who report to them (Morris 2004, 509–534). The distinction between librarians who are classified as administrators and those considered faculty has more to do with the school's acceptance of the managerial aspects of a librarian's job than with the job itself. When a school has classified its head librarian as an administrator, it has recognized that its library as a department requires the leadership of a seasoned senior staff member with the expertise to shape the the department's direction. This classification has nothing to do with the size of the library or the number of staff members. It does, however, have to do with the quality of the library program, the services offered, and the library's presence in the school community. The stronger the presence, the more the school needs a library administrator. A school that recognizes the strong impact of the library program on other aspects of administration is more likely to designate the librarian an administrator.

Library administrators are not, or should not be, novice librarians. As administrators, these librarians will be year-round employees with standard vacation schedules. Library administrators are vocal members of the school community who work to build a library program that extends beyond the walls of the library; they have honed their advocacy skills and are not afraid to use them. Library administrators generally work in libraries with several staff members. They organize staff schedules and supervise librarians,

> When a school has classified its head librarian as an administrator, it has recognized that its library as a department requires the leadership of a seasoned senior staff member with the expertise to shape the department's direction. This classification has nothing to do with the size of the library, or the number of staff members. It does, however, have to do with the quality of the library program, the services offered, and the library's presence in the school community.

clerks, perhaps a cataloger, an archivist, or volunteers. These librarians may manage libraries with larger budgets and oversee larger library spaces, or they may use their expertise to create a large impact with a smaller budget and find innovative ways to maximize use of a smaller library space.

The library staff, whether trained professionals or not, benefit from the leadership of a library administrator. Administrators act as mentors to colleagues, help them build curricula, and teach them how to deal with student and teacher behavior. Their knowledge of books and student reading interests is broad and deep. Library administrators offer internal leadership for library staff, as well as external leadership that demonstrates to the larger faculty why library use is essential to a strong education.

Library administrators generate goodwill for the library with departments that may not use library services on a regular basis. School libraries are (or should be) the heart of the school. There is no aspect of the school curriculum that

> *There is no aspect of the school curriculum that libraries do not support, there is not one student librarians ignore, and there are no teachers whom libraries cannot support.*

libraries do not support, there is not one student librarians ignore, and there are no teachers whom libraries cannot assist. Many library administrators participate in other school activities, such as Academic Senate, accreditation committees, and advisory and technology counsels. Librarians have a vast store of knowledge at their fingertips, knowledge that can bring perspective to administrative discussions ("Staffing and Hours Questions" 2009). Librarians are also more aware of "student overflow issues"—study hall, extended-day, makeup tests, free time—and can bring a concrete grounding to administrative discussions of these issues. They will ask hard questions, such as, how does the decision to allow students to stay on campus until 6:00 pm affect library staffing?

Librarians as Faculty

In most schools, librarians are classified as faculty. This means they are contracted employees who only work in the library when school is in session. Faculty librarians hold a master's degree in library science. A librarian's contract will also identify any other duties and responsibilities of the librarian in a given school year, such as hours of work, participating in student supervision, chaperoning field trips, and attending staff meetings. As faculty, librarians have the ability to teach students how to access, evaluate, and use information through library materials, both print and online sources. These classes are referred to as library skills, research skills, or information literacy programs.

Although not all librarians teach structured classes, most independent schools do expect librarians to do some teaching. Many elementary school librarians have regular teaching schedules. Often elementary schools include librarians with the "specialists," referring to a subject specialist who teaches all students in the school a specific enrichment curriculum like art or music. Specialists teach a progressively more challenging "library skills" curriculum to all students in the school. Librarians with fixed schedules such as these are closest to standard faculty in job description.

This model works best for elementary schools, whose teaching staffs work collaboratively to enhance the student learning experience. This constant schedule offers librarians a guarantee that every child will visit the library at least weekly for books; some teaching time will be included during the visit. This schedule also ensures that the librarian has an active voice among the faculty dealing with curriculum as applied to the student body. Many librarians find that they provide insights about behavior and reading habits to classroom teachers that the teachers would not have gleaned from other school situations. However, this schedule is not without its drawbacks. Although elementary school librarians usually have regular access to students, their fixed schedule limits their flexibility to welcome classes at the last minute to support unexpected research opportunities. Professional literature recommends that we have more flexible scheduling for libraries ("AASL Position Statement" 2009). Each school has to find its own balance between the two needs. In addition to teaching duties, elementary librarians are also responsible for the circulation management and collection development aspects of the library.

Librarians who work in middle and high schools are less likely to have scheduled time with students, requiring them to structure their teaching responsibilities differently. As students' progress in school and their schedules become more complex, so do librarians work with specific faculty members to facilitate lessons tied to specific projects. These librarians reach out frequently to faculty to plan collaborative lessons that extend the course content while building useful research methodology. Middle and upper school faculty librarians function as a part of the academic team, supporting student learning and monitoring student behavior. Secondary libraries see a steady stream of solo students, small groups, and full classes; they may be coming for books to read, quick information, makeup tests, computer access, student center, and other miscellaneous reasons. The librarians offer readers' advisory, ready reference, tech support, and disciplinary supervision ("Staffing and Hours Questions" 2009).

Freedom of access to school libraries for students creates an obligation on the part of librarians to supervise student behavior. Although all independent school librarians deal with supervision of students during "free periods." this supervision issue can be more challenging on high school campuses, where students have free periods and no designated student center ("Staffing and Hours Questions" 2009). Librarians supervise a free-floating collection of students who visit the library throughout the day for myriad reasons: makeup tests, free time, small group research (Morris 2004, 54–58). When librarians are not working directly with students, they have many other duties that keep them very busy. They collaborate with many members of the school community: with teachers on class curriculum and with the school technology department, on computers, library software, databases, and other online resources.

A large part of a librarian's work involves maintaining the library's physical and virtual collections. Librarians work closely with faculty to make sure the library collection supports classroom curriculum. This process includes evaluating potential sources, testing new electronic databases, reading reviews and previewing books, and conducting curriculum mapping activities. Depending on the number of staff members working in the library, librarians may also have to catalog all new library materials.

Although many school libraries may be small in numbers of staff, they are large in terms of per-pupil resources and annual budgets.

Librarians are managers of space and people. The librarian works with library colleagues to make sure the library is clean and the environment inviting. Interesting displays entice the school's many patrons into the library. Although many school libraries may be small in numbers of staff, they are large in terms of per-pupil resources and annual budgets.

Librarians as Staff

Librarians classified as staff members have very different job responsibilities than librarians classified as administrators or faculty. Most schools use a staff designation for those employees who do not teach students, including office workers, part-time employees, counselors or educational therapists, and custodial staff (*Membership Directory* 2009).

Staff often do not have annual contracts and are at-will employees. Staff members may be year-round employees, hourly employees, or employees without benefits who are required to work during school breaks, when students and faculty are on vacation. Within the library, this classification is given to part-time librarians who are not expected to teach classes but act as support to full-time professional staff. This classification is also acceptable for library staff members who do not regularly interact with students and faculty, such as catalogers or archivists.

However, this classification is problematic for full-time librarians working in any school setting. The library is an academic department. The manager of this department needs to be able to interact with students and faculty from a position of authority and respect. Classifying the supervisor of the library facility as merely staff impedes that librarian's' ability to connect with students on an academic level and with teachers as an equal colleague.

When librarians are classified as staff, the school may see them as supervisors of space and materials, but not as teachers or educators; this classification is antithetical to the librarian's true role within the school community. For example, a librarian in Southern California holds an MLIS, but is classified as staff. As a staff member, she is required to work on all noninstructional days, including the Christmas and Easter holidays. As the only library employee, she must ask a colleague to staff the library when she has lunch. If she is absent, "they would have to close the library, which would be a hardship for the students." She does not teach students during the school year, but does offer a library skills class before school starts in the summer ("Hours and Staffing Questions" 2009).

Sometimes schools expect library staff members to teach and handle all the professional aspects of a library job without according them the respect of faculty status. These librarians may be sole practitioners (library supervisors who have no additional staff support) or paraprofessionals with the title of librarian but not the requisite credentials. A staff classification is not just a title. Staff members are paid on a different pay scale than faculty. Librarians who contribute to their communities as faculty should be appropriately compensated for their work.

Paraprofessional Staff

Library clerks and assistants staff a circulation desk, provide general circulation support for students and teachers, or manage the clerical load for librarians ("Library Technicians" 2009). They may also assist with copy cataloging and materials processing. Where do libraries find library clerks? Several types of people gravitate toward these positions. Some library students (working on an MLS) may take jobs as clerks to gain practical library experience. Some long-term library volunteers transition into paid employees when they realize how much they love the work—or the library staff. An assistant teacher may move to the library looking for a change. Libraries post these positions on the same Web sites used to find a professional librarian. Responses to these postings probably include people who have experience with libraries or who really want to work in libraries.

A great deal of time and attention is devoted to the contributions of the librarian, but the efforts of the library's support staff make a significant difference in the quality of service that a librarian can offer students and faculty. There are not enough hours in the day to complete all the tasks it takes to run a successful library program. Having quality assistance allows librarians to delegate responsibilities to make sure all areas of service are adequately supported.

> *[T]he efforts of the library's support staff make a significant difference in the quality of service that a librarian can offer students and faculty.*

In the minds of the students and faculty in a school, anyone who works in a library is considered a librarian. Whereas the duties and title of an associate teacher are clearly distinguished from those of a classroom teacher, librarians and library clerks perform duties that look very similar from the perspective of our patrons. All library staff members sit behind a service desk, support student learning, work with classes, and supervise student behavior (Eberhart 2006, 132).

However, clerks, assistants, and volunteers provide tremendous services in the library and to librarians that patrons may not see. Libraries that have ample support staff are able to offer additional service hours, manage additional library programs, and run quality information literacy programs. Additional staff allows the librarian to move more freely throughout the school for meetings and class presentations, and even clubs, while staff members supervise the circulation desk and physical library space.

Staff members also support maintenance of the library's collection: they process books, repair damaged books; search for lost materials; shelve, shift, and pull books for classes or displays; and make a detailed inventory manageable.

Staff members are also valuable to students. Students may know library staff just as well as, or even better than, the school librarian, because the nonprofessional staff member is often the one sitting at the desk to remind students about overdue books. A staff member who just processed the new book order may remember the kind of books the student likes and that a new one just arrived. Staff members save books for students, talk to students about their day, help students study, and contribute to a supportive library atmosphere that draws students to the library (Eberhart 2006, 209).

Professional and Part-Time Librarians

Cataloger

Many independent schools will employ a cataloger. Catalogers can be degreed librarians or library technicians who have taken cataloging classes. Cataloging requires the same attention to detail as accountancy. A cataloger's primary responsibility is to catalog new library materials, assigning the catalog number that locates the item in the collection, adding subject headings that make the item as accessible as possible to users via the library's catalog, and adding the record to the online catalog. Catalogers also make sure that materials in the collection have continuity. This is extremely important for school libraries where students find many of their resources by "browsing" the stacks (Fourie and Dowell 2002, 123).

> *Cataloging requires the same attention to detail as accountancy.*

For elementary and smaller libraries, having a cataloger is not a necessity. Much catalog information is available online, through either the materials vendor or a subscription service attached to the school's integrated library system. However, upper school and larger libraries with more academically advanced collections find having a staff cataloger indispensable ("Hours and Staffing Questions" 2009). Few school librarians have the time or inclination to do on-site cataloging. Having a staff member whose primary responsibility is to make sure that all new materials are cataloged guarantees that other library staff can spend more time with faculty and students, while ensuring that new materials are available in a timely manner. One school librarian commented that due to her teaching responsibilities, "I need someone to catalogue and deal with the organization and processing needs of the library" ("Staffing and Hours Questions" 2009).

Most cataloging positions in a school library are part-time, because only the largest of school libraries has need for a full-time cataloger. Schools that employ several staff members may make cataloging part of one full-time employee's duties. Finally, although cataloging can be a duty for a paraprofessional, this would generally be copy cataloging: downloading precataloged records from a cataloging service and adding minimal original information. Any original or complicated cataloging would be completed by a degreed librarian.

Archivist

An archivist collects, organizes, and maintains control over a wide range of information that reflects the school's

The older a school, the richer its history.

history and is deemed important enough for permanent safekeeping and easy retrieval. Independent schools are developing more and more special collections. Whether this material is documents from the school's history or a special collection left to the school by a donor or alumni, schools are creating archives and special historical collections. The older a school, the richer its history is, a history that needs to be preserved.

In independent schools, archivists manage school historical documents such as school newspaper collections, yearbooks, photos or video of school events, and even collections of old uniforms or textbooks, cheerleading pom-poms, and more artifacts of the school's early years. School archives can be used in many ways to promote school activities. For example, at Crossroads School in Santa Monica, the archivist works closely with the school's development department to create movies for high school reunions and alumni events (*Paul Cummins Library* 2009). As digitization becomes easier, independent school archives are beginning to put displays online for alumni around the world to view. An archivist who can organize a school online video or pictorial archive is a very helpful resource.

The Taft Education Center (Taft School, Watertown, CT (www. taftschool.org/tec/nonap.aspx#09C09) offers a summer week-long introductory course in school archives.

Many librarians have general archival training, but the responsibilities of an archive can become overwhelming over time. Especially at the beginning, when time must be spent with basic organization and location of materials, a trained person whose job description includes time for archiving will be more successful than someone borrowing time from an already full assignment ("Archivists, Curators, and Museum Technicians" 2009).

Library Clerk

A library clerk may be known as a circulation assistant, library assistant, library aide, library media assistant, or library monitor. A library clerk or assistant is a library employee who does not possess an advanced library degree. The clerk may be expected to circulate books, add new patrons, send out overdue notices, troubleshoot computers, assist librarians with classes, process books, copy catalog, clean or straighten the library, repair damaged books, help students with projects, supervise student behavior, shelve materials returned, and help students find library materials. Library clerk positions may be full- or part-time ("Library Technicians" 2009). The job of library clerk requires no previous training. Librarians train clerical staff to complete tasks to their library's specifications.

Library Monitor

The library monitor is nonprofessional staff member whose primary responsibility is dealing with student behavior. Because libraries are often asked to absorb all "loose" students (those who have makeup work, are behind in an assignment, are waiting to see an administrator for a disciplinary matter, or can't attend PE, etc.), there may be students in the library who are not in need of reference support but do require supervision to prevent malingering on the Internet or noisy behavior. Some schools regularly have monitors in other areas of the school (hall monitors, lunch monitors, crossing guards); these schools just add library monitor to the list so that the library can focus on its real job of supporting the academic curriculum and reference needs of the students. One librarian found that assigning that disciplinary supervision to one person raised the morale of the entire staff; the students were well supervised, and the staff could get the work done ("Staffing and Hours Questions" 2009).

> *Because libraries are often asked to absorb all "loose" students, . . .there may be students at the library who are not in need of reference support but do require supervision to prevent malingering on the Internet or noisy misbehavior.*

Unpaid Staff: Interns and Volunteers

Whether the volunteers are parents, students, interns, or interested elderly people, library volunteers are a valuable asset to school libraries. They are often people who love books and want to stay connected to the world of children and libraries, or who have a history with the school and want to contribute somehow. Because library volunteers can be trained to do almost any task in a library that a clerk would do, they can fill in any small assignment. This service is particularly helpful on days when the library is short-staffed.

Librarians work to cultivate long-term volunteers. Many school librarians began their library careers as volunteers in their child's school library. They became so excited by the library's central role in lifelong learning that they began taking classes and—before they knew it— had an MLS and a full-time job. A librarian for a large independent school in Santa Monica California followed that exact track, finally retiring after seventeen years to play with her grandchildren (Friedman 2007).

Library volunteers also allow smaller libraries, and libraries with smaller budgets, to expand their services without overextending the school's staffing budget. Some volunteers hold full-time jobs in other fields, but those skills can be hugely helpful in library advocacy and program development. For example, the librarian at Sequoyah School was thrilled to have a library volunteer who was an art/artist coordinator. This volunteer helped her create dynamic displays and did all the decorations for the school's annual book sale. This parent's contributions make every library event look spectacular.

Using volunteers in the library is not without its problems. The nature of a volunteer job includes the option not to show up. No matter how much the librarian needs a reliable set of volunteers, not all library volunteers are reliable. Not all parents are able to take orders. Library volunteers must be trained, and not all volunteers understand the need to shelve correctly, for example, or to place the spine labels exactly as explained. Some volunteers will not want to clean or straighten. Parents and teachers have a very clear relationship, even when volunteering, but the relationship is a little different between parents and librarians. Parent volunteers in the library may be more interested in supporting their own child than in accomplishing broader tasks that benefit a larger part of the school, or they may be more interested in chatting among themselves than in supporting student needs (Eberhart 2006, 133).

Although many librarians value the contributions of volunteers, some prefer not to have volunteers in their libraries. Some librarians are uncomfortable working with parents, or they may feel pressured by certain volunteers to alter their library programs ("Hours and Staffing Questions" 2009). Others just become frustrated fixing the mistakes of volunteers, as they can create more work for librarians by shelving books in the wrong location or making processing errors.

Every librarian needs to decide individually about volunteers: How many can you handle? How many are effective? How can you train them most efficiently? What can you ask them to do with confidence that it will be done correctly? Carefully articulate the library's needs and any concerns to your volunteer coordinator so that you feel comfortable with the volunteers that you receive.

Make sure that volunteers understand their commitment before they begin. Expect to lose volunteers to work commitments, illness, boredom, and vacations. Create a volunteer manual that clearly details all the responsibilities of your volunteer staff and answers the most

> *Every librarian needs to find his or her own way with volunteers: How many can you handle? How many are effective? How can you train them most efficiently? What can you ask them to do with confidence that it will be done correctly?*

common questions. Holding a training session for new volunteers allows you to assess their skills and give them tasks on a par with their skill levels.

Finally, make sure to acknowledge volunteer contributions throughout the year. Some schools hold volunteer appreciation lunches; others donate books to the library's collection in their honor. If you want to do something with a more personal touch, try sending thank-you cards to all your volunteers at the end of the school year, signed by the entire library staff.

The most important thing to remember about volunteers is that they are not permanent. Even the most dedicated volunteers will leave when their children have graduated—unless they have become hooked on the library atmosphere and you can find a way to hire them! At Annunciation Orthodox School in Houston, one long-time volunteer (eight years) was ready for a part-time job after her daughter graduated; she is now a part-time nonprofessional cataloging assistant and an important part of the library staff ("Hours and Staffing Questions" 2009). Although cultivating a stable of long-term volunteers is an asset to any library, it is also important to have a plan in place to organize volunteer responsibilities and to manage without them should they stop coming.

Interns

Students in library or related programs often work in a library to get practical experience. Based on the classes that they have taken, interns can be given more professional responsibilities, such as cataloging, supervised reference service, participating in collection development, and supervising students. It is important to remember that interns leave when they have completed their program, so you will have regular turnover ("Staffing and Hours Questions" 2009).

Student Volunteers

Depending on their age and level of enthusiasm, students can participate in any normal volunteer activities. Student volunteering activities can include cleaning, shelving, helping with displays, working at the circulation desk, and reading and reviewing books.

Determining Your School's Staffing Needs: Qualities, Size, and Coverage

The size of the staff needed in a library depends heavily on the services the school expects the library to support. The school must understand what it takes for a library to perform these services. The library staff will need an ongoing advocacy program to keep the school aware of what current staff levels can accomplish and what services could be added if additional staff members were hired. Typically, schools will hire one librarian per division (elementary, middle, or high). Each librarian is expected to develop a comprehensive library program for that division; this quality program will include a strong collection and an active teaching program that supports the needs of the core academic curricula of the division. This traditional model for independent school libraries may be changing based on technology and student use.

Hiring library staff members should always be a collaborative process between the library and the school's administration. The librarian and the administration must have a clear mutual understanding of the overall library job description: one librarian can accomplish a limited set of tasks in the finite hours of a school week. Having additional staff enables greater support of academic functions. When head librarians lead in the hiring of new library staff (i.e., posting ads, reading résumés, conducting interviews, and making hiring recommendations), they should have a clear understanding from school administrators of the job descriptions. Conversely, when heads of school or other administrators make hiring decisions about library positions, they should consult existing library staff to get a sense of what skills are needed and what schedule will work best. This is particularly important when hiring part-time staff members, as they tend to need more flexibility in scheduling. For example, will a new hire be available for after-school coverage for the five days a week that are listed in the job description? All staff members should have a job description that details expected duties and the education necessary for the position. Librarians should work closely with school administrators to make sure that the job descriptions are current and meet the needs of both the school and the library. Information about library job descriptions can be found on the ALA Web site (ALA.org) and in the *Occupational Handbook* published by the U.S. Bureau of Labor Statistics, Office of Occupational Statistics and Employment Projections (see also Eberhart 2006, 80–99).

How many staff members does the specific school need to accomplish the best level of library service?

When looking for staff for a school library, there are some general qualities that all library staff members should have:

1. **An affinity for children, young adults, or teens.** This is more than just "liking kids." Having an affinity for children and young adults refers to a genuine respect for people under the age of eighteen and the ability to work with them at their level. Working in a school library includes continued contact with the same students for several years. Librarians need to be comfortable with many stages of child and adolescent development. School librarians who don't like children won't bring a passion for learning to the kids. This affinity for children has to be genuine. Kids know if the librarian doesn't like children; that dislike will affect the library's ability to serve your core user group.

2. **Knowledge.** Library staff members have to know everything. This includes the name of every student in the school, the curriculum for all grades, the names of teachers, the programs, and how to answer reference questions.

3. **Patience.** The most powerful tool in a librarian's arsenal is patience. Successfully navigating a school year is a marathon, not a sprint. The librarian needs patience to maintain a sense of team with other library staff members and to cultivate productive relationships with faculty and students. Patience supports a positive attitude when working as the only librarian on campus; when your department has been left out of the loop on an important decision . . . again; when you are explaining to parents why they have to pay for books that their children have failed to return; and when you are sending out your annual reminder to faculty to give the library copies of their assignments. Those patiently cultivated relationships with library staff and faculty allow humor to rescue difficult situations and mutual understanding to dominate ongoing conversations.

4. **Persistence.** We work persistently to be a central part of every curriculum and an essential extension of textbooks and lectures. We are academic support, and that support comes in many different ways. Our persistence also shows in our often extended hours and our efforts to maintain balance as teachers, tech support, occasional janitors, disciplinarians, and faculty colleagues sitting on committees. And unlike classroom teachers, we constantly have to prove our worth to all the stakeholders in the school community, including parents, teachers, students, and administrators.

5. **Flexibility.** Flexibility is needed to deal with a myriad of situations that can affect a library's schedule, including changes in the school's schedule, being available to teach at a moment's notice, classes that cancel at the last minute, and field trips. As academic support, library staff members have to be comfortable with the constant fluctuations and changes in a school day. Librarians and staff members who are not flexible tend to become very frustrated when working in independent schools, where situations change all the time.

6. **Energy.** Whether you are working with small children or older teens, librarians and library staff members need energy and a positive attitude to get through the day. Our patrons exhibit great enthusiasm that is not always directed toward study, and we have to find ways to channel that energy while they are in the library. This could be a scavenger hunt (for younger children who just can't sit still) or finding ways to calm and focus an older student who is excited and full of caffeine.

7. **Willingness to do it all.** There is no interlibrary loan officer; it's you. There is no acquisitions librarian; that's you, too. For that matter, there is no serials manager, no additional reference librarian. Many librarians are accustomed to the framework of public and academic libraries, which separates work into various departments. In independent school libraries, those other library departments may not exist. The independent school librarian is responsible for all the duties those departments would handle, without the additional help.

Independent school libraries are similar to public school libraries, except that public school librarians have a support system of other people who do the same job, can compare notes, and offer mutual support to their colleagues across the school district. They also have a supervisory structure at the district level that spells out some core elements of how things need to be done (Morris 2004, 211). Independent schools glory in their independence, as do their librarians. We can work directly with our campus administration to solve problems and improve services. We build solid working relationships with our administrations that allow ongoing support of a growing program in support of the school and library missions. We are given more autonomy, but with that comes more responsibility.

Although we serve a finite population (total number of students plus faculty), we often work alone, with few or no coworkers who share our educational background, work experience, or philosophy on information and collaboration. Librarians new to independent schools must adjust to the unique environment as they learn to be vocal and consistent advocates for their library programs. They will learn to let go of the public/academic library framework. A teacher transitioning from the classroom has a different learning curve; a teacher without any library training will need strong community support and will look to other librarians to face the many challenges along the way to building a strong library program.

Formal training in a library program is important because it allows librarians to maintain continuity between our libraries and those of our brethren in public and academic institutions.

In many schools, moving teachers from the classroom to the library is considered a great idea. Teachers have a sense of curriculum, and they already know the faculty, staff, and students. Although the pressures of school librarianship are very different than those of other school positions, they are not less. As school librarians, we always have to remember our obligation to inspire lifelong learning and use of information. We want our patrons to know how helpful librarians can be so that they return to libraries throughout their lives. Formal training in a library program is important because it allows librarians to maintain continuity between our libraries and those of our brethren in public and academic institutions. Paraprofessionals also need links to colleagues in other similar libraries.

Size and Collection

Independent school libraries can be classified by the number of books or materials in the library's collection, the square footage of the library's space, the size of the library staff, and/or the number of services offered by the library. The need for staff is directly tied to the other measures in combination with the number of student patrons served by the library. Your school administration needs a clear understanding of how many staff members it will take to adequately support the curricular collaboration, the collection, and the supervision needs of the facility. It is always a good idea to know the ratio of books to pupils, the ratio of students to librarians, and the ratio of librarians to teachers. These statistics are strong indicators of how many people the library staff are expected to support and the size of the collection they are expected to maintain.

In general, a school library runs best when there are at least two employees. Librarians who work alone must close the library when they need to attend a meeting or have a lunch break ("Staffing and Hours Questions" 2009). Libraries with small collections can adequately support student learning with a staff of two. A staff of two may not be able to do the cataloging in-house or offer services before or after the school day. A two-person staff allows consistent coverage; one person can meet with a teacher, take a quick break, or concentrate on a lesson plan while the other covers the desk and the tables. Many elementary school libraries follow this model (*Membership Directory* 2009). Smaller libraries also rely on parent or student volunteer support for services such as processing books, shelving, and keeping the library open during lunch and before and after school.

> *In general, a school library runs best when there are at least two employees.*

Libraries with larger collections will not function adequately with one librarian. Not only do these libraries have coverage issues, but they will need larger support staffs to manage student supervision, teacher collaboration and classroom support, new materials processing, shelving, weeding, book repair, shifting, and inventory. Librarians with larger collections also need to spend more time evaluating sources, reading reviews, and shopping for materials to support currency and curricular support, as well as supporting AV and tech functions and circulation. Finally, these libraries often have extended hours of library coverage, which one librarian cannot support. For example, the school library at Philips Exeter Academy has nine floors, houses over 160,000 volumes, employs seven librarians and fourteen support staff members, and is open seven days a week (*Library* 2009).

Libraries that are similar in square footage and collection size may have drastically different needs in staffing, based on school schedules, student needs, and student behavior. Librarians who work with secondary students may need more staff simply to deal with the volume of students who need library support at the same time. Boarding schools that keep their libraries open up to sixteen hours a day, nights, and weekends will also require more staff due to the sheer number of hours that they operate. Some schools have begun to hire part-time support for those one-person libraries to cover the times when the librarian needs to be away from the library, whether for collaborative meetings, lunch, or the opportunity to catch teachers quickly for updates on their needs for the week. One librarian stated, "Yes, I would like to have a part time clerk so I would have more time to work with teachers. I also think the library should be staffed during all the hours it is open" ("Staffing and Hours Questions" 2009). Too many libraries are forced to leave the library unsupervised for lack of adequate staff, which is a liability issue for the school. "I wish my assistant position was full-time; she comes in only 4 days a week and we are stretched thin on the day she is not here. Most people don't realize what goes into selecting, acquiring, processing and teaching/promoting the many sources of information we provide to the community" ("Staffing and Hours Questions" 2009). Libraries that open for longer than the school day require more staffing and staggered starts to cover the additional hours.

Although a staff of two is the minimum coverage needed by libraries today, too many libraries have only one librarian.

Every school would love to have several professional librarians, but many schools have found the cost of having several professional librarians prohibitive. Hiring part-time staff members allows the library to have qualified professional staff at a price that the school can better afford; not only is the cumulated hourly rate lower than a full-time salary, but no benefits are added to the total (Eberhart 2006, 98–100).

Although having enough staff to adequately cover all aspects of service is the ultimate goal of all librarians, having a plan in place to offer service given the actual number of staff available is the working reality. Cultivate a quality staff of volunteers. Work with school administration to have qualified substitutes. Hire library school interns to stretch staff while helping to cultivate future librarians. Be realistic about staffing: take a serious look with your administration at the library's hours of service.

Part II—Library Service Hours and Staffing Concerns

Setting your library's hours of service is as important a decision as whom you hire. School libraries facilitate academic support, but the library itself is also a physical space within the school that has a variety of uses. Libraries are visually beautiful and tasteful, and exude an appearance of educational excellence. They are generally accessible and easy to find. Finally, your library's layout probably makes it a ready-made space for meetings, presentations, or conferences because it is open and has numerous chairs, tables, and computers.

In any library, hours of staff service will dictate the number and type of services it can provide.

Considering all these factors, every librarian should expect his or her library to have a second life, possibly a night life. Independent school libraries are essential to school families because of the constant support we provide during nonschool hours. Students have come to expect the library to be open early enough for them to finish projects, print homework, and check out or return books. Parents have come to rely on independent school libraries to be an adult-supervised space for their children to be until they can be picked up at the end of the day. Teachers and administrators often see the library as a school space for meetings, after-school functions, and class presentations.

It's the librarian's job to take all these expectations and create a cohesive service model for the library and its staff for the school year. This cohesive service model is not just about keeping the library open during the school day as long as possible. It is about weighing the physical resources and staff at the librarian's disposal against the reality that the library itself is a physical space that can be used by other departments in the school for various activities that are not necessarily library-related, anything from meetings of the Girl Scouts to meetings of the board of trustees. What effects might the need for extended hours and services have on library staff availability?

The Library Service Model

Hours of service of elementary and middle/high school libraries vary. All school libraries are open during the proper school day, and most school libraries, regardless of student population, will open their doors before the school day begins. High schools may open their libraries as much as one hour before school begins, but elementary school libraries may only open fifteen to thirty minutes early (*Membership Directory* 2009).

It would be a rare elementary school library that would have extended after-school hours, but high school libraries are typically open up to three hours after the end of the school day. Some libraries offer evening services as well. Whereas high school libraries would never close early for after-school programs, elementary school libraries frequently find their space co-opted by after-school programs such as day care. Finally, elementary schools tend to be closed during the summer, whereas many high school libraries have summer hours and year-round staffing needs (*Membership Directory* 2009).

What effect might these extended-hour services have on library staff availability?

Although it is clear that there is a vast difference between elementary and high school libraries, there is one very important similarity: in any library, hours of service will dictate the number and type of services the library can provide. Every library needs a cohesive service model. Your library's service model acts as a road map for library service. It includes practical information such as hours of services, library closure dates and times, and staff scheduling (based on a full-time employee model or FTE). The library service model also tackles more complicated issues: type of services the library can offer, such as extended morning or evening hours or an information literacy program; types of staff needed, such as cataloger or clerk; space issues, such as how a cub scouts meeting might affect students doing research or the realities of middle and high school students sharing the same space at the same time. Finally, the service model should help you determine priorities in service, based on your school's curriculum and any special events or activities that may affect your year. For example, if the library is planning to update its automated library software, how might the process affect basic library services? What time of year is best for the change? If your library is being renovated, how will you handle the upcoming renovation? What implications will this have for your staff, or the services you can offer? A service model can help you prepare for these situations.

Hours and Staffing Challenges

Unlike other departments in a school, libraries operate both as a part of and outside of the regular school schedule. The library is obviously a vital part of the regular school day as a physical space, but it may play an equally vital role during the evening hours of school life. It is important to think of the library not simply as a library, but as a multi-use facility. With that in mind, it's important to think about how the overall service model will affect your staff, and what you need to do to minimize or eliminate such problems if necessary.

> *It is important to think of the library not simply as a library, but as a multi-use facility.*

Scenario 1: While opening the library at 7:00 am, the librarian receives a message from the afternoon clerk that he is ill. How can the librarian rearrange staff assignments to keep the library open for its regular 10.5-hour a day schedule with only her remaining staff?

Scenario 2: In the middle of the work day, a member of the facilities department comes in to set up the library for an evening event. The librarian is not expecting the event and has a full slate of classes for the afternoon, as well as the usual extended day crowd. The evening event requires that the library close early, and no plans are in place for students who use the library in the afternoons. The hourly staff scheduled to work in the afternoon lose valuable hours and pay.

Scenario 3: The library has scheduled six classes to come sequentially throughout the day. Mrs. X arrives with her students to study dinosaurs; she is not on the schedule but intends to stay. Mr. J sends his advanced students for individual project research. And an unexpected group of parent volunteers comes to help with book processing.

Scenario 4: Librarian Jones has both morning carpool duty and lunch/recess duty outside on the day the fifth grade decides to send twenty students to the library during the lunch recess to finish a project that has run behind. The students arrive to find an unsupervised space.

These are examples of staffing issues that every library has to face at one point or another. For some libraries, getting qualified substitutes is a real problem. For many librarians, the solution has been to work longer hours and shuffle existing staff. Libraries can inadvertently be left out of the loop in event planning by other departments. Librarians are very proactive about scheduling classes for research lessons, but there are always times when classes show up unannounced. In all these situations, it can be very difficult for the library staff to accommodate the needs of a large number of people at the same time.

All schools have a master calendar, on which major school activities and events are posted. Making sure that the librarian is informed of any events on the master calendar that will affect the library is essential. This will ensure that the library can schedule staff accordingly. In addition, the librarian should consult the master calendar regularly for changes.

Sometimes librarians can be victims of their own success. Working hard to create an open, supportive environment for student and staff can translate into a busy library with an overwhelmed librarian. For example, a librarian from Northern California states, "Our library seats 180 students. We are at full capacity before and after school, and at lunch.

During lunch we have teachers who take turns supervising, but they sometimes forget to show up. . . . We have 5 staff members, some are part time. Sometimes it seems we can't get to our other work, as we are walking around the library supervising students" ("Staffing and Hours Questions" 2009).

"Where schools would never think to leave seventy students alone with two classroom teachers for an hour, they do not hesitate to do this to Librarians."

One of the biggest issues librarians face is the expectation that they will supervise students who are not in class during the school day—students in study hall or making up a test or waiting for a tutor or . . . . This is mainly an issue with upper school libraries on campuses where students have free class periods with no structured activity or supervised place for them to go. School administrators see the library as a perfect solution to a challenging problem: Who is going to watch these kids? Libraries are fully staffed, which means there is always someone to supervise student behavior. Libraries have adequate seating for students in an environment conducive to studying or holding quiet conversations. However, what seems to be an ideal solution from the perspective of the school administrator can be a very challenging issue for library staff members ("Staffing and Hours Questions" 2009). "Where schools would never think to leave seventy students alone with two classroom teachers for an hour, they do not hesitate to do this to Librarians."

The issue of student supervision permeates every aspect of the secondary school library experience. Librarians with teaching responsibilities always have to be aware of how their teaching responsibilities affect their other library services, especially library supervision. For many libraries, student supervision has become one of their highest priorities. When a librarian is teaching, colleagues have to rearrange their duties and responsibilities to make sure the library is fully covered ("Hours and Staffing Questions" 2009).

Weather can play an important role in student supervision. Students will socialize outside when it's warm, but not during cold or rainy weather. When asked, one librarian commented that no matter what her library rules are, all bets are off in bad weather: "My students simply have no other place to go. On rainy days we cancel classes, and all we can do is try to keep the students occupied" ("Hours and Staffing Questions" 2009). This is likely not the image independent schools intend to project, of the library as a "holding tank" for students with no academic interest for the period (Lau 2002).

Library supervision is even more important for schools with night, weekend, or summer hours. Independent schools can be year-round institutions, providing morning and evening day care and summer classes. If your school intends to use the library for any of these activities, a librarian needs to be included to ensure the safety of the collection.

This is particularly important for boarding schools where the library hours are extensive. Boarding school librarians have more flexible rules for hours of service than day schools do. Many boarding school libraries are open from 6:30 am to 10:30 pm, only closing for evening meals. The library may be used for study hall or as a student lounge. Even with the tremendous number of hours many boarding school libraries offer, some still only employ two or three library staff members and rely on teachers to proctor the library in their absence. " School ends by 3 pm, the librarians are here until 4 pm and then we have library assistants (usually trained upperclassmen from the library advisory board) staff the library from 4 pm to 6 pm. We close at 6 pm [for dinner] and reopen from 7:30 to 9:30 for evening study hall (Monday thru Thursday) where there is a librarian on duty. We do also have Sunday hours from 2 pm to 5 pm. You can imagine with only two librarians and all our hours it's a little tiring. I do three nights a week and the other librarian does one night a week" ("Hours and Staffing Questions" 2009).

Every school wants to see the library space and materials used constantly.

Librarians should work closely with deans and other school administrators to make sure that library staff members are not being taken for granted or mistreated. Every school wants to see the library space and materials used constantly; the school administration may need to be reminded of the library mission, which does not include babysitting but focuses on academic enrichment. It is also important to address this issue in your service model and to readdress it every year, as it will affect your staffing needs and service hours.

Creating Your Library's Hours of Service

Create a Staffing Schedule

1. Tie your hours of service to the number of staff members that you have to cover your service day. Give the administration detailed staffing schedules—to illuminate any gaps in coverage for specific weeks, months, or years.

2. Plan staff vacation times and school schedules. Look at all the activities that need staff assistance in a given week and schedule your staff accordingly. Maximize your staff to support the busiest times of day. Inform the administration when the library can't cover expectations without asking for additional hours or personnel.

3. Schedule staff time to manage collection development and maintenance, as well as teacher collaboration. Schedule information literacy classes. Share the various duties among the staff to keep morale high. Remember that ten-month librarians must complete their collection development efforts during that ten-month period. Twelve-month librarians can complete those duties during summer months when the student load is lower.

4. Make time in your schedule for staff development. There are many quality conventions and workshops available to school librarians and paraprofessional staff. Participating in staff development gives librarians a look at the greater library community and creates opportunities for librarians to expand their services based on new ideas or methodologies.

5. Make time to meet with staff regularly. It may seem that you and your staff are always chatting, but this is not the same as a structured meeting to discuss library issues. This time is helpful for library staff and can give librarians much needed insight into aspects of staff duties and challenges that they may not have seen.

Library Statistics

Library statistics, including door logs and circulation statistics, are indicators of student and faculty use of space and materials. For example, library circulation software keeps track of the number of books checked out in a given day, week, month, or year.

Libraries that employ door monitoring systems also have an internal counter that can tell you how many people are coming to and going from your library in a given day. Knowing how many books you are circulating in a given day or week (and at what hours) offers insight into student use of the library. To complement your circulation statistics, count the books left on tables from student research efforts. Couple those data with statistics on how many people are coming into the library during the day and when, to develop an understanding of how the facility is being used and how much supervision is needed. This information can be used to advocate for additional support at peak usage times or for closing the library an hour earlier because no one is coming then. If a huge number of kids came and went but no books were circulated or used, the library is being used mostly as a social center; use the data to demonstrate this to the administration. Being able to provide actual numbers for

> *Being able to provide actual numbers for library services and usage gives school administrators something tangible to use when evaluating library requests for increased staffing and different hours of service.*

library services and usage gives school administrators something tangible to use when evaluating library requests for increased staffing and different hours of service. For example, a large independent school located in Los Angeles, California, reviewed its hours of service to see if the library could close an hour earlier every day, making the day 7:30 am to 5:00 pm. The librarian kept an actual count of the number of students in the library between 5:00 pm and 6:00 pm and found that a significant number of patrons used the facility then, so closing early was not a viable option to solve the coverage issue.

Using Information from Other School Librarians or Library Organizations

Many school librarians belong to local consortiums that meet regularly to discuss library issues they all deal with and to bounce ideas for service and curriculum off each other. Librarians also belong to various listservs and national organizations (like ALA/AASL/ISS, AISL, and NAIS), where they can ask practical questions of fellow library professionals. Smart librarians compare notes about hours of service and staff levels. When the data they collect informally point to a trend in similar schools, their administrators may be more receptive to proposed changes.

Conclusion

It is important to remember that libraries have boundaries. Although we would love to offer library services for ten hours a day, that may not be possible. Just like teachers, library employees need downtime, free from students. The library being closed to students does not mean the work day has ended for the staff. When setting library hours, make sure that you have a clear idea of your limitations and the limitations of your staff. This is particularly important for libraries that employ part-time staff and those that rely on volunteers to fill in the gaps for extended service.

The most important thing to remember about staffing your library and setting hours of service is communication. Make sure that whatever efforts you are putting forth in your library, you are chronicling them to the head of the school or supervising body. Invite teachers, deans, and division directors into your classes to see your teaching skills and your rapport with students. Ask for help when you need it; your colleagues will never know of or appreciate your personal sacrifices. Make sure you are chronicling all library efforts to your head of school; use your Web page to good advantage, showing successful students engaged in reading and research. Staffing an independent school library with quality staff members can be a challenging endeavor. But the rewards of a strong library program are immeasurable and will help to provide the quality of education your independent school dispenses.

References

AASL Position Statement on Flexible Scheduling. 2009. American Library Association. Available at www.ala.org/ala/aasl/aaslproftools/positionstatements/aaslpositionstatement. htm. Accessed October 24, 2009.

"Archivists, Curators, and Museum Technicians." 2009. Available at http://www. bls.gov/oco/ocos065.htm. Accessed May 10, 2009.

Bryant, Alice. 2008. Interview by Joyce Valenza, "Issues for the Independent." April 13. Available at www.schoollibraryjournal.com/blog/1340000334.html. Accessed March 22, 2009.

Eberhart, George M., ed. 2006. *Whole Library Handbook 4: Current Data, Professional Advice, and Curiosa about Libraries and Library Services.* Chicago: American Library Association.

Education and Continuing Learning Brochure. 2007. American Library Association. April 19. Available at http://www.ala.org/ala/aboutala/missionhistory/keyactionareas/ educationaction/educationcontinuing.cfm. Accessed October 24, 2009.

Fourie, Denise K., and David R. Dowell. 2002. *Libraries in the Information Age: An Introduction and Career Exploration.* Greenwood Village, CO: Libraries Unlimited.

Friedman, Linda. 2007. Interview with author, October.

"Hours and Staffing Questions." 2009. Independent School Library Exchange listserv. March 22.

Lau, Deborah. 2002. "What Does Your Boss Think About You?" *School Library Journal* 1 (September): 52-59.

"Librarian." 2009. In *Occupational Outlook Handbook, 2008–09 Edition.* U.S. Bureau of Labor Statistics, Office of Occupational Statistics and Employment Projections. March–April. Available at www.bls.gov/oco/ocos068.htm. Accessed May 10 2009.

Library. 2009. Phillips Exeter Academy. April–May. Available at www.exeter.edu/ libraries/4513.aspx. Accessed August 19, 2009.

"Library Technicians." 2009. In *Occupational Outlook Handbook, 2008–09 Edition.* U.S. Bureau of Labor Statistics, Office of Occupational Statistics and Employment Projections. March–April. Available at www.bls.gov/oco/ ocos316.htm. Accessed May 10, 2009.

Membership Directory. 2009. National Association of Independent Schools. March–April. Available at www.nais.org/about/index.cfm?ItemNumber= 151032. Accessed August 19, 2002.

"Mission Statement." 2009. In *Oxford English Dictionary.* 2nd ed. Available at http://dictionary.oed.com/. Accessed October 24, 2009.

Moorman, John A., ed. 2006. *Running a Small Library: A How-to-Do-It Manual.* New York: Neal-Schuman.

Morris, Betty J. 2004. *Administering the School Library Media Center.* Westport, CT: Libraries Unlimited.

Paul Cummins Library. 2009. Crossroads School for Arts and Sciences. Available at www.xrds.org. Accessed March 23, 2009.

Sequoyah School. 2008. *A Community of Learners.* Pasadena, CA: Sequoyah School.

"Staffing and Hours Questions." 2009. ISS Discussion List. American Association of School Librarians. Available at iss@ala.org. Accessed September 29, 2009.

Taft Education Center: Non-AP Courses. 2009. Taft Education Center. February. Available at www.taftschool.org/tec/nonap.aspx#09C09. Accessed November 14, 2009.

Visit http://lu.com/excellence for supporting links and occasional updates to all essays in this book.

Aquita Winslow Tyler is the Director of Learning Resources for Crossroads School. She has been a professional librarian for fifteen years. Aquita holds a bachelor's in legal studies and philosophy from the University of California at Santa Cruz, a master's in library science from Simmons College, and a juris doctor from Loyola Law School. Aquita is also an adjunct faculty member at Pasadena City College, teaching bibliographic instruction in the Shatford Library (http://www.xrds.org/).

The Many Faces of Advocacy for School Libraries

Dorcas Hand, Annunciation Orthodox School (Houston, TX)

If you were a school librarian about to lose your job, what would you do? If you are a teacher-librarian, how can you convince teachers to collaborate with you to build assignments with strong information skills imbedded? What if instead of those massive cuts, you must convince the board that you need a new multi-million-dollar facility? For another perspective, if you are a head of school facing massive budget cuts, why should you not shrink or eliminate your library program? The answers to all of these questions involve advocacy. In independent schools, the library staff has a much more direct and immediate connection to all stakeholders including the board of trustees. The smaller bureaucracy allows us to effect changes more quickly than in public school districts with many layers of hierarchy. We not only teach in independent schools; we work independently in collaboration with our administrators, faculties, parents, and students. This immediacy is a gift we frequently appreciate. It is also a responsibility: independent school librarians must continue to be consistently responsive to the needs of the students and faculty of our schools. How can we be the strongest possible advocates for our students? That can be restated as, How can we be the strongest advocates for our programs?

The rest of this book discusses in depth many ways a library helps its students and its school. This essay discusses what advocacy is and how it overarches every activity of the library to help the students and their school. Without artful advocacy, the library is likely to be a nice room off to the side that holds books, counted for accreditation visits, rather than a heavily used space that contributes daily to student achievement.

What Is Advocacy?

In its simplest definition, advocacy is public relations and marketing. It is selling library services to all the library's constituents: students, teachers, administrators, and the larger community of families and alumni. It is convincing students to read and to borrow materials from the school's library, and to use library research tools to support their assignments. It is also persuading faculty to plan assignments that use library resources, as well as to tell the library staff what resources are needed for specific courses. It is proving to faculty that the library has the best resources for their assignments because the librarians collaborated with faculty to write the curriculum and then remained aware of the curriculum as written, as well as of requests by teachers for specific resources. It is demonstrating to parents that the librarians understand student needs and interests, and that they work to encourage a lifelong love of reading and learning. And it is showing administration at every level that library funds are carefully spent to maximize student learning in many learning styles and support current pedagogy. Advocacy is advertising in concrete terms that the library supports student progress so that school graduates are ready to move on to the next level. It focuses on providing the students with the best possible programs, instruction, and resources rather than on the need for libraries or librarians; it is telling the community in concrete terms the impact of the library program (*Teacher Librarian* 2008).

> *Advocacy is . . . telling the community in concrete terms the impact of the library program.*

Ruth Toor and Hilda Weisburg's *New on the Job: A School Library Media Specialist's Guide to Success* includes a chapter on advocacy aimed at new school librarians. They discuss the similarities and overlap among public relations, marketing, and advocacy (2007, 118–24), a discussion that can better inform us all. Their analysis suggests that PR "tells people what you are doing well" in the immediate short term, announcing all your events and programs as they develop and succeed. According to the AASL Advocacy Training program, PR is, "This is who WE are and what WE do; this is when, where, and with whom WE do it." Marketing is "selling your program"; it is a specific plan like the American Library Association's ALA "@ your library" campaigns, which are implemented for a finite period, and which organize your ongoing programming under the umbrella of library services available to the school community. Marketing is who are YOU and what do YOU need? HOW, WHEN and WHERE can we best deliver it to YOU? PR and marketing are steps up the ladder to true advocacy, which is "an ongoing way of being" (Toor and Wesiburg 2007, 119).

> *PR is, "This is who WE are and what WE do; this is when, where, and with whom WE do it." . . . Marketing is who are YOU and what do YOU need? HOW, WHEN and WHERE can we best deliver it to YOU? . . . advocacy . . . is "an ongoing way of being."*

Advocacy works in collaboration with library stakeholders to promote community awareness of library strengths and importance. Toor and Weisburg further suggest that a library should not focus on defending needs (budget, space, staff), but rather on building alliances and demonstrating the importance of the library to the educational progress of a successful graduate. AASL supports these recommendations, suggesting that advocacy requires a common agenda, proposed and effected by a spectrum of library supporters.

The independent school community is tremendously varied. We include schools of all levels; schools for special audiences, from learning challenged to high performing; single sex and coed schools; boarding schools and day schools; religious; secular; and military schools. This variety of audience means that our applications of the concepts underlying advocacy will be equally varied. Bloom's Taxonomy is a classic pedagogic tool that assists curriculum and lesson development to push students beyond the basic concrete awareness of facts to a deep understanding of how those facts work together to make the world. We can apply the same framework to advocacy topics. I can talk about any library topic in very concrete terms or with reference to research and evaluation of that topic. Both discussions may be useful, depending on need, audience, and goal. Both are essential to the complete advocacy program. If librarians only give administrators data without interpretation, they cannot expect the administration to provide the answers they are hoping to hear. If they only give administrators interpretation without data, they cannot expect the leadership to understand how the librarians reached the specific conclusions. Administrators must be able to defend every project in the school. Strong analytic support of project design will make that easier and show the librarian and library resources as strong contributors to the curriculum. Parents want to know their students are learning and enjoying the process of learning; when they know the library contributes to that process, they will be strong library supporters. At the very least, librarians must understand the issues. To be a successful advocate, a librarian must have analyzed, evaluated, and synthesized the effects of the proposed application on the campus. This consideration separates the PR, marketing, and analytic levels of advocacy and demonstrates that higher level advocacy relies on a foundation laid by the lower levels.

Applied to our libraries, Toor and Weisburg's statement that "advocacy is an ongoing way of being" translates to a

> [T]ell . . . the community who WE are . . . ask . . . what services THEY need.

directive to coordinate our ongoing PR, marketing, and more analytic efforts to build a comprehensive program of advocacy that places our library solidly in the essential services list when budget and staffing decisions are made. We must constantly be telling the community who WE are as well as asking what services THEY need; those PR and marketing efforts contribute to a strong, overarching program of advocacy that includes other data in support of our efforts to consistently improve our library facilities and programs. Collaboration is an essential element of strong advocacy.

Certainly librarians must collect data—about student patrons and curriculum needs, faculty teaching styles, and current trends in pedagogy. If the library only does that and presents the data from only the perspective of a library protecting its turf, the administration and faculty will be wise to remain somewhat skeptical. A library that builds strong alliances with other departments is in a much stronger position to request additional resources; those allies will support the requests because the requests support the needs of other departments. The library may need a budget increase to support more databases for use with the senior history paper, for example. Or the library may need an additional staff person to work directly with middle school classes, especially now that the school has instituted research as an important thread in the curriculum map for middle school. When teachers and department heads speak in favor of library budget requests because those funds indirectly support departmental needs, administrators are much more likely to listen.

Advocacy focuses on the research into how libraries support student learning, as evidenced in test scores and graduate placements. The Colorado Studies of 1993 and 2000 compared achievement data to library funding, collection, and staff, finding that schools with higher achievement scores have libraries with stronger funding, collections, and staff. Independent schools often analyze their ERB scores to see where curriculum is weak; these scores can also give clues to library strengths. The school community includes current and prospective parents as well as administrators, accrediting agencies, and the general population. The ultimate product of a strong school is thoughtful, caring graduates who know how to locate and apply information as they become adults; library advocacy ensures that the school and the community understand the role the library plays in accomplishing that product.

WORKING DEFINITION OF ADVOCACY: An ongoing program of collaboration with the goal of ensuring that the school community is fully aware and reminded regularly of the library's strengths.

Following are stories of effective advocacy, including examples of PR, marketing, and more sophisticated data collection. Specific examples offer all of us a world of possibilities as we seek ideas to improve our existing library programs.

Professional Organizations

Professional Community

National Level

- The American Association of School Libraries (AASL), with its Independent Schools Section (ISS), offers ongoing professional support and development, as well as national standards and guidelines (*Standards for the 21st-Century Learner in Action*). AASL and ISS have listservs and wikis that regularly ask and answer questions posed by members, questions ranging from the philosophical to the mundane. www.aasl.org

- The Association for Independent School Librarians (AISL) is a smaller group specifically focused on independent schools and their libraries, which also offers a listserv, a ning, and an annual conference that visits independent school communities around the country. www.aislnews.org

- The National Association of Independent Schools (NAIS) is the umbrella accrediting organization for many nonpublic schools. www.nais.org

State and Regional Levels

- Most states have a school library association as part of the state library organization.

- In Texas, the Texas Association of School Librarians (TASL) advocates for school library funding at the legislative level. www.txla.org

- The New England School Library Association (NESLA) combines the efforts of the local affiliates in all six of the New England states. http://neschoollibraries.org/

Local Groups

- There are local independent school library groups all over the country that work together to support best practices and advocate in the community for excellence in libraries. See at the Web page associated with this book for a more complete list (http://l u.com/excellence).
- Houston has the Houston Area Independent School Library Network (HAISLN). www.haisln.org

International Groups

- The International Association of School Librarians (IASL) provides an international forum for those interested in promoting effective school library media programs as viable instruments in the educational process. http://www.iasl-online.org/

How can a librarian stay abreast of changes in best practices for independent school libraries? Our professional organizations offer us a rich community of colleagues who work in similar situations and face similar challenges. The organizations are advocates on our behalf. The AASL, ISS, and AISL published the following statement in September 2009, in response to a school that chose to abruptly eliminate the book collection of its library in favor of entirely electronic resources. Librarians combined our voices through these organizations to make a statement stronger than any one or several of us could have done alone:

> First of all, individual libraries are built intentionally, over time, by trained professionals, and resources are selected with the needs of the community that the library serves in mind. Such collections are vibrant entities that continually expand and contract. Many resources are available electronically but many are not and may never be. In addition, books go out of print quickly, databases stop archiving material without notice, and e-book collections are compiled by corporations that do not differentiate one school from another. Once a library has purchased and has on its shelf a book that perfectly meets the need of a group of users and has the potential for continued relevance, what does an institution gain by discarding that book? More to the point, what does it lose?

In 2005 ISS conducted a survey of independent school libraries across the country, discussed in essay 3, that is pertinent to this discussion of advocacy. The survey is tremendously useful to our community as we look beyond our individual campuses for appropriate data to support changes in the direction of best practices. An independent school librarian can support professional advocacy in the larger community just by participating in such a study and contributing data from a single school's library (or libraries); the same librarian can benefit from the results of the study some months later by using the collected data to institute change in the individual school.

Another demonstration of advocacy by a professional group that benefits a school directly is the pamphlet developed by ISS for distribution by an admissions office when prospective families tour their school. The pamphlet provides criteria visitors can use to evaluate whether a library will offer the best possible informational resources and programming. The school offering them this list of criteria tells a family that the specific school is confident it provides a library program that best supports the individual school's mission, and that this specific school thinks a strong library program is an essential facet of a strong academic program. The pamphlet, "A Student and Parent's Guide to Evaluating Libraries in Independent Schools," is available from ALA at www.ala.org/ala/mgrps/divs/aasl/aboutaasl/aaslcommunity/aaslsections/iss/resources.cfm.

The Texas Association of School Librarians (TASL) advocates for school library funding at the legislative level. Although that funding does not directly affect independent schools, its absence would detract from the strength of school libraries in all schools in Texas. TASL advocates for funding for databases and other purchasing consortia statewide that benefit the public school libraries as well as nonpublic schools. Many vendors offer private schools pricing comparable to that offered through the state consortium for public schools, because they understand that our students need the same access.

Schools that pay dues to these professional organizations will be repaid in many ways as the quality of the campus library programs improves and approaches best practices. Even if the librarian only scans journals and lurks on the listservs, the school will still benefit from increased awareness of new ideas and materials. If the librarian becomes active in the organizations, attending conferences and serving on committees, the resulting collegial networks will continue to build strong advocacy support groups and bring great new ideas into the schools. All these connections with the broader world of school libraries provide the library with a toolkit to strengthen ongoing advocacy on individual campuses. Our advocacy programs cannot be successful in a vacuum, and we pick and choose the parts that can be applied to our individual situations. Then we can build our programs, one day at a time, one smile at a time, one book at a time, one teacher collaboration at a time, and ultimately one student success at a time.

AASL Advocacy Toolkit,
  www.ala.org/ala/mgrps/divs/aasl/aaslissues/toolkits/aasladvocacy.cfm

AASL Crisis Toolkit,
  www.ala.org/ala/mgrps/divs/aasl/aaslproftools/toolkits/crisis.cfm

---

Evidence

Another set of resources for independent school librarians is the many journals devoted to our profession. *School Library Journal* (*SLJ*) hosts an annual summit conference at which building-level librarians mix with administrators and professors to consider the big questions about where we are and where we should go from here. In the April 2008 issue of *SLJ*, Ross Todd summed up the fall 2007 summit: "If librarians can't prove they make a difference, they may cease to exist." We must show value to maintain support, and that is the ultimate purpose of advocacy: to show value. Besides using our own library data to reinforce the understanding that we make a difference, we can use data published in these journals, including the annual *SLJ* survey of book costs and average per student budget estimates from schools across the country.

The July 2008 issue of *Booklist* focused on readers' advisory (RA), which is certainly at the core of library programs; it is "the pleasure of talking about books and the rediscovery of the importance of story in our lives." A good RA program will bring students back to the library day after day, and those students who use the service informally most often will be your biggest supporters. This makes RA a great tool for advocacy: give your readers what they want, and you have more credibility when you go to teach them what they don't yet know that they need to know. Even better, give your reluctant readers books they can enjoy, and you have them hooked as well. The process of listening to what the students want and need offers you raw data to use as you decide what to buy more of, what to suggest teachers add to the curriculum, and how to better advocate for student success in the library. Success can be measured in circulation statistics, more accessible shelves, students who can competently locate information, comfortable chairs filled with students reading for pleasure reading, or a variety of other concrete results.

Statistics

What then are the concrete tools of advocacy? Certainly the standard statistics, including circulation and attendance, collection size and age, hours and virtual availability, are basic building blocks. Alice Bryant of Harpeth Hall reminds us to keep track of what we do all day: how many classes and how many individual students; what were they doing? Were we teaching a group, or one on one? How many teacher collaborations? This time analysis, in combination with circulation details, provides us with a full complement of tools to build some really excellent reports, and we're not talking a dull list of statistics. We analyze the data to show trends that support collection development, staffing, or facility needs, and we tie the analysis to student achievement. Local data, in combination with the statistics from ISS and AASL, build a powerful case to support our requests. The word "needs" does not necessarily translate to new purchases, but can instruct artful weeding or reorganization to better support current usage. That kind of analysis can be shown to faculty, administration, and parents to encourage understanding of library functions and strengths. To maximize success, every effort at advocacy must focus above all on the students, getting the students the best possible programs, instruction, and resources. When we focus on student achievement as the bottom line, we show rather than tell why library programs and staff are essential components of a vibrant school program.

The spring 2009 issue of *Texas Library Journal* includes an interesting article by John Pecoraro that suggests that public libraries teach patrons about the value of services they enjoy, value that can be analyzed in a very personal way. The Maine State Library offers an online tool patrons can use to see the cumulative value of various services they enjoy, like borrowing one book/week for a year: $20 x 52=$1040. There is also a link other libraries can use to adapt the application for local use. Independent school libraries may not want to go this far, but the analysis can be a revealing exercise, especially in any situation where funding is at stake. It would not be useful information in isolation; combine the value analysis with circulation statistics to demonstrate a need, for example, for additional materials funding or additional staff to support increased circulation. (See table 6.1.)

Table 6.1. Estimated or Average Maine Values with Explanations		
Item	**Estimated Retail Value**	**Values Explained**
Book Borrowed	$27.00	Average cost of hardcover for adults
Paperback Book Borrowed	$ 7.00	Average cost of paperback for adults
Children's Book Borrowed	$20.00	Average cost of hardcover for children
Magazine Borrowed	$ 3.50	Average cost to purchase a popular periodical issue
Audio Book Borrowed	$30.00	Average cost to purchase an audio book
Computer Use, e.g., Internet and MS Word per Hour	$12.00	Sample hourly rate at a copy center
Reference Questions	$15.00	Estimated cost per question

Return on investment for public libraries: http://www.lrs.org/public/roi/; http://www.lrs.org/public/roi/usercalculator.php; http://www.lrs.org/public/roi/calculator.php

Source: www.maine.gov/msl/services/calexplantion.htm

Action Research

A recent issue of *Knowledge Quest* (2008), the journal of AASL, focused on "Action Research." These articles emphasize the fact that we all do "action research" every day as we make decisions based on what we observe in our space, classes, and circulation statistics; the particular examples don't happen to be specific to independent school libraries, but the core concepts can be seen at most independent schools. Independent school libraries do not have a journal to publish our specific successes, but we can benefit from remembering that we have as much in common with public school libraries as we have differences.

These articles report on action research used to update a summer reading program and draw in the English teachers in the process. Carol Gordon took the "I hate summer reading" comments from students as a personal catalyst to make the goal of more reading more of the time more pleasurable to more students. She did some quick research on why "the more you read the more you know" and took her results to the teachers. They were inspired to collaborate on some new ways to talk with kids about the books they read and ways to make it less onerous for them to actually do the talking. She also worked with the teachers to revamp the booklists to include more popular titles. This article exemplifies advocacy at every point. Carol advocated for her students to be more satisfied with the assignment; she collaborated with the teachers to build an assignment more likely to be successful for more students, an assignment that also better accomplished the teachers' goals; and she advocated for the library to play an essential role in the entire process. She also let the teachers know that she valued their expertise, and that a collaboration of talents would strengthen the final project and the final results in terms of student success, as well as easing the planning process for both the teacher and the librarian.

The same *KQ* issue described a Connecticut library's application for the National School Library Media Program Year. The application is an internal evaluation that is then sent out as a contest entry. Maureen Snyder and Janet Roche examined the interaction of their Simsbury High School library with test scores on the Connecticut Academic Performance Test, looking particularly at social studies and science. They wanted to be sure that students would be explicitly taught database search skills and citation skills in the context of social studies, as well as several interpretive skills that supported the science curriculum. Examining their current overall program in the context of the school curriculum, they determined a specific area in need of improvement: test scores on the state-mandated exam in science and social studies. Collaborating with science and social studies teachers, they designed units to target those skills. Test scores improved in those areas the following year. This success will enable further team efforts with other departments. The entire effort may be titled "evaluation," but it is an excellent example of "advocacy." These two librarians advocated for stronger student success as demonstrated by improved test scores; the advocacy process allowed them to also advocate with increased support of the teachers and the curriculum. This particular project was derived directly from the Colorado study mentioned earlier in this essay.

Journals That Support Advocacy in School Libraries

KnowledgeQuest (KQ)—the journal of AASL

School Library Media Research (SLMR)—the research journal of AASL

School Library Journal (SLJ)—articles of interest as well as book reviews

Teacher Librarian—the journal for school library professionals

Amy Jensen's article in the same *KQ* issue on the dreaded annual report demonstrates what an essential piece of advocacy this report is. The annual report is an opportunity to describe succinctly what happens in the library: how many books are circulated, how many bodies come and go in a day, how many teachers bring classes to use the space and resources and how many of those teachers collaborate with librarians to build a better project, how many new books the library has, how many outdated books have been weeded, and budget considerations going forward. Anything we need to say to the administration can be said in the annual report. We need to make it an exciting document with anecdotes to support the data. These anecdotes bring individual students our administrators know to life in the library program and allow us to continue to build on the library's successes. The administration will want to show the annual report to the board because it demonstrates how much the library does for the students and how well the budget is spent.

The ten-year accreditation questionnaire intended to summarize the Annunciation Orthodox School (AOS) library's strengths and weaknesses was a ready-made opportunity to look closely at current conditions that might need to change. Pluto had just been demoted from planet status, making much of the 520 section of the library out-of-date. Collection age was the first big question to consider. Some book vendors now offer free online collection analysis tools that provide very clear statistical results, as well as comparisons to a hypothetical perfectly balanced collection. AOS took advantage of such a tool, and the resulting analysis demonstrated that the AOS libraries were overall in pretty good shape, but that the science and technology sections had an average age of eleven to twelve years. State standards and professionally accepted methods (CREW: Continuous Review, Evaluation, Weeding) recommend ten years as the desirable average age of the collection. The staff focused on the 500s and 600s first, evaluating all items over ten years old and keeping only those items for which there was strong justification—curricular needs, browsing material, or historical relevance. Some subjects were weakened, such as drug awareness and the planets. Standard professional reviews and sources easily located replacement titles with recent dates. A second collection analysis revealed the new average age of those sections to be 9.5 years. The complete process took the concrete data through analysis back to concrete and back to analysis; the results for the annual report and for the visiting committee were easy to understand and demonstrated what the AOS Library has done to ensure the collection is appropriately current for faculty and student needs. The administration, which also saw the documentation, was assured that the budget moneys are well spent maintaining a collection that is up to date for student interests and curricular support. The admissions office can point to the currency and accuracy of the collection as strengths of the AOS Library, another reason to choose our school.

Technology

Libraries are more than physical spaces; they have a virtual component as well. Essay 8 discusses in detail how to build and manage the technology aspects of a strong school library, but here we need to consider how the technology affects our program of advocacy. How can I analyze my facility to be sure it is doing the best for the students? How can I use the analysis to demonstrate to teachers or administration how we could better support the curriculum? Our best practices recommend that we assist students with the full spectrum of the research process, from topic design through final paper to self-evaluation; our library best practices do not suggest we provide a word processing lab for our students. When students are sent from class to "type something," the workstations are not available for research needs. The extent and vibrancy of the library program will control in part whether the noncore uses can be accommodated. The librarian wanting to follow best practices will look at the big picture and seek creative solutions through discussion with administration. Library data can advocate for the decision that is in the best interests of the students, a decision to add a laptop cart or other access points to technologic supports of student achievement.

When the Annunciation Orthodox School (AOS) Brown Foundation Library was built in 2001, connections for five student workstations were included for the K–4 library; in 2008 database research demands for third and fourth grades could not be met with only five workstations. Students used the computer lab for database access, but that curtailed the computer curriculum. The library staff was able to demonstrate that a laptop cart would supplement the five workstations, allowing the entire class online access at once. The librarians can now teach database use, and the computer teacher can focus on computer applications, like graphing and page layout including pictures. This is an example of advocacy that took a basic fact (only five workstations) and used it with judicious analysis and synthesis to request a new laptop cart. Student access was the bottom line, along with the full range of the existing curriculum. The new cart went into use immediately; students and teachers were thrilled at the improved hands-on access and teaching time.

A library advocate must also look at the virtual space available to the school community. How can the Web page be best designed for ease of navigation and access? How many databases are enough or too much? How can the library best make the databases accessible 24/7? What does the library's Web page look like? Is it buried in the school's Web site, carefully branded in ways that make it difficult to use? Can the library Web page be redesigned in any way to minimize those problems? Can you imbed Web 2.0 tools for student access? As a school's library works its way along the continuum of improved Web and database access, the questions change to those about the number of workstations needed by students, and perhaps to the possibility of becoming a laptop school.

What student interests can I support that reasonably fall within the school's reach? Each school will make its own decisions about how much campus access is appropriate. Bandwidth and workstations are the first and most concrete concerns, but quickly filtering, cybersafety curricula, and appropriate age restrictions also affect decision making. Web 1.0 access has become pervasive in the last ten to fifteen years; Web 2.0 is becoming the new standard. Where do libraries need to go from here—3.0? 4.0? Essay 9 examines these issues in depth, but they play an important role in advocacy as well. Will social networking sites really become the "way it is done," as some advocate today? Will curricular content be conveyed through online "gaming?" School libraries have been leaders in technology almost as long as there have been school libraries, but especially in the last fifteen years, as computers and Internet access arrived in our library facilities and classrooms. Well into the future, part of our library facility will be a digital, virtual presence available to our student patrons from workstations, dumb terminals, laptops, cell phones, and many other as yet unknown access points. As we continue to advocate for appropriate new technologies and age-appropriate access, we must stay aware of ongoing developments in our peer libraries and in the wider field of technology hardware and software. Without appropriate current technologies, the library will be unable to supply useful current information to students of any age.

Honest Work

Another recent issue of *KQ* (2009) focused on "Doing Honest Work." Because libraries sit at the nexus of students, information, and required academic projects, we also sit at the nexus of teaching skills that encourage the use of information and ideas while providing appropriate credit to the sources of the ideas. As we advocate for strong community standards, broad access to information, and tolerance as students approach controversial ideas, we must offer our students and faculty tools to support their learning, tools that encourage skillful note taking and complete bibliographies as projects are constructed. These tools include discussions of plagiarism, copyright, and ethics; they teach citation styles for works cited and consulted. Such efforts demonstrate that librarians are strong advocates for the students, for their skills and the library program that builds those skills. What magazines interest students beyond their academic requirements? Is it reasonable to subscribe to *Seventeen* or *Elle* if it draws students in who may discover *Americas* or some other title on the display—or even just because it pleases them to read it? Will a skateboard magazine encourage a reluctant reader to try something else? What research might I do to support such expansion of my print subscription list? Or is the question, "Should I cancel all print subscriptions in favor of online access only?" What are the broader implications of such a decision for academic concerns and budget? How can I use these results to further advocate the importance of the library in the broader structure of the school? Students deserve access to resources they find rewarding, interesting, and entertaining, as well as those that support their curricular needs.

Many schools now subscribe to long lists of databases. We make every effort to offer the students digital information that has been as carefully checked as the printed resources we traditionally offer. We do that even as we recognize that the students prefer the ease of a basic search engine that doesn't require passwords and offers millions of "hits" per query. They don't realize why the databases are so much better than any open search engine. The long list of databases can be too overwhelming to know which one is best for this question today; it requires them to develop selection and evaluation skills. We need to advocate with the students to compare and contrast the weaknesses of the search engines and the databases. And we need to advocate with the teachers to build assignments that require the use of specific databases, because it takes practice with anything to develop the skill required for successful searches. We also need to continue to observe and analyze usage of the databases to be sure we are selecting the best tools for the students, faculty, and curriculum. We must continue to monitor the wikis, blogs, and social networking sites available for education applications; which if any of these will be our best choices?

Parents

One useful approach is to educate parents and students about the breadth of our database offerings, sorted by discipline (history, science, general encyclopedias) at the same time that we post pathfinders for student assignments. Pathfinders are nothing new, but being able to post them to library and teacher Web sites is a convenient development. This gets the teacher into the loop of recommending the specific databases that are most useful for a topic and makes the pathfinder that much more accessible to students. This is marketing based on sophisticated thinking and planning; it is also advocacy on behalf of the students getting the best resources 24/7 and a school's curriculum that requires only the best resources. By increasing parent awareness of our digital resources (databases, etc.), we encourage them to support the remote use of the complete access that we provide—and we begin to teach parents the merits of databases over basic search engines. This parent education can come back to us in comments to administrators about how wonderful the library is, or how much the student appreciates the ease of finding the information needed for homework or projects, not to mention in successful completion by students of sophisticated research assignments using the databases provided by the school.

A *Teacher Librarian* article (Johns 2008) discusses "P + M = A," which translates to "Promotion + Marketing = Advocates," with Advocates defined as "others who take up your cause because they *know* [the] students will not . . . be able to use information well without you[r program]." We expend energy every day to build the programs we know our students need, but if no one knows how the students benefit—that is, analytically how and statistically how much—then our programs are forever at risk. Tell your success stories: the anecdotes that demonstrate student "aha" moments in the research process as well as those documented successes that tie your program to improved academic performance. Be sure that the school community—the students, the faculty, the administration, and most of all the parents—knows that the library is an essential aspect of an excellent education. Parents and students are some of our best advocates. Parent–teacher organizations can be excellent additional sources of funding, which is a form of advocacy, for our programs. According to the AASL advocacy Web page, "True advocacy is when stakeholders stand up and speak out for you on behalf of a cause, idea, program or organization." Think about those parents we just taught about the databases, for example. Be sure to honor your volunteer advocates in a way that suits you and your school's personality. The *KQ* "Storytelling" issue (2008) offers a creative way to feature our most reliable advocates: Ogre Awards. The name certainly got your attention, didn't it? Find your own unusual approach.

Rude Awakening

> Here's a totally bizarre situation. We are a 350-girl college prep school that has been in existence for over 160 years. We have money issues brought on by the economy and lower than desired enrollment. Our President (we have a President-Principal model) has decided that staffing cuts were in order to offset our money problems. She dictated that [3 teachers] should be cut plus [three who] will work only ½ time. But the most sweeping and radical dictate was to eliminate me from the staff PLUS the library will NOT exist. No more budget and coverage will be English teachers monitoring the room. By the way, this President is in her second year here having NEVER been an educator. What we think led our search committee to select her was that she was local and had been the Chief Financial Officer at a local school. (Antal 2009)

This true story was posted on the AASLForum listserv on May 15, 2009. The author contacted AASL as soon as the news was announced, which tells us this author was already connected to the existing advocacy network, but the head of this school didn't care. This account offers the rest of us a strong incentive to never let up on our efforts at PR, marketing, and advocacy, all year and every year. We need to be sure we are reaching all our constituents to ensure they will speak for us if the going gets this tough. We are talking about collaborations with teachers, readers' advisory, and research support for students, efforts that improve student achievement. We are talking about being sure the administration is always aware of our effects on student learning. As long as we keep our communities aware of our impact on student achievement, we are less likely to be subject to wholesale elimination.

Conclusion

In sum, Bloom's Taxonomy offers a framework to better understand the elements of advocacy: PR, marketing, and the ongoing analysis that complete the spectrum. The process of advocacy also requires that we in the library advocate to and for various audiences: library staff, students, faculty, administration, admissions, parents, alumni, and the greater community. In the *NAIS Guidelines of Professional Practice for Librarians* (2008), numbers 10 and 11 point directly to advocacy (see Appendix A).

10. Partners with the school administration to provide knowledge, vision, and leadership to plan for change and the future success of the library program and thus guarantees that the library facilities, collection, and staffing will continue to meet the needs of the school over time.

11. Assesses the effectiveness of the library media program on an ongoing, regular basis.

Advocacy is at the core of everything we do. We want our students to have the exact resources that will best support their academic achievement of the specific school curriculum. We also want our students to have access to interesting, timely informational and recreational resources. Our faculty should have access to the support they require to teach the curriculum we have collaboratively designed and implemented, which will further the academic success of their students. Parents want to know that their students are getting exactly what they need from the library for their classes and their pleasure. The library must be an outstanding aspect of the school, a highlight for admissions tours, a place that will appeal to the prospective student. We want the administration and the board to recognize and fund the library's ongoing efforts to maintain a collection that supports the needs of the school. Library staff members participate in professional organizations and continuing education to grow their skills and knowledge to lead the library forward into the future. Advocacy is convincing our patrons to use all of our services and offering all of the services they need; it is also convincing our administration and leadership exactly how our program is essential to the successful education of all students. It is just one little word, but what a word: Advocacy.

> *Advocacy is convincing our patrons to use all of our services and offering all of the services they need; it is also convincing our administration and leadership exactly how our program is essential to the successful education of all students.*

References

American Association of School Librarians. 2009a. "Guidelines or Standards." In *Standards for the 21st-Century Learner*. Available at www.ala.org/ala/mgrps/divs/aasl/guidelinesandstandards/learningstandards/standards.cfm. Accessed March 16, 2009.

———. 2009b. *School Libraries Count!: AASL's Longitudinal Study*. AASL. Available at http://aasl.org///////.cfm. Accessed March 22, 2009).

Antal, Jim. 2009. "Re: RE: RE: RE: RE: RE: Ironic Library Economic Stories." E-mail to aaslforum@ala.org, May 15.

Bryant, Alice. 2009. E-mail to author, October 19.

Gordon, Carol A. 2008. "A Never-ending Story: Action Research Meets Summer Reading." *KnowledgeQuest* 37, no. 2: 34–40.

Hand, Dorcas. 2008. "Keep Everyone in the Loop: Constant Advocacy." *Teacher Librarian* 36, no. 2: 26–27.

Houston Area Independent School Library Network. 2009. *Recommended Reading Lists for Preschool–12th Grade Students*. Houston Area Independent School Library Network. Available at http://haisln.org/.html. Accessed March 22, 2009.

Independent Schools Section, American Association of School Librarians. 2009a. *ISS Data Committee Survey*. Available at www.ala.org///////slsections//.cfm. Accessed March 22, 2009.

———. 2009b. "ISS Resources." In *A Student and Parent's Guide to Evaluating Libraries in Independent Schools*. American Association or School Librarians. Available at www.ala.org/ala/mgrps/divs/aasl/aboutaasl/aaslcommunity/aaslsections/iss/resources.cfm. Accessed March 16, 2009.

Jensen, Amy. 2008. "Presenting the Evidence: Librarian's Annual Report to the Principal." *KnowledgeQuest* 37, no. 2: 28–32.

Johns, Sara Kelly. 2008. "What Can Teacher Librarians Do to Promote Their Work and the School Library Media Program? Offensive Formula: P+M=A." *Teacher Librarian* 36, no. 2: 30–31.

Knowledge Quest. 2008. 36, no. 5. Issue on Storytelling.

Knowledge Quest. 2009. 37, no. 3. Issue on Honest Work.

Lance, Keith Curry. 1993. *How School Librarians Help Kids Achieve Standards or Impact of School Library Media Centers on Academic Achievement*. San Jose, CA: Hi Willow Publishing.

Lance, Keith Curry, Marcia J. Rodney, and Christine Hamilton-Pennell. 2000. "How School Librarians Help Kids Achieve Standards: The Second Colorado Study." *Library Research Service* April. Available at www.lrs.org/documents/lmcstudies/CO/execsumm.pdf. Accessed March 7, 2010.

Maine State Library. 2005. *Maine Values and Explanation for Library Use Value Calculator.* Maine State Library. Available at www.maine.gov/msl/services/calexplantion.htm. Accessed November 23, 2009.

National Association of Independent Schools. 2008. *Guidelines of Professional Practice for Librarians.* NAIS. Available at www.nais.org/about/seriesdoc.cfm?ItemNumber=151374. Accessed March 16, 2009.

Pecoraro, John. 2009. "What's It Worth? The Value of Library Services as an Advocacy Tool." *Texas Library Journal* 85, no. 1: 8–9.

Saricks, Joyce. 2008. "At Leisure: Readers' Advisory—Flash in the Pan or Here to Stay?" *Booklist* 104, no. 21: 12.

Snyder, Maureen M., and Janet Roche. 2008. "Roadmap for Improvement: Evaluating Your Library Media Program." *Knowledge Quest* 37, no. 2: 22–26.

"Taxonomy of Educational Objectives." In *Wikipedia, the Free Encyclopedia.* Available at http://en.wikipedia.org//.php?title=Taxonomy_of_Educational_Objectives&oldid=275838233. Accessed March 8, 2009.

Teacher Librarian: The Journal for School Library Professionals. 2008. 36, no. 2. Issue theme: Advocacy and the Teacher Librarian.

Texas State Library and Archives Commission, and Texas Education Agency. 2008. "The Needs of Public School Libraries Report: Executive Summary." *Texas Library Journal* 84, no. 4: 146–47.

Todd, Ross. 2008. "The Evidence-Based Manifesto for School Librarians: If School Librarians Can't Prove They Make a Difference, They May Cease to Exist." *School Library Journal* (April). Available at www.schoollibraryjournal.com.//html?q=summit. Accessed March 16, 2009.

Toor, Ruth, and Hilda K. Weisburg. 2007. *New on the Job: A School Library Media Specialist's Guide to Success.* Chicago: American Library Association.

More Tools for Advocacy

AASL Advocacy Toolkit. 2009. AASL. Available at www.ala.org/ala/mgrps/divs/aasl/aaslissues/toolkits/aasladvocacy.cfm. Accessed March 27, 2009.

AASL Crisis Toolkit. 2009. American Association of School Librarians. Available at www.ala.org./ala/mgrps/divs/aasl/aaslissues/toolkits/crisis.cfm. Accessed March 27, 2009.

Visit http://lu.com/excellence for supporting links and occasional updates to all essays in this book.

Dorcas Hand grew up in independent school; she has attended or been a librarian at seven independent schools located in Florida, Georgia, Massachusetts, and Texas. Her library career has included three schools and two public libraries, as well as a tour as editor of SLJ*'s* Adult Books for Young Adults*. She has been active in ALA/AASL/ISS and TLA/TASL (Texas) since 1978. She is in her twentieth year as Director of Libraries at Annunciation Orthodox School in Houston, Texas (www.aoshouston.org).*

Advocacy Through Assessment: Library Professional Practice and the School Mission

Ann Weber, Bellarmine Preparatory (San Jose, CA)

Accountability builds success. It allows all parties to ascertain how well goals and aspirations are being met. Independent schools must be accountable to a plethora of interested parties, including students, parents, benefactors, and other educational institutions. Within the school, accountability is assessed on many levels, including individually. Assuming that the whole is equal to the sum of its parts, the collective assessments of the school's workforce would equate to the accountability of the institution as a whole. Though assessments and evaluations are seldom eagerly anticipated by either the person being assessed or the assessor, they can be constructive tools that build relationships. From the assessor's point of view, an assessment should promote understanding of the work that is expected relative to the work is performed. For the person being assessed, an assessment should reinforce exemplary work and draw attention to tasks that need improvement. In a perfect world, an assessment would be a win-win activity.

School librarians have often fallen through the cracks when it comes to assessment in their institutions. One reason is that the school librarian is often the sole librarian in the institution and therefore does not fit into a class of employees whose work is normally evaluated. Many schools use a faculty evaluation form for the librarian, and others use an administrative form. We librarians are often considered faculty for contract purposes, but our duties include many administrative tasks (see essay 5). School librarians manage staff, space, and collections and administer budgets that are often larger than other academic budgets. A librarian's role in a school is unique, and many school administrators don't know what it is that librarians do, let alone how to assess their work.

Accountability builds success.

In an informal poll taken in 2009 by Dorcas Hand, director of libraries at Annunciation Orthodox School in Houston, Texas, independent school librarians were asked if and how they were evaluated. Surprisingly, many replied that they had not had an evaluation, and some for as long as twenty years. Several librarians replied that they reported library usage to administrators in lieu of having an evaluation of their work. Some were assessed by surveys of faculty and/or students, and some were assessed with tools specific to the work of school librarians. The results of this informal poll revealed a lack of consistency in assessing the work of school librarians.

Many school libraries report detailed statistics of use (how many books circulated, how many classes taught, how many single students) in lieu of work assessments, but those reports only indicate how librarians spend their time and how their facilities are used. These numbers don't provide any analysis of how librarians might best spend their time; what changes in either the program or the facility might improve service; or, most important, how library service might best support the school mission. The analysis is what leads to professional development and program improvement. Surveys of faculty and staff can give librarians a sense of popularity but do not lead to improvement of either staff service or facility goals, unless the results are analyzed in the context of the school's mission and the library's goals. Independent schools and their students are best served when an honest and relevant assessment or self-assessment of staff and program in the context of the particular school mission and curriculum is performed on a regular basis.

From Hand's poll, three types of assessments emerged as most compatible to the librarians who responded: customized administrative/faculty tools, individual goal setting and review, and tools designed particularly for librarian assessments. Librarians have a passionate desire to contribute to and support the mission of their schools. For that reason, librarians are comfortable with assessment tools that assess based on community values and are similar to tools used for other professionals in the school community. Goal setting and reviewing progress at the end of a school year produced genuine satisfaction. If all members in the school community participate in goal setting, the process contributes to team spirit and camaraderie. Setting goals at a particular time and reviewing progress toward the goals at a specific later date facilitates professional development plans and leaves no time for procrastination. This process is concretely useful within any assessment method.

> *These numbers don't provide any analysis of how the librarian might best spend his or her time; what changes in either the program or the facility might improve service; or, most important, how library service might best support the school mission.*

Types of Assessments

- Customized administrative/faculty tools
- Individual goal setting and review
- Tools designed particularly for librarian assessments

The most appreciated types of assessment tools were tools specifically designed to assess the work of librarians. Librarian assessment tools can take a variety of forms, including rubrics. Educational consultant Charlotte Danielson (2007) designed a rubric assessment tool specifically for librarians. Her rubric for librarians is similar in structure to other rubrics that she designed for teachers, breaking the work into four domains, each with six components that describe aspects of the librarian's work. Within each component, descriptions of a librarian's performance that would be assessed as unsatisfactory, basic, proficient, and distinguished are provided. A librarian and/or the librarian's supervisor could easily identify the rubric level that best describes the quality of the librarian's work in each component. Those components that are judged less than proficient or distinguished can become areas for professional development.

Danielson's Four Domains

- Planning and Preparation
- The Library Environment
- Communicating Clearly and Accurately
- Reflecting on Teaching

Following completion of a rubric domain, the action plan for improvement can be spelled out in a table listing action(s) to be taken, persons/resources needed, documentation, and a timeline. This action plan provides the librarian with details of essential professional development to amend any gaps in the formal assessment. In the directions that precede the rubric, Danielson states that the professional growth plan must be tied to standards. She explains that the purpose of the evaluation process is to improve student learning by strengthening instruction. In the world of independent schools, school standards are

> *[The] professional growth plan must be tied to standards.*

interpreted within the context of the school mission; librarian assessment must also be tied to direct support of the school mission. The rubric for librarians provides a clear path to forming student-centered professional development plans.

Danielson's method is the clearest and most library-oriented published evaluation system available. However, in 2008 the National Association of Independent Schools (NAIS) adopted the new *NAIS Guidelines of Professional Practice for Librarians,* with fourteen criteria integral to ideal school library service (see appendix A). The librarian at Bellarmine College

> *In the world of independent schools, school standards are interpreted within the context of the school mission.*

Preparatory in San Jose, California, immediately thought that they would add substance to her yearly self-assessment. When she forwarded the guidelines to the administration, proposing to use the NAIS guidelines as a new self-assessment tool, her proposal was met with enthusiasm.

In the past, the Bellarmine librarian had been evaluated by a generic self-assessment form designed for administrators at the school. Having been designed for administrators, the form perfectly described administrative duties, yet administration is only part of the librarian's job. The administrative self-assessment tool did not offer the librarian any opportunity to reflect on the many other important responsibilities of a professionally trained school librarian. She decided to combine her school's administrative form with the new criteria from NAIS to develop a tool easily recognized by her administration but better targeted to her work as librarian in content (see appendix B).

As a Roman Catholic Jesuit high school, Bellarmine administrators and faculty are committed to modeling the principles articulated in the Graduate at Graduation (Grad at Grad) profile. All administrative and faculty assessments employ the principles of the Grad at Grad profile (Jesuit Secondary Education Association). Performance criteria are classified within those principles, effectively tying administration evaluation to the school's specific mission. The librarian assessment tool now includes both criteria specific to working in a Catholic Jesuit school environment, as well as criteria specific to the work of a librarian.

Principles of Grad at Grad

Open to Growth

Professionally and Intellectually Competent

Committed to Doing Justice

Loving

Religious

Pursues Leadership Growth

The newly designed Bellarmine librarian's self-assessment table allows for the librarian to be assessed along a spectrum ranging from exceeding the school standard to unsatisfactory for every standard. At the conclusion of each section, space is provided for comments so that the librarian can further explain the self-assessment or the supervisor can add comments. The last section of the self-assessment form provides an opportunity for the librarian to summarize strength and areas for growth. The areas for growth, in particular, supply seeds for a professional growth plan. This assessment form has proved to be most satisfying for the librarian and the administration.

As she developed the form, the Bellarmine librarian considered her answers to the self-assessment guide. She identified two guidelines on which she felt she needed improvement; both require the librarian to reach out to faculty in new ways:

1. As a member of the faculty, partners with teaching colleagues to integrate information, technology, and research skills into the curriculum.

8. Utilizes a variety of interactive tools to provide services, information, and tutorials to the learning community.

Already the *NAIS Guidelines of Professional Practice* were proving valuable in their inclusion of twenty-first-century technology skills for a librarian's toolbox. The librarian saw the usefulness of the criteria in building a library program of excellence and took that charge as inspiration to develop increased expertise in her perceived areas of weakness, technological collaboration and Web 2.0 tools. She would extend additional research help to every faculty member who scheduled time in the library, not just those who were already receptive. She would also learn more about Web 2.0 tools so that she could implement them in her teaching. To that end, she enrolled in a workshop to learn Audacity (http://audacity.sourceforge.net/), a multimedia tool that records demonstrations on using the many databases available at Bellarmine. (Audacity® is free, open source software for recording and editing sounds.) An open-ended GPP such as the NAIS list will continue to offer her new challenges as each school year brings new technological and traditional challenges, but when her annual self-assessments come due, she will have a ready tool to catalyze her thinking.

The core GPP/Grad at Grad assessment tool can be tweaked for every Bellarmine library job description. Every library task contributes in some way to the final product, a "Graduate at Graduation." This method keeps the student learner at the center of staff evaluation, as well as the school's independent perspective on successful education. Staff members can then identify their own strengths and areas for growth, and plans can be made to improve library service by improving targeted skills through professional development.

When a self-assessment form uses criteria that are tailored to fit the school and specific responsibilities, the self-assessment process becomes much more valuable. Any school can do this; any librarian can do this. Take your own school mission, your library goals, and the NAIS GPP to build an assessment tool to suit your individual

> *Every library task contributes in some way to the final product, a "Graduate at Graduation."*

institution. The assessment acknowledges strengths and areas for improvement and is the basis for activities designed to enhance growth in knowledge and experience. School librarians who are assessed in the context of the *NAIS Guidelines of Professional Practice for Librarians* and their specific school's mission derive satisfaction from achievements in their local context and set realistic goals for the future. These librarians can also take satisfaction that such an assessment tool offers administrators strong insights into what best practices in a library should be, which will improve communication about all library issues. Assessment is one key element of a superior independent school library.

References

Audacity. 2009. SourceForge. Available at http://audacity.sourceforge.net/copyright. Accessed November 14, 2009.

Danielson, Charlotte. 2007. *Enhancing Professional Practice: A Framework for Teaching*. Alexandria VA: Association for Supervision and Curriculum Development.

National Association of Independent Schools. 2008. *NAIS Guidelines of Professional Practice for Librarians*. Available at www.nais.org/about/seriesdoc.cfm? ItemNumber=151374. Accessed December 18, 2008.

"Profile of the Graduate at Graduation." 2009. In *Faculty Handbook*, 6–10. Bellarmine College Preparatory. August. Available at www.bcp.org/data/files/ gallery/FacultyFiles/FacultyHandbook.pdf. Accessed November 15, 2009.

Visit http://lu.com/excellence for supporting links and occasional updates to all essays in this book.

Ann Weber has been the Library Director at Bellarmine College Preparatory (www.bcp.org/), a Catholic Jesuit high school for boys, in San Jose, California, for ten years. She is a frequent contributor to School Library Journal*'s Media Review and* Library Journal*'s Book Review.*

Faster Than a Speeding Bullet: Technology in Independent School Libraries

Patt Moser, Sidwell Friends School (Washington, DC)

> *1922:* The "New" high school library has a library classroom, adjoining the main reading room where a lantern and bulletin boards make the use of pictures and slides possible with the least inconvenience, as all the material is at hand in the library.
>
> This room is fitted with tablet arm chairs which can be moved, and is equipped with dark shades at the windows for darkening the room, white wall curtain for showing pictures, reflectoscope, Victrola, and cases for holding slides, postcards, Victrola records, etc.
>
> —Wilson (1917/1922, 13)

> *1963:* With regard to media, we have learned that today we must have immediately at hand a full spectrum of learning and information resources including books, magazines, and other forms of printed material; pictorial and graphic aids; motion pictures, discs, and recordings; television and teaching machines.
>
> Television can, and is now being used successfully in teaching more than one-fifth of American youngsters.
>
> Computers are actually being used experimentally, for example, by the Systems Development Corporation in California, not only to make available a full range of modern techniques for storage, retrieval, and correlation of information, but also for instructional sequencing and the simultaneous recording of student response to any form or combination of forms of instructional media presentation.
>
> —Stone (1964, 4–5)

1986: Bring technology into your programming particularly in the schools. Use interactive video to involve an entire school building in a project on reliving history or taking a trip into space. Connecting a videodisc, video-tape, filmstrip, or slide projector to a microcomputer allows the student to make interactive decisions involved with a scenario. Think of the possibilities.

Does your school or library have cable access and capabilities? Besides routine school newscasts, instructional demonstrations, and story programs, how about having students present book reviews on the air and running them as spot announcements during the day or in the school cafeteria at noon time?

—Cummins (1989, 36)

2009: As regular folks store more data and rely more and more on the cloud, librarians would be well-served to spend some time pondering what this means for services and access. As movies and music become downloads from the great jukebox in the sky, what happens to the AV department? As documents and data find their way to the ether, how can we provide a means to use them? Some implications from the "Cloud" post:

- *Understand converged devices are everywhere.*
- *Allow unfettered access to the cloud.*
- *Understand that the cloud may also be a valuable information resource.*
- *Utilize the cloud to save time and money.*

—Stephens (2009)

School libraries have striven for over a century to keep up with the latest and most useful technologies that promote learning. As is evident in the quotes above, trying to describe a library with the ideal selection and amount of technology is like trying to catch a speeding bullet—impossible. In the first decade of the twenty-first century, technology has changed so swiftly, with new applications and equipment appearing daily, that it seems almost fruitless to try to prescribe the best technology for school libraries in these static pages. It is easy to imagine a school librarian several decades from now selecting a quote from this essay to show how "quaint" school library technology used to be in the 2010s. Despite this daunting challenge, this essay takes the plunge into crystal ball gazing and recommends seven essential tools for the independent school library. Their use will vary depending on the grade level each library serves, yet all are needed in varying degrees. These tools are

- books,
- ILS (integrated library system),
- reliable online information sources,
- a computing device available for each student and staff member,

- wireless access to the "cloud,"

- great relationships with your IT (information technology) department members, and

- flexibility and experimentation.

That's it! Let's examine them in some detail.

Essential Tools for the Independent Library

Books

We all know the predictions: books are doomed to disappear from our daily lives, relegated to dusty museum exhibits and underground vaults for their protection, safely kept away from the hands of the public. Indeed, one independent school in Massachusetts made headlines when the headmaster declared that they were about to remove all the books from the library and replace them with a coffee shop, flat screen TVs, and e-book readers. However, consider the cover of *The New Yorker* on June 8, 2009: A space alien is visiting a ruined New York City and sits in a pile of broken monitors, keyboards, e-book readers, and cell phones, reading the only technology that still works, books (Clowes 2009). What other foolproof method of recording information do we have that can be decoded without worrying about the correct operating system, the correct physical format, indeed, even electricity? Books will be around for a long time to come. Your library needs books. Your students need books. Period.

That said, it is fun and exciting to explore and experiment with the many digital book formats now available, such as e-book readers, books online, books on smart phones, books on computers, books in audio formats that play on a variety of equipment, even books written on cell phones using text messaging at 140 characters per "page." With so many different formats for books—from print to e-ink to audio recordings—"reading" can now be done

> *Books will be around for a long time to come. Your library needs books. Your students need books. Period.*

under almost any circumstances: alone in a room with a book, in a noisy gym while running on a treadmill with a personal music device, on the subway with your cell phone, or on a trip around the world with your personal library on your e-book reader. Audio versions of books recorded by lively narrators bring life to stories for reluctant readers. The advent of free digital downloads of audio books from public libraries means patrons have many format options: burn them to CDs, listen at their computers, or download to their personal audio devices (MP3 players, iPods, iPhones, Blackberries, etc.). Playaways, small MP3 players containing the audio version of just one book, are particularly popular in school libraries. In short, great books for all ages are available in multiple formats. School librarians should continually be aware of the formats and experiment with them to determine which may be useful for their students.

Books in digital format can be a lifesaver for a student trying to complete a research project from home. Resourceful school librarians include links on their library's Web pages to free sites on the Internet with full-text versions of books, usually those in the public domain. Project Gutenberg (www.gutenberg.org/wiki/Main_Page), founded by Michael Hart in 1971, is one of the largest collections of free online digital books available in multiple languages and formats. For decades volunteers have typed the full texts of books and uploaded them to the site for the use of anyone who needs them. Of course, Google Books is the great online experiment to scan and digitize all of the world's books. Because of copyright restrictions, only portions of the books still under copyright are available for readers and, as of this writing, Google intends to make access to the full text of these books a pay-per-view event—not a model that librarians take to very kindly. In addition, many vendors sell digital books to libraries either as a yearly subscription or as a file the library "owns" in perpetuity for a onetime fee and a yearly Web site maintenance fee.

Books on e-readers such as Amazon's Kindle, Barnes and Noble's Nook, and Sony's e-reader are gaining popularity. Many independent school libraries are experimenting with them, checking them out to students so they can try the format and see how they like it. As more and more newspapers disappear from our doorsteps, reading online versions of the nation's most important newspapers on a large format e-reader may become the closest thing we will have to the actual experience of reading a newspaper in print. Moreover, there is a potential market for online textbooks on e-readers. Currently the need for a larger screen and color e-ink are barriers to successfully transferring textbooks to e-readers. However, as this book goes to press, Apple, Inc. has just announced the release in April 2010 of their newest product, the iPad, which looks like an overgrown iTouch or iPhone. The "coolness" factor of the iPhone cannot be overestimated, and it may transfer to the iPad. If the plan to open an Apple bookstore is as successful as the iTunes store, then reading may become an entirely new experience on the iPad, and Amazon's current domination of the e-reader audience will be severely challenged. In addition, Apple seems poised to capture the textbook market with the iPad and the Apple bookstore, without having to worry about color e-ink. This rapidly changing e-reader market is a great illustration of how fluid the technology market is and how necessary it is for school librarians to be constantly on the alert for such changes.

To sum up, books in their print format will be a staple in libraries for years to come and will remain a valuable research tool for our students, but the many electronic formats that books are assuming are useful and convenient in a variety of situations and for a variety of students. Libraries that offer a range of book options allow their students to choose the best format for their specific situation: reading a printed book at home for a research paper, listening to a novel while exercising, or reading a textbook on a Kindle because they left theirs at home. Independent school librarians should make it a practice to try the new formats and encourage their students to do the same. But how do we keep track of all of those books, both in print and online? The answer, of course, is tool number two: the integrated library system.

> *Libraries that offer a range of book options allow their students to choose the best format for their specific situation.*

ILS—Integrated Library System

Every school library needs an integrated library system or ILS so students can easily find the books they need and librarians can keep track of who has which book or any other item the library manages. An ILS typically has multiple functions: circulation, cataloging, online public access catalog (OPAC), report writing, overdue book notification, and inventory procedures. Features to look for include the ability to copy MARC records from various libraries, especially the Library of Congress; the ability to automatically send overdue notices via e-mail; an option to integrate pictures of book jackets, reviews, table of contents, and links to outside sources for each title listed; the option of different interfaces for different age groups; and accommodation for video clips, icons, photographs, and educator-approved Web sites. Newer features allow students the option of sending citation information to their cell phones via text messaging, uploading their own reviews, and placing holds on books they want that are already checked out.

Ensuring that the software is fully compatible with the student information system (SIS) software used in your school will make it easy to import names, contact information, and pictures for all students. Look for ILS software that is "SIF" (Schools Interoperability Framework) compliant. The SIF format is a standard created for school information systems that allows the easy flow of information across databases that are SIF compliant, no matter which vendor created the software.

A number of companies offer ILS software appropriate for school libraries. A search of the literature will bring up numerous articles comparing the merits of each vendor's system. School librarians should work with the IT staff when selecting new ILS software. The IT professional can look for any hidden problems and help determine which software is most compatible with the school's other enterprise systems. In addition, the librarian and the IT staff may want to consider an open-source ILS. Open source is defined by the Open Source Initiative as "a development method for software that harnesses the power of distributed peer review and transparency of process. The promise of open source is better quality, higher reliability, more flexibility, lower cost, and an end to predatory vendor lock-in." As Michael Stephens wrote in his *Tame the Web* blog, "Sometimes, it seems to me, we are very quick to run to vendors and spend money on solutions that might be available for the cost of participating in an Open Service Software (OSS) project. It's not free—I readily admit that—but a very different way of managing resources and the future" (Stephens 2009). He argues that using an open source ILS keeps the librarian closer to the actual developers of the software, because the software is constantly undergoing improvements submitted by its many users who are savvy enough to create improvements in the programming language itself. When librarians are closer to the developers, they are more likely to have their needs met. The downside, of course, is that librarians using open source software will need to have some programming experience and be willing to work with user groups to solve problems rather than turning to technical support contracts with vendors.

Currently three open source ILSs are Koha (www.koha.org/) supported by LibLime, Evergreen (www.open-ils.org/) supported by Equinox, and OPALS (OPen-source Automated Library management System). There are many pros and cons to using open source software, and librarians

> *[L]ibrarians will want to carefully consider whether the free nature of open source software outweighs the necessity of having someone on staff who has the knowledge and time to troubleshoot problems and load updates.*

will want to carefully consider whether the free nature of open source software outweighs the necessity of having someone on staff who has the knowledge and time to troubleshoot problems and load updates. The devil is in the details, and sometimes the details of dealing with open source software quirks may make paying money to an ILS vendor who will keep your software running look like a bargain.

The OPAC (online public access catalog) is a vital ingredient for a successful school library, or any library, for that matter. It is how patrons know what books are in the library, what format they are in, and whether or not they are checked out or available. OPACs can also contain cataloged Web sites with active links to information useful to students in the school. Besides being readily available on dedicated computers in the school library, the OPAC should be available on the Internet so students and teachers can research it from any computer with an Internet connection. In a survey conducted of independent school libraries in 2004–2005 (see essay 3), 94 percent responded that they had an automated catalog; however, only 52 percent of the school libraries said their catalogs were available remotely (Williamson and ISS 2009). Remote access to the library catalog is essential for students and teachers alike. In schools with one-to-one laptop programs, all students and teachers will have ubiquitous access to the school library catalog through their laptops. Even students with smart phones or personal digital assistants such as iPhones or iTouches should be able to access the library catalog.

The OPAC . . . is a vital ingredient for a successful school library, or any library, for that matter.

Federated searching, while not yet perfected at the time of this writing, is an idea of interest to many librarians. This one-stop-search function allows a student to enter a set of keywords into just one Web screen to search across all of the library's holdings and subscription databases. In other words, a search for "American revolution" will find library books; digital books the library subscribes to; and magazine, journal, and newspaper articles from the library's subscription databases. No longer must a student conduct separate searches in each type of resource and compile the results from separate lists. One list is created, saving time and frustration for the student researcher. Software developers who create federated search engines must develop agreements with a wide variety of database vendors to ensure that the search engine is capable of correctly searching every database to which a library decides to subscribe. As with all endeavors involving multiple vendors, this has been accomplished with mixed success so far, but many librarians have their fingers crossed in hopes of success in the near future. On the flip side, with federated searching there is the fear that a student's searches will return a large number of "hits," overwhelming them with too many choices, much like a Google search. Younger students in particular may do better with concentrated searches in specific databases, because fewer results make learning how to assess the relevance of a resource easier. Fortunately, assuming that good federated searching becomes an affordable reality, librarians can choose whether or not to use it when teaching research skills to their students, based on the age and ability of the class in front of them. Students can choose to use it or search in individual databases depending on which method they find most useful.

A more recent trend in OPACs is "faceted" searching, which many online retailers have already adopted. Faceted searching allows patrons to drill down into a particular topic to get precisely what is needed. For example, a search might begin with the keywords "Abraham Lincoln." The OPAC then gives the patron the option not only of narrowing the meaning of what information is needed (assassination versus biography), but also what form the information should come in (books, database, journal articles, etc.). This is similar to ordering a sweater from your favorite online clothing store. After you choose the style you want (Lincoln's biography), you need to choose the color and size (book or journal or online source, etc.). Several university libraries are developing their own open source software in an effort to create the most useful OPAC for their patrons. Hopefully, these ideas and concepts will trickle down to the school library level so that we may take advantage of them.

So far, with our first two tools, our library has books available to our students in a variety of formats, a way for students to find the books they need, and a way for the librarian to know who has which books. Beyond books, our student researchers need encyclopedia, journal, magazine, and newspaper articles, as well as primary sources. That leads us to the third essential tool.

Reliable Information from Online Resources

The independent school librarian endeavors to create self-sufficient, discerning researchers who will thrive while doing college research and, indeed, research throughout their lives. The Internet may be a treasure trove of information, but it can just as easily be a cesspool of misinformation, as every librarian knows. Teaching our students how to find reliable information is a primary goal. This must be done using both free information on the Internet, as well as subscription databases for which the library pays. Upper school students need access to scholarly databases for their research. Many of these will be the same databases they will find in their college libraries; thus they will be better prepared for their college research careers. Middle and lower school librarians will want to subscribe to databases from vendors who create resources especially for younger children. Because these databases should be chosen to carefully match the curricular needs of the school, the lists will vary from school to school. The best ways to explore available products are to visit other independent school libraries; take time to meet with vendors at conferences; and take advantage of free trials so that you, your students, and teachers can try them out and give relevant feedback.

Of course, to teach our students how to use these databases and then give them practice in using them for their research assignments requires computers, the fourth tool necessary for a school library.

> *The Internet may be a treasure trove of information, but it can just as easily be a cesspool of misinformation, as every librarian knows. Teaching our students how to find reliable information is a primary goal.*

A Computing Device Available for Each Student

"What I hear I forget. What I see I remember. What I do I understand" (Bennett n.d.). Seeing may be believing, but doing is knowing. Students cannot just watch the librarian conduct an online search; they need lots and lots of practice so that they gain skills in finding the information they seek. The only way practice is possible is to ensure that there is a computer available for each student to use while in the library, whether as part of a class for a research lesson or on his or her own. There are several ways to provide this one-to-one computer access. If the school has a one-to-one laptop program, in which every student has a personal laptop computer to use in all classes, then students should bring their laptops to the library and use them for research classes. If this is not the case, the school may have a laptop cart available for the librarian to borrow, or there may be a computer lab either in the library or in the school that can accommodate a class of students. A cheaper alternative that is more easily affordable for any school is a classroom set of netbooks. These small, lightweight computers cost not much more than a smart phone yet have the capabilities of most full-sized laptops. A class set can easily be stored on a small shelf or cart, and when they are not scheduled for use in a class, they can be checked out to students to use in the library or school.

But of course having a computer for each student solves only half of the problem. These computers must be able to connect to the Internet, and that is where tool number five comes in.

Wireless Access to the "Cloud"

Ironically, to stay connected one needs to disconnect, the network cable, that is. We want to be connected to an instant and ubiquitous source of information and to our social networks wherever we go, but to do that we need wireless networks that allow us to connect anywhere, anytime. When a school library has a wireless network and a set of laptops or netbooks for students' use, then students can do research anywhere in the library—curled up in a comfy chair or seated at a desk. The information follows them. When the entire school has a wireless network, then the entire building becomes one large virtual library, because digital library sources are accessible from any point in the building via a laptop connected to a wireless network. Even the print collection becomes more accessible, because students can search their OPAC remotely, determine if the book is on the shelf, and pop in to check it out. School librarians should be loud cheerleaders for their IT department's efforts to maintain a good wireless network in the school.

Cloud computing can happen anywhere the student can connect a computer to the Internet.

When students have ubiquitous access to a wireless network, they have ubiquitous access to the "cloud." So much of what is done with computers is migrating to cloud computing. The cloud is basically the Internet with a twist. Technology companies are rushing to create applications that live only on the Internet, eliminating the need to download software to one's computer. Google has created numerous "apps" (applications), and Microsoft created its Office Live services, just to name two of the biggest companies. These cloud applications allow one to do word processing, create spreadsheets and presentations, send e-mail, keep calendars, and so much more. The software is free and allows groups of people working on the same project to collaborate on the same documents. These documents never need to be downloaded to a personal computer because companies offer storage space on their servers either for free or for a nominal fee. Students with netbooks and wireless connections can access all of the library's resources except for the pages of its print collection, all of the free resources on the Internet, the applications they need for a research project, and the actual files that make up the project to be turned into the teacher. Cloud computing can happen anywhere students can connect a computer to the Internet.

In addition to cloud computing, social networking keeps students connected, not just to each other, but potentially to their school and their librarians. Increasingly institutions, both small and large, have begun spreading their messages via social networking sites like Facebook and Twitter. Students are accustomed to getting their information in this manner, and they get it while they are on the move using handheld devices such as iPhones, iTouches, smart phones, and netbooks, which connect to either a wireless network or wireless broadband through a cell phone company. School librarians who make use of

Facebook and other social networking sites to share information with their students will be connecting with the students where they live and play. (See essay 9.)

Social Networking:

Twitter: http://twitter.com/

Facebook: www.facebook.com

My Space: www.myspace.com/

Social Bookmarking:

Diigo: www.diigo.com/

Delicious: http://delicious.com/

Photo Sharing:

Flickr: www.officelive.com/en-us/

Picasa: http://picasa.google.com/

Video Sharing:

You Tube: www.youtube.com/

Teacher Tube: www.teachertube.com/

Video calling:

Skype: www.skype.com

Wikis:

PB Works: http://pbworks.com/

Wiki Spaces: http://www.wikispaces.com/

Wikipedia: http://en.wikipedia.org

Free Software Applications:

Google Apps for Education:www.google.com/a/help/intl/en/edu/

Microsoft Office Live: www.officelive.com/en-us/

Moodle: http://moodle.org/

One more reason for students to have ubiquitous access to a computer and the cloud is the increasing use of collaborative Web applications that enable them to work with others to create new information for their school assignments. Wikis, blogs, Google apps, Microsoft Office Live, social bookmarking sites like Diigo, and video conferencing sites like Skype enable students to collaborate as never before. Students can now pool their research on a wiki, discuss its meaning in a blog or on Skype, and collaboratively create projects with applications accessible in the cloud, giving their school work a real-world context. *Wikipedia*, despite its flaws, is a wonderful example of a vast array of information created collaboratively by experts and amateurs from around the world.

A word of caution is needed here. Independent school librarians and, indeed, their schools, struggle to balance participatory Web 2.0 global collaboration and communication with students' and families' needs for safety and privacy. Many independent schools' rosters contain the names of children of wealthy or famous public figures or even children and young adults who are famous in their own right. When students use publicly accessible wikis, blogs, and other social networking sites for their collaborative projects at school, their privacy may be violated by strangers who may find them online. For this reason, most schools refrain from publishing a student's full name online and carefully choose the student photos they put on their Web sites. For collaborative class projects, course management systems like the open source and free Moodle or fee-based Blackboard allow control over who is viewing, editing, and collaborating on the site. Students'

> *Independent school librarians and, indeed, their schools struggle to balance participatory Web 2.0 global collaboration and communication with students' and families' needs for safety and privacy.*

identities can be protected, and therefore students can more freely make their comments. These course management systems have a wiki component built in, as well as forums, journals, discussions, and so much more. They can be ideal social networking tools for both the classroom and the library while protecting our students' identities at the same time. Librarians can make use of these tools for their research skills classes as well as for student sharing about good books they have read—all within the protection of the school's course management system.

All right, we have books, an ILS, online databases, computers, and wireless access to the cloud. So what's next on our list of essentials for the independent school library? A diligent, resourceful, and knowledgeable IT team is the sixth tool.

Warm Relations with the IT Staff

All of the first five items in this list of seven essential tools for the independent school librarian depend, to varying degrees, on technology working properly. Even accessing our library books is dependent on the ILS for location, checkout, and recall. Very few school librarians possess the in-depth knowledge of IT skills, not to mention the time, necessary to keep the network and computers running. This means that the librarian's closest friends and collaborative partners should be the members of the school's IT department. Without their competence and expertise, it would be next to impossible to locate the information we seek.

Information technology (IT) refers to those professionals who keep the school's network functioning, the computers operational, and the school's connection to the Internet viable. Consider the Venn diagram in figure 8.1.

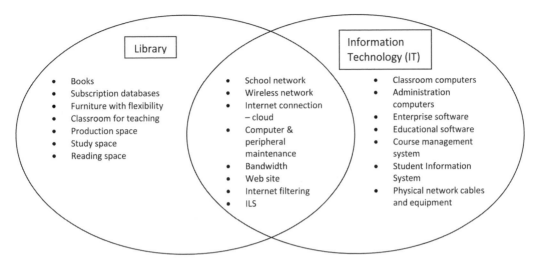

Figure 8.1. Library and IT Intersections

In the left circle are the main tangibles the librarian is responsible for but which do not involve IT in any major way. They include collection development for both books and subscription databases, the furniture and atmosphere of the library, study spaces, reading spaces, production spaces, a classroom for teaching, and the use of the ILS. In the right circle are those tasks for which the IT department is responsible and which do not involve the library staff in major ways. These include the maintenance of the classroom and administrative computers; the enterprise and educational software such as the course management and student information systems; and the physical parts of the network including cables, servers, routers, etc. Where the circles intersect are the many ways in which the IT staff and librarians must interact as a well-functioning team if the library is to be the gold mine of information it should be. As discussed above, a wireless network, a school network, an Internet connection, computers, and an ILS are essential to the school library. Teaming with the IT staff to make sure these are all functioning is crucial for the school librarian.

Additional items of mutual concern involve the school's Web site, Internet filtering, and bandwidth. The Web site is one of the primary ways the librarian has to communicate with students, parents, and the outside world. Working with the IT staff to ensure that your messages are ever-present on the school's Web site is important. The IT department is usually responsible for monitoring Internet filtering for the school, if it exists. No matter where you stand on the issue of filtering, you need to be involved in helping to make decisions about this process, especially since filtering, at times, can deny students and teachers access to important information that may have accidentally been trapped in the filter.

With the shift to cloud computing, wireless networks, social networking, and bandwidth-hogging applications like video-sharing Web sites (YouTube.com, TeacherTube.com, etc.), the most highly coveted resource is bandwidth—the speed with which information can flow over our networks. Schools and institutions, even homeowners, all over the country are discovering that no matter how wonderful an application may be, if you do not have enough bandwidth to run it, the results will be dismal. The school librarian

> *Whereas the IT staff deals with the nuts and bolts of a school network, the educational technology staff helps teachers and students use technology as a learning tool in the classroom.*

should be educated about bandwidth and support the IT department to ensure that the school has the amount of bandwidth it needs to provide the educational experiences our students need.

If your school is lucky enough to have educational technology integrationists, this is another set of people who should be the librarian's best friends. Whereas the information technology (IT) staff deals with the nuts and bolts of a school network, the educational technology staff helps teachers and students use technology as a learning tool in the classroom. When the school librarian works collaboratively with the educational technology integrationist and the classroom teacher to develop a project-based lesson involving research skills, the power of the lessons is palpable. The librarian works with the classroom teacher to help design a curriculum unit that requires independent inquiry and research. The technology integrationist works with the students to help them create a final product, which may be a paper, a digital slide presentation, a video, a podcast, a wiki, or any number of projects. In schools without a technology integrationist, the librarian may have to play both roles in collaboration with the classroom teacher. The outcome will be a powerful project-based lesson in which students will have utilized their library resources, their librarian, and technology to inquire, think critically, gain knowledge, draw conclusions, create new knowledge, and share that knowledge with others.

The last vital tool in the school librarian's tool box is the one that makes all the other tools possible.

Flexibility and Experimentation

Staying Current

Associations:

- American Library Association (ALA): www.ala.org/
- American Association of School Librarians (AASL): www.ala.org/ala/mgrps/divs/aasl/index.cfm
- Independent School Section (ISS) of AASL: www.ala.org/ala/mgrps/divs/aasl/aboutaasl/aaslcommunity/aaslsections/iss/iss.cfm
- Association of Independent School Librarians: www.aislnews.org/aisldefault.html
- ISTE Conference (International Society for Technology in Education): www.iste.org/

Journals:

- *Knowledge Quest*: www.ala.org/ala/mgrps/divs/aasl/aaslpubsandjournals/knowledgequest/kqweb.cfm
- *School Library Journal*: www.schoollibraryjournal.com

Online

- *American Libraries Direct* weekly e-newsletter: www.ala.org/ala/alonline/aldirect/aldirect.cfm
- *The Wired Campus* from *Chronicle of Higher Education*: http://chronicle.com/blog/wiredcampus/5/
- Doug Johnson's *Blue Skunk Blog:* http://doug-johnson.squarespace.com/
- Joyce Valenza's NeverEndingSearch: www.schoollibraryjournal.com/blog/1340000334.html
- Kathy Schrock's *Kaffeeklatsch*: http://kathyschrock.net/blog/
- Will Richardson's *Weblogg-ed*: http://weblogg-ed.com/
- National Association of Independent Schools (NAIS) Ning: http://isenet.ning.com
- *NAIS Guidelines of Professional Practice for Librarians*: www.nais.org/about/seriesdoc.cfm?ItemNumber=151374
- *The Horizon Report* and *The Horizon Report: The K–12 Edition*: www.nmc.org/horizon

The final tool in the librarian's top seven list is not a technology but an attitude, a way of thinking. With technology changing every moment, we have to be flexible enough to realize that library tools are in flux, as is learning in general. Flexibility goes hand in hand with a willingness to experiment and try new things. Even if our experiments fail, we learn something new and move forward.

In terms of the physical library, flexibility is important for the design and furnishings of the school library. Just as classroom desks are no longer nailed to the floor, library furniture should be movable so that it can meet the needs of the moment, from single readers, to small study groups, to entire classes. Computers have to move for the same reasons—to accommodate a group of three students working together on a project in a quiet corner or an entire class learning how to search an online subscription database. Our school libraries must be flexible spaces run by flexible minds to meet the challenges that technology and our broadening understanding of learning are giving us.

Flexibility necessitates experimentation. Try out that new social networking site. Get a parent to donate an e-reader to check out to students. Stay current with what is going on in all types of libraries and in technology. Attending association conferences is one of the best ways to learn about new ideas and technologies. The annual American Library Association (ALA) conference and the biannual American Association of School Librarians (AASL) conference are both chock full of new ideas and vendors selling their latest products. As important as the workshops and vendor exhibit areas are, the opportunity to network with your colleagues and learn what they are doing is invaluable. Joining the Independent School Section (ISS) of AASL and the Association of Independent School Librarians (AISL), attending the independent school tours offered at national conferences, participating in the listservs, and volunteering to help the organizations is a fantastic way to meet your colleagues in independent schools

Flexibility necessitates experimentation.

across the country. Once you have gathered these contacts and created friendships along the way, you will have a network of people to turn to for questions and to learn new ideas for your experiments.

Stretching yourself in directions you may not normally think of is part of being flexible. Consider attending the annual International Society for Technology in Education (ISTE) conference. One look at their program will convince you that, on the national scene, libraries and technology have been married for years. Many of the "rock star" librarians we flock to see at conferences have their own blogs, Facebook pages and/or Twitter feeds that you can follow and learn from. Among the most popular are Doug Johnson's "Blue Skunk Blog," Joyce Valenza's "TheNeverEndingSearch," Kathy Schrock's "Kaffeeklatsch," and Will Richardson's "Weblogg-ed." Of course, reading the journals devoted to our profession is another way to keep up. To look far into the crystal ball, search the Internet for *The Horizon Report* (http://wp.nmc.org/horizon2009/), published every year by The New Media Consortium and Educause, in which "leaders in the fields of business, industry, and education" seek "to identify and describe emerging technologies likely to have a large impact on teaching, learning, research, or creative expression within learning-focused organizations" over the next year, two to three years, and four to five years. Some of the technologies on the horizon are mind boggling and will truly give you a deeper perspective into the future than ordinary journal articles. This year for the first time, there is a *Horizon Report* just for K–12 education, and it is interesting to compare and contrast the two reports. Your teaching colleagues and students can also be a source of new ideas for technology. All of us have learned that our students are often our best teachers when it comes to learning new computer skills.

To sum up, staying flexible and conducting your own technology experiments is one of the strongest tools you have in your toolkit. Keep the best that libraries have always offered, but also be a school leader in trying new technologies and searching for new learning possibilities. Your students and colleagues will admire your adventuresome nature, and your library will be seen as an indispensable lighthouse of technology and learning.

What Technology in School Libraries Looks Like Today

Having considered the importance of these seven tools, let's take a look at where school libraries and technology are in 2010. Currently, most independent school libraries fall somewhere along a continuum from a one-computer library to a full-fledged information commons (see essay 10). The amount and type of technology a school library has in both the physical and virtual senses depends on a number of factors, including

- the grade levels the library serves,

- the primary mission of the library program,

- the school's culture and its vision for learning,

- the amount of money the school can afford to spend on technology,

- whether or not the school has a one-to-one laptop program for its students,

- whether or not the school has a technology integrationist who works with students and teachers to integrate technology into the classroom, and

- the level of the librarian's interest in emerging technologies.

Each school and each librarian must carefully weigh these factors to determine what technology will best meet the goals of the library's mission and the school's vision for student learners.

Lower School

Perhaps the biggest factor affecting how much technology a school library needs is the grades the library serves. Just as a library built for primary school students includes desks and chairs built to the scale of children's bodies, the lower school library program is designed to meet the needs of emerging readers and nascent researchers. The primary emphasis is on students' reading skills and developing a love of reading that will hopefully last for their entire lives. One of the "Common Beliefs" stated in the AASL *Standards for the 21st Century Learner* (2009) is, "Reading is a window to the world . . . a foundational skill for learning, personal growth, and enjoyment." The book collection is the primary focus of the lower school librarian, whose students check out books at a prodigious rate each week. Consequently, librarians need to keep their collections robust and updated to satisfy their students' enormous reading needs. Understandably, the computer and other technologies may take a back seat to this essential mission; however, there is still a critical need for some basic technology. An online public access catalog (OPAC) enables both teachers and students to find the books they need, and an integrated library system (ILS) makes it possible to manage circulation, overdue books, and cataloging. Because lower school libraries typically have the highest circulation levels when compared to middle and upper school divisions, an ILS is essential as a time-saving tool for keeping track of who has which book and making sure the collection suffers a minimum of losses each year.

The ILS software, of course, requires computers for both the librarian and the students. Multiple computer stations available at a child's eye level for students to search in the library's OPAC for a book they would like can also serve double duty as Internet research tools for older students under the supervision of adults. Netbooks may well be the best tool for this use. The smaller keyboards are a great fit for little hands, the cost is much less than that of a normal sized laptop, and the mobility provides the ultimate in flexibility. The low cost of netbooks may even make it possible to purchase a class set so that all students can learn on their own computers when visiting the library as a class. A projector to which the librarian can connect a computer will make it much easier to display lessons to all the students in the class. Even better, an interactive white board can make those lessons come alive when students are asked to demonstrate their library knowledge by writing on the white board or interacting with its objects. I have seen a lovely lesson in which young students sort a "shelf of books" according to the Dewey Decimal System—all on the white board while other students are looking on.

In addition, the library will need a computer for volunteers to check out books as well as one for the librarian. Having a laptop for the librarian will enable him or her to take it home, to conferences, and to classrooms if needed. When the lower school library in my school was being used for classes during a construction project, the librarian took her program to individual classrooms by bringing baskets of books and checking them out to the students on her laptop.

Middle School Libraries

In middle school, students are already readers and, if a thirst for reading has been ignited in the lower school, they are often still avid leisure time readers. One of the principal jobs of the middle school librarian is to continue to foster this love of reading by gently guiding students into the world of young adult literature. As in the lower school library, the ILS and computers for its access are needed for this mission.

But middle school is also the place where research begins to get more serious and technology skills are used more heavily in most subject areas. Collaboration between the librarian and the classroom teacher on research projects is essential. Online database subscriptions that meet the curricular needs of the classroom and the age appropriateness of the students are mandatory and form the heart of a virtual library available 24/7 to students.

> *[M]iddle school is also the place where research begins to get more serious and where technology skills are used more heavily in most subject areas.*

Students need librarians to teach them how to use these databases efficiently. It naturally follows that school librarians are teachers, and teachers need classroom tools and a space to teach in. A projector that connects to a computer that connects to the Internet is essential for teaching library research skills. An interactive white board or a tablet PC can enliven the lesson by providing interactivity. Wireless or "networked" projectors make lessons even more interactive by allowing students' computer screens to be projected at the click of a mouse.

A separate space or attached classroom that can accommodate an entire class allows multiple activities to take place in the library at the same time. The librarian can teach research skills to a class in the library classroom, while other students and classes may be in the library continuing research already begun. As discussed in the section on tool four, to make the lesson even more powerful, every student should be seated at his or her own computer to practice using the databases as the librarian teaches their use. In the middle school library, netbooks have the same advantages as those described in the section on the lower school library: small keyboards for little hands, low cost, and mobility. A computer lab in the library or a laptop cart would accomplish similar goals. When students come back to continue their research, they can check out a laptop or a netbook to use anywhere in the library.

Upper School Libraries

Although upper school librarians continue to encourage a love of reading for reading's sake, the upper school experience emphasizes the research process in more sophisticated ways. Students are often expected to locate, understand, and cite scholarly articles and books in much the same way as a college undergraduate. Indeed, one of the primary duties of the upper school librarian is to ensure that the school's graduates will be able to find reliable research materials while in college. The upper school library, therefore, is a more sophisticated version of the middle school library. The basics are all there: the ILS, the OPAC, and computers for all students to use. In addition, if possible the upper school library should have a separate classroom for learning research skills, as described in the middle school section. To be truly a place for one-stop shopping, the upper school library may include production facilities.

Production Tools

In the 1960s school libraries often became "library media centers," where students could not only read books but watch films, filmstrips, slides, etc., and produce their own audiovisual materials such as slide shows and audio tapes. Today's libraries are also production centers that include tools ranging from the lowly stapler to high-end computers with video editing capabilities. Students and teachers should look upon the library as a one-stop shop for finishing any type of project. For research papers, students need computers for word processing, printers for printing the papers (for those teachers who do not accept digital versions of papers), USB keys to transfer files, staplers, hole-punchers, scotch tape, and paper clips. For digital projects, students may need digital cameras to take photos to insert into digital slide shows; scanners to add images on paper; video cameras, tripods, and external microphones to create their own videos; audio digital recorders to conduct interviews or create podcasts; headphones for listening without disturbing others; and computers for video editing. Because digital picture, video, and audio files take enormous amounts of storage space, external hard drives are needed to store the projects while students are working on them. Projectors and large screen monitors are great ways to display student projects.

> Today's libraries are also production centers that include tools ranging from the lowly stapler to high-end computers with video editing capabilities.

A number of these production tools will need to be checked out to students and teachers for use outside the library. An easy way to manage this process and keep track of equipment is for librarians to catalog these items in the ILS and check them out in the same way books are checked out to all patrons. Generous supplies of backup batteries, battery chargers, cables, blank tapes, and blank DVDs and CDs are essential to maintain the production facilities and prevent interruption of classroom projects.

Information Services Departments: Integrating Libraries, Educational Technology, and IT

Increasingly, independent schools are creating combined departments that incorporate the libraries and technology in varying ways and are called by various names, such as "information services." In a number of cases the department is led by one of the school librarians. Many of the advantages of working together in one department are described above. To get a fuller sense of how it all works, consider the comments of Marilyn Meyerson (2009), head of libraries and technology for twelve years at the Key School in Annapolis, Maryland (www.keyschool.org/); Anne Macdonell (2009), academic technology coordinator and head librarian pre-K–12 for the past eight years at St. Andrew's

Episcopal School in Potomac, Maryland (www.saes.org/index.aspx); and Karen Douse (2009), director of library and information services at Harpeth Hall School in Nashville, Tennessee (www.harpethhall.org/podium/default.aspx?t=23587). These women hold MLS degrees and are librarians by training, but their willingness to explore and learn have led them to a technology leadership position in their schools. Marilyn commented that she got her MLS many decades ago and has completely reinvented herself to keep up with the many advances in technology. She was and is the first person to hold this position and actually wrote the job description for it. The philosophy behind the creation of the Libraries and Technology Department at the Key School has always been, "With more and more information, how do we help kids get control of it? How do we funnel it through the library, because the librarians are the information specialists?" Marilyn's duties include overseeing three libraries, one for each division, and academic technology, as well as teaching various library classes or a media literacy elective. She supervises the divisional librarians, the technology integrationists, and two IT people. Although a separate IT director oversees the administrative aspects of technology, she and he evaluate the IT staff together. The librarians and technology integrationists are evaluated by the principals with input from Marilyn. To help accomplish all of her tasks, Marilyn works two weeks over the summer. Although she reports to the head of school, two of the divisional heads are responsible for evaluating her. Marilyn describes her department as "very tight, like-minded, and in and out of each other's spaces" all day long. "All of the technology integrationists came out of the libraries. I hired them and we all have the same world view. We believe in the importance of student research and in students vetting the authority of the sources they use. It's a natural thing: we're together; we're interdisciplinary throughout the school; we teach information literacy and media literacy together; and we collaborate on a lot of projects throughout the school."

> *"With more and more information, how do we help kids get control of it? How do we funnel it through the library, because the librarians are the information specialists?"*

As head librarian, supported by three part-time assistants, Anne Macdonell oversees three libraries serving students from preschool through twelfth grade. In her additional capacity as academic technology coordinator for the entire school, Anne supports faculty in their use of technology; trains students; facilitates and initiates technology projects in the classroom; and collaborates on strategic, as well as budget, planning for academic technology. In her school, administrative technology is handled separately by a staff of four IT department members. As a third facet of her position, Anne is the school archivist, aided in the summer by paid student employees. "It sounds like three separate heavy responsibilities, for an entire Pre-School–12 school, but actually the work dovetails nicely. It's all about the flow of information—both in print and digitized—and teaching and learning the best ways to find it, organize it, evaluate it, and present it . . . just in different contexts," wrote Anne in an e-mail about her position. "Since I am alone in this position for the school, it means that we all share responsibility for staying up-to-date with technology in our content areas and classrooms, and all the faculty become technology experts and help each other."

> *"It's all about the flow of information—both in print and digitized—and teaching and learning the best ways to find it, organize it, evaluate it, and present it . . . just in different contexts."*

Karen Douse has been the director of library and information services at Harpeth Hall School for over ten years, managing all of the administrative and educational technology on campus, as well as the schoolwide library program. The academic side of her department includes the librarians and technology integrators. Additional support staff includes the network administrator, technicians, a part-time Web coordinator, and an administrative assistant. Her duties involve visioning, management, and promotion of the department's programs, and supervision of and collaboration with the library and technology staff. She serves on both the Administrative Team and the Curriculum Committee. In addition, she tries to keep a finger in all aspects of her department, assisting at times with teaching classes; providing professional development to teachers, staff, and administrators; and even doing a small amount of tech support. In Karen's view, "The key to a successful joint department is a collaborative attitude—we are a team and work together to be sure that our teachers, staff, and administrators have the resources, services, and equipment they need to do the very best job possible while keeping student learning as the central goal."

In my school, Sidwell Friends, in Washington, D.C., I am the director of information services, a department created four years ago to combine all three divisional libraries, all three divisional technology integrationists, and the IT Department consisting of a director and four support members. My contract describes my duties as being divided into 0.4 FTE for information services and 0.6 FTE as upper school head librarian. In truth the ratio could be reversed, because of the many aspects of overseeing technology for the entire school. Fortunately, my extraordinary full-time co-librarian and full-time library assistant keep the upper school library humming along. The impetus behind combining all three departments was to create better communication among them, collaborate on a technology vision for the school, and work together to provide the best information services we can. Our monthly meetings with the three librarians, the three technology integrationists, and the IT director keep us on track, give us an opportunity to learn what each person is up to in his or her division, and plan ways in which we need to collaborate on a variety of projects from teacher training to curriculum planning. This collaboration has led to a schoolwide research procedure for our students ("8 Steps to Research Success"), a coordinated scope and sequence for learning technology skills that are integrated into the classroom curriculum, coordinated teacher training both during the school year and in the summer, and a move toward consolidation of enterprise software to enhance the hands-free flow of student data. My primary function is to establish and maintain the lines of communication among all of the parties who use technology in our school.

"The key to a successful joint department is a collaborative attitude."

When librarians step into technology leadership roles in their schools, they gain a bully pulpit for educating administrators about the importance of the school library.

When asked what benefits Marilyn and Anne found with their combined technology and library departments, both said that the arrangements are entirely beneficial for the school, essential, and "a natural fit." Anne commented that it "is extraordinarily satisfying. The skill sets blend better every year." As for whether or not this is the right choice for every school, both women remarked that the decision to combine libraries and technology has to grow out of a school's culture. Marilyn acknowledged that the idea "has to come from the school itself; it has to make sense; and it is a good way to protect the school's libraries." This last point, perhaps an obvious one, is certainly worth remembering. When librarians step into technology leadership roles in their schools, they gain a bully pulpit for educating administrators about the importance of the school library.

Conclusion

In the opening paragraph of this essay I complained that trying "to describe a library with the ideal selection and amount of technology is like trying to catch a speeding bullet—impossible." I take that back. Although it is difficult to predict where technology will take us next, and although each school library has its own unique set of circumstances that will shape its use of technology, there are some indispensable tools and an indispensable attitude that will keep the library at the forefront of learning in any school. These tools include research sources both in print and online, the equipment and networks needed to access these sources, a great relationship with the IT staff, and a librarian with insatiable curiosity who values flexibility and experimentation. No matter what century we are in, these tools are essential to a successful independent school library program.

References

American Association of School Librarians. 2009. *Standards for the 21st-Century Learner.* American Library Association. Available at www.ala.org/ala/mgrps/divs/aasl/guidelinesandstandards/learningstandards/standards.cfm. Accessed September 29, 2009.

Bennett, Kim. n.d. "What I Hear I Forget, What I See I Remember, What I Do I Understand." In *The Phrase Finder.* Ed. Gary Martin. Available at www.phrases.org.uk/bulletin_board/55/messages/669.html. Accessed October 25, 2009.

Clowes, Dan. 2009. *The New Yorker,* June 8 (cover image). Available at www.cartoonbank.com/2009/New-Yorker-Cover-682009/invt/133044. Accessed October 26, 2009.

Cummins, Julie. 1989. "Design of Youth Services." In *Managers and Missionaries: Library Services to Children and Young Adults in the Information Age.* Comp. University of Illinois Graduate School of Library and Information Science. Ed. Leslie Edmonds. University of Illinois, Urbana-Champaign. Available at www.archive.org/stream/managersmissionaalalle/managersmissionaalalle_djvu.txt. Accessed September 29, 2009.

Douse, Karen. 2009. E-mail interview with author, August 15.

Harpeth Hall School. n.d. Harpeth Hall School. Available at www.harpethhall.org/Default.asp?bhcp=1. Accessed October 26, 2009.

The Key School. n.d. The Key School. Available at www.keyschool.org/. Accessed October 26, 2009.

Macdonell, Anne. 2009. E-mail interview with author, September 27.

Meyerson, Marilyn. 2009. E-mail interview with author, August 1.

Open Source Initiative. n.d. Open Source Initiative. Available at www.opensource. org/. Accessed September 29, 2009.

Sidwell Friends School. n.d. Sidwell Friends School. Available at www.sidwell.edu/. Accessed October 26, 2009.

St. Andrew's Episcopal School. n.d. St. Andrew's Episcopal School. Available at www.saes.org/index.aspx. Accessed October 26, 2009.

Stephens, Michael. 2009. "Ten Trends & Technologies for 2009." *Tame the Web: Libraries, Technology, and People.* January 12. Available at http://tametheweb. com/2009/01/12/ten-trends-technologies-for-2009/. Accessed September 29, 2009.

Stone, C. Walter. 1964. "Research and Practical Experiences of Recent Years That Support the Concept of the School Library Materials Center." In *The School Library Materials Center: Its Resources and Their Utilization.* Comp. University of Illinois Graduate School of Library Science. Ed. Alice Loher. University of Illinois, Urbana-Champaign. Available at www.archive.org/stream/schoollibrary matalalle#page/n7/mode/2up. Accessed September 29, 2009.

Williamson, Susan, and Independent School Section, comps. 2009. *ISS Data Committee Survey.* American Association of School Librarians/American Library Association. Available at www.ala.org/ala/mgrps/divs/aasl/aboutaasl/ aaslcommunity/aaslsections/iss/data.cfm. Accessed September 29, 2009.

Wilson, Martha. 1917/1922. *School Library Management.* 3rd ed. New York: Wilson. Available at www.archive.org/stream/manageschoollib00wilsrich/manageschool lib00wilsrich_djvu.txt. Accessed September 29, 2009.

Visit http://lu.com/excellence for supporting links and occasional updates to all essays in this book.

Patt Moser has been Upper School Head Librarian at Sidwell Friends School (http://www.sidwell. edu/) in Washington, D.C., since 1998. In 2006 she also assumed the position of Director of Information Services and now oversees the three divisional libraries, the three divisional technology integrationists, and the IT department. Prior to moving to Washington, Patt was head librarian at Concord-Carlisle High School in Concord, MA, a public school serving students in two small but culturally rich towns. If you delve deep into her past, you will discover that she ran local access cable television operations for both Chelmsford and Methuen, MA, before becoming a school librarian.

Sea Changes in Technology Services and Learning

Debbie Abilock, Consultant & Editor-in-Chief, Knowledge Quest
Elisabeth Abarbanel, Brentwood School (Los Angeles, CA)

What sets evolving, visionary, technology-oriented, future-focused libraries apart? Open-minded, flexible librarians who focus with laserlike clarity on excellence. They evaluate new tools for discovering, managing, and presenting information; design new instructional strategies and services; collaborate with their colleagues; and share widely with other library professionals. As fast as they absorb one set of tools, new ones are introduced, pushing traditional library services in new directions. Whether operating on a shoestring budget or with a full spectrum of technology and resources, today's independent school librarian aims for excellence in support of teaching and learning.

In independent school libraries, teaching, learning, and research are participatory, integrated, experimental, ethical, and independent.

From its beginnings, the Internet has supported social interaction on a global scale. Web 2.0 has shifted the platform from a predominantly "read only" information highway to a continuously evolving "read-write" Web in which it is easy for everyone to interact and produce, collaborate and create, and remix and share. Inspired by participatory tools that support collaborative academic work, called "social scholarship" (Cohen 2007), independent school librarians are experimenting with user-focused services and group projects that benefit learning and literacy. They envision Library 2.0 (Miller 2005) as a dynamic intellectual commons, a center for learning and teaching, that supports the school community by integrating the resources and personalized help of the physical place with responsive, well-managed online services and systems.

The McCullough Library (Jack McCullough '25) is a place where students feed their curiosity, enhance their research skills, sharpen their ability to think logically, and enjoy reading. Aligning with our mission and our equity pedagogy, the library strives to be a warm, welcoming, inclusive environment that students and faculty view as a place to connect, converse, and grow.

The mission of the library is to support and enrich the school curriculum; to engage the students in the process of lifelong learning; to support and encourage lifetime reading habits; and to empower the students as library users.—Mission Statement, Lick-Wilmerding High School, San Francisco, CA (www.lwhs.org/podium/default.aspx?t=106751)

Setting the Stage for Learning

The independent school's Web site serves as a recruiting tool for new families and a source of timely information for current families. At the turn of the millennium, a library's static list of databases with a link to the catalog and information about staff, hours, and policies, was good enough. Today the library's Web pages must serve learners, teachers, and the curriculum with continually updated resources, targeted help, and few barriers to access and use.

The library learning space is not just a place

"Our physical library is small and busy with students borrowing materials —it cannot accommodate classes I'm teaching. But there's really no need to be 'in the library.' I design lessons carefully, pull the topic/inquiry books for classroom use, and ask the class to access my Netvibes resource page with their laptops."

—Katie Day, teacher-librarian at United World College of SE Asia, Singapore

To market library services, the librarian designs "sticky" experiences, which entice users to come, come back, and stay longer in both the physical and virtual spaces. Once there, learners can examine and question information with peers, reflect and write for authentic audiences, and synthesize and create together with support when needed. Some virtual libraries are staffed during evening hours, providing the personal service that students and teachers have come to expect from their in-school experience.

If the library's Web pages cannot be integrated directly into the school's official Web site, the librarian works with the technology or communications department to design a complementary, easy-to-update library Web site, which might be a blog, a wiki, a NetVibes landing page, or a LibGuides home page that serves as the virtual starting point for student research and collaboration.

A participatory environment for students, teachers, parents, and librarians. Find out about new resources, and learn about locating, evaluating, and using information effectively.

—Wildwood School, *The Library Blog*
(http://thelibrary.typepad.com/)

Wildwood School in Los Angeles uses a blog as the complete library Web site. Librarian Michelle Simon Frommé explains, "I started it because I didn't like the way our internal page functioned. It wasn't user-friendly and it required a password, which students never remember. I want the library to be a place for all things . . . for everything students need."

Just as the walk-in patron stops to browse a timely book display or observes a presentation of student work, the virtual user is enticed by interactive components like widgets, surveys, blog-style narratives, pictures, and video. The environment conveys information in interesting ways and features library services. In the physical library, one librarian might place *Wordle* posters next to each Dewey section's subject headings to show the relative importance of topics in books that are shelved in that area. Another might mount a digital summer reading list in *issuu*, which simulates a print magazine to lure students into browsing the lively annotations and book covers. Yet another might decide to migrate to a social public access catalog (SOPAC) so that students can write reviews, rate books, and tag them with their own subjects. Technology draws curious students into exploring both physical and virtual resources.

Experimenting with Social Software

"Jumping into this public 2.0 ocean can be intimidating. I was embarrassed to tell the kids I was on their turf. I felt that everything I tried was so public. And yet, as I paddle, I grow proud of my skills, my networking, and my discoveries—and I welcome new risks at work. My advice to others just beginning? Vary your experiments using tools for different purposes. Dip a toe in as you feel comfortable —it's less scary than taking a plunge!"

—Elisabeth Abarbanel, Brentwood School, Los Angeles, CA

Because independent schools encourage their faculty to be innovative and may place fewer limitations on their networks than do school districts, a dauntingly wide array of technology tools is available to the librarian. Little empirical data exist on the depth of school change required to use technology effectively in learning (Lempke, Coughlin, and Reifsneider 2009, 5) and the worth of certain social tools may only become evident after intensive use by thousands of users. Notwithstanding these considerations, independent school librarians are experimenting with new technologies, aware that technology motivates their students to learn more deeply when the right tool matches the teacher's goals and the learner's characteristics and needs (Abilock 2007). But social tools have a wide range of "affordances," a term used by designers to mean that users expect tools to work flexibly for many purposes. Therefore the "fit" of a particular tool for a specific function is less obvious than with earlier, less-flexible technologies. As one school librarian has said, "It's obvious that I can't hammer a nail in with a screwdriver, but with ten hammers available, how do I choose?"

Consequently librarians are taking calculated risks without the benefit of rigorous data, experimenting alongside their students, teaching along with their faculty. Because their students' informal learning experiences are shaped by highly interactive digital media, librarians embrace participatory culture as a window into how their students play and learn. Typical of these risk-takers, Elisabeth Abarbanel of the Brentwood School (Los Angeles) readily experiments with Web 2.0 technologies:

> I started a blog for my library and, as I learned to use it, I promoted it and explored its uses for the library. Then I deliberately volunteered to advise a student life blog whose purpose was to highlight sports, performing arts, and community service events because I suspected it could support students' sharing of school experiences. Of course, I did 'sneak' library-related stories and information into the blog. For example, I published one of our new READ bookmarks there, with a link to the library blog to see the rest and I added a widget that displays covers of our library's new books via LibraryThing.

Free Web services are easy to learn superficially and then build out incrementally with add-ons that work with each other, a characteristic called "interoperability." With little instruction, her students participate as co-designers, adding widgets, slideshows of their school events, original music, and weekly videos and podcasts about student life. "When my student journalists learned to embed a slide show and post stories and polls on their blogs, their enthusiasm grew. Now we also teach blogging to tenth graders for a United Nations simulation, and remark on how easily they pick up technology skills and make blogs their own." Experimentation and observation uncover the potential for social scholarship and allow Elisabeth to test teaching strategies in an informal setting.

Characteristics of a 2.0 Independent School Librarian

Flexible—willing and able to adapt to change in curricula, services, and tools.

Brave—willing to put new ideas to the test, and able to learn from mistakes.

Involved—willing to publicize new ideas to the community in collaboration with others, and to take the library curriculum into classrooms.

Friendly and collaborative—willing to work with faculty and the technology department to get the job done and able to work with students in an open dialog.

Creative—willing to create content for the Web site/wiki/video/ podcast, and able to assist others in learning to do so.

Visionary—able to sort through the tools and ideas and create a vision for your library, at your school, in your school curriculum.

Fostering Social Relationships

Seeking to holistically understand the impact of a networked social environment, independent school librarians look beyond the library's walls and hours to cultivate durable personal relationships with students. As a by-product, they hope to encourage students' full use of the library's resources. CD McLean, the library director at Berkeley Prep School (Tampa, Florida) is available to her students on Facebook, "to provide my Middle School advisees with another opportunity to converse with a safe adult who will be objective about things in a way that parents or relatives cannot—just what an advisor's role should be—a friendly adult, who cares, not a friend, per se." She "friends" all who ask because "it gives me access to students I rarely see in the library—but who 'live' on Facebook. They're more likely to ask for research help online, request a book or retrieve a password on a wall post, or using Facebook's internal e-mail or chat."

According to Helen Adams, author of a book on intellectual freedom in school libraries (2008), the librarian has a professional obligation to educate minors when they are learning or socializing in an environment with ill-defined norms and few guidelines:

> Although CD's students may appear to be adept in social networking, her presence is vital to their safe navigation in a constantly shifting technological landscape. Not only is she modeling and guiding how to use popular social networking tools ethically in school and online settings, but she is also providing the 'safety net' as middle school students grow into new online academic and personal social situations.

Others disagree. They believe that supervision of media practices outside of school is best left to parents. "For the most part, the existing mainstream strategies that parents are mobilizing to structure their kids' media ecologies . . . are more than adequate in ensuring that their kids do not stray too far from home" (Ito et al. [2009]). Yet librarians may be able to provide insights that can help students grapple with virtual norms since they, themselves, are struggling with what to reveal or conceal. The very features that make these technologies attractive—personalization, transparency, and interactivity—reduce privacy. CD argues that her students ought to be explicitly considering how much personal information they reveal when they ask to "friend" her in a social network. "After all, they know I am a faculty member and they are opening up their page, should I choose to look at it."

In the field of educational technology a creepy tree house is an institutionally controlled technology/tool that emulates or mimics pre-existing technologies or tools that may already be in use by the learners, or by learners' peer groups. Though such systems may be seen as innovative or problem-solving to the institution, they may repulse some users who see them as infringement on the sanctity of their peer groups, or as having the potential for institutional violations of their privacy, liberty, ownership, or creativity. Some users may simply object to the influence of the institution.

—Stein (2008)

What is defined as private is in flux, and some administrators are concerned about their schools' liability if faculty were to become aware of "situations" that should be reported, so they develop policies that forbid faculty from "friending" a current student. Other librarians, like Laura Pearle at Hackley School (Tarrytown, New York), delineate this boundary for themselves by maintaining a separate list of student "friends" who have requested a link. "It blocks them from seeing almost all of what I'm doing while allowing them to leave me a message asking for research help or a book recommendation. In reverse, I 'hide' them from my newsfeed so I don't see what they are doing."

Other schools require librarians to use password-protected services that are closed to all but the school's users. CD disparages private microblogging platforms like *Edmodo*, opting instead for public technology because "students respect teachers and librarians who actually use the same technology in their everyday lives that they do for classes." She argues that the cachet she gains as an early technology adopter gives her added credibility when she teaches online research or talks to an advisee.

However, not all students welcome these incursions of power and authority into their social culture (Stein 2008). Indeed, because users' practices and expectations define the technologies in which they are embedded, danah boyd, social media researcher at Microsoft and a fellow at Harvard University's Berkman Center for Internet and Society, warns that repurposing social technology for school use may "rupture norms in the classroom" in ways that are "socially or educationally harmful."

They don't use del.icio.us (sic) or Second Life or Ning or Twitter as a part of their everyday practices. And the ways that they use Facebook and MySpace and YouTube are quite different than the ways in which you do. We each approach technology based on our own needs and desires and we leverage it to do our bidding. In this way, we actively repurpose technology as a part of engagement such that rarely does one technology fit all. Yet, when we introduce technology in an educational setting, we often mistakenly assume that students will embrace the technology in the same way that we do. This never works out and can cause unexpected strife. Take social network sites as an example. You use this for professional networking; teens use it to socialize with their peers. Putting Facebook or MySpace into the classroom can create a severe cognitive collision as teens try to work out the shift in contexts. Most problematically, when teens are forced to navigate Friending in an educational setting, painful dramas occur because who [sic] you're polite to in school may be very different than who [sic] you socialize with at home.

—boyd (2009)

Given that intellectual freedom is a core value of librarianship, school librarians have voiced concerns about minors' First Amendment rights: "Despite the technology protection measures required by the Children's Internet Protection Act (CIPA), students still retain their First Amendment right to receive information whether in print or online in a school library" (Adams 2008). According to *Minors and Internet Interactivity* (2009), social software poses "two competing intellectual freedom issues—the protection of minors' privacy and the right of free speech." Adams supports "school librarians like CD and Laura who are online alongside their students [and] are in the best position to help their students learn to strike a balance between their First Amendment right to free expression and the need to retain a degree of personal privacy as they interact with 'friends' online."

In the absence of empirical evidence to substantiate the positive effects of repurposing social tools for academic learning or hard data on the most effective ways of scaffolding students' ethical and safe behavior within social networks, most independent school librarians depend on the sharing of tacit knowledge in informal networks by professionals like CD and Laura.

Developing Collections Collaboratively

Typically, early use of a new technology replaces an older way of accomplishing the same task. Because collection development is another core responsibility, many librarians have gravitated toward Web-based collection tools to manage their resources. Social bookmarking services like Diigo and delicious allow users to tag, save, manage, and share Web links. Customizable Web pages like LibGuides, PageFlakes, or Netvibes employ browser add-ons and drag-and-drop functionality to aggregate and update resources and services on the fly. Given the ease of use of these tools, librarians rarely maintain just-in-case lists on a static Web page; rather, they seed pages with authoritative resources and targeted help that match a particular assignment or project.

Katie Day, the International Baccalaureate Primary Years Programme (PYP) teacher-librarian at United World College of SE Asia in Singapore, has assembled widgets, Web sites, blogs, search engines, photos, videos, and podcasts into an Endangered Animals page on Netvibes for her first graders' Animal Research unit (www.netvibes.com/ uwcsea#Grade_1%3A_Animal_Research). She admonishes librarians to make the selection of technology and resources the last step in designing a unit. First she and the curriculum coordinators identify which units of inquiry need a research component. Because the PYP "transdisciplinary" skills (skills that work across the curriculum) match well to information literacy skills, Katie is able to plan instruction that addresses both. In certain cases she begins with a mini-research-cycle project that models a larger unit to follow. In other cases, teachers will ask for specific lessons: "I might be part of the tuning-in process where students learn skimming and scanning or come in later for online searching and note-taking." Finally, just before the unit begins, she creates a Netvibes home page, selecting tools, resources, and services based on the large goals of the curriculum, the needs of the project, and the characteristics of learners.

Social aggregation tools invite collaborative collection development. For a unit on beliefs, Fiona Collins, librarian at Shanghai Rego International School, asks students to add resources to their unit's home page. She teaches them to search the Library OPAC for reliable Web sites, to bookmark and store searchable copies of Web pages, and to evaluate the information on these pages to give each site a rating. After the first iteration of this project, a Furl database of teacher- and student-vetted Web sites had been created for use the following year. Unfortunately, Furl closed its services in April 2009, and Fiona had to migrate her list to Diigo (www.diigo.com/user/librarianfchk/Beliefs). Since that unsettling experience, she has become more cautious about using free Web services, which usually offer no assurance that contributed work will remain available if the company's business model changes.

That's one reason why Elisabeth Abarbanel chose to use a subscription service called LibGuides: "I feel that the company is likely to feel more responsible to its subscribers than a free service." Unlike a printed pathfinder handout or static and unattractive list of links, a project's LibGuide is easily updated by the librarian or teacher with information in almost any format, and as a plus for students, they can access it without a password.

> The interface is attractive and easy to use—I can link to or embed all types of media and even upload word-processed documents I've created. Students can recommend new links for a guide and their names are not visible, respecting student privacy while still enabling their collaborative work. An added benefit is that I can see other LibGuides on the same topic created by other librarians and either modify them for my own use or just discover other professionally selected resources.

A consistent interface for all projects, with access from the library's blog, homepage, Facebook page, and the school's Moodle, has standardized where students begin research and go for help:

> In just one school year, everyone has become accustomed to go to their LibGuides. When students are absent from a research mini-lesson they can find the lesson, their homework and, indeed, everything they need. I even embedded a Google Calendar of the library and lab's schedules, so that teachers at home can plan class visits and students know when they will be able to work on research during school.

Teaching Information Literacy

Print reference books, once the bread and butter of the physical library, are rapidly migrating to computers and other devices. Large-scale digitizing efforts include volunteer transcription and editing of classic titles for Project Gutenberg, scanned books by the Internet Archive and Google Books, vendor repurposing of reference books as reference databases, and the mounting of static e-books by publishers and authors. After Cheri Dobbs, the middle school media specialist at Detroit Country Day School, provided her students with access to Gale's middle- and high-school collections and the e-books included with ABC-CLIO social studies databases, she found her students "receptive to using digital reference books because they had access 24/7."

To improve their access, she added the Gale Virtual Reference Library to the library's research page, "but I had to continue to eliminate barriers if I wanted them to be well used," she recalls. "I added Gale's e-book search widget to the library's home page so that everyone has a way to do a 'quick and dirty' search of e-books. Then I downloaded MARC records from Gale so that each e-book now appears within the library's online catalog." In preparation for a project or lesson, Cheri works with teachers to identify resources, then organizes an e-book subcollection and directly links to relevant e-book titles, complete with thumbnail images. As sixth graders begin their World Tour geography project, they find focused and age-appropriate information about countries, cultures, world cities, and foods, tailored to what they will need to know and be able to do. In addition to making e-book searching "as easy and 'in-your-face' as Google searching," Cheri shows students how to download e-books to their laptops and then teaches them to take notes and cite sources in NoodleTools.

Like published print books, e-reference sources lend themselves to traditional evaluation of authority and credibility, a prime focus for Cheri's collaborative units in French, social studies, study skills, and science. "We examine authoritative results from a digital reference book and contrast them with open-Web results so that our students are acutely aware of the value of vetted sources," she reports. "In fact," she adds, "if you ask our sixth graders to list three adjectives that describe a resource that is valuable for their research, most of them will reply 'reliable, authoritative and useful'—or some version of that—and mention our e-reference books." Cheri's analysis of her students' understanding is based on more than anecdotal evidence. On a recent sixth-grade assessment, 85 percent of her students demonstrated that they knew what made a source authoritative and reliable.

As software programmers develop new interfaces for e-book content, the content is becoming more difficult to evaluate. "Snippets" of e-content are delivered out of the context of a chapter's logic. Evaluation can involve examining metadata (the descriptive data about the source), which can be as diverse as a MARC record and user-generated tags. Further, authors are disseminating original digital books that have not gone through a publisher's editorial review, copyediting, and fact checking. Undoubtedly Cheri will need to further refine her teaching of reading, source evaluation, and note taking when everything is indeed "miscellaneous" (Weinberger 2007).

"Our 9th grade history teacher wanted to emphasize the potential unreliability of Wikipedia, so we set up an ancient history wiki that her students could contribute to, based on their research on a particular historical topic. Each student created her own page, uploading text, images and links about their topic. Fellow students could read and comment on each other's pages, but time and constraints of the assignment did not provide for sharing or adding to the information. Nonetheless, they began to understand the process of a wiki and were able to see the potentials and the pitfalls of creating and using shared information."

—Joann Davis, middle- and upper-school librarian,
Archer School for Girls, Los Angeles, CA

In coordination with a content-area teacher, librarians at Archer School for Girls (Los Angeles, California) are teaching information evaluation through the collaborative creation and transparent review of content in a wiki. They wanted students to view and comment on each others' work as they published and revised information on African countries. When asked to read each other's wikis and comment on similarities among their countries, students were motivated to carefully evaluate what they had written and produce more accurate information.

Initially students had been focused more on the superficial design features of a wiki, like changing font colors and adding pictures and maps. The ease of examining classmates' pages and sharing artistic tips with one another resulted in personal comments such as, "Ooh, I like your page color" or "cool avatar," at the expense of evaluating the quality of their peers' information. Perhaps their interest in design elements is a natural response to the novelty of using a wiki, just as students in previous classes experimented with the capabilities of a word processor or PowerPoint when these tools were first introduced. Rather than just refocusing the students on content evaluation, educators have an opportunity to draw parallels to large-scale research findings on information evaluation that show that many adults also rely heavily "on the surface qualities of a Web site to make credibility judgments" (Fogg et al. 2002, 24–25).

Within the wiki interface, the Archer team was able to use the revision history to observe both group and individual progress, ask or answer questions, and give feedback. School librarian Joann Davis acknowledges that, without comparative data, she cannot definitively evaluate "whether students learned the content any better than with a traditional paper." She believes that the project "raised students' comfort level in navigating and evaluating Web sites and using the computer for research," foundational skills for later, more sophisticated units. As students create, maintain, and add to a collaboratively written and continuously updated record of what they know, the Archer librarians and teachers are also learning the tool's features and refining how to teach information evaluation through wiki peer production.

Engaging Readers and Leading Literacy

Book clubs, book fair events, picture book writing projects, and any number of special activities and celebrations testify to the strong place that reading motivation has held in independent school library programs. It is no surprise to see early uses of new media focus on reading promotions and readers' advisory services. School librarians help elementary school children share books in *StoryTube* videos and podcast poems for two voices with a Book Buddy. Older students are encouraged to comment on book blogs, write reviews on Amazon, or create *MakeBeliefs* short comic strips as visual book reports.

Librarians create motivational virtual displays of banned books, promote state reading award programs on *VoiceThread*, and add *LibraryThing* feeds for new titles and blog about them as they are shelved. To develop young children's understanding of a picture book story, Lauren Collen projects digitized pages from the International Children's Digital Library (ICDL) collection during early childhood storytime. She finds that all students, not just those closest to the book, begin to raise questions about the interaction of illustrations and text (2006, 14–16).

Some teaching teams are assessing students' margin notes as part of their reading instruction. "We located collections of digital folk and fairy tales and asked 6th grade students who have laptops to use Diigo, a social bookmarking and annotation tool, to 'dog-ear' important pages, ask questions, reflect, and analyze the story by inserting their comments, then view and respond to the comments of their peers," said Sarah Hanawald, the technology and learning specialist at Greensboro Day School (North Carolina). Later the team used the "Extract Annotations" feature to collect highlighted passages, review the annotations, and evaluate students' thinking.

Strong reading programs developed by librarians are focused on developing skillful lifelong readers and writers. Although some programs are extracurricular (see essay 13), others are embraced as core curriculum. The librarian becomes a respected literacy leader, responsible for a unique school- or division-wide initiative that is essential to the literacy goals of the school.

For over three decades, students at the San Francisco Bay Area's Nueva School have met weekly in mixed-grade groups (third and fourth grades, fifth and sixth grades, seventh and eighth grades) to discuss student-selected literature. Using mixed teams of administrators, parents, and teachers to facilitate small-group student discussions (www.noodletools.com/debbie/consult/articles/litclub.html), this weekly program is administered by the librarian, Marilyn Kimura, who gives booktalks and provides in-service to the year-long adult volunteers on reading comprehension and questioning, annotation skills, facilitation techniques, and assessment strategies. Currently few independent school librarians are attempting online book discussions for older students, although they are common in postsecondary classrooms. Perhaps because face-to-face book group discussions in K–12 independent schools have a low adult-to-child ratio, there is little to be gained by taking the discussion online. One librarian, who did not want to be identified, explained that her attempts at a book discussion blog were "artificial and impoverished because the body language, expressive language, and immediacy of our sustained face-to-face discussions were missing."

"The physical book creates links thru memory and imagination, the web creates [links] to electronic destinations."
—Interview with Hugh McGuire, co-founder of BookOven.com and founder of LibriVox.org

Dorcas Hand (Annunciation Orthodox School, Houston, Texas) has reshaped the school's writing and research curriculum in collaboration with her teachers. Dissatisfied with yearly author visits that had no relationship to what students were learning and determined to revitalize her library research at the same time, Dorcas led the creation of "History as Story," a library program that transforms author visits into curriculum-related master classes related to the AOS schoolwide focus on writing across the curriculum. It also includes an authentic assessment of the research process that has redirected her teaching of research skills. As a result, each year an author is invited to teach four days of master classes directly relevant to teacher-assigned writing projects for which students have already researched historical information. Each master-class author teaches writing techniques that students can use in their own writing to help their readers understand the significance of the facts they've gleaned from their online note cards in NoodleTools. "Within literary nonfiction," Dorcas explains, "while every fact and idea is attributable to various research sources, the 'story' of history embeds real people and settings in a narrative. In every grade, as students and their readers read, write and research, they are developing a deeper understanding of an historical time and place." She plans to create a student wiki of her eighth graders' writing about a broad range of American artists from the first half of the twentieth century because the wiki will facilitate a broader understanding of how these artists influenced each other—Ella Fitzgerald and Langston Hughes, Les Paul and Jerry Jeff Walker—and show their continued influence on American culture.

Collaborating to Create Knowledge

Some independent school librarians are helping teachers move successful assignments online. Although the initial assignment may appear substantially unchanged, the transparency and social nature of networked technology begins to impact important aspects of instruction and learning. Shannon Bomar (Colorado Springs Christian School, Colorado Springs) developed an assignment with freshman English teacher Mason Young in which students would individually own the responsibility for learning grammar conventions and collaboratively improve their wiki writing skills. The teacher identified six conventions for the wiki based on the Six Trait writing guidelines for capitalization and punctuation: 1) capitalization rules; 2) abbreviations and end marks; 3) commas; 4) semicolons, colons, dashes, and parentheses; 5) quotation marks and underlining; and 6) hyphens and apostrophes. Each group developed a *Wikidot* wiki page about an assigned grammar convention, including usage rules and examples, then added a *MyStudiyo* interactive quiz to test readers on the content of their page. Each student was responsible for reading and understanding the writing conventions and taking the student-created quizzes. When the guide was finished and the quizzes completed, students would be able to refer to it throughout the year for other writing assignments.

Bomar (2009) notes that the online implementation of this project changed the number and nature of students' collaborative interactions. Because all student interactions and work were visible, hyperlinked together in one place, date- and time-stamped with the student's name, and archived with a revision history, the teacher and librarian had ample data to evaluate both individual and group work. The student's grade was based on the quality of his or her wiki content, the average quiz grades received by classmates for the group's section of the wiki guide, and the student's own quiz scores. By providing an authentic purpose and audience, the wiki motivated students to do better work so Bomar plans to use this assignment template for other projects.

In another example, Archer School's senior AP English classes began using wikis as "collaborative online study guides." Realizing that the AP class had no time to discuss two important novels prior to the AP exam, teachers asked students to read *Lolita* and *The Age of Innocence* independently during class. Students' written responses were archived in a wiki chapter-by-chapter, allowing everyone to follow the emergence of ideas and make connections across the texts. According to middle- and upper-school librarian Joann Davis, students made the wiki their "study destination" as they prepared for this demanding test.

The insight gained from this use of a wiki encouraged the Archer librarians to suggest to the English Department that they use the software again as a means of increasing discussion depth. "Probably the first real wiki conversation," recalls Joann, "was our 'Wykyssey' in which students were required to comment on each of the books in the Odyssey. . . . We saw what they were finding or not finding, saying or not saying . . . [and] watched their evolving work without dealing with paperwork."

Archer English teacher Genevieve Morgan saw additional benefits: "A wiki discussion works especially well for the shy kids who don't want to speak in class but have much going on in their heads." In asynchronous literature discussions, more reserved, or perhaps academically weaker, students are able to take the extra time that they need to thoroughly read and think about others' comments before they respond. Because the wiki discussion is archived, the teachers and librarian can monitor and evaluate all students' contributions unobtrusively.

In contrast to the earlier AP wiki, which simply archived the thinking of individual students, this one became a place for lively discussion. Wikis promote "unmediated" discussion, because students publish first and edit later. If educators fade back online while continuing to follow the conversation, students' ownership of "their" discussion grows. To confer legitimacy on peer-directed discussions, some independent school librarians deliberately quote students' online comments during face-to-face class discussions to show that they are following online exchanges and take them seriously.

Testing New Presentation Formats

Librarians have long recognized that multimedia formats can facilitate teaching to multiple intelligences (Gardner 1993) and help teachers differentiate instruction (Tomlinson et al. 2002). Presentation tools may be used by students in culminating displays of learning or by teachers presenting content in preparation for a class discussion. Participatory tools offer added opportunities to teach multiple literacies (Abilock 2007), because one interacts with content as both a consumer and creator. PowerPoint, a desktop presentation tool, is being replaced by less powerful, but nonetheless adequate, online slide show programs like Slideshare and Prezi, which hold images, documents, and video.

More flexible tools, like Google Earth, enable students to collaboratively create tours of ancient ruins; report on current events or world hotspots; and display immigration patterns, troop movements, or bird migrations. VoiceThread, a popular tool among educators because of its low barrier to entry, lets a Web audience leave comments (subject to the creator's approval) using a microphone or telephone or add text comments, drawings, or audio or video files. In the two examples that follow—a teacher's lesson and a student's writing assignment—the school librarian grounds the use of the presentation software in sound pedagogy and thoughtful reflection.

Constance Vidor, director of library services at Friends Seminary in New York, produced a multimedia lecture to complement a music teacher's fifth-grade unit on classical composers. Her narration, images, text, and music connect elements of Johann Sebastian Bach's life and music with Paul McCartney's contemporary music. The screencast pauses to ask questions that are prompts for her class's face-to-face discussion. "The students were very engaged and had a lot to say about each of the slides and each of the questions," reports Constance, "so my lesson was successful in this respect."

Her second goal was to demonstrate to faculty how one might use this presentation tool to compare and contrast two composers or, for that matter, two people from another field or from different eras. "I can see its potential for effective and intellectually engaging student work," she observes, "beyond the traditional composer report that our Middle School students are currently assigned."

After her class discussion, Constance began to think about ways to strengthen her lesson. She focused on how to develop her students' listening skills. "It was hard to get the students to refocus after listening to the Beatles excerpts," she remarks wryly, "so perhaps I could add prompts about the purpose for listening to the musical excerpts." She also wondered if the design of her questions contributed to students' misconceptions:

> Disconcertingly, some of my open-ended questioning in the *VoiceThread* opened the door for some students to say 'Paul McCartney is a better composer than J. S. Bach.' Of course, it is valid for students to prefer one composer over another. However, is it educationally sound to give students the impression that they are qualified to make a judgment about one composer being 'better' than another? Their responses spotlight some of the complexities of developing open-ended questioning in multimedia.

Constance decided to initiate a follow-up discussion with students about "the difference between personal opinions and mature, informed judgment." She used their initial comments to "explore with them the purpose of background knowledge and how one marshals evidence to construct an argument . . . an important part of an information skills curriculum."

Unlike Constance, the library media specialist at Colorado Springs Christian School (Colorado) is teaching students to use VoiceThread as a presentation tool. Shannon Bomar's students are comfortable creating online content and regularly engage in formal presentations during class. Like many teens, they believe they understand what kind of language is appropriate in a given context (Lenhart et al. 2008). Yet Shannon found that their presentations employed the informal language of the social Web, rather than the academic voice that they ought to realize would be appropriate for a school presentation. Some scholars have argued that new literacies reshape communication and establish new practices and ways of thinking that result in new forms of rhetoric (Lankshear and Knobel 2006, 17, 25). However, Shannon contends that, even in new media, an academic purpose should have a scholarly tone, and that one of her goals is to "help student learn to modulate their narration for different audiences, since they will be entering a workforce that will increasingly conduct formal business over multimedia channels."

Like Shannon, librarian Annette Counts and her teaching partner, Cora Antonio, are observing peer-group culture become a powerful driver of what is learned when learning becomes more social. Cora, teacher of a required tenth-grade religion course called Christian Scriptures at Bishop O'Dowd High School (Oakland, California), proposed to Annette that students use Facebook applications to fashion multimedia profiles of biblical characters from the New Testament, who would then converse with each other online. She felt that the fresh format for displaying their research and peer-to-peer interactions would result in a deeper understanding of these biblical characters' lives and impact beyond what their textbook presented.

The team began with a whole-class brainstorming of elements that make one Facebook page more expressive or illustrative than another. Their list was posted in the classroom throughout the project.

Cora developed a rubric for students that enumerated requirements such as "five personality traits represented by three quotations, two songs, and five examples from the scriptures or from evidence found during research." The visual depiction of the character would be evaluated for accuracy and authenticity:

> We told them to avoid glorified portraits with halos and other unrealistic features imposed by later artists. We asked them to evaluate pictures by considering questions like: Was the clothing typical of first-century life? Does Martha belong in fancy Renaissance garb? Wrong time period and social class. Does Luke have a stethoscope or does the image contain people from a different time period? Anachronisms.

The rubric also required "appropriate and insightful comments or questions" on five other characters' walls. In turn, the recipients would reply to at least five posts. The social aspect spilled easily into face-to-face interactions in the classroom. "When a student found a great image or piece of research for another character," Annette recalls, "we loved the way he or she would say, 'Who has Martha? There's great information about her on this site.' It felt like a learning community!"

However, without more guidance about what it means to "share and comment," the students experienced a certain cognitive dissonance between school and social norms. Although some student walls displayed insightful comments and questions, many used superficial, breezy dialogue. "Cora and I need to figure out how to teach everybody to make substantive remarks rather than 'Hey, how was prison, Paul?' "

To teach students to write unstilted, content-rich dialogue in new media involves striking a balance between the timeless artistry of English composition and the dialogue of participatory culture. Many educators wonder about the long-term effects of electronically mediated communication on academic discourse. According to Baron (2009, 42), there are currently few observable effects in essay writing. As alternative writing genres supplant traditional essays, and new media shape communication, one assumes that there will be an escalating impact on both writing and thinking.

When asked to evaluate their Facebook project, Cora and Annette's students asserted that the technology had helped them "learn more." However, Annette observes, "Some kids omitted important aspects of a character, for example one student focused on Luke as a physician, but neglected his role as Christian leader and evangelist." Distinguishing between seeing students *engage* with their characters, the biblical text, and the time period, and having students *demonstrate understanding* of the characters' influence on the Christian faith is key to assessing instructional design using technology. "Further," cautions Annette, "teachers and librarians should not overestimate students' abilities in using new technologies." This group of high school students had little previous experience with Facebook in any systematic way. "Even our savvy technology users had trouble setting up their pages to accommodate the project's requirements," Annette recalls. To address these issues, Cora and Annette plan to unblock Facebook earlier, begin the unit by showing students some examples of quality pages, post this year's criteria for a good Facebook page, and invite students to revise them as they learn more. In addition, they will double the class time to two eighty-minute periods so that students won't feel pressure to comment quickly on each other's postings. During the extended classes the teacher and librarian plan to be online, offering guidance and feedback on students' comments in real time.

What makes a successful Facebook profile in a school project?

- Compelling details and interesting vocabulary
- Photo captions that provide background or information about what was happening, rather than a list of names
- Regular updates about activities and insights
- Annotated links to other sites that have relevant, interesting information
- Lots of action, responses, and comments from other users

Some of the school librarians we interviewed ignored the users' agreement when asking students to sign up for social software. Others resented the subterfuge, arguing that all Web 2.0 applications should have an education site just as Glogster, an online multimedia poster-creation tool, has done. Rather than teaching students to ignore click-through agreements, educators could ask students to create fictional characters within, for example, "Facebook School Projects."

Partnering for Inquiry

Not so long ago it was common to hear independent school librarians say they were responsible for resource selection and the information literacy process, whereas the content would be handled by their collaborating teachers. Research on learning does not support this dichotomy, because reading comprehension, content knowledge, and cognitive evaluation interact dynamically as a learner accesses, evaluates, and uses information to "make meaning." An artificial separation of content from process can only diminish the potential for student learning. Fortunately, the online environment presents librarians with the opportunity to renegotiate arbitrary or traditional roles so as to become full partners in instruction (Montiel-Overall 2008, 16–18).

Barbara Jansen, chair of instructional technology and upper school librarian at St. Andrew's Episcopal School, Austin (Texas), is a full collaborative partner who is involved in planning, implementing, and evaluating student work. When the ninth-grade history teachers proposed that students do research and report on the Indian caste system, Barbara began by asking what she asserts is *the* critical question for any project: "How will students add value to the information that they find in their sources?" As Barbara explains, "In the last analysis, it is only when original thinking emerges from critical analysis, that students value their contribution." Barbara's commitment to inquiry doesn't end there:

> If teachers want to give students questions to research, I suggest that we ask students to create a list that they think is appropriate for the task, a technique I have used with students since I was an elementary school librarian. For

example, in the Indian caste assignment, students brainstormed a list of questions (http://casteproject.pbworks.com/Student-generated-questions) that they would need to investigate in order to write authentic-sounding journal entries about the caste system. When they e-mailed the list to us for review, their questions were so on-target and creative that we hardly had to edit them at all!

Barbara is describing an information inquiry process in which one "seeks answers to questions, raises new questions and further questions the content" (Callison and Preddy 2006, 5). Unlike information literacy, in which a learner finds, evaluates, and uses information, and then absorbs knowledge created by others, students are actively constructing insights that are new to them (Callison and Preddy 2006, 5–9). When they recognize that they can apply their knowledge to authentic tasks, their learning is transformational (Abilock 2007).

Reductive and formulaic reports invite plagiarism, so Barbara's teaching team spent a great deal of time crafting their assignment for the caste journal entries so that they would elicit students' original ideas, require higher-level thinking, and stimulate student interest. Initially she may construct a wiki, adding graphics and uploading many documents, but the teaching team will also add and edit content. Their wiki becomes the focal point for the teaching collaboration and the inquiry process, as evident in the wikis for an Islam project (http://islamproject.pbworks.com/FrontPage) and the Indian caste system (http://casteproject.pbworks.com/FrontPage). They are one-stop assignment pages for students who are "absent, disengaged or just plain forgetful," as well as a question bank of writing prompts to inspire students' journal writing, thus deepening everyone's thinking about the topic.

Barbara is quick to point out that wikis are not a replacement for face-to-face teaching; the team discusses all aspects of the assignment directly with their students and co-teaches skills at the point of need. In addition, Barbara uses Meebo, an embedded instant messaging (IM) reference service that does not require downloading any software, to make herself available to each student at his or her virtual point of need:

> During class I ask students when they are most likely to be working on a project at home and I offer virtual office hours during those times. Since I have been part of the design team, co-introduced the project alongside the teachers, and am teaching the skills needed for accessing and using sources, as well as coaching students on how they might present their results, I am trusted as a reliable source of help; students will IM or e-mail me about any aspect of the project. They know, too, that I will be assessing their notes, bibliographies, and parts of the final presentations, so they consult me as much as their subject-area teachers.

The team understands that note-taking is critical to both synthesis and creativity. Notes are required and monitored, with feedback given often, so that students learn to organize and think about their information. Believing that the best way to teach ethical behavior is through practical application, Barbara explains that "We're proactive so they won't procrastinate . . . because desperation and ignorance are what lead to plagiarism." She sees little point in copyediting student bibliographies or taking points off a grade for punctuation, because "those errors are best handled by the citation software." Rather,

Barbara is interested in spending her time on the relationship between the notes and sources: "I check to see if the sources in the notes are included in the bibliography. Then we actually examine the sources they've used, evaluate the quality of the information taken from the sources, and observe how this has informed the student's conclusions." Summarizing and note taking are among the most important instructional strategies that enhance student learning in all subject areas and grades (Marzano et al. 2001, 7).

Although the current collaborative partnership and curricular design at St. Andrew's Episcopal School result in impressive student learning gains, Barbara would like to find an authentic audience beyond the classroom for these projects. "We have tried, so far unsuccessfully, to get students from Indian and Islamic communities to help our students learn about these cultures. I cannot help but believe that networked culture will provide us with an opportunity to enhance this curriculum with a global connection."

Designing Professional Development

In the past, software was likely to have been deployed by a technology director or network administrator, along with a subset of other faculty who became informally responsible for tools they believed were related to their job descriptions. Technology specialists selected and maintained, and sometimes taught workshops on, general productivity software. Librarians took ownership of specialized software related to library services. And content-area teachers gravitated toward discipline-specific tools. However, the explosion of Web-based, easy-to-learn communication tools like blogs and wikis, media creation and sharing tools, and a multiplicity of handheld gadgets and platforms has rendered it unlikely that any small group within a school could remain responsible for selecting tools and training the faculty, students, and administration. In fact, Laura Pearle argues, although the librarian can now bring new tools to the attention of their colleagues and train them in how to best use them, ultimately every educator must become responsible for maintaining and, indeed learning, the classroom-specific toolkit:

> As far as our services are concerned, I tend to agree with Walt Crawford: libraries cannot be all things to everyone, and librarians cannot do all things for every teacher. Wikis? Nings? I'm all for showing faculty what tools are out there, and how to use them, but if teachers aren't interested in managing and developing them, why would and, indeed, how could we do it for them?

Librarians who do assume professional responsibility for teaching faculty to use technology know that their task is not to conduct workshops about tools but rather to develop "habits of learning" (Fullan 2001, 179) using tools. Moreau Catholic High School (Hayward, California) was in its second year of a three-year, schoolwide rollout of laptops when Susan Geiger, the librarian, noticed that some teachers were having more difficulty than others integrating technology into their curriculum. There had been strong administrative support for staff development on the educational applications of Mac iLife productivity tools and Moodle, an open source course-management system. Now she realized that sustained, intensive, more individualized instruction could scaffold learning to *teach* in a ubiquitous computing environment.

Schools that take a systematic and planned approach to using technology to support learning achieve better outcomes with technology than other schools. These "e-mature" schools have a well-developed vision for learning and lead and manage their use of technology in support of this. They develop teacher skills and curriculum support to build habits and competency in using technology effectively in independent learning.

—*Evidence* 2009

To learn new ways of teaching, faculty members need time to practice and share, so she and her two library assistants adapted a version of "23 Things," developed by the California School Library Association (CSLA) under a Creative Commons License. The original version of "23 Things," designed by Helene Blowers, technology director, Public Library of Charlotte & Mecklenburg County in North Carolina, provides nine weeks of self-paced instruction in Web 2.0 tools. Participants blog about their progress and experiences. "Moreau Learning 2.0 (http://moreauteachers.edublogs.org/the-23-things/) kept most of the instructional content intact," Susan reports, "but we changed the examples and graphics to reflect our school and updated some of the social bookmarking tools. I also started a wiki, MCHS Learning Resources (http://mchslearning.wikispaces.com/), as a companion to our blog."

"I knew that we needed to publicize our idea and garner enthusiasm for participation, since this was voluntary," she remarked. "With the blessing of our Assistant Principal for Instruction we were able to offer two perfect incentives: T-shirts and jeans." With a relatively strict dress code, wearing jeans was a significant privilege at Moreau, even for teachers. Participants would be able to wear jeans every Friday during the nine-week program along with a T-shirt displaying the school logo and the tag line, '23 Things for 21st century learners.'"

During an important staff development day at the beginning of second semester, library staff members were given a ten-minute slot in which they showed a five-minute video they had shot and edited of faculty and staff members' responses to the question "Do you have 23 things?" "We used the other five minutes to do a Letterman-style 'Top Ten Reasons Why You Should Participate'," Susan said, "and wrapped up our promotion with information about how to sign up." During the first week, modeling the use of a tool from "23 Things," they produced an Animoto music video celebrating the first thirty-three sign-ups and e-mailed the link to all computer users in the school along with a reminder of how to sign up. "Peer pressure began to kick in when the secretaries and office staff joined us," Susan confided, "but I knew things were really going well when the entire administrative team signed up. Everybody wanted to wear jeans on Friday!"

From the moment the program began in February, the library staff began sending regular messages to all computer users, but directed toward the "23 Things" participants. On Thursdays, it was a reminder to wear jeans and T-shirts. On Fridays another e-mail announced that there were treats in the library for those needing "23 Things" help. And every Monday the library blog highlighted some of the interesting faculty blog posts and reminded everyone that library staff members were there to help.

"We were really busy," said Susan. "We went into classrooms and offices all week offering 'roadside assistance.'" Every Friday the library took on a festive atmosphere, crowded with faculty learners in jeans and T-shirts, and, Susan confessed, "We learned as much as we taught!" When in-service is tailored to the needs and abilities of the learner, it markets the value of the library. "In one sense we were cheerleaders." said Susan. "As teachers generated blog posts, we used the commenting function to encourage their efforts and, in fact, all forms of communications including e-mails, blog posts, and videos were branded with 'brought to you by the library'."

In turn, Susan and her staff received schoolwide recognition for these efforts, summed up in this blog post from the principal:

> First and foremost I would like to offer my gratitude and joy to the library staff for bringing 23 Things to life. I have observed first-hand how Susan, Connie and Anne have been reaching out, offering to help everyone keep on track and get their blogs set up. If Susan had not paid me a special visit this morning, *In Tenebris Lux* [his blog] would still be just a motto. So thank you to the wonderfully patient, techno wonder women of the library for launching this professional development experience for everyone.

Not everyone completed all twenty-three tasks in the allotted nine weeks. Research on how schools adopt change reports that it takes at least three years to resolve early concerns and see later ones emerge. However, the library had become a hub of learning in a relatively short time, and the library staff was exhilarated but exhausted. Looking back over second semester, Susan spoke to the successes of this professional development effort: "Everyone gained confidence using Web 2.0 technology. Our library's visibility and popularity grew—we're now the 'go to' experts." This year they are continuing to build on the momentum by conducting monthly "Techno Fridays," during which individuals may seek help for specific integration issues while other faculty can work on curriculum together. To complete this professional development cycle and continue the change process, the faculty should be asked to systematically analyze how student learning has been enhanced by this infusion of technology.

Exploring Professional Development Options

Most independent school librarians report that they first learn to use new media tools at home. To share information, ask questions, and mitigate their own professional isolation, they may join listservs for school librarians (e.g., LM_Net, the Independent School Section of the American Association of School Librarians, the Association of Independent School Librarians, local consortia listservs) and join or create social networks hosted on platforms such as Ning, Linkedin. Google Groups, and Moodle. Some groups are limited to independent school librarians, but others, like the Teacher-Librarian Network, the Australian School Library Association, and the Colorado Teacher Librarian Ning, include both public and private school librarians. Because collaboration with faculty is an important part of their jobs, independent school librarians may join groups that include both teachers and librarians, such as the Independent School Educators Network, First Grade Teachers, and the National Council for the Social Studies or participate in nings that focus on education topics like the Global Education Collaborative, ISTE, Classroom 2.0, and Making Curriculum Pop, which is about incorporating popular culture into curriculum.

Many are loosely organized social groups in which members create a personal profile and post asynchronous messages inviting comments. Hard-working moderators like Jim Burke (English Companion), Ryan Goble (Making Curriculum Pop), Laura Summers (21st Century Teacher-Librarians), and Demetri Orlando (Independent School Educators Network) are impressive facilitators who are able to create flourishing professional learning communities, which offer everything from lesson plans, resource lists, moderated discussions of professional books, and discussions about teaching practice, to personal support for novice teachers and librarians. Steven Hargadon, founder of the Classroom 2.0 social network, was hired by Elluminate to demonstrate the value of its online meeting software by artfully moderating real-time interviews and panels in which librarians join notable experts and authors to discuss the impact of technology on society and culture.

2.0 Resources Mentioned Here

Animoto: http://animoto.com/

Animoto: for Education http://animoto.com/education

Delicious: http://delicious.com/

Diigo: www.diigo.com/buzz/hot

Diigo Educator: www.diigo.com/education

Facebook: www.facebook.com

Gale Virtual Reference Library: www.gale.cengage.com/gvrl/

Glogster EDU: http://edu.glogster.com/

GoogleEarth: http://earth.google.com/

issuu: http://issuu.com/

LibGuides: www.springshare.com/libguides/

LibraryThing: www.librarything.com

Moodle: http://moodle.org/

Myspace: www.myspace.com/

MyStudiyo: http://mystudiyo.com/

Netvibes: www.netvibes.com/#General

Ning: www.ning.com/

NoodleTools: www.noodletools.com

Pageflakes: www.pageflakes.com/Default.aspx

Second Life: http://secondlife.com/

Twitter: http://twitter.com

VoiceThread: http://voicethread.com/#home

Wikidot: www.wikidot.com/

Wordle: www.wordle.net/

The English Companion Ning: http://englishcompanion.ning.com/

Making Curriculum Pop Ning: http://mcpopmb.ning.com/

Independent School Educators Network: http://isenet.ning.com/

21st Century Teacher-Librarians Ning: http://21centurylibrarian.ning.com/

Questions, Now and in the Future

These teaching and learning snapshots are both inspiring and unsettling. On the cusp of transformative changes, how will school librarians make wise decisions about technology? Does a focus on social scholarship privilege collective over independent work at the expense of the unique individual? Will a richly realized physical and virtual space that says "Welcome to the Library" indeed lead administrators to conclude that print is "outdated technology, like scrolls before books?" (Abel 2009). Are the professional ethics and enduring values of librarianship robust enough to keep librarians afloat as they plunge into an ocean of tools?

1. What should I know about technology diffusion that can help me select and use tools?

Gartner, Inc., a leading information technology research and advisory company, has developed a Hype Cycle (1995) model to help companies understand how technology diffusion occurs. With some modification, the independent school librarian can apply it to planning for networked technology (see figure 9.1). When early adopters use a new tool, they are enthusiastic and likely to over-project the tool's potential to change long-standing instructional practices or overhaul the librarian's role. As it becomes clear that the tool cannot fulfill this unrealistic potential, these early users enter the "Trough of Disillusionment," during which some will push back against or reject the technology because it has failed to solve entrenched school problems or catalyze sweeping reforms. This is followed by a period of enlightenment and consolidation; users see how the tool can, in fact, be used successfully and integrate it into their practice. The Gartner cycle ends with a "Plateau of Productivity," when widespread use of the technology is demonstrated and accepted. According to this consulting company, "The technology becomes increasingly stable and evolves in second and third generations. The final height of the plateau varies according to whether the technology is broadly applicable or benefits only a niche market" (Gartner 2009).

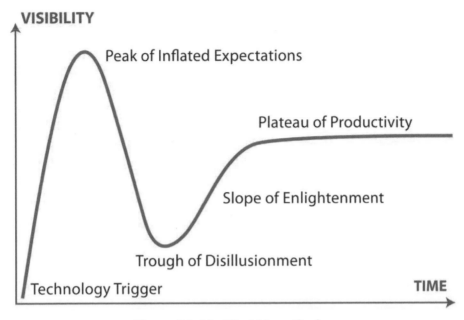

Figure 9.1. Modified Hype Cycle.

What Gartner's cycle misses is that new online technologies remain in "perpetual beta"; that is, they are continually being modified and updated while at the same time users are figuring out how to incorporate them into services and practices. School librarians who are realistic about the potential of inherently unstable tools are better able to develop a beta-tolerant school culture and pragmatically lead technology diffusion, taking calculated risks based on focused goals and preparing for uneven growth and rapid change with equanimity.

Cathy Rettberg, the head librarian at Menlo School in Atherton, California, is a teaching administrator who attends curriculum, technology, and division meetings. Although she does not always take the lead in using new media personally, she is respected as a risk taker and collaborative teaching partner who will put in the time to learn a new tool that she thinks might augment the research component of a curricular project. Cathy has taken a particular interest in cloud computing applications because they are platform-neutral and interoperable. For the last two years she has worked on integrating free Google applications into her laptop school so that students and teachers can learn, interact, create, remix, and publish without software barriers. She's aware of the pitfalls of using free services that are not locally managed. A service could decide to withdraw a particular tool, charge a fee, or change the terms of service. When she learned recently that students in several colleges were able to access and read each others' Gmail accounts (Perez 2009), she faced the fact that her school's investment in cloud computing necessitated a trade-off between privacy protection and free services. Yet she can imagine the synergistic potential of learning groups composed of individual students and teachers with their own dashboards and access to shared and individual calendars and multiple, interactive applications like Google Wave. They could plan and work together, simultaneously communicating and collaborating in real time, as well as playing back a collaborative sequence for someone who was absent. In this learning "cloud," students and teachers could gather and share sources; locate, create, and edit audio, vodcasts, and images; free write, revise, and comment on text, sound, or images in an editor or a wiki; analyze data in a spreadsheet; and then, using any number of presentation options, publish and remix. The potential of this schoolwide model of communities of practice, she argues, outweighs privacy concerns.

Cathy says, "What I appreciate is that the teacher participates *with* students as they learn—these integrated online apps take the 'guide on the side' concept to entirely new levels." When such technology is unleashed in schools and adopted by faculty, it has the potential to transform instruction and redefine schooling—and not just in the school library.

However, tools alone do not guarantee substantive changes in education. For example, comments and trackbacks on a blog may be disabled if a librarian uses it only to post assignments, in effect turning a participatory tool into a "broadcast" medium. If independent school librarians hope to make schoolwide changes in teaching and learning, they must be unafraid to question how and why a technology is being used, or even if technology should be used, and insist on assessing its value and congruence with learning goals.

2. Is teaching with new media different from teaching with other technology?

Unlike the first generation of digital software, whose greatest value for the school librarian was its ability to manage and organize information, new media's biggest impact is on "relationships between people and between organizations" (Lankshear and Knobel 2006, 48–49). Although school librarians are enthusiastic about a participatory Web with independent, self-directed, collaborative students, few appreciate the deep relationship shift that a "flat" school library might entail. Librarians often see themselves as coaches and co-learners, but as yet there has been little disruption of the hierarchical relationship among librarians, teachers, and students: decisions to ban or integrate technology are made by educators, not students. Decisions about what is studied are made by adults, not children. Ultimately the librarian manages the school library, the teacher manages the classroom. The adults are responsible for imparting skills, assigning work, and evaluating learning outcomes. The students are responsible for "doing it."

In reality, viewing these technologies through the lens of "information" is dangerously myopic. The value of the Internet and the ever-expanding World Wide Web does not live mostly in bits and bytes and bandwidth. To say that the Internet is about "information" is a bit like saying that "cooking" is about oven temperatures; it's technically accurate but fundamentally untrue.

—Schrage (2001)

The library director at the Head-Royce School in Oakland, California, has done her share of experimenting with various new tools, but Mary Goglio is not satisfied that she has designed assignments that make full use of their potential in ways that resonate with her school's culture, the library's goals, and users' needs:

> Part of the reason I'm having such trouble is that we're twelve grades with teachers and students all over the place in terms of 2.0 abilities, interests and understanding. I'm not sure that teachers or students who are using these tools think of themselves in terms of communities of practice with the potential for distributed cognition and collective knowledge generation. I think both groups, at this point, are just responding to bright shiny objects.

Can the peer-to-peer learning that is happening online and outside the classroom exist in schools? Some librarians argue that only "radical trust" (Fichter 2006) with learners as designers can enable "knowledge construction, not reproduction; conversation, not reception; articulation, not repetition; collaboration, not competition; [and] reflection, not prescription" (Jonassen et al.,1999, 16, quoted in Kimber and Wyatt-Smith 2006, 19). If we are indeed in the midst of a new age of learning in which students will exercise their freedom to question; design their environment and direct their own learning; and harness the "wisdom of student crowds" for collaborative evaluation of information, distributed problem solving, and self-assessment, then independent school librarians must face disruptive changes in control and power.

That's not to say that independent school librarians aren't questioning the focus of their teaching. Rather than teaching students to incorporate new technologies into their repertoire, some ask if they should be aggressively teaching information evaluation in an ocean of unfiltered, erroneous information coupled with an insidious infusion of advertising. Others worry that media pyrotechnics will inundate their learners and educators, preparing the way for massive societal ADD. Ought the school librarian to teach students how to manage "continuous partial attention," or how to resist impulses to multitask? What does it mean practically to teach students to use information "ethically," when copyright law is broadly contested and fair use is an ill-defined guideline? And still others ask whether the library can continue to serve the whole child; can it support both intellectual rigor and independent reflection while purveying social tools and collective wisdom?

Anne Letain, primary teacher-librarian at the Inter-Community School, Zurich, writes to her colleagues:

> I daydream about my next computer—what bells and whistles I want, what kind of monitor I'll have, how I'll network it with my existing computers. Maybe I'll add a little netbook to the collection, or I might gift myself an IPhone on my next birthday. I think about open source versus shareware, about wikis and blogs and RSS feeds and social bookmarking and other interactive media that comprise my Web2 life. Will I migrate to Chrome?

> But increasingly, I find myself questioning my unwavering loyalty and fidelity to the wireless world. For inexplicable reasons, I have found myself resisting invitations to Facebook, Twitter and LinkedIn.

After setting up blogs on both Blogger and Word Press, I quickly put them to death after noting that 537 other teacher-librarians already had a presence. Surely, I was not needed. I never deny the validity or worth of any of these beta and otherwise apps and have signed on to many. But, this niggling doubt about the magnificence of being "on" 24/7 has been festering inside me. What is the REAL point of being immersed in this enormous ocean of largely unfiltered information?

Human attention is indeed finite. We cannot multitask ourselves into a new age of enlightenment. Learning is a pyramid of historically based fundamentals (like philosophy, geography, art, science, mathematics, et al.) culminating at its apex with acquired meaning and context. In a nutshell, how will this generation and those that follow become "learned" when the fundamentals have gone astray? In other words, what does it matter that a second grader can embed a video into a personal PowerPoint presentation but doesn't understand why he chose that particular YouTube segment or what the significance of the content is for our society? This is my kind of daily dilemma.

3.   Where should I focus my attention?

Independent school librarians have focused their time and energies in a variety of ways. Some use an information inquiry research model to guide students in constructing new insights. Others make choices about which tools to use, inspired by a vision of schoolwide learning. Two important concepts, implicit in many of these examples, can focus these efforts. The first, "backward design" (Wiggins and McTighe 2005), is a method of planning curriculum so that students learn what the librarian or team intend, rather than just what might emerge. First the team identifies what students should be able to know and do; then they pinpoint evidence that will show that students have indeed achieved these goals; and finally they design experiences, choose tools, and select instructional strategies that will scaffold students' learning toward these goals. The content and steps of the project *enable* students to understand the important ideas and understandings that were identified as essential (Wiggins and McTighe 2005, 17–20). See figure 9.2.

Researchers find that extracting the full learning return from a technology investment requires much more than the mere introduction of technology with software and web resources aligned with the curriculum. It requires the triangulation of content, sound principles of learning, and high-quality teaching—all of which must be aligned with assessment and accountability.
>   —Lemke, Coughlin, and Reifsneider (2009, 6).

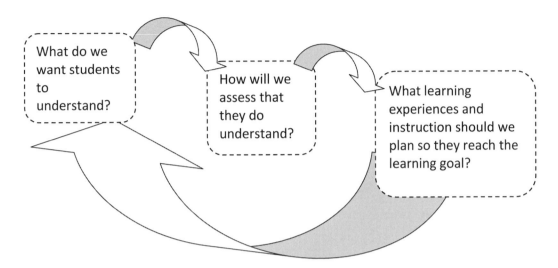

Figure 9.2. Backward Design. Based on the curriculum design model of Wiggins and McTighe (2005)

The second idea relates to selecting teaching strategies that have been proved effective. *Classroom Instruction That Works* (2001) distills decades of educational research findings into nine research-based teaching strategies, listed in descending order of their impact on student learning:

1. Identifying similarities and differences
2. Summarizing and note taking
3. Reinforcing effort and providing recognition
4. Homework and practice
5. Nonlinguistic representations
6. Cooperative learning
7. Setting objectives and providing feedback
8. Generating and testing hypotheses
9. Questions, cues, and advance organizers

Many of these strategies appear in our snapshots, but "intentional" curriculum design means that these are used explicitly and systematically in every unit or project. By planning backward and using effective instructional strategies throughout a project or unit of study, then assessing and documenting the results, the independent school librarian can be certain of enhancing learning for students and teachers, whether online or face to face.

Conclusion

Social technologies and participatory culture stand to transform how students, teachers, educational technology professionals, and librarians work together in libraries. Interaction, rather than information, is emerging as a primary driver of collaboration for learning. In untested waters, independent school librarians are thoughtfully choosing technology to improve their services and instruction. A few are using tools in ways that destabilize their authority and power with the goal of reinventing their school libraries as dynamic learning commons. As librarians negotiate their online presence, balancing privacy, responsibility, and free speech, they must be willing to expose their experiments, reveal their tacit knowledge, and honestly assess their efforts. Through informal networks, sharing strategies and insights, independent school librarians can identify best practices of social scholarship.

Interaction, rather than information, is emerging as a primary driver of collaboration for learning.

We return to the beginning to reiterate the sea changes that technologies are bringing. In independent school libraries, teaching, learning, and research are increasingly:

- **Participatory**—Experiences both inside and outside the curriculum are designed for inquiry and collaboration to promote knowledge creation and global citizenship.

- **Integrated**—Learning with new and traditional sources and formats is both multiliterate and multidisciplinary.

- **Experimental**—A beta-tolerant culture allows for the assimilation and frequent assessment of new technologies that are deployed to enhance learning.

- **Ethical**—Issues like plagiarism, privacy, and copyright are discussed as ethical dilemmas involving the public good, economic incentives, transformative online creation, and scholarly attribution.

- **Independent**—Students and teachers become independent, self-reflective learners, whose learning is "transformational" when they can "find, understand, evaluate, and use information in various forms to create for personal, social or global purposes" (Abilock 2007).

School library 2.0 = (access
+ books, stuff 'n' tools
+ PLC
+ social scholars
+ radical trust
x inquiry

www.hetemeel.com

References

Abel, David. 2009. "Welcome to the Library. Say Goodbye to the Books." *The Boston Globe,* September 4. Available at www.boston.com/news/local/massachusetts/articles/2009/09/04/a_library_without_the_books/. Accessed April 4, 2010.

Abilock, Debbie. 2007. "Information Literacy Building Blocks of Research: Overview of Design, Process and Outcomes." In *21st Century Literacies.* NoodleTools. July 13. Available at www.noodletools.com/debbie/literacies/information/1over/infolit1.html. Accessed April 4, 2010.

Adams, Helen R. 2008. *Ensuring Intellectual Freedom and Access to Information in the School Library Media Program.* Santa Barbara, CA: Libraries Unlimited.

American Association of School Librarians. 2009. *Empowering Learners: Guidelines for School Library Media Programs.* Chicago: ALA.

———. *Standards for the 21st Century Learner.* 2007. American Library Association., Available at www.ala.org/ala/mgrps/divs/aasl/guidelinesandstandards/learningstandards/standards.cfm. Accessed April 4, 2010.

Baron, Naomi S. 2009. "Are Digital Media Changing Language?" *Educational Leadership* (March): 42–46. Available at www.ascd.org/publications/educational_leadership/mar09/vol66/num06/Are_Digital_Media_Changing_Language%C2%A2.aspx. Accessed April 4, 2010.

Bomar, Shannon. 2009. "The Grammatically Correct Wiki." *Knowledge Quest* 37, no. 4: 51. Available at aasl.metapress.com/content/l4w1h11158647287/?p=ce5bee3e156d42d3bab7ef5cdf1ccd98&pi=3. Accessed April 4, 2010.

boyd, danah. 2009. "Some Thoughts on Technophilia." *Apophenia: Making Connections Where None Previously Existed* (August 20). Available at www.zephoria.org/thoughts/archives/2009/08/20/some_thoughts_o_1.html. Accessed April 4, 2010.

Callison, Daniel, and Leslie Preddy. 2006. "Information Inquiry: Concepts and Elements." In *The Blue Book on Information Age Inquiry, Instruction and Literacy,* 1–16. Westport, CT: Libraries Unlimited.

Code of Ethics of the American Library Association. 2008. American Library Association. January 22. Available at www.ala.org/ala/aboutala/offices/oif/statementspols/codeofethics/codeethics.cfm. Accessed April 4, 2010.

Cohen, Laura. 2007. "Social Scholarship on the Rise." In *Library 2.0: An Academic's Perspective.* University at Albany Libraries, SUNY. April 5. Available at http://liblogs.albany.edu/library20/2007/04/social_scholarship_on_the_rise.html. Accessed April 4, 2010.

Collen, Lauren. 2006. "The Digital and Traditional Storytimes Research Project: Using Digitized Picture Books for Preschool Group Storytimes." *Children and Libraries* 4, no. 3: 8–18. Available at www.ala.org/ala/mgrps/divs/alsc/compubs/childrenlib/index.cfm. Accessed April 4, 2010.

Crider, Lissa. n.d. *About the Library.* Lick Wilmerding Library. Lick Wilmerding High School. Available at www.lwhs.org/podium/default.aspx?t=106751. Accessed April 4, 2010.

Evidence on the Impact of Technology on Learning and Educational Outcomes. 2009. Becta. July 13. Available at http://partners.becta.org.uk/upload-dir/downloads/page_documents/research/impact_of_technology_on_outcomes_jul09.pdf. Accessed April 4, 2010.

Fichter, Darlene. 2006. "Web 2.0, Library 2.0 and Radical Trust: A First Take." *Blog on the Side* (April 2). Available at http://library2.usask.ca/~fichter/blog_on_the_side/2006/04/web-2.html. Accessed April 4, 2010.

Fogg, B. J., et al. 2002. *How Do People Evaluate a Web Site's Credibility? Results from a Large Study.* Consumer Reports WebWatch. Consumer Union. November 11. Available at www.consumerwebwatch.org/pdfs/stanfordPTL.pdf. Accessed April 4, 2010.

Fullan, Michael. 2001. *The New Meaning of Educational Change.* 3rd ed. New York: Teachers College Press.

Gardner, Howard. 1993. *Multiple Intelligences: The Theory in Practice.* New York: Basic.

Gartner Research. 2009. *Research Methodologies: Hype Cycles.* Gartner. Available at www.gartner.com/it/products/research/methodologies/research_hype.jsp. Accessed April 4, 2010.

Hall, Gene E., and Shirley M. Hord. 2005. *Implementing Change: Patterns, Principles and Potholes.* 2nd ed. Boston: Allyn & Bacon.

Ito, Mizuko, et al. 2008. *Living and Learning with New Media: Summary of Findings from the Digital Youth Project.* Digital Youth Research. John D. and Catherine T. MacArthur Foundation. November. Available at http://digitalyouth.ischool.berkeley.edu/files/report/digitalyouth-WhitePaper.pdf. Accessed April 4, 2010.

———. [2009].*Final Report: Conclusion*. Digital Youth Research. John D. and Catherine T. MacArthur Foundation. Available at http://digitalyouth.ischool. berkeley.edu/book-conclusion. Accessed April 4, 2010.

Kimber, Kay, and Claire Wyatt-Smith. 2006. "Using and Creating Knowledge with New Technologies; A Case for Students-as-Designers." *Learning, Media, & Technology* 31, no. 1: 19–34. Available at www.tandf.co.uk/journals/titles/ 17439884.asp. Accessed April 4, 2010.

Lankshear, Colin, and Michele Knobel. 2006. *New Literacies: Changing Knowledge and Classroom Learning*. 2nd ed. Philadelphia: Open University Press.

Lempke, Cheryl, Ed Coughlin, and Daren Reifsneider. 2009. *Technology in Schools: What the Research Says: An Update*. Cisco Systems. Available at www.cisco. com/web/strategy/docs/education/tech_schools_09_research.pdf. Accessed April 4, 2010.

Lenhart, Amanda, et al. 2008. *Writing, Technology and Teens*. Pew Internet & American Life Project. April 24. Available at www.pewinternet.org/Reports/ 2008/Writing-Technology-and-Teens.aspx. Accessed April 4, 2010.

Loucks-Horsley, Susan. 1996. "The Concerns-Based Adoption Model (CBAM): A Model for Change in Individuals." In *The National Academies*. National Academy of Sciences. Available at www.nationalacademies.org/rise/backg4a.htm. Accessed April 4, 2010.

Marzano, Robert J., Debra J. Pickering, and Jane E. Pollock. 2001. *Classroom Instruction That Works: Research-Based Strategies for Increasing Student Achievement*. Alexandria, VA: ASCD.

McGuire, Hugh. 2009. Interview by Sean Cranbury. In *The Future of Publishing*. Toronto: Open Book. September 11. Available at www.openbooktoronto.com/ magazine/fall_2009/articles/future_publishing. Accessed April 4, 2010.

Miller, Paul. 2005. "Web 2.0: Building the New Library." *Ariadne* 45. Available at www.ariadne.ac.uk/issue45/miller/. Accessed April 4, 2010.

Minors and Internet Interactivity: An Interpretation of the Library Bill of Rights. 2009. American Library Association. July 15. Available at www.ala.org/ ala/aboutala/offices/oif/statementspols/statementsif/interpretations/minorsintern etinteractivity.cfm. Accessed April 4, 2010.

Montiel-Overall, Patricia. 2008. "Toward a Theory of Collaboration for Teachers and Librarians." *School Library Media Research* 8 (April). Available at www.ala. org/ala/mgrps/divs/aasl/aaslpubsandjournals/slmrb/slmrcontents/volume82005/ theory.cfm. Accessed April 4, 2010.

Perez, Sarah. 2009. "Whoops! Students 'Going Google' Gets to Read Each Others' Emails." In *ReadWriteWeb*. Richard MacManus. September 18. Available at www.readwriteweb.com/archives/whoops_students_going_google_get_to_read _each_others_email.php. Accessed April 4, 2010.

Schrage, Michael. 2001. "The Relationship Revolution." In *Merrill Lynch Forum*. ManyWorlds. Available at http://web.archive.org/web/20030602025739/http:// www.ml.com/woml/forum/relation.htm. Accessed April 4, 2010.

Stein, Jared. 2008. "Defining 'Creepy Treehouse'." In *Flexnology*. Learningfield.org. April 9. Available at http://flexknowlogy.learningfield.org/2008/04/09/defining-creepy-tree-house/. Accessed April 4, 2010.

Tomlinson, Carol Ann, et al. 2002. *The Parallel Curriculum: A Design to Develop High Potential and Challenge High-Ability Learners*. Thousand Oaks, CA: Corwin.

"Using and Creating Knowledge with New Technologies: A Case for Students-as-Designers." 2006. *Learning, Media and Technology* 31, no. 1: 19–34. Available at www.tandf.co.uk/journals/titles/17439884.asp. Accessed April 4, 2010.

Weinberger, David. 2007. *Everything Is Miscellaneous: The Power of the New Digital Disorder*. New York: Times.

Wiggins, Grant, and Jay McTighe. 2005. *Understanding by Design*. Expanded 2nd ed. Alexandria, VA: ASCD.

Visit http://lu.com/excellence for supporting links and occasional updates to all essays in this book.

Elisabeth Palmer Abarbanel is in her thirteenth year as Librarian for the middle and upper schools at Brentwood School in Los Angeles, California (www. bwscampus.com—school; www.bwscampus.com/academics/library_east.aspx-library). She has worked at two other Los Angeles independent schools and as a public librarian in both adult and children's reference. Elisabeth writes about her school library experiences and issues relevant to school librarians in her blog, Archipelago (www.archipelago.blogspot.com).

Debbie Abilock is Editor-in-chief of Knowledge Quest, *the journal of the American Association of School Librarians, and co-founder of NoodleTools, Inc. (www.noodletools.com/debbie/bio/), which designs Web-based tools to support students' academic research. She received an American Memory Fellowship and* Time *Magazine's Grand Prize for innovative online curriculum, and is a* Library Journal *Mover & Shaker. She has conducted workshops and given presentations throughout the United States and Europe and works with schools and nonprofits on inquiry teaching and learning based on her experience as a teaching librarian, director of a unified library/technology department, curriculum coordinator, and school administrator.*

Information Commons and Independent School Libraries: Opportunities for Excellence

Alison A. Ernst, Northfield Mount Hermon School (Gill, MA)

Introduction

What is an "Information Commons" (IC)? What, if anything, could such an entity do for an independent school library? For nearly two decades colleges and universities have experimented with combining the departments of information technology (IT), media services, and the "traditional" library. These efforts have resulted in the development of Information Commons. Is this combined IT/media/library model appropriate for K–12 schools? Do current school library programs already embody this kind of integrated teaching and learning, or are there new components we should consider for twenty-first-century school library service? Is "Information Commons" merely a new term for the same traditional library services, window dressing rather than substantive change? Even if it is simply a name, is it useful?

The Information Commons emerged in the higher educational library scene during the early 1990s. Examples abound of colleges and universities implementing

> *Is "Information Commons" merely a new term for the same traditional library services, window dressing rather than substantive change?*

areas providing "one-stop shopping" for students' academic technology needs. But why should we in primary and secondary independent schools care about what happens beyond K–12? Because most of our charges are college bound, we should pay attention to what students will experience as they move to the next level of education. An elementary or high school library should not necessarily be modeled after that of a research university. However, it benefits our students to think of their education in terms of K through 16 and beyond. Different kinds of libraries can and should learn from each other. Paying attention to advances in all areas of librarianship (including public libraries) is appropriate and sensible.

What about an Information Commons in higher education might be useful to public school and independent school libraries? What ideas are emerging about transforming school libraries for twenty-first-century learning? Consider the example of a public high school in Massachusetts that established a Learning Commons, and Northfield Mount Herman School's effort to create and adapt an Information Commons. The Northfield Mount Hermon example will *not* be a "how they did it good" report, but a case study about the impetus, vision, reality, successes, and disappointments along the way. Instructions on how to implement an Information Commons in your school will *not* be provided. Rather, there will be questions about how to provide your students with the best twenty-first-century library experience you can muster in your institutional situation. How might the underlying principles of service discussed here best inform your long-term vision and implementation of all or parts of the Information Commons structure?

> *[T]here will be questions about how best to provide your students with the best twenty-first- century library experience you can muster in your institutional situation.*

The following examples are high schools; you the reader may be serving a K–8 population. Should you skip this essay? No! Our unified mission as librarians is to connect users with what they need and want regardless of grade level. How we facilitate a library program in the school setting does indeed vary based on the age of our constituents. Our objectives in an IC model include the fostering of information literacy skills and cultivating reading for pleasure, both traditional library functions.

An e-mail survey of independent school librarians asked if any of their institutions had experimented with creating an Information Commons. The most prevalent response was, "What is an Information Commons?" An Information Commons is a place where information technology, media services, and traditional library services intersect, providing students with the technology tools, information sources, and human resources needed to do their best work. Reactions on the library listserv were passionate as well as varied. One camp declared our libraries already do this work of integrating academic technology, and it is simply a matter of semantics. This cohort voiced strong concern about diluting the idea and reality of "library" with verbal wordplay. Other voices countered insistently that libraries need to redefine and respond to the reality of digital-native millennials. Still others wanted to explore more about what an Information Commons is, and why/how it may differ from a library. Clearly this is a provocative topic. The discussion may not lead to a definitive answer, but is important because the ultimate focus and beneficiaries of our machinations are the students we are preparing for college and life, the students we are supporting in their current work at our schools.

> *An Information Commons is a place where information technology, media services, and traditional library services intersect, providing students with the technology tools, information sources, and human resources needed to do their best work.*

Information Commons 101

During the late twentieth century, much of librarianship became reliant upon IT to function. Examples include the emergence of online catalogs, periodical databases, and integrated library systems. Congruently, college and university students as well as faculty began using computer technology and eventually online resource technology to do their work. When I started college in the early 1980s, I wrote on a typewriter, depending on whiteout and erasable paper to facilitate revisions. By the time I earned my undergraduate degree, I word-processed my senior thesis and was extremely grateful for cut and paste revision, as well as the spell-check tool. Academic technology as an educational reality emerged and thrived. Libraries in higher education both instigated and responded to the opportunities and demands of the IT-dependent information age.

Beginning in the early 1990s, some colleges and universities experimented with combining IT and library department functions. In some cases the motivation was simply cost management, an institutional decision not necessarily grounded in strategic planning nor trying to cultivate the best environment for student learning. Several institutions physically consolidated departments with the head of IT and library director becoming one position (see essay 6). A person filling this new post had either an IT or a library background, not necessarily both. At some establishments, the consolidation worked well. At others, library and IT department members felt threatened, and cooperation was not highest on their list of accomplishments. However, in other cases, particularly when the decision to combine IT and library management was part of a strategic planning process involving key stakeholders, the result was innovation and transformation. The product of this dynamic integration resulted in a facility or program, which may or may not be located physically in the universities' libraries, where academic technology, library, and media services came together in one location. This model became known as an "Information Commons" (IC).

Several sources in professional library literature define Information Commons in similar ways. A 2004 entry in *The Encyclopedia of Library and Information Science* states:

> Information commons are a new type of library facility. They commonly include a large number of computer workstations that provide access to productivity software as well as the Internet and electronic library resources. Often, they are formed through a partnership with IT and the library and employ professionals from both areas. Help is provided for the technology as well as information research. They first appeared in the early 1990s and are being adopted by university libraries at a rapid pace, as *they seem to meet the emerging needs of today's students.* (Emphasis added.)

A 2007 entry in the *Dictionary for Library and Information Science* affirms this definition:

> A new type of technology-enhanced collaborative facility on college and university campuses that integrates library and computer application services (information, technology, and learning) in a single floor plan, often equipped with a wireless network and, in some cases, equipment for multimedia production. Most ICs are designed to support librarians engaged in assisting individual students and in teaching research skills to groups,

teaching assistants helping individuals and groups of students with class assignments, and individual students and groups independently accessing information in print and online. Some ICs are open 24/7, synonymous with integrated learning center.

The descriptions are consistent, but are focused on higher education. The later entry brings up the issue of terminology. What's in a name? Information Commons seems to be the most frequently used phrase to describe the integrated service model of library, IT, and media resources. However other idioms in use include "learning commons," "teaching commons," and "knowledge commons." One of my colleagues insists an entire library is an Information Commons, so why use this term to designate one area of a program? I am sure the professional debate will continue. For the purpose of this essay, IC will describe a distinct area or program providing one-stop shopping for students in terms of academic technology, media resources, and library services, particularly since the moniker is used in higher education regularly as well as in library literature.

> *IC will describe a distinct area or program providing one-stop shopping for students in terms of academic technology, media resources, and library services.*

In the professional library literature there is a growing body of work extolling the Information Commons as an effective means of fostering information literacy instruction as well as providing responsive customer service to students and faculty in this digital age. The Information Commons, what it stands for in terms of providing integrated services as well as facilitating collaborative work, is not a fad or an anomaly. It has become a staple library service at the higher educational level. So, what could this mean for secondary and elementary school librarianship?

School Library Conditions

Before exploring the opportunities and possibilities for the Information Commons model to be translated into school library practice, consider some of the environmental and cultural issues in school libraries. Over the past few decades, the librarian often served as the technology leader in a school, as well as providing most media support. (See essay 8 for more discussion.) Computers in schools may have made their first appearances in the library, particularly if availability of space precluded a separate computer lab. It is a broad generalization that public school librarians became de facto IT contacts for their institutions as well as the media managers. But it is useful in contrasting their work with that of independent school librarians.

As readers know, one of the great things about independent schools is indeed their independence. Yes, independent schools are accredited by a regional body with national affiliation. Best practices in all areas of independent school life are regularly developed and updated by NAIS. But the kind of certification requirements in play in public schools are absent in the sphere of independent education. The implication for an independent school library includes a range of who might be staffing the program. Is a professional librarian with a master's of library science or related degree, who is versed in the principles of librarianship and stays abreast of developments in the field, at the helm of a school's library program? Is an intelligent, talented, well-read teacher of English, history, or some other discipline in the head librarianship role along with other school duties? The size and funding of an independent school will certainly affect the kind of library program and who is planning and implementing it, as well as the number of individuals staffing it. These factors will also determine whether an independent school has a distinct IT department or academic and institutional technology is managed as added duties to those with other roles. Is there a separate media department that facilitates video editing and provision of films for classroom use, or has this traditionally been managed by the library? These variables will all come into play when considering the applicability of an Information Commons to an independent school.

Commons Model in School Libraries

At this writing there are few publications in the library literature about schools and Information Commons specifically. There is, however, recent work advocating creating "learning commons" in school libraries. To understand what this phrase means, first look at the elements of an Information Commons:

- Physical location in or near the library

- Access to traditional library services (e.g., reference collection and assistance, print and electronic resources, etc.)

- A technology-rich environment (e.g., computers, scanners, printers, digital cameras)

- Multimedia hardware, software, and support (e.g., PowerPoint, Photoshop, video-editing packages)

- Productivity software (e.g., Word and Excel)

- Collaborative learning and work spaces (Bailey and Tierney 2008, 2)

Bailey and Tierney define "learning commons" as a further developed Information Commons:

> [R]eflect[ing] a shift in learning theory from primarily *transmission* of knowledge to patrons toward a greater emphasis on *creation* of knowledge by commons staff and patrons' self-direction in learning. A learning commons includes all aspects of the information commons but extends and enhances them. (Bailey and Tierney 2008, 2)

In light of this, it appears that the phrase "learning commons" is an evolution of "Information Commons."

In December 2008, a Learning Commons dedication and opening was held at the public high school in Chelmsford, Massachusetts. The Learning Commons essentially replaced the school's previous traditional library, both in terms of facility and services. Librarian Valerie Diggs spent the previous five years thinking deeply, strategizing about library service and taking programmatic steps to cultivate change:

> Many people have asked me how I was able to create such a space. How did I decide to call the library a Learning Commons and why? My response is that

> I did not decide; the program did. A recent article in Teacher Librarian describes the vision of a true learning commons as "the showcase for high-quality teaching and learning—a place to develop and demonstrate exemplary educational practices. It will serve as the professional development center for the entire school—a place to learn, experiment with, assess, and then widely adopt improved instructional programs." Our program defined us and the definition of what we did every day transformed our space into one that we now call a Learning Commons. (Diggs and Loertscher 2009)

The Chelmsford High School Learning Commons has elements of the Information Commons model, including technology rich collaborative space, as well as providing access to traditional library resources and services. The focus on creation of knowledge is in line with the recent AASL *Standards for the 21st-Century Learner*.

In *The New Learning Commons*, library educator David Loertscher and educational consultants Carol Koechlin and Sandi Zwaan advocate for a reworking of school libraries into a more client-centered, responsive organization appropriate for the ways this generation of learners interacts with information (e.g., Googling). Though the authors don't specifically reference higher educational Information Commons, their learning commons proposal is a school-centered version of the integrated, responsive, and collaborative learning spaces now a fixture in college and university libraries.

Some librarians do indeed balk at the idea of losing the L word, library. Many independent school library leaders advocate retaining the term "library" to describe the facility and program. However, most agree it is crucial to transform the definition of what a library is, as well as re-envisioning and continually developing the program and facilities of a library. Following is a discussion of how the Information Commons was conceived and implemented as part of the library system at the Northfield Mount Hermon School.

The Information Commons at NMH

One of the truisms of independent schools is that by their nature they tend to have unique circumstances, organizationally and culturally. In 1999 the Northfield Mount Hermon School was the largest boarding school in the country, set on two campuses five miles apart, with two libraries and two media centers on the two campuses. The library system's collection was approximately 100,000 items, and the content level was more similar to a small liberal arts college library than a school. The library personnel team consisted of fourteen professional and paraprofessional workers. More than half of the faculty and staff of the library had an MLS degree. At this writing the school has consolidated onto one campus, with half the previous number of students and correspondingly fewer faculty and staff. As of the 2010–2011 school year, there will be five library personnel working in the one library facility.

[I]ndependent schools . . . by their nature . . . have unique circumstances, organizationally and culturally.

Just prior to 1999, the school's IT department was deciding to absorb the media department (considered part of the library), as equipment and functions of this unit were so technology heavy. Instead, the IT director and the library director decided to co-manage the media functions of the NMH Library System. The two directors began to plot and plan how to provide cutting edge services to the school community. They were both very interested in effective models for providing students and faculty with the facilities, programs, and services to do their best possible work.

At the beginning of the IT/library consolidation, students commonly walked all over at least one campus to accomplish all the parts of a research project. If a student had a paper assignment but also needed to prepare a PowerPoint presentation on the same topic, he or she would do research in one of two libraries, word processing either in the library or a dorm room, but then have to go to one of the media centers for assistance with the visual presentation. On one campus this meant stepping next door to the library, but on the other it required going to an entirely different building. Laptop trouble required tech support in yet another building! The NMH Library System had already developed a strong customer service focus, based on best practices identified in public and academic libraries.

During the spring of 2003, the NMH Library System engaged the school community in a strategic planning process, during which the following goals were identified:

- Ensure students at NMH acquire and apply the information literacy skills necessary to be successful in school, college, and life.

- In order to support the academic and student life program, as well as personal interests of the NMH community, continually develop a strong and relevant collection of resources in a variety of formats (print, multimedia, electronic) that are readily accessible to the NMH community.

- Develop a cohesive and creative team of library, media, and IT personnel to provide the NMH community with excellent service.

- Create a visionary, cutting edge facility designed for integrated library/media/ technology programs and services, a signature campus building, and a physical and virtual crossroads for the NMH community.

The Information Commons opened in the NMH Libraries in the fall of 2003 as an extension of this planning process; the implementation is ongoing, as is the nature of libraries.

As part of the preparation for creating the NMH Information Commons, the directors of the library and IT visited liberal arts colleges that had successfully implemented either an Information Commons or a combined library/IT management. These visits included Wellesley College in Massachusetts, which had recently moved IT functions into the library. The library, media services, and instructional technology, as well as computing, are all under the auspices of the Wellesley College Information Services, headed by a VP of information services as well as the college librarian. Kalamazoo College in Michigan had at the time a management structure with one director responsible for IT and library operations. Wellesley's director came from a library background, and Kalamazoo's was IT. Mount Holyoke College in western Massachusetts featured a distinct Information Commons. The Mount Holyoke example became the physical model for the NMH effort. The NMH directors also did extensive reading and research about these integrated spaces at colleges and universities across the country.

In collaboration, the IT and library directors developed the following vision: a technology-rich space within each library, high-end computers with an array of presentation software, staffed by rotation of IT and media personnel, with librarians nearby. Following is what it looked like initially.

Campus A: The Information Commons was more theoretical than actual; no new equipment (except for software upgrades) or renovation:

- A bank of computers adjacent to the reference collection and close to the circulation desk and distinct from the public access terminals used primarily to connect with the online catalog.

- Scheduled afternoon hours: Media faculty and a Latin teacher serving as a liaison between IT and other teachers

Campus B: A significant Information Commons model was implemented:

- A wing of the facility designated as an Information Commons space.

- An IT help desk area installed at one end of the room, with regularly scheduled hours for walk-in assistance.

- Round computer tables with high-end PCs and an array of presentation software installed.

- Collaboration stations: long, rounded tables (to accommodate group work) with a large screen at one end. Wireless keyboard and mice enable multiple users.

- Scanners and printers available onsite.

Students trained in technology sharpshooting were also assigned hours at both Information Commons on the two campuses to provide support and presentation software guidance to users.

In fall 2004 the Northfield Mount Hermon School completed a strategic consolidation onto one campus, previously referred to as Campus B. The NMH Library System contracted to one library facility. The campus's offsite media center integrated into this library. The consolidation provided opportunity for IT personnel from campus A to be relocated into the library on campus B. This was a chance to implement the vision of a truly integrated library and IT department. At NMH this consolidation of the two departments did not work as an ongoing management strategy; on other campuses like Sidwell Friends in Washington, DC, this strategy is very successful.

The following worked well after the NMH campus and library consolidation:

- An IT professional was available in a central location in the library for walk-in help for students and adults.

- Collaboration stations with large screens were used heavily, by students with group projects and adults, both faculty and staff, for trainings.

- It became a very popular destination/location with student users.

- It became a distinct and definable place within the library, pointed out on admissions tours.

Six years later, the initial vision has not been fully realized. This is not necessarily a bad thing, as the reality of implementing an idea is bound to include amendments, modifications, and adaptations. Following are examples of what was intended and what actually occurred:

Vision:

- Librarians/media and IT personnel working one-on-one with students and faculty in Information Commons morning through evening.

Reality:

- Adult staffing not available to the extent hoped, student support of each other informally was consistent, though (as the digital native millennials were more comfortable and capable with the technology tools).

Vision:

- Area primarily for academic work.

Reality:

- Students using the Info Commons for group gaming in the afternoons.

  - Pros: student attachment and investment in space

  - Cons: could get loud/heated; intimidating to other nongamer students, who found other places in the library to call their own.

On the institutional level, the best-laid plans are sometimes scuttled by circumstances beyond our direct control. In our case there was turnover in IT leadership, and institutional support of academic technology decreased due to other pressing needs. IT staff moved out of the cramped library space, though one IT position continues to have hours in the Information Commons. Life happens. Key administrators leave the school, institutional priorities shift, school staffing is cut across the board due to national and global economic crises. An independent school library director must adapt while still aiming for excellence.

The polar opposites "success" or "failure" do not do justice to the NMH Information Commons experiment. Certainly there were pleasant surprises and triumphs as well as disappointments. Perhaps the most important experience to note is that of continual tweaking. This is part of the effort to redefine and evolve library service to meet the realities of twenty-first-century learning.

> *On the institutional level, the best-laid plans are sometimes scuttled by circumstances beyond our direct control.*

At this writing, the Northfield Mount Hermon School's library is zoned. A reading room housing the print fiction collection, comfy chairs, and large tables for academic work is relatively low tech. Though students bring laptops into the space, there are few public access computers. Then there's the thriving Information Commons, a technology-rich workspace, tables of computers, the IT help desk, as well as the graphic novel collection (and a chess set between two comfortable chairs). The reference area houses a robust print collection, as well as a bank of computers for students to do online research. There is also a collaboration station with a big screen at one end for group projects. This is a hybrid area.

By the time you read this, the layout in the Information Commons will have changed. Immediately, Macs (prized for their digital editing capabilities) will replace the PCs, and the collection of DVDs will migrate into the Information Commons, while the PCs will be redistributed throughout the library. Over ten years, many more changes could occur. But this is indeed the nature of an Information Commons and twenty-first-century librarianship, continual evolution pointed toward excellence.

Lessons Learned

If you are intrigued with the commons concept and are interested in exploring its applicability to your independent school library situation, ponder the following:

- Are your efforts aligned with the school's mission and based on strategic planning?

- Is there institutional support and interest in forward-thinking approaches to integrating academic technology?

- Is an IT director, academic dean, or someone else in a significant administrative role interested in collaborating to implement best practices for learning with technology?

Also consider taking these actions:

- Identify interested faculty partners.

- Cultivate student input and management—tap into the technological strengths of millennials.

- Visit other schools and/or colleges and universities for ideas.

- Troll the library literature for work on Information Commons, learning commons, information literacy, and any other topics that will inform your work.

And remember:

- Change is the only constant—plan for the flexibility to adapt while growing.

Conclusion

Librarianship is an evolving art. School librarianship requires a commitment to information literacy as a multidisciplinary endeavor. Explore your own school environment to determine what might be the best means of fostering information literacy. The teaching and practice of multiple literacies require an effective library space and program that includes sufficient resources and skilled librarians. The Information Commons model, successful in higher education, has possibilities for improving library service in schools. Whether a space within a library or a whole library itself is called an Information Commons, a learning commons, or any other name, the most important thing for independent school librarians to keep in focus is providing the best possible service and learning environment to our students. Remaining flexible and being willing to revise and experiment with service models is essential as we work with the millennials in the information age.

References

Bailey, D. Russell, and Barbara Gunter Tierney. 2008. *Transforming Library Service through Information Commons: Case Studies for the Digital Age.* Chicago: American Library Association.

Beagle, Donald Robert, Donald Bailey, and Barbara Tierney. 2006. *The Information Commons Handbook.* New York: Neal-Schuman.

Chelmsford High School Learning Commons Homepage. 2009. Chelmsford High School. June 19. Available at www.chelmsford.k12.ma.us/chs/library/index.htm. Accessed June 27, 2009.

Diggs, Valerie, and David V Loertscher. 2009. "From Library to Learning Commons: A Metamorphosis." *Teacher Librarian* 36, no. 4: 32–38. Available at http://0search.ebscohost.com.library.simmons.edu/login.aspx?direct=true&db=. Accessed June 27, 2009.

A Field Guide to the Information Commons. 2009. Ed. Charles Forrest and Martin Halbert. Lanham, MD: Scarecrow.

"Information Commons." 2007. In *Online Dictionary for Library and Information Science.* Ed. Joan M. Reitz. Libraries Unlimited. November 19. Available at http://lu.com/odlis/. Accessed June 27, 2009.

Koechlin, Carol, Sandi Zwaan, and David V Loertscher. 2008. "The Time Is Now: Transform Your School Library into a Learning Commons." *Teacher Librarian* 36, no. 1: 8. Available at http://infotrac.galegroup.com/itweb/?db=AONE. Accessed June 27, 2009.

Loertscher, David. 2008. "Flip This Library." *School Library Journal* 54, no. 11: 46–48. Available at http://0search.ebscohost.com.library.simmons.edu/login.aspx?direct=true&db=lih&AN=35226058&site=ehost-live. Accessed June 27, 2009.

Loertscher, David V., Carol Koechlin, and Sandi Swaan. 2008. *The New Learning Commons: Where Learners Win! Reinventing School Libraries and Computer Labs.* Salt Lake City, UT: Hi Willow Research.

The New Learning Commons. 2008. Available at www.lmcsource.com/isell3/product.php?id=88&locatekey=cbc84bb307b238d879096d7ccdc3b852. Accessed June 27, 2009.

Palfrey, John, and Urs Gasser. 2008. *Born Digital: Understanding the First Generation of Digital Natives.* New York: Basic Books.

School Library Teacher Program. Department home page. Available at www.simmons.edu/gslis/academics/programs/teacher.php. Accessed June 28, 2009.

White, Peggy, Susan Beatty, and Darlene Warren. 2004. "Information Commons." In *Encyclopedia of Library and Information Science.* Ed. Marcia J. Bates, Mary Niles Maack, and Miriam Drake. Informaworld. Available at http://0www. informaworld.com.library.simmons.edu/smpp/section?content=a713532120&f ulltext=713240928. Accessed June 27, 2009.

Visit http://lu.com/excellence for supporting links and occasional updates to all essays in this book.

Alison Ernst has served as Director of Library and Academic Resources at the Northfield Mount Hermon School in Massachusetts (http://www.nmhschool.org/) for over a decade. Ms. Ernst is committed to facilitating exceptional library service for all types of libraries through consulting work and participation in national and international library organizations. She is passionate about strategic planning, life-long learning, writing, and libraries.

To Collaborate or Not to Collaborate: It's Not a Question!

Barbara Weathers, Duchesne Academy (Houston, TX)

Collaboration is a word that has been buzzing in the school library world since 1988 when the American Association of School Librarians released *Information Power*, which marked a dramatic shift in the role of the librarian. Suddenly "teaching" and "collaboration" were part of the job. Until that time, "library skills" were taught randomly and often out of context with the curriculum. Students learned about how to physically locate information in their library because there were neither electronic resources nor an Internet, and student access to library materials was strictly defined by the four walls of the location and what print volumes were contained within them.

Initially, many librarians ignored teaching and collaboration because they just didn't know where to begin. To be sure, private school librarians were already recognized for their strong reading and enrichment programs and their efforts to engage students to become curious readers. However, there were few, if any, classes or seminars to assist this transition to teaching through collaboration and fewer practitioners who had already begun to do it. Many librarians hoped the concept of collaboration would just go away, but with every update of the standards, the role of librarian as teacher and collaborator was even more strongly emphasized. The latest guidelines, *Standards for the 21st-Century Learner* (AASL 2008), continue to articulate this responsibility.

NAIS Guidelines of Professional Practice for Librarians

At the heart of the independent school library program is a professionally trained librarian who

> One. As a member of the faculty, partners with teaching colleagues to integrate information, technology, and research skills into the curriculum.

Three. Teaches information-seeking, critical analysis of sources, citation methods, synthesis, and the ethical use of information, and is thus a strong resource to students, teachers, and the school.

Approved by NAIS in 2008

In 2008 private school librarians welcomed the *NAIS Guidelines of Professional Practice for Librarians* (see appendix A), which had as point 1 a professionally trained librarian who "as a member of the faculty, partners with teaching colleagues to integrate information, technology and research skills into the curriculum." Later, in point 3, the librarian is described as teaching "information-seeking, critical analysis of sources, citation methods, synthesis, and the ethical use of information, and is thus a strong resource to students, teachers, and the school." This clearly mandates collaborative work, as stated by the primary independent school accrediting group in the country. However, the core questions still remain for many independent school librarians: How do I collaborate on curriculum development with the classroom teachers? What standards or models do I use?

Making Collaboration Work

Several factors must be in place for successful collaboration to happen. Nothing is more important than the support of administrators. Some private school administrators are not aware of the roles that librarians now fulfill in teaching information literacy and research skills, so the librarian may need to provide documentation, such as the previously mentioned AASL standards or the NAIS guidelines. This can be the beginning of explaining the value that this work brings to an academic program. Value is the key point for an administrator, and it will take time and several meetings for the librarian to make his or her case with the head of school.

Documentation

In addition, parents have become more critical consumers when selecting private education for their children, so a strong program of instruction in the library takes on greater importance. Parents want to know whether their children will be taught to select and evaluate Internet resources. They are pleased when told there is a curriculum that allows their children access 24/7 to carefully selected electronic resources. And they are impressed to learn that the librarian teaches in collaboration with the content teachers to prepare their children for a complex, electronic world, as well as that students will be ready to use college and university resources when they have completed their high school career. These strengths are marketable points that the head, the Admissions Department and even the Department of Institutional Advancement can point to as distinguishing advantages in the selection of the right private school.

Value

The second essential element for successful collaboration is the librarian's knowledge of the curriculum. This knowledge is never completed and is constantly shifting, as curriculum does, but a librarian who knows when units are taught, understands the learning objectives that are required, and effectively communicates the value of information literacy in strengthening learning is a good partner in collaboration for a teacher. Although this does not guarantee

Knowledge

that every teacher will want to collaborate, it is well known that a successful collaboration is noticed in a school community and often leads to requests from other teachers for similar collaborative opportunities. In addition, private schools tend to have the advantage of libraries that are richer in both print and electronic resources than many public schools, so the librarian is likely to already have materials in the collection to support the collaboration.

Another essential requirement for creating a collaborative environment is having teachers who are open to partnering with librarians to create successful learning experiences. New teachers may be more willing to collaborate, possibly because they have had more exposure to technology that makes them flexible in using new methods to improve instruction. They know information literacy is essential for everything from student success to work

Partner

in their adult lives. But collaboration cannot be limited to new teachers. The advice most often given is to find teachers who are open to collaboration or have seen its positive effects. Some recommend that the librarian ask faculty friends to work on projects, stressing that sharing the load in the planning and teaching stages—perhaps even the evaluation stage—makes the job easier and learning richer. The assumption in all these recommendations is that the partnering of the librarian and teacher in collaboration has shown itself to be valuable to successful learning, as well as advancing the teaching of information literacy. Documentation of these successful partnerships—both through mapping (discussed later in this chapter) and through coverage in school publications, displays, or presentations—brings positive notice to good teaching on the part of both the teacher and the librarian, as well as highlighting collaboration.

Is collaboration easy? Does it happen quickly and simply? The true answer to these questions would have to be "no." Collaboration takes time, formalized training, careful building of faculty relationships, and continued efforts on the part of the librarian. It requires being open to new ideas and techniques for teaching information literacy and is based on the librarian's attendance at and participation in department meetings, grade level meetings, and even random conversations in the hall! There are librarians who have worked consistently to make collaboration succeed in their schools. How do they do it? Following are just a few strategies:

- **Offer updates of resources for established assignments**. Always look for electronic and print resources that would be useful for established assignments that could do with a bit of refreshing. Share them with the teacher(s) involved and offer to assist in teaching the students how to use the new material.

- **Meet with departments** and listen to their discussions for concerns and needs that you may be able to address. Share lists of everything from lists of pertinent, new books in the library to opportunities for using technology in their work. Offer your assistance in reaching student success. This develops trust and indicates that the librarian has knowledge of the curriculum, which can lead to growing collaboration(McGregor 2003).

- **Suggest journals and articles in the various academic disciplines** so that teachers can keep up in their fields. This is definitely a commitment of funds and time spent looking for the articles that engage you and the faculty in a learning-centered conversation that builds toward collaborative projects.

- **Offer the best resources you can find for each assignment**. If teachers request library time without having included you in project planning, ask them to share the assignment so that it can be reviewed to be sure it is designed for student success. Discuss resources that may be added to the assignment. What is more frustrating to the students—and the librarian—than when an assignment is impossible to complete because little information exists or it is based on an unrealistic expectation of what is accessible? Removing frustration from the process adds to collaborative success and strengthened learning.

- **Focus on one content area or one teacher** and present the teacher with the information literacy skills that need to be taught and would strengthen student work. This may take a year or two to stabilize. After a period of two years of collaboration between the librarian and the teacher, juniors at one private school are assigned a research paper that lasts from the beginning of school until February. Every student selects a topic, asks a question about that topic, and develops the answer using a variety of resources and techniques. Research skills are built into the grading rubric and require the students to show that they can use peer-reviewed journals, evaluate appropriate content, show ethical use of scholarly information, and make good use of supporting resources. When these students are seniors and working on their English research papers, they are more confident, start faster on their topics, and use their skill base to transition to a university library after exhausting the school's resources. Feedback from alumni indicates that they are ahead of other students in their university classes because they aren't intimidated by research and can do it well.

- **Keep the faculty informed** of major changes in citation formats and offer to teach their students how to ethically and accurately cite the resources used in research assignments. Assist teachers in transitioning to the next editions of the style manuals as they are released.

- **Schedule breaks and lunch** once or twice a week to coincide with those of the classroom teachers so that you can learn about their projects, what they are teaching, new techniques they are trying, etc., and offer resources and research techniques that could strengthen their students' learning.

Every independent school librarian will find other ways to uniquely serve the individual school, ways that address a specific mission but build on these core suggestions.

What Standards and Methods Should Be Used?

One of the big differences between private schools and public schools is that there is a tremendous amount of freedom and autonomy from standards. Private schools guard and value this freedom. It is thought to lead to greater learning, independent thinking, and stronger graduates. However, from the librarian's point of view, having standards to guide work isn't a bad thing and can actually be a key ingredient in helping the librarian successfully collaborate with teachers. Standards may lend more authority to the role. Needless to say, the least desirable way to teach research and information literacy would be to do so randomly, out of context, and in isolation, with no collaboration or mapping. Teaching this way leaves the students confused and unsure of exactly how to apply the information they have been taught, negating the work that the librarian has done. The following approaches are part of the spectrum of methods that librarians may employ to fulfill their responsibility for teaching information literacy skills. They begin (1) teaching from a scope and sequence, possibly created by the librarian who is working toward (2) teaching officially recognized proficiency-based standards but out of context with the curriculum and finally attaining the goal of (3) teaching proficiency-based standards in collaboration with individual teachers in the school.

In the first part of the spectrum, the librarian charts the research and information literacy skills as they are taught in the school. He or she usually bases the progression on the teachers'

> **Scope and Sequence**

curriculum. In independent schools, this library curriculum may or may not be tied to any state or national standards, but one of its values is that it provides documented evidence of the teaching that the librarian does to strengthen learning in the school community. The scope and sequence may be unique to the private school where it is created and, although it may be shared with other schools as an example, it rarely can be exactly duplicated because private school curriculums can be very unique. Drop in on any of the major independent school listservs, such as the Independent School Section listserv of AASL, and you will often see requests for sharing or feedback on the success of having a scope and sequence to chart when and how skills are taught. These samples are great places to start when you are beginning to create a scope and sequence.

Moving along the spectrum, a librarian begins the quest for a comprehensive library curriculum, which may include skills that are recommended by guidelines such as *Standards for the 21st Century Learner* or the *National Educational Technology Standards for Students* (ISTE 2007), without collaboration or documentation; the standards provide an overview of the final product, but a product that has not yet been tweaked to suit the librarian's campus mission. To be sure, they are

> **Standards**

important skills, such as learning to evaluate information from a variety of resources, or to ethically cite that information, but they are not taught in connection with assignments (i.e., no collaboration), because the librarian may not yet have won over the faculty and administration. Because the librarian is beginning wherever possible, the content may not be presented to an entire grade level; curricular documentation will then show that only some students were exposed to certain specific content or skills. Some students may completely miss the information, whereas others may meet it several times. This is an inefficient way to approach teaching research and information literacy. However, by beginning to teach without broad support for the full program, the librarian can point to specific student achievement to

> **Proficiency-Based Standards Taught out of Context**

support the need for a more complete program. Improved ability to locate information for the next assignment can lead a single teacher to see the advantages of the new approach, and this can build a bridge to a resistant administration. Without administrative leadership, the librarian must teach students in this scattershot way because there is no other way to even begin the process. Private schools that are struggling economically, have not committed to a full-time librarian, and have not been shown what a fully collaborative librarian can do, are often in the position of making choices that keep the librarian from being fully vested in the collaborative process. Are there librarians who don't care to collaborate and document?

Yes and, sadly, they short change both their school and their students, as well as reflecting badly on all school librarians. In addition, independent schools that have not committed to a full-time librarian, whether for financial or philosophical reasons, have made a choice that limits the librarian's participation in the academic program and ultimately limits the school's program potential.

The strongest section of the spectrum is where the librarian puts standards, whether AASL, ISTE, state, or others, in place and becomes a collaborative part of the instructional team, with the students reaping the rewards. This is when some really amazing learning takes place. Exposure to a wide range of electronic and print resources and new ways of showing knowledge, differentiated learning strategies—something that private schools are increasingly implementing—and other strategies can be customized to the assignment, resulting in work, whether traditional reports or digital films or blogs, showing some really exciting thinking on the part of students. Successful collaboration is a joy to behold, and administrators love to showcase the work to the community. There is only one piece lacking here, and that is mapping.

> **Proficiency-Based Standards Taught in Collaboration**

When proficiency-based standards are taught in collaboration and mapped via use of a curriculum mapping tool, a school has the ultimate prize of collaboration. Mapping is a methodology employed by a growing number of private schools. It has several strong benefits, among them reflecting proficiency-based standards integrated into content, tracking of information literacy skills, and visible documentation of the work of the librarian.

Mapping

A curriculum map is a visual picture of the subjects and skills taught during a school year. A curriculum map shows where you are with the curriculum, where you need to go, and how you will get there (Vlasis 2003). Most people who work on these maps will admit that they are not quickly done. Many will say that mapping is one of the hardest things they have ever done. However, there is nothing quite like the moment when the map reflects a visual expression of the work that the librarian has done in collaboration with teachers.

There are many products available for facilitating the process. All are Web based. The original mapping programs were expensive, but the benefits included making upgrades and improvements available to users while keeping the maps on the vendor's server. Now there are one or two open source programs on the Web, but they lack the stability and support, as well as the security, of a fee-based program.

A school begins by making decisions about how the map will be constructed. Generally there are several columns, but the number of (as many as eight or as few as four) and the headings for these columns are decided locally. The maps are not intended to be a duplication of a teacher's lesson plans, but rather to show the content, skills, and assessment that occur month by month in a classroom. Every faculty contributor has password access to his or her map, and it is not "shared" or "made public" until the administrators decide that it is ready, often after a period of three to four years of work by the teachers. Parents may then access a school's map and see each content area and what is being taught on each level. In private schools completed maps are a great opportunity to show parents of current students, as well as parents of potential students, exactly what the curriculum of the school covers and how it is taught.

The in-house value to the faculty is that overlaps become obvious. Repetitions of content as well as overlooked content also show up when the maps are shared in a department. This starts discussion about how to make the curriculum more efficient for the learners, a process known as "alignment."

For the librarian, this is a golden opportunity to show collaboration and how it strengthens the work of the students, as well as how information literacy skills such as evaluation, citation, and research techniques are taught in the school. In some schools the decision is made to chart the skills in both the information literacy and the content areas. The benefit is that the teaching done by the librarian is shown both independently as well as within the content map. Some teachers are not always open to having the skills shown on "their" pages, but doing so makes the work—and learning— stronger. Some schools only show the information literacy skills in the library section. And some schools, sadly, have chosen to not include the work of the librarian at all. In such a case, the librarian should work toward the goal of becoming a part of the mapping initiative by establishing a presence on the map.

What is the ultimate value of the work involved in mapping information literacy and research skills? First, the map shows that the school has accepted accountability for teaching its students the research skills that will equip them for life in the twenty-first century, such as locating, evaluating, and ethically using information, . These are the same needs that more and more parents ask about when they tour private schools. A school that provides this infrastructure of skills, preparation, and resources is ahead in the admissions choice. Second, mapping is a visible indication of the librarian's work, and the value that it brings to the students strengthens the role of librarian in the school as learning partner. Third, the community sees the work of teachers and librarians joined in mapping, which creates the expectation that collaboration is normal and will continue.

Questions Parents Ask When Touring School Libraries

- How do you teach my child to be a good Internet user?
- How do you get my child ready for work in a college environment?
- What are the resources that my child can access for academic work?
- Are these resources available to students 24/7?

Outcomes of Collaboration

There are numerous positive outcomes of collaboration and few, if any, pitfalls. It is known, for example, that student learning and fluency with multiple formats can be the result of collaboration, even for students as young as kindergarten. Digital presentations, using print and electronic resources to make new ways to organize and display data, and creating digital video are great examples of collaborative efforts that can work at any grade level in either public or private schools. However, in private schools there are greater possibilities for collaboration because the school structure is not tied to a public school model. Private schools can be more creative in their approach to learning and often have greater flexibility and stronger resources, whether through funding or staffing, to achieve deeper learning through nontraditional means. These outcomes include the following:

- **A more articulated role in the community for the librarian.** Old stereotypes fall away as the dynamic work of a fully collaborative professional becomes a normal part of the life of the school.

- **Strengthened visibility for the library itself and the programs it conducts.** Parents are delighted by the vitality that energizes libraries when programs reflect strong learning.

- **Inclusion of all collaborative work in the library's annual report, also presented to the head of school.** It shows visible work that is woven into the curriculum throughout the school.

- **Student success as they transition to college work.** With most private school students targeted for higher education, it is real value for them to be grounded in information literacy and research skills. Lack of preparedness for doing research is increasingly observed by college and university librarians as they struggle to instruct students who come to them without any skills. A recent report states that "research seems to be far more difficult to conduct in the digital age than it did in previous times" (Head and Eisenberg 2009).

- **Collaboration as a selling point for the admissions process.** Schools with a collaborative librarian in place have an admissions edge with prospective families because they clearly show the positive outcomes that flow from collaborative work.

- **Use by the offices of institutional advancement of the energy projected by the collaborative librarian as a marketing tool for fund-raising,** particularly when parents have seen the impact of collaboration on their students' work

- **Feedback from alumni indicating that their success at other schools and in college flowed from the research and information literacy skills they acquired at the private school.** One student reported that when she took her first film class at UCLA, she was the only member of her class who was familiar with electronic indexes, knew how to effectively use them to do research, and was ultimately asked by her professor to demonstrate how to use the resource.

Overcoming the Negatives

In preparation for this chapter, a request was sent to the ISS listserv (Weathers 2009) for responses to a series of questions. The results were limited, but rich in observation and insight. Some spoke of the frustration that came from the desire to do more collaboration in school environments that lacked a supportive administrator or willing faculty. Some responses were clearly from librarians who had succeeded and were enjoying every collaborative moment. Some were from librarians who were struggling with what collaboration meant in their schools. Following are both thoughts from the respondents and ideas, based on observation, formed from studying the responses. This is definitely an area where fuller study is needed in private schools.

- Few of the librarians who sent comments used the word *teach*, instead using terms like *talk*, *show*, and *demonstrate*. This is undoubtedly modesty about their work, but it is essential to own the word "teach," because that is what is being done. Students are taught to find information, taught to use technology, taught to be alert for bias and to avoid the unethical use of information. These are critical skills in today's world. Respect for the contributions of librarians to collaboration is based on the assumption that they are teachers. Language is important.

Teach

- Instead of words like *enrich* or"*support*, why not use *strengthen*? The implication of the first two words does not exude the vitality of "strengthen." This comes back to the issue of value and the fact that the collaboration of the librarian, done well, adds tremendous strength to learning.

Strengthen

- Don't say *library* project or even *library skills*. The limits of four library walls no longer exist, so it is important to name the work for what it is: *history research* or *English research* or *information literacy*. The scope of the work is far broader than it once was.

Information Literacy

- Time has become a huge issue in private schools. It seems there is less and less of it, with ever-expanding activities to be fitted into the academic schedule. Often teachers react with horror at the thought that a whole class period will have to be used to integrate research into their collaborative assignments. Offer to go to the classroom to emphasize the importance of this time investment, perhaps only part of a class period, for the strengthening of student research skills and efficiency, and ultimately for stronger content learning. If a teacher says he or she will teach the students about resources to save time, find a way to make clear that you are prepared to teach it and can do it more efficiently and quickly because this is your content area. No teacher knows as much about resources as you do, and your contribution of expanded content extends the impact of the lesson without additional work on the teacher's part.

Time

- Attend curriculum meetings, grade level meetings, and any other situation in which teachers are talking about planning or content changes. Volunteer for curriculum committees. Use every conversation, no matter how informal, to interest teachers in resources or strategies for their students. The librarian often knows the curriculum better than anyone else on the faculty. Use this knowledge to offer assistance through planning and collaboration. And don't be satisfied with "pulling books off the shelves"; that is not collaboration.

Curriculum Committees

- It is often repeated but still very true: do one collaborative project with a willing teacher and market it as an example of what you can do. David Loertscher, a well-known figure

| Marketing |

in creating the concept of collaborative work, has said that a librarian cannot do more than three really good collaborative projects a semester. As one respondent to the listserv questions said, "Start small and build" (McLean 2009). Each year, plan to build more collaborative work, venturing into working with teachers whom you may not know well or who have previously seemed uninterested in anything collaborative. These collaborations are meant to build and change with passing years; change is the nature of curriculum collaboration over time.

- Think out of the box about who might collaborate in your school. Teachers of English and social studies are not the only possibilities. Responses to the questions on the

| Outside the Box |

ISS listserv included projects in biology, foreign languages, spirituality, health, math, drama, and more.

- Library Web pages are an ideal place to post descriptions of collaborative work—preferably with pictures—in addition to electronic resources (hopefully with universal electronic passwords for your users), citation guides that your students will need, pathfinders for specific assignments, access to e-books and the electronic catalog, area university catalogs, library blogs,

| Library Web Pages |

librarian contact information, and anything else that will be helpful to student work.

- Moodle-based course management programs, such as Remote Learner, offer librarians a great opportunity for collaborating with teachers to post assignment-specific resources, Web sites, electronic resources, etc., through links on both the teachers' pages (a new form of collaboration) as well as the librarian's page. As this new area develops, it may even surpass the library Web page for creating a highly

| Remote Learners |

functional work space in which students have a specific collection of research tools and Web sites for their work. A school that implements this type of program is able to continue instruction when hit by flu outbreaks, hurricanes, or other disasters, thereby minimizing lost time in the classroom and continuing the program.

- Use surveys for both faculty and students to evaluate the effectiveness of instruction and resources. In addition to surveys, one ISS posting cited "listening to students talking about

| Surveys |

resources they are using and then matching those demands up to projects and assignments."

Conclusion

It should be very clear that collaboration takes constant, sustained work on the part of the librarian. It should also be acknowledged that it takes a lot of effort on the part of teachers who may not be accustomed to collaborating. Collaboration is the goal of a spectrum of change that begins with the "old school" methodology of library skills and progresses through coordination with the classroom teacher to actual collaboration that imbeds the information literacy in the core curricula. Every respondent to the ISS listserv survey said the same thing: the work is valued for what it gives to students to carry forward in academics, as well as "everyday life research." To collaborate brings strength and vitality to the work of the librarian, as well as to the role of the library in the private school.

References

American Association of School Librarians (AASL). n.d. *Independent Schools Section.* American Library Association Available at www.ala.org/ala/mgrps/divs/aasl/aboutaasl/aaslcommunity. Accessed October 2, 2009.

———. 1988. *Information Power: Guidelines for School Library Media Programs.* Chicago: American Library Association.

———. 2008. *Standards for the 21st-Century Learner.* Chicago: American Library Association.

Head, Alison J., and Michael B. Eisenberg. 2009. *Finding Context: What Today's College Students Say about Conducting Research in the Digital Age.* Washington, D.C.: Project Information Literacy Progress Report.

International Society for Technology in Education. 2007. *National Educational Technology Standards for Students.* 2nd ed.Washington, DC: ISTE.

McGregor, Joy. 2003. "Collaboration and Leadership." In *Curriculum Connections Through the Library.* Ed. Barbara K. Stripling and Sandra Hughes-Hassell, 199–219. Westport, CT: Libraries Unlimited.

McLean, C. D. 2009. E-mail to author, May 13.

National Association of Independent Schools. 2008. *NAIS Guidelines of Professional Practice for Librarians.* Available at www.nais.org/seriesdocPrint. Accessed December 12, 2008.

Scudder, Judy. 2009. E-mail to author, May 13.

Vlasis, Charlotte C. 2003. "Librarian Morphs into Curriculum Director." In *Curriculum Connections Trough the Library.* Ed. Barbara K. Stripling and Sandra Hughes-Hassell, 107–17. Westport, CT: Libraries Unlimited.

Weathers, Barbara. 2009. E-mail questionnaire to Independent School Listserv, May 13.

Visit http://lu.com/excellence for supporting links and occasional updates to all essays in this book.

Barbara Weathers has been active in private school libraries for most of her career as well as having served as a university adjunct professor for many years. She has been elected to positions in the American Association of School Librarians, the Texas Library Association, the Houston Area Independent School Librarian Network, the Catholic Library Association, and the Network of Sacred Heart Schools. She has been a presenter in the field for many groups, including the National Association of Independent Schools, and has been active as an editorial advisor, contributor, and writer of articles. She is currently the Upper School Librarian at Duchesne Academy in Houston, Texas (www.duchesne.org).

Are They Ready for the Next Step? Bridging High School to College

Martha Daly, Connelly School of the Holy Child (Potomac, MD)

A quick look at mission statements found on independent school Web sites reveals certain phrases repeated, including "preparing students for the twenty-first century" or for "lifelong learning." Ask any school librarian to tell you how integral the library's role is in fulfilling the mission of the school. Buzz words of most educational trends in the last thirty years, such as critical thinking, affective learning, problem-based learning, and even time management, are concepts that have been part of the library information skills program all along. So the library's mission is inextricably linked to the school's mission. How are we doing? Are we succeeding in preparing our students for the next stage of learning? How will we know if we are succeeding? The assumption, even if it is not specifically noted in the school's name, is that students are being prepared for college, where their education will continue. Let us consider the standards and practices of high school libraries, the skills needed for college as perceived by college librarians and professors, and what we can do to close any gap identified between high school and college information literacy skills. We know we can make our students college *eligible*, but our goal is to make them college *ready* with skills they will need to succeed.

> *Are we succeeding in preparing our students for the next stage of learning?*

Information Literacy Defined

As with any educational practice, the term used to describe that practice is subject to change as people continue to refine its meaning and scope. What was once called "research skills" morphed into information literacy skills, media literacy skills, digital literacy, and "Information Communications Technology" (ICT) (Allen 2007, 19). ICT seems to be the most recent and encompassing of the terms. However, for the purposes of this essay, the term *information literacy* is used to describe all of the facets covered in most high school programs. The American Library Association defines information literacy as being able to recognize that information is needed and be able to locate, evaluate, and use effectively the needed information (ACRL 2000, Information Literacy Standards 1–3). In practice most librarians have expanded this basic definition, either with the help of standards such as AASL/AECT, or through common sense, to include all of the subskills needed to achieve information literacy.

Standards

There are a number of recognized standards for information literacy. The American Association of School Librarians and the Association for Educational Communications and Technology developed "Information Literacy Standards for Student Learning" in 1998. The Association of College and Research Libraries developed its guidelines, *Information Literacy Competency Standards for Higher Education*, in 2000. Both documents address the skills needed to be a responsible and effective information consumer and producer. Each set of standards has its strengths, but both are important in that they are mutually complementary and scaffolded to support the goal of independent learning and thinking. Taken together, there is a continuum of operational and thinking skills that cover students from kindergarten through college. It is fairly easy to parallel both of these standards' core competencies. Ellysa Cahoy maps the ACRL standards relative to AASL standards and enjoins us to "consider reading them consecutively to confirm or clarify the presence of certain skills within your curriculum" (2002, 14).

AASL/AECT and ACRL standards were written primarily for the library audience. The standards combine aspects of traditional library literacy, including research methods, with technology. AASL/AECT's "Information Literacy for Student Learning" details three categories of standards: information literacy, independent learning, and social responsibility (1998, 1). ACRL's *Information Literacy Competency Standards for Higher Education* are self-described as "an intellectual framework for understanding, finding, evaluating and using information" with the goal of enabling learners "to master content and extend their investigations, become more self-directed, and assume greater control over their learning" (2000, 2).

Reports from educational organizations, like the North Central Regional Educational Laboratory publication *Engage 21st Century Skills: Literacy in a Digital Age* (2003) and "Understanding University Success" (a report sponsored by the Association of American Universities and The Pew Charitable Trusts), inform practitioners of user skills and attitudes for a broader audience and perspective. A close look at documents of this nature reveals their essential content to be similar to the *Standards for the 21st-Century Learner*. These new AASL standards encompass the skills associated with successful learning but go well beyond by including "the disposition to use those skills, along with an understanding" of student responsibilities and self-assessment strategies (2007, 1).

Many of the reports and publications are organized by discipline and make no mention of the broad term "information literacy," let alone the library, but when reviewed by a librarian, these standards correlate closely with the skills taught and competencies sought in any library curricula. The fact that this correlation exists can be viewed positively or negatively. The close correlation is a reminder of the reason and benefits of collaboration.

Librarians need to advocate for teaching the concepts and skills they are expertly qualified to teach, mainly because those skills and concepts are being written into curricula for specific disciplines like English, social studies, and science. In reality, most high school librarians receive time for direct group instruction mainly through a collaborative project with a core teacher. Although the teacher and librarian help each other achieve educational goals on individual projects, the wholesale commitment by a school to this type of integration is what will produce the results called for by the standards and other educational studies and reports. Again, librarians must be proactive in promoting their expertise and in collaborating. The twenty-first-century citizen must be equipped with the skills, attitudes, and practices of an independent learner. Susan Allen sums it up: "The definition of information literacy has expanded beyond technical and toolset skills to performance for understanding. To succeed in college, career, and the twenty-first century life, students need to be information savvy, not tech-savvy. Information literacy is a curricular initiative, not a library or technology initiative . . . many goods schools continue to focus too narrowly on technical skills and research skills. Teaching students to think should be the ultimate goal of the twenty-first century" (2007, 24).

"Information literacy is not a school task but a lifetime habit of mind."
—Abilock (2004)

The Technology Piece

Where does this leave the other core set of competencies expected of the literate adult? Technology has grown as exponentially as the availability of information; in some ways there is a symbiotic relationship. Technology fluency is an explicit outcome of ACRL standards two through five. The AASL standards state that, "Today's students need to develop information skills that will enable them to use technology as an important tool for learning both now and in the future" (2007, 1). Technology skills are interwoven into the skills section of each standard. Librarians acknowledge the role of technology in accessing and producing information and often are the expert users of educational technology in the building. The standards, which make collaborating with classroom teachers so important, exist for technology too. The new National Educational Technology Standards are conceptually similar to the AASL standards. Although it is comforting to know that the standards are becoming more aligned, in some schools technology literacy and information literacy are allowed to date, but not get married. Warning lights should be going off if this is happening. As Allen comments, "its coordination with the curriculum is both necessary and possible" (2007, 24). Viewing technology literacy and information literacy independently is a situation that needs to change, as collaboration through the whole information literacy process, across all disciplines, is essential to its success.

[C]ollaboration through the whole information literacy process, across all disciplines, is essential to its success.

However, there are two pitfalls that must be considered when merging technology literacy and information literacy into the general curriculum. Most educators rightly consider technology, and its effective use, as tools for learning. Developing skill with technology use is secondary to what it can do to enhance learning. Weis comments that "while some states use *NETS for Students* as models for developing technology integration standards, more often they use these standards to focus on acquiring and developing skills using technology tools rather than using tools to acquire learning skills" (2004, 13). The updated NETS standards promote learning as a primary goal with technology skill as a by-product of that goal. Assuming that students are technologically literate because they are constant users of multiple technologies is another trap. Allen points out that "the assumption among many high school teachers is that technology skills are purely technical, while, in fact, using technology tools to analyze and understand information more deeply is the defining skill of ICT literacy" (2007, 23). In Allen's study students had trouble locating relevant pages on a Web site, judging the usefulness or sufficiency of information, considering the audience in a presentation, judging the authority of materials, and using an academic database. The casual observer might see students navigating through the resources and assume more competence than is warranted. The ability to access information is just the initial skill in the spectrum of information literacy. Today students can be "successful" even when they haven't mastered the skills necessary to be truly information literate, because the law of averages is in their favor. Usually, with a little persistence even a mediocre search will produce something that can be used, but finding information by luck or settling for any information that remotely satisfies the information need should not be classified as efficient or effective use of information.

> *Assuming that students are technologically literate because they are constant users of multiple technologies is another trap.*

Attitudinal Skills

Librarians understand intuitively how important it is for students to feel comfortable in their surroundings. They try to strike a balance in providing an atmosphere that allows study, encourages exploration, and values new ideas. Librarians know that when the library is perceived as intimidating, students will feel uncomfortable using its resources. One of the most important roles of a librarian can be helping the student make the progression from anxiety to self-confidence and satisfaction. These affective responses to the information search process were first identified and explained by Carol Kuhlthau in *Seeking Meaning* (2003). Other affective factors, including Costa and Kallick's "16 Habits of Mind" (2000), can provide a framework for developing and evaluating a library's environment.

Librarians who have established a relationship with students and a student-acknowledged purpose for the library as it relates to students' needs and interests will be better positioned to help students smoothly make the transition from uncertainty to satisfaction in the research process. In 1986 Constance Mellon coined the term "library anxiety." In describing Mellon's study, Ellysa Cahoy said, "In her study she found 75 to 85 percent of the surveyed college students used words like 'scary, overpowering, lost, helpless and confused' to describe the way they felt in the library" (2004, 26). Citing this information from 1986 is important for two purposes. First, the phenomenal changes that have occurred in the amount of and access to information can only accentuate the feelings described by students more than twenty years ago. Second, it literally demands a personal update on our part. To be sure, library anxiety still exists, but how prevalent is it in our own schools, and are there practices that have or can be taken to make this less of an issue for students? Individually, do we know what students think of the library?

Esch and Crawford state that "university libraries report that the two questions most often asked are 'Where is the bathroom?' and 'How do I print my paper?'" (2006, 22). High school librarians have to work to assure that students feel comfortable enough and practiced enough to ask more meaningful questions of the librarian in any setting. If students do not feel comfortable in the library or do not get sufficient practice in using the library in high school, it is a stretch to assume that they will do so at the college level. If the Internet is the "new library" for many students, librarians have to help students understand how the quality resources provided by libraries can be accessed 24/7 through the school's library Web site or a local public library. Other services like "ask a librarian" or pathfinders pointing students to invisible-Web resources need to be part of the student's vocabulary. Knowing when and how to ask a question is a vital skill given that today's students often prefer to work outside of the physical library. Froudy's 2006 study suggests that "while students are likely to begin academic research with their campus library's online databases, they are not likely to connect those resources with the physical library or librarians. That is, they will probably turn to the library resources first when doing research, but they will only ask a librarian a question as a very last resort, and it usually never occurs to them to do so" (quoted in Byerly, Downey, and Ramin 2006, 593).

> *High school librarians have to work to assure that students feel comfortable enough . . . to ask meaningful questions of [any] librarian.*

Today's Library User

Many studies have been published that give us a snapshot of how our students, the NextGen generation, process and use information. OCLC conducted a study and published *Perceptions of Libraries and Information Resources* in 2005. A subset of the data gathered in that study was compiled into the section "College Students' Perceptions of Libraries and Information Resources." The report findings are striking. Despite librarians' attempts to dissuade students from using the free Web as a first source of information, the study found that 89 percent of the students begin their research using a search engine, with only 2 percent responding that they begin their search on the library Web site (OCLC 2005, 6-2). What does this say for the electronic resources provided for the students by the library? It is particularly sobering to consider the efficacy of these resources when the study also reports that the students are well aware that the library is "wired" and that both high school and college students use the library regularly to access the Internet. The study reports that college students are more likely to use the library and more aware of the resources that can be found there than is the general public. Yet even with the students' fairly consistent information need, "libraries are not seen as the top choice for access to electronic resources, even among college students who have the highest level of awareness of those resources." Libraries are predominantly identified with books and as a place to do homework (OCLC 2005, 6-3).

"By the time a student graduates from high school, his research habits—for better or for worse—are often ingrained."
—Evan St. Lifer, editorial in *SLJ*, quoted in Morriston (n.d.)

Most students do not differentiate between the quality and trustworthiness of the content on the free Web and the resources offered at the library. Despite teaching students to be critical users by evaluating information and its source, students trust the information they get from libraries and search engines equally. This generation has been raised in a self-serve, self-reliant culture, and their actions reflect that. More than half of the students responded that they do not request assistance when using either a physical or virtual library. Most adults know that, in certain areas of commerce, customers must request help from the staff to get the items for use or purchase. Asking for help is not a foreign concept to anyone born before the advent of big-box stores or discount warehouses. Some of the best merchandise was in the "back" or "behind the counter." Older users of the library have had the benefit of searching for "just the right" item under both systems. Today's student does not have the same experience and needs to be shown or invited to ask for personal help when what he or she is searching for is not found.

The most frequent response about their method of judging the trustworthiness of information was relying on "common sense and personal knowledge" (OCLC 2005, 6-4). In a recent article James Rettig notes that college "librarians also observe students' lack of knowledge and skills they need to succeed, in particular their lack of information-retrieval and information-evaluation skills" (2009, 1). This does not speak well for high school librarians' efforts to help students learn to choose the type of resource to use and then evaluate the information they find. If the information literacy message is right, then what inference can be drawn from the results reported in the OCLC study? Students use the unexamined Internet because it is fast, it is available when and where they want to use it, and they believe it provides "better quantity and quality than librarian-assisted searching" (OCLC 2005, 6-4). This fits with the way they live and the way they have learned to learn. These are habits of this generation of learners, and habits are very difficult to break. The question then becomes, what can be done to convince students to use the library for the information goldmine that it is? How do libraries become a seamless part of the information process for your student users? Achieving this requires a two-prong strategy of learning more about our users' habits and working collaboratively with teachers to make information literacy skills, processes, and attitudes habit-forming. Excellent articles abound on the habits, lifestyles, and mindsets of the NextGens. One such article, "Born with the Chip," identifies nine aspects of NextGens' behavior that differentiate them from earlier generations of library users. NextGens are format agnostic, nomadic, multitasking, experiential, collaborative, integrated, principled, adaptive and direct (Abram and Luther 2004). Information literacy lessons should be run through a filter of these behaviors to address the relevance of the lesson to the student. This list is by no means the only source, but it is an interesting description of this generation of library users. Whether through professional literature or conference attendance, librarians must become knowledgeable and focused on the users' learning traits and behaviors. It is not enough for librarians to note a change in learning behaviors of their students; they must thoroughly

[W]hat can be done to convince students to use the library for the information goldmine that it is?

understand the attitudes and traits of their students. That will lead libraries and librarians to provide instruction and systems of information delivery that make sense to the students, who are expected to be information and communication literate for the twenty-first century.

Constant evaluation is the key. Librarians need to evaluate their knowledge of the users and the many systems of delivery for information and instruction. If information is power, librarians and libraries need to be seen as powerful. The insight gleaned from evaluation is not only imperative for information literacy instruction, but as a master of the schools' curriculum and the schools' chief curriculum collaborator, librarians must bring this knowledge into every collaboration and discussion they have. It is also important for the librarian to ensure that instruction is happening when and where it is most appropriate. Informal evaluation

> [E]valuation is the key. . . . What librarian has time to spend on instruction or projects that are only marginally effective?

of lessons or collaborative research projects addresses the effectiveness of the sessions and helps to coordinate the sequence and scaffolding of these experiences. Evaluations take time, but it is time well spent when you take into consideration the time and effort expended in organizing and delivering instruction. What librarian has time to spend on instruction or projects that are only marginally effective? Not only are the demands on a school librarian's time substantial, but time allotted for research instruction by the classroom teacher has often been hard won.

What has worked in the past will not always work in the future. Students, information, and delivery systems are changing at a dizzying speed. Ongoing evaluation is vital, and the one evaluation that librarians should not put off is that by the end user. It can be as simple as having a teacher give you a copy of students' bibliographies after the completion of a research project, with their opinions noted as to the most helpful resources found and their most difficult-to-find information needs. Sending short Web-based surveys is also very effective and allows you to target specific individuals, groups, and segments of the process. This is another way of conveying to the students the "service" nature of the library and your desire to make it excellent in every way.

Without question, librarians must assess whether the skills and attitudes necessary for college success are reaching the students they do not regularly see in the library. Librarians are in a position to see how information literacy is being realized across the curriculum and raise the alarm if certain segments of the student population slip through the cracks.

The Academic Perspective

In any situation knowing, where you are presently is as important as knowing where you want to go. School systems and individual teachers expend time and effort developing, following, and refining the scope and sequence of curricula or curriculum maps.[1] It is an agreed upon principle that this natural progression of knowledge and skills affords the best hope of mastering a subject area or reaching a goal. Although its component attributes are addressed in many disciplines, reaching the goal of information literacy follows the same roadmap for success. As practitioners at the high school level, where we are should be known to us. Where is it that we need to go?

The College Freshman

There are, of course, suggestions for what college freshmen should know before they come to school. It is beneficial to first look at how the work of college students might vary from that of high school students. "In their first semester they must read reams of difficult text, take comprehensive exams that require analysis not covered in the class, and write papers that synthesize ideas from multiple resources" (Fitzgerald 2004, 19). Terms like *read, understand, analyze,* and *synthesize* are part of the library and information literacy vocabulary. A good number of independent high schools are preparing their students for college, offering honors and advanced placement courses that presumably mirror the tasks expected of a first-year college student. The courses offered in high school should promote daily practice of reading, writing, critical thinking, and habits of mind necessary for college. It would be a mistake to assume that all students have mastered these skills, and a bigger mistake to assume that all high school classes present students with opportunities to practice these skills.

"In their first semester they must read reams of difficult text, take comprehensive exams that require analysis not covered in the class, and write papers that synthesize ideas from multiple resources."

The biggest change between high school and college may be the degree to which all of the skills students have been practicing in discrete environments will be integrated. In addition, assignments often will not come with detailed instructions, requiring students to apply what they know and to be able to ask for clarification when they are uncertain. The synthesis of textbooks, lectures, class readings, and the students' own ideas will be their task and may not be mediated in a class discussion (Esch and Crawford 2006, 23). The ability to synthesize must extend to integrating prior knowledge and experience with new information (*Academic Literacy* 2002, 16). There will be an expectation on the professor's part that sources for everything will be evaluated and that students will be able to defend their choices as well as properly cite sources used (Esch and Crawford 2006, 23).

It is a fairly well established idea that teenagers and college-age adults tend to feel invincible. They take risks and do not see dangers that are apparent to others. There is a technology corollary to that idea. Technology can make a student feel overconfident in his or her ability to find information. Students can and do accept "dangerous" information without scrutiny and find themselves with products that lack academic rigor. This may be a librarian's most challenging task: to take students who feel confident, but lack all the literacy skills to be discerning, and help them see value in spending the time to be cautious and scholarly in their approach to research. Achieving a balance between blind confidence and caution is not easy. Push too hard, and the student may think it is easier to avoid the library and stay with the more familiar realm of the Internet, which does not challenge his or her assumptions (Fitzgerald 2004, 21).

Technology can make a student feel overconfident in his or her ability to find information.

Assignments may differ in college. Homework may be assigned but not collected; required class readings may never be discussed. Students may be assigned more annotated bibliographies, presentations, and research proposals. Assignments often will have a short turnaround time. Students will find the sheer quantity of writing assignments, class readings, and research requirements a departure from high school, where the workload is often managed for the students. For example, a high school may have a policy about not assigning long-term projects over school holidays, faculty members may agree to limit the number of tests a students can have on one day, or consideration may be given for major school events such as a school play or sport tournament. Workload management is rarely practiced in college. The types of assignments and the independent nature of some of the college work suggest a set of expected skills for the incoming freshman. Many independent schools have adopted class work and structure similar to that of colleges, but each independent school librarian must judge that individually. Some schools may apply "college" standards to only a small portion of the student body. How are the remaining students prepared for the transition?

Preparing the student who has been in a mostly structured environment for the independent work required in college is a task that did not just start with this generation or because of recent changes in society. Consider the following: "In 1983, Dr. Edward Bloustein, then president of Rutgers University, in his 'President's Statement on Pre-College Preparation,' stated that 'nationwide, too many graduates are coming to college inadequately prepared for college level study'" (quoted in Goodin 1991). This quote appears in an article that expands on students' lack of the necessary preparation by noting more specifically that students are ill-prepared to make effective use of an academic library. More than twenty-five years have passed, and the problem persists.

Faculty Perspective and Expectations

The standards for both high school and college exist, but what does the practitioner at the college level see? The following comments from *Academic Literacy*, a report from California's public colleges and universities, are reminders that vigilance is necessary if we are to prepare students for college. Narrative comments include the following:

> "[S]tudents are more diligent than in the past, but less able to tackle difficult questions, and much less curious."

> "[S]tudents today seem unwilling to engage in the hard work of thinking, analyzing, unless it is directed to their most immediate interests."

> "[Students]overemphasize the skill dimension of the discipline and ignore the communication dimension."

> "[T]hey do not know how to seek help." (2002, 14)

The report continues: "83% of faculty say that lack of analytical reading skills contributes to students' lack of success in a course" and "only one third of entering college students are sufficiently prepared for the two most frequently assigned writing tasks: analyzing information or arguments and synthesizing information from several sources" (2002, 4).

Jean Donham sums up the thoughts of many when she notes that students should "be able to focus on a topic, compose a thesis statement, support an argument, evaluate sources of information and develop a cohesive research paper into which they integrate information that they have found" (2003, 32). Many small steps are required to make that happen, and numerous authors have cited the more discrete skills or competencies that students would be well-served to have as they enter college. Most high school and college librarians would agree on a similar list. A list generated at a workshop on transition to college research at George Washington University (Nutefall et al. 2004) does not differ significantly from the list in figure 12.1.

- Recognize the difference between popular and scholarly material.
- Know what libraries provide for free.
- Understand citations: the types and their use.
- Know what constitutes plagiarism.
- Acknowledge that copyright laws apply to everyone and everything unless explicitly stated otherwise.
- Differentiate between what is common knowledge and intellectual property.
- Discern when to paraphrase and when to quote.
- Know what a reference source is.
- Understand topic development, including narrowing a topic.
- Understand the function of a reference librarian.
- Know where to look for help online.
- Use a subject specific encyclopedia to begin research.
- Ask intelligent questions.
- Bring a copy of the assignment to the library.
- Understand your choice of sources and be ready to defend your choice.
- Make critical distinctions between key points and illustrative examples (in reading, writing, and listening).
- Comprehend instructions and communicate academic needs by seeking help, requesting clarification, and asking questions.
- Distinguish fact from fiction in online and print resources.
- Know the significance of domain names.
- Practice effective development of search strategies (search terms and structure).
- Develop evaluation skills for Internet use.
- Differentiate between the Internet and databases.
- Understand the difference between aggregated and edited databases.
- Know the difference between search engines and directories.
- Use and understand what constitutes a primary source vs. a secondary source.
- Understand the role of advertising on the Web.
- Know the value and purpose of indexes and bibliographies.
- Understand concepts and practice time management.
- Understand how search engines work and apply intelligent search methods.
- Use technology tools to communicate and collaborate efficiently (RSS, blogs, application-based visual programs, bulletin boards, etc.).

Figure 12.1. Essential Skills.

Reading is repeatedly identified as a most significant factor in the success of students in their college classes. Three fundamental reading competencies prove essential: reading for literal comprehension and retention; reading for depth of understanding; and reading for analysis, and interaction with the text (*Academic Literacy* 2002, 17). Librarians, particularly at the high school level, can be school leaders in monitoring how practice in those skills is being accomplished across the curriculum. At a bare minimum, librarians need to be certain that they keep the reading competencies in mind as they construct curricula and give as much attention to understanding information as to finding it.

What do we want students to know besides the list of skills in the standards? Constance Mellon, the author of a landmark qualitative research study on students' attitudes to library research, provides the following list (quoted in Goodin 1991).

1. An understanding of the intrinsic role of library research in undergraduate education

2. A sense of benefit to result from effective library use

3. The development of an attitude of library competence in the student

4. An appreciation of the reference librarian's professional role and the complexity of academic libraries

5. An understanding of library research as challenging rather than frustrating

6. A redefinition of library success as competence in research processes rather than as number of items retrieved

Librarians "get it." They get the library: its value, its personal and collective power, its ability to change and shape ideas and lives. Any librarian feeling that she or he had succeeded in accomplishing Mellon's list with students could rightly be satisfied. The understanding of a library's value and the transferability of that knowledge to all aspects of a student's life is profound.

Survey of High School Librarians

In a recent online survey,[2] independent school librarians were provided with a list of skills. They were asked to decide which skills they thought they covered in high school and in a second question which of those same skills are essential for college success. The statistical results are shown in table 12.1.

As shown in table 12.1, high school librarians taught the skills that they thought would be essential for college research in 50 percent of the topics listed. For those topics for which there was not a strong correlation between what librarians felt were essential skills and what they taught, individual respondents wrote in the *comments* field of the survey that those skills are classified as part of the research process and taught by the English department in their schools. One of the flaws of this survey was not providing for a response where participants could have indicated that a particular skill was taught at the high school, just not necessarily as part of any library instruction. The number of comments indicating that the research process was being taught, albeit not solely by the librarian, removes most of the anomalies shown and allows a generalization to be made: high school librarians feel that the skills essential for college freshmen are being taught at their high school. If the skills are included in the high school course of study, why do colleges feel that students are coming to college ill-prepared?

Table 12.1. Survey Results on Skills: What Topics HS Librarians Cover in School and What Topics Are Essential for College

Topics	HS	College	Difference
Bibliographic citation format	92.2%	82.9%	9.3%
When/where to cite	74.4%	89.1%	14.7%
Academic integrity	83.7%	96.1%	12.4%
Paraphrasing	51.2%	79.8%	28.6%
Main idea	30.2%	64.3%	34.1%
Broaden/narrow search	81.4%	83.7%	2.3%
Database versus "free" Web	92.2%	92.2%	0.0%
Journal versus magazine	72.9%	76.0%	3.1%
Primary versus secondary source	81.4%	81.4%	0.0%
Subject versus keyword search	74.4%	75.2%	0.8%
Fact versus opinion	52.7%	79.1%	26.4%
Types and use of print resources	77.5%	78.3%	0.8%
How to use a catalog/OPAC	90.7%	88.4%	2.3%
Library classification (Dewey/LC)	55.0%	55.0%	0.0%
Evaluate resources	90.7%	93.8%	3.1%
Define information need	58.1%	82.2%	24.1%
Identify possible sources	72.1%	81.4%	9.3%
Prepare search strategies	66.7%	82.9%	16.2%
Boolean and proximity searching	58.1%	69.8%	11.7%
Research process	79.1%	93.0%	13.9%
Note taking	34.9%	72.1%	37.2%
Formulate topic/thesis	40.3%	74.4%	34.1%

Several possible answers to why students are not exhibiting the skills taught in high school come to mind:

1. Students don't think it is important and therefore don't make the effort to learn the skills.

2. Students recognize the concepts, but haven't mastered them, which would allow a transfer to new situations.

3. Skills are not taught in a coordinated manner, which prevents practice and ensures mastery.

4. Students experience a larger "college anxiety" along with "library anxiety," which makes them less effective in putting the skills they do have to good use.

5. Some students are not receiving the instruction, whether due to lack of an established framework for instruction or simply because the students are falling through the cracks.

The answer may be one of the possibilities mentioned above or some reason specific to the school's situation, but the most important issue is to discover what the reason or reasons are and work to correct the situation. The survey results, while lacking statistical rigor, do hint that there are inconsistencies in how the skills are being taught. Considering Einstein's definition of insanity, doing the same thing over and over again and expecting different results, it would be prudent for every librarian to take stock of the situation at his or her school. Identify a scope and sequence for the skills considered essential for college success. Use the widest possible definition of skills, including reading, research, critical thinking, habits of mind, and technology related to access and presentation. Determine who is responsible for the presentation of these skills. Collaborate and work to build in redundancy, practice, and application across the curriculum. Evaluate, adapt, experiment. Sound the alarm if too many roadblocks are put in the way.

Included in the survey were the librarians' responses to several questions aimed at gauging how high school librarians are collaborating with their counterparts in academic libraries. Forty-five percent of the respondents have attended a workshop on student transition from high school to college. Table 12.2 shows who sponsored the workshops that the librarians attended. It is interesting to note that only seven respondents answered that they attended a workshop sponsored by a local high school or school district.

Table 12.2. Sponsorship of Workshops

If you have attended a workshop on students transitioning from high school to college, was the workshop sponsored by

Answer Options	Response Percent	Response Count
a local college or university	33.9%	20
a local high school or school district	11.9%	7
a local professional organization	37.3%	22
a national or state professional organization	40.7%	24
other	5.1%	3

Forty percent of the survey respondents said they had contact information for a local college librarian who worked predominantly with freshmen. The percentage may have been higher if the word "local" had been dropped from the question. The librarians who have contacted college librarians have been almost twice as likely to discuss college expectations as they have been to actively engage the college librarians in an interaction with high school students. The comments indicate that some successful partnerships have been established. A number of schools are acquainting their students with college resources by establishing borrowing privileges with a local college or university. In addition, some high school librarians are arranging college research visits for senior or AP students where the college librarian is involved in their research process. Several librarians spoke about hosting a college librarian at their schools, again an effective way to give high school students a college perspective. Another good example of librarians' resourcefulness was the comment submitted in the survey by the librarian who observed college freshmen receiving library instruction for a class in the social sciences. Making choices based on your school's situation is the most practical approach, and taking the initiative in developing a partnership is empowering.

The survey attempted to sample whether simple measures had been taken to expose high school students to college libraries and resources with two questions: "Do you provide a link to college catalog Web sites on your Web site?" and "Do you provide information for your students on borrowing policies, hours of operation, and resources of local colleges?" Approximately 47 percent of the respondents answered positively to both questions.

Although the survey could certainly be improved, given the self-imposed requirement that it be quick and easy to take,[3] it provided many insights and could be valuable to all who participate when the results are shared. In this world where it is difficult to take the time to attend meetings with colleagues, surveys can be the poor man's version of dialogue and collaboration.

Reflections from College Librarians

In a random sampling of college librarians (conducted via phone and e-mail) who deal predominantly with incoming freshmen, many of the results from the high school librarian survey were confirmed. Table 12.3 shows the correlation between the topics marked in the high school survey as "essential" for college students and the comments of college librarians about the essential skills. All of the skills listed in the table are considered essential skills by the surveyed college librarians.

Table 12.3. College and High School Correlation: Topics Labeled Essential by Both HS and College Librarians

Topics	HS	College
When/where to cite	74.4%	89.1%
Academic integrity	83.7%	96.1%
Database versus "free" Web	92.2%	92.2%
Journal versus magazine	72.9%	76.0%
Primary versus secondary source	81.4%	81.4%
Types and use of print resources	77.5%	78.3%
How to use a catalog/OPAC	90.7%	88.4%
Evaluate resources	90.7%	93.8%
Identify possible sources	72.1%	81.4%
Prepare search strategies	66.7%	82.9%
Formulate topic/thesis	40.3%	74.4%

Instruction at the College Level

"Information resources at the college and university levels are more extensive, more specialized, and more diversified than those supporting learning at the high school level. Thus, even students who have had exposure to information literacy skills in elementary and secondary school need additional education and concrete learning experiences before they are able to take full advantage of available resources" (Smalley 2004, 193). For the college librarian, the task is daunting. To modify an often quoted phrase, "So much information, so little time." The college librarian too must collaborate and bargain for time to acclimate new students to the college's library resources. Information is key. There are very few philosophical arguments on this point. Providing library resources and literacy information is important and should happen sooner rather than later. "Most of us in higher education would agree that high on the list of essentials for collegiate success are the abilities to find, manipulate, and use information—not just information that can be easily downloaded from the Web, but information that meets the standards of accuracy and academic rigor"(Barefoot 2006, B16).

"Most of us in higher education would agree that high on the list of essentials for collegiate success are the abilities to find, manipulate, and use information— not just information that can be easily downloaded from the Web, but information that meets the standards of accuracy and academic rigor."

How college librarians accomplish introducing their libraries' unique assets as well as helping students and teachers with all manner of information needs varies from college to college. In reviewing college library Web sites and discussing library instruction with former students and college librarians, three main avenues are used: orientation information sessions, online tutorials, and required information literacy or research classes. Similar to what is done in many high schools, direct formal instruction by the librarian in college is often done in conjunction with the freshmen English classes as the class is structured to coincide with a research paper or presentation. Sometimes this class is required and built into the curriculum. At other colleges, all direct instruction is done in collaboration with the individual professors or instructors at their request, and instruction is designed to address a particular research or information need of the class. Many librarians in the phone and e-mail survey commented that although they did not get as much formal instruction time as they would like, their respective faculties are cooperative and well aware of the value of information literacy instruction. However, the general consensus was that there is a major drawback to this type of instruction: not all students receive the same information, leaving some students at a disadvantage unless they are incredibly motivated and seek help individually.

Regardless of which type of instruction is offered, it is imperative that new students get some exposure to the library. The number and extent of the resources, the complexity of a large university system with multiple libraries, and new services like e-reference (ask a librarian, live chat) or government documents archives, are fundamentally so different from students' high school experience with libraries, that it is difficult to expect students will somehow learn this on their own. There is a point to mentioning this besides empathizing with fellow librarians who share a similar instructional plight: high school librarians can set their graduates on a course for success in college by teaching a strong understanding of college level library resources, both how to find the right research tools and then how to learn to use them. Some suggestions appear in the next section.

Developing a Roadmap for Success

The simple days (pre-Internet) are gone forever, and we have to deal with the information stream, which is constant and can seem ready to bury us. Teachers too have seen greater demands for their curriculum time as they strain to keep producing better results on SATs and in AP courses. Something has to give. Often teachers are not spending as much time on research projects, which in turn means that library instruction time gets cut. That results in librarians giving hurried directions and the most cursory information before students begin the research process. Gaps in student knowledge are sometimes filled in by one-on-one instruction, but that is unacceptable if librarians are to remain true to their mission. Basic information literacy, essential for a world whose technology and information needs can only be imagined at this point, cannot merely be given lip service. In fact, as independent schools with predominantly college-bound students, there should be a higher standard of information *fluency* rather than literacy (Pearle 2002, 11). The challenge is before us, and to meet it requires not only excellent pedagogy, but collaboration, evaluation, and advocacy.

Starting Partnerships Outside School

Dialogue is a first step. Both college and high school librarians face similar challenges and have found solutions that can be shared. Discussion needs to be nurtured. Possible topics include scheduling instruction, collaboration with faculty, creating quality assignments in library research, designing Web pages for resources for instructional use, and assessing student performance (Donham 2003, 32). Many high school librarians write a professional development plan at the beginning of the school year. Make this the year that your goal is to attend a workshop on transitioning to college or pick up the phone and call a college librarian. Collaboration is a two-way street, and either side can make the initial gesture. If your local school library association has not sponsored a meeting to which college librarians have been invited, work to make such a meeting possible.

> "Our school, public and academic libraries form a unique integrated info-ecosystem that offers universally accessible lifelong learning opportunities. As in any eco-system, weakness anywhere in the system threatens the whole."
>
> —Rettig (2009)

"Since 1998, an AASL/ACRL Task Force on the Educational Role of Libraries has emphasized the importance of information competency instruction for the entire K-16 spectrum" (Smalley 2004, 194). Academic and high school librarians have been urged to work together, and many partnerships exist. Educational and association conferences at both levels have been dotted with sessions and workshops calling for or detailing stronger working relationships. Articles written by and about collaborators attest to the fact that partnerships can be established and bear fruit. Even if you do not have a college in close proximity to your school, it is important to explore possible ways to collaborate with college librarians. Martha Ameika describes her collaboration with four colleges, which brought college professors and librarians to her school to speak to seniors (2008, 408–9). With so much information available online, a possible collaboration could take place remotely by using a college's catalog, database, or special digital collection or archive. Additional examples of college–high school partnerships are numerous and can be found in professional literature, online, and through networking and professional organizations.

If you have the time to think outside of your school, consider the possibility of collaborating with a college librarian. For librarians with colleges and universities close by, make a plan to visit. If AP students are not making use of college library resources, work with their instructor to ensure that resources at the college level are required in the course and then set in motion a way for students to become familiar with these types of resources. One such visit is described by Margaret Tabar (2002). Visiting a college library requires preparation work with the students before you go and good coordination with the instructional or outreach librarian at the college. Figure 12.2 is designed as a checklist for the high school librarian who wants to provide a college library experience for his or her students (Nutefall 2001, 315–17).

Arrange for the visit with the college librarian:

- Schedule a mutually beneficial time for the HS students and the library staff.
- Determine the number of students visiting to ensure that staff and facilities can accommodate.
- Determine if there is a recommended chaperone ratio for HS teachers/ librarians accompanying their students on the visit.
- Ask about photocopying policies and procedures.
- Ask for a brief orientation to begin any visit.
- Send a copy of the students' assignment, if at all possible.
- Ask about borrowing privileges.
- Complete all necessary forms (such as for guest borrowing privileges) in advance.

Before the visit the HS librarian needs to provide:

- A handout of key reference sources that are unique to the college/public library being visited.
- A map of the library building for the students.
- An explanation of the difference between Dewey and LC classification, if necessary.
- An explanation of any library policies such as costs for photocopying.

Ensure that both the HS teachers and HS librarians are available for the visit. After the students have exhausted the sources in the high school library, the students need to:

- Compile a list of further sources from bibliographies found in their school library sources.
- Print out titles of books from the online catalog of the library to be visited.
- Review the database list of the library to be visited for possible use.
- Prepare a list of questions to be answered or information still needed.

Figure 12.2. Suggestions for Making a College Library Visit.

"The Last Semester" or "One Last Opportunity for One New Beginning"

Getting students ready for college library work has been on the radar of some librarians for a long time. Kathleen Craver describes a three-session program covering Internet searching, using the catalog, and database searching in which students gained experience using university resources (1998, 34). The hands-on aspect of using the college catalogs and database descriptions for the selection of appropriate resources cannot be overestimated. As seniors, students may not be interested in "reviewing" aspects of research in their high school library, but working in the college library is like test driving a new car.

Organize a "boot camp" for graduating seniors: know where (which colleges and universities) your students have been accepted[4] and do a quick scan of those libraries' Web sites. Have the students work through the library Web site at their new college to discover special features of the library. One library Web site recently visited has a feature that allows students to text the catalog information about resources to their cell phones. Features that are unique or a feature that students just haven't had experience with at your school, like "ask-a-librarian," need to be publicized, and you can help your students become aware of them even before they set foot on campus.

Have students look at the number of subscription databases offered at the college. Have them find one database that they don't know and determine what it contains. Find out what kind of orientation is done or what kind of classes are required or offered. Have them use the OPAC for their new school, find a book, and explain the details of what is in the catalog entry, such as library, collection, or any other locational aids. This is a great opportunity to talk about the switch to LOC cataloging (Craver 1998, 34). Have them search for a campus map and locate the library or libraries on campus. The possibilities are numerous.

The article "My Senior Is Your First-Year Student" stresses two requirements for effective teaching. The instruction must occur when the student is motivated to learn and should be constructed with students' direct active involvement (Donham 2003, 23). Having a senior days away from graduating actively doing something on the Web site of his or her new school will be motivating and fun.

Partnerships within School

The value of collaborating with faculty at your high school cannot be overestimated. Any instruction will be more productive if coupled with a "real" assignment. This may become more difficult to do in a university setting, and that is why it is so important for the high school librarian to accomplish. Not only are students more receptive and motivated if literacy instruction occurs at the onset of the need for information, they also will begin to see the connection of literacy to all research endeavors when there is an institutional, multidisciplinary approach. Doing so will make the transferability of their skills become real for the student, and transformative education will take place. "Students who exercise these [information literacy] skills in every area of study will be preparing themselves not only for college but for a lifetime of seeing the interconnections among the disciplines" (*Academic Literacy* 2002, 35).

"We are what we repeatedly do. Excellence, then, is not an act but a habit."

—Aristotle

One of the most important steps in collaboration is follow-through. Do what you say you will, on time and with a positive attitude. Truly listen to the teacher's needs and expectations and plan for the most effective lesson you can to teach. Treat each opportunity as just that: a golden opportunity to connect with a teacher and students. Just as any good teacher would, make backup plans in case part of the lesson runs into a problem. If a teacher's lesson is successful with your help, your input will be indispensable when that teacher is planning another research assignment. You may only get one shot at making yourself that teacher's instructional partner. Give it your best effort.

Another important step in collaboration is evaluation. Be sure that you give both teachers and students the opportunity to evaluate the content and format of lessons as well as the library resources available. Providing an opportunity to evaluate reaffirms that you value the collaborative effort the teacher has made. It also signals to students that you value their time and are interested in helping them with their information needs. Finally, it provides you with the type of feedback you need to develop even better lessons. Be flexible and receptive to student and teacher suggestions. (See essay 11.)

Quick Tips 1: Collaboration

- Volunteer to grade the bibliographies or online source evaluation forms.
- Make it a point to ask to read several of the students' finished products or attend the presentation of the reports generated from students' research.
- Expand your own knowledge of the college research environment.
- Stress the quality of resources; don't accept questionable material.
- Use blogs or other technologies, like Google Docs, for information sharing.
- Offer to combine information literacy lessons with a new technology application.
- Create online pathfinders for students and bibliographies for teachers.
- Offer individual help to any teacher who feels uncomfortable with the technology or other aspects associated with the research process.

As a footnote to the discussion about collaborating with high school teachers and librarians and faculty from universities, we should not forget that we can and should collaborate with teens about information literacy. Social Web sites are real and very popular and already have the audience we want. In 2005 the Pew Internet & American Life Project published a report. The study found that more than half of online teens are content creators (Lenhart and Madden 2004). The passage of time has probably increased the number of teens who create content for the Web, whether it is a Web site, a blog, or a sharing on a social network. We need to tap that resource: learn from our users and access them wherever they can be found. (See essay 8.) In addition, we have to recognize things they value. Don't dismiss Google or *Wikipedia*. Both resources have their place and purpose;

just make sure students realize the limitations along with the strengths. "Regular discussion with teens about reading, information literacy, the Internet, and other issues in technology would be a rich source of guidance and policy if only teachers and librarians would take the time to ask, and then listen carefully. If this does not occur, teens relegate libraries to nonentity status" (Loertscher and Woolls 2002, 34).

Pedagogy

Librarians from high school do have an impact on college success. In a study done by Smalley (2004) in California, students attending Cabrillo College's information research class who had librarians in their high schools fared much better than the students who did not attend schools staffed by a librarian. So some of what we are already doing is working. But each day the world changes, the amount of information increases, and its access points change, not to mention the changes experienced by the user. Staying abreast of information products, delivery systems, and user needs and attitudes is no mean feat and requires continual research and education.

How and what we teach must be examined. Frances Jacobson Harris, the librarian at the University of Illinois's University Laboratory High School, comments: "Like critical thinking skills, information literacy skills must be taught and practiced in multiple ways and in a variety of settings over time. Because of the complexity of information in today's world and the variability of the information problems students encounter, information literacy must be learned as a tool of strategy rather than a tool of procedure" (quoted in Smalley 2004, 197). Carol Gordon concurs: "The information skills our college-bound students need are not only mechanical skills, also thinking skills" 2002, 18).

Quick Tips 2: Pedagogy

- Work with students to generate questions from the material they read.
- Collect and examine undergraduate research assignments (Gordon 2002, 17).
- Encourage students to use a combination of media in resources (i.e. print and online; audio and print).
- Model the use of the "help" screen in databases and search engines.
- Brainstorm with students.
- Share your thought process when searching with students.
- Make sure students understand the "anatomy" of a citation.
- Remove jargon from your lessons. Search engine optimization (SEO) won't mean much to your students. Speak plain English.
- Require students to create a time management plan for a big research assignment with a log for reflection on their progress.
- Move past assignments that require answers and "reporting" to assignments that require critical thinking and creation (Gordon 2002, 19).

Evaluation

"In information-rich environments, a human interface between teen and technology is still a critical asset to information use and student improvement. . . .The human interface must concentrate on critical thinking, analysis, synthesis, using and reporting. The wise professional does an analysis of the quality interactions that are actually occurring, then works to maximize such interactions" (Loertscher and Woolls 2002, 34). See what works well and go from there: work smarter, not harder. There are a number of evaluation tools available to the librarian: performance assessments like pre-post tests, observation, and worksheets; portfolios; and self-assessment tools like surveys and research journals.

Obviously you can depend on observation for initial feedback. Every teacher and librarian knows the "information overload" or "huh?" look. One drawback is that sometimes it is difficult to discern problems for students who exhibit low affect, and with students who are quite sure they know what they are doing but whose confidence belies their ability. A survey has its place because it can help gauge how students and faculty feel or how they self-assess their skills. Some type of performance assessment in which the learning results are more demonstrable allows the librarian to monitor student improvement, clarify what has been mastered, and consider course revisions for improvement.

The Tool for Real-Time Assessment of Information Literacy Skills (TRAILS) and Standardized Assessment of Information Literacy Skills (SAILS) are tests that have been developed for school and academic students at their respective levels. TRAILS is designed for sixth- and ninth-grade assessment. Although SAILS was developed to measure the traditional information literacy skills of locating, evaluating, and using information at the college level, high schools interested in determining whether students are college-ready might consider using this instrument. Both are multiple choice tests and can be taken several times to determine both baseline and proficiency measurements. Another test, which is more expensive to administer, has recently been developed by the Educational Testing Service (ETS.) The Information Technology and Communication Literacy Assessment measures the traditional literacy skills as well as the skills needed to communicate information in a digital world (Seymour 2007, 33–34). The test is taken on a computer and is a simulation lasting seventy-five minutes. The scoring is similar to the SAT and ranges from 400 to 700. The average score in 2006 was 550 (Heyboer 2007).

The point is to make sure that some form of assessment is done so that your program can be evaluated and you can feel confident that your students are in a good position to succeed in a college setting. "Assessment is extremely important at both the high school and college level, but particularly at the high school level if we want to be sure that we are preparing our students to make the transition" (Donham 2003, 32).

Quick Tips 3: Evaluation

- Experiment with different types of evaluation.
- Remember to have all constituents evaluate an activity.
- Consider investing in an online survey instrument.
- Commit to the time it takes to do evaluation.
- Share results.

Advocacy

Become an expert on what is needed for success at college. If the administration feels that the librarian is knowledgeable and working toward that end, your voice becomes more important. Teachers and administrators are always more willing to listen to requirements from the outside—statistics grounded in research and anything tied to their mission statement—than they are to any plea we might make about valuable skills. They do not want to ignore us; they are just being pulled from too many directions, and we need to give them a compelling reason to listen to us. Teachers feel a degree of comfort in making time for something that relates directly to national or state standards. Correspondingly, librarians are sure to win a new ally if collaboration either enhances the teacher's instruction or improves student output. Students, especially juniors and seniors, become more engaged if the topic involves something in their sphere of interest. College is in that sphere.

Know who is teaching what and make sure that the best person suited to the task takes it on. Byerly, Downey, and Ramin tell us that the English teachers at one university were charged with teaching standards three, four, and five of the ACRL standards, which primarily involve students turning their library research into a product following appropriate ethical and legal requirements regarding information. The English teachers also guide students through "identifying key concepts and terms that describe their information need" and "understanding resource formats" (standard one). In addition, the English faculty taught selecting the appropriate information resource, designing and refining good research strategies, understanding information retrieval, and extracting the information needed (standard two) (2006, 593). This seems like a lot of the research process to turn over to the content teacher, at least when it is not taught in collaboration with the librarian. Some of these skills are very dependent on current and constant use. Librarians, by the nature of their job, are much more apt to be aware of changes in search engine features, monitor closely copyright issues, and have consistent practice refining search strategies and are logically the best suited to know and explain what resources are available in the library collection. Joyce Valenza has said, "We have not done as good a job as we could promoting ourselves—the value of our services, our instruction, or the array of online resources we provide" (Everhart and Valenza 2004, 55). Make sure that faculty and administrators know that you can contribute to preparing students with inquiry and information skills.

Quick Tips 4: Advocacy

- Lobby for a review of how literacy is being taught throughout the curriculum. If you are not on the school's curriculum committee, join!

- Present a workshop for your faculty and administration on what college faculty are saying about your graduates.

- If you are not already, become part of the research/writing process throughout the curriculum. If no one is coordinating that at your school, volunteer!

Conclusion

Ellysa Cahoy has asked, "Will Your Students Be Ready for College?" (2002). This is a question that anyone in education has asked in relation to his or her discipline and grade level. Everyone wants to answer "yes," but ensuring that students are college ready continues to be hard work and an elusive goal. Are we doing everything possible to make it happen? Are we working smarter, not harder? With so many questions, it is time to get some answers even if the answers only apply to our personal situations and students. Change is called for, and we are in the position to make changes. Cahoy gives us five steps that will start the process:

1. Evaluate the scope and sequence of your school's library skills curriculum.

2. Explore and implement performance-based assessment methods.

3. Reach out to other schools in your area.

4. Collaborate with librarians at different educational levels.

5. Seek out professional development opportunities. (2002, 14–15)

To be effective, experience with information literacy strategies has to be part of the entire educational experience. School librarians and school library programs are key educational components (Smalley 2004, 197). Librarians can influence how successful students will be in both direct and indirect ways. It is incumbent on librarians at all levels to help students become fluent with information. Beyond that, librarians need to help develop in students a flexibility and adaptability to fairly constant change in the ways information is stored, retrieved, and interpreted. Accomplishing all of this will take knowledge, collaboration, integration, assessment, and advocacy. It is an extremely large task but, as it goes to the core mission and values of librarians, it is a challenge that must be faced.

Will our students be ready for college? Yes, because we will make it happen. Just as our libraries have grown outside our physical spaces, so too have our curriculum and the possible scope of our influence. As librarians in independent schools we can move quickly, experiment, and innovate. We need to be agents of change in our schools. No one else is as uniquely positioned to connect the dots among information, evolving technologies, student learning traits, and the academic realities of our schools.

Notes

1. Many independent schools have spent a year or more in curriculum mapping in one form or another. The role that the library can play is often highlighted when a school goes through this process.

2. This survey was conducted by the author during the second half of May 2009. The survey was sent out to AISL and ISS e-mail list-serves with requests to forward the survey to any other independent school library association; 129 independent school librarians responded to the survey.

3. No more than ten questions/minimal writing/less than five minutes to take.

4. Carolyn Hilles (Wheeler School, Providence, RI) suggested using the schools accepting your students as the "pool" of librarians to contact to discuss what they see, or don't see, in incoming freshmen. I had been using the Web sites of several local universities to do this "boot camp," and realized after seeing Carolyn's suggestion that I was missing the opportunity to personalize this exercise and actively engage the students in learning. This works much better when students are going to their own college Web sites.

References

Abilock, Debbie. 2004. "Information Literacy From Prehistory to K-20: A New Definition." *Knowledge Quest* (March–April): 9–11.

Abram, Stephen, and Judy Luther. 2004. "Born with the Chip." *Library Journal* (May 1). Available at www.libraryjournal.com. Accessed June 10, 2009.

Academic Literacy: A Statement of Competencies Expected of Students Entering California's Public Colleges and Universities. 2002. Sacramento, CA: Intersegmental Committee of the Academic Senates (ICAS). Academic Senate for California Community Colleges. Available at www.asccc.org/Publications/Papers/AcademicLiteracy/AcademicLiteracy.pdf. Accessed May 30, 2009.

Allen, Susan M. 2007. "Information literacy, ICT, High School, and College Expectations." *Knowledge Quest* (May–June): 18–24.

Ameika, Martha. 2008. "Introducing College Research at the High School Level." *VOYA* (December): 408–9.

American Association of School Librarians (AASL). 2007. *Standards for the 21st-Century Learner*. American Library Association. Available at www.ala.org/ala/mgrps/divs/aasl/guidelinesandstandards/learningstandards/standards.cfm. Accessed March 28, 2009.

American Association of School Librarians (AASL) and Association for Educational Communications and Technology (AECT). 1998. "Information Literacy Standards for Student Learning (Chapter 2, excerpt)." In *Information Power: Building Partnerships for Learning*. Chicago: American Library Association. Available at www.ala.org/ala/mgrps/divs/aasl/guidelinesandstandards/informationpower/InformationLiteracyStandards_final.pdf file. Accessed March 28, 2009.

Association of College & Research Libraries (ACRL). 2000. *Information Literacy Competency Standards for Higher Education*. American Library Association. Available at www.ala.org/ala/mgrps/divs/acrl/standards/informationliteracycompetency.cfm. Accessed May 28, 2009.

Barefoot, Betsy. 2006. "Bridging the Chasm: First-Year Students and the Library." *Chronicle of Higher Education* (January 20): B16. Available at http://search.ebscohost.com/. Accessed May 28, 2009.

Byerly, Gayla, Annie Downey, and Lilly Ramin. 2006. "Foothills and Foundations: Setting Freshmen on the Path to Lifelong Learning." *Reference Services Review* 34, no. 4: 589+. Available at http://proquest.umi.com/login. Accessed May 28, 2009.

Cahoy, Ellysa Stern. 2002. "Will Your Students Be Ready for College?" *Knowledge Quest* 30, no. 4: 12–15.

———. 2004. "Put Some Feeling into It!" *Knowledge Quest* 32, no. 4: 25–28.

Carr, Jo Ann, and Ilene F. Rockman. 2003. "Information-Literacy Collaboration: A Shared Responsibility." *American Libraries* (September): 52–54.

Conley, David T. 2007. *Toward a More Comprehensive Conception of College Readiness.* Eugene: Educational Policy Improvement Center.

Costa, Arthur L, and Bena Kallick. 2000. *Habits of Mind.* Alexandria: ASCD.

Craver, Kathleen W. 1998. "Internet Search Skills for the College-Bound." *School Library Journal* (November): 33–35.

Donham, Jean. 2003. "My Senior Is Your First-Year Student." *Knowledge Quest* 32, no. 1: 32.

Eissinger, Richard. 2005. "Library Research Skills Needed by New College Students." Paper presented at the Mountain Plains Library Association Annual Conference, Oct0ber 12–15, Jackson Hole, Wyoming. MPLA. Available at www.mpla.us/documents/handouts/2005. Accessed May 28, 2009.

Ercegovac, Zorana. 2003. "Bridging the Knowledge Gap between Secondary and Higher Education. *College and Research Libraries* 64, no. 1: 75-85. Available at www.ala.org/ala/mgrps/divs/acrl/publications/crljournal/2003/jan/ercegovac.pdf. Accessed April 4, 2009.

Esch, Carrie, and Amy Crawford. 2006. "Helping Students Make the Jump to University Level Research." *Multimedia & Internet@Schools* (March–April): 21–25.

Everhart, Nancy, and Joyce Valenza. 2004. "Internet-Savvy Students and Their Schools." *Knowledge Quest* 32, no. 4: 50–55.

Fitzgerald, Mary Ann. 2004. "Making the Leap from High School to College." *Knowledge Quest* 32, no. 4: 19–24.

Goodin, M. Elspeth. 1991. "The Transferability of Library Research Skills from High School to College." *School Library Media Quarterly* 20, no. 1: n.p.

Gordon, Carol. 1999. "Students as Authentic Researchers: A New Prescription for the High School Research Assignment." *School Library Media Research* 2: 1–21.

———. 2002."A Room with a View." *Knowledge Quest* 30, no. 4: 16–21.

Head, Alison J., and Michael B. Eisenberg. 2009. *What Today's College Students Say about Conducting Research in the Digital Age.* Project Information Literacy. The Information School, University of Washington. February 4. Available at http://projectinfolit.org/publications/. Accessed May 28, 2009.

Heyboer, Kelly. 2007. "Tech-savvy kids? New Test Shows Shortcomings in Cyber Literacy." *The Star-Ledger,* February 12, n.p.

Knowledge Quest. 2002. 30, no. 4. Issue theme "One Step Beyond: From High School to College."

Knowledge Quest. 2004. 32, no. 4. Issue theme "Information Literacy K–20."

Knowledge Quest. 2007. 35, no. 5. Issue theme "Assessing Information and Communication Technology."

Kuhlthau, Carol. 1993. *Seeking Meaning: A Process Approach to Library Information Services.* Norwood, NJ: Ablex Publication Corp.

Latham, Don, and Melissa Gross. 2008. "Broken Links: Undergraduates Look Back on their Experiences with Information Literacy in K-12 Education." American Library Association. November 11. Available at /www.ala.org. Accessed May 10, 2009.

Lenhart, A., and M. Madden. 2004. *Teen Content Creators and Consumers.* Ed. Pew Internet & American Life Project. Available at www.pewinternet.org/Reports/2005/Teen-Content-Creators-and-Consumers.aspx. Accessed April 16, 2009.

Loertscher, David C., and Blanche Woolls. 2002. "Teenage Users of Libraries." *Knowledge Quest* 30, no. 5: 31–36.

Morriston, Terry. n.d. "Preparing Your High School Student for College Research." Ebsco Publishing Customer Success Tools. Available at www.ebscohost.com//dbTopic-288.pdf. Accessed May 30, 2009.

North Central Regional Educational Laboratory and Metiri Group. 2003. *EnGauge 21st Century Skills: Literacy in the Digital Age.* Green River Regional Educational Cooperative. Available at www.grrec.ky.gov/SLC_grant/engauge21st_Century_Skills.pdf. Accessed November 21, 2009.

Nutefall, Jennifer E. 2001. "Information Literacy: Developing Partnership across Library Types." *Research Strategies* 18, no. 4: 311–18.

Nutefall, Jennifer, et al. 2004. "My College Freshman Is Your High School Senior: Starting the Transition Conversation." Paper presented at District of Columbia Library Association Meeting, Washington, D.C., December 3.

OCLC Online Computer Library Center. 2005. *Perceptions of Libraries and Information Resources.* OCLC. June. Available at www.oclc.org/us/en/reports/2005perceptions.htm. Accessed June 10, 2009.

Pearle, Laura. 2002. "The High-C Connection: Research Skills Last a Lifetime." *Knowledge Quest* 30, no. 4: 11.

Pew Charitable Trusts, and Association of American Universities. 2003. *Understanding University Success.* Eugene, OR: Center for Educational Policy Research. Standards for Success. Center for Educational Policy Research. Available at http://cepr.uoregon.edu/cepr.uus.php. Accessed November 22, 2009.

Phillips, Karen, Esther Grassian, and Lynn Lampert. 2006. "What Do Our Students Need to Know for College?" Paper presented at CAIS 2006 Southern Regional Meeting, North Hollywood, California, March 13. California Association of Independent Schools. Available at www.caisca.org/events_resources.asp? PrintFriendly=YES&event=115. Accessed May 28, 2009.

Rettig, Jim. 2009. "Frame of Reference: School Libraries and the Educational Ecosystem." *Change* (March–April). Available at www.changemag.org. Accessed June 10, 2009.

Schroeder, Robert. 2007. "Information Literacy: The K-12 College Continuum." In *OASL Conference Proceedings*. Paper presented at the OASL Conference, October 13. Available at www.oema.net/conferences/2007/saturday.htm#infolit. Accessed May 12, 2009.

——. 2009. "Frame of Reference: School Libraries and the Educational Ecosystem." *Change* (March–April): n.p. Available at www.changemag.org. Accessed June 10, 2009.

Seymour, Celine. 2007. "Information Technology Assessment." *Knowledge Quest* 35, no. 5: 32–35.

Smalley, Topsy N. 2004. "College Success: High School Librarians Make the Difference." *The Journal of Academic Librarianship* 30, no. 3: 193–98.

Tabar, Margaret. 2002. "Rite of Passage." *Knowledge Quest* 30, no. 4: 29–30.

Weis, June Pullen. 2004. "Contemporary Literacy Skills." *Knowledge Quest* (March–April): 12–15.

"What Is SAILS?" 2009. In *Project SAILS*. Kent State University. July 22. Available at www.projectsails.org/pubs/brochure.pdf?page=aboutTest. Accessed September 22, 2009.

Visit http://lu.com/excellence for supporting links and occasional updates to all essays in this book.

Martha Daly has been the Librarian at Connelly School of the Holy Child (http://www.holychild.org/home/home.asp) in Potomac, MD, for the last fourteen years, opening a new library in 2002. She belongs to numerous professional organizations and is currently the nonpublic school representative to the Maryland K–12 Digital Library Project. She received an MLS from the University of Maryland and was a fellow in the Leadership in Technology program at Harvard. Prior to becoming a librarian, she taught school in grades 6–12 in the United States and overseas.

What Else Can We Do? Library Programs Beyond Curriculum Foster a Culture of Learning

Mary G. Milligan, St. Luke's Episcopal School (San Antonio, TX)

The library is the soul of a school's academic life, and the way a library is used says a great deal about the degree to which a school values independent learning and prepares students to be lifelong learners. As each independent school has its own unique character, with traditions and a curriculum designed to fit that school's mission, the independent school works to fulfill the needs and mission of that school. Each independent school library serves a community with a unique purpose and specific library needs that are central to the school's character. Just as no two independent schools are identical, no two independent school libraries will be the same. Keeping those needs at the forefront of all library planning, the independent school librarian has the freedom to customize the library's services to fit the needs of the community.

Each independent school library serves a community with a unique purpose and specific library needs that are central to the school's character.

Extracurricular programming that occurs within the school library, usually led by the library staff, extends the impact of the library beyond its direct involvement in the curriculum and sometimes beyond the school day. These extra programs may be official school clubs with a librarian as the sponsor or they may be semiregular gatherings that evolved from the interests of their members. Although these gatherings may be extensions of activities that occur during the school day, they are normally geared to special interests, with voluntary participation. Meetings may occur before or after school, during lunch, or on weekends or school holidays. Scheduling is often a critical issue. To guarantee a well-attended gathering requires flexibility. Ruth Sagebiel (formerly at Saint Mary's Hall Lower School, San Antonio, TX) points out that typically younger students have very limited unscheduled free time. Having worked at both public and private schools in elementary and middle school, she has observed that younger private school students "have more scheduled activities, lessons, sports, tutoring, and special classes, making scheduling programs after school

213

difficult. Once they are in high school, although they are still busy, they have a little more freedom to follow up on their interests." Arranging meeting times around other school events and student activities can also be challenging, but successful book clubs find that advance notice and consistent meeting times help attendance.

Think of libraries, and reading is the first activity that comes to mind. With home access to library online materials, the school library program is able to support the school's reading collection 24/7. Recognizing that the reading experience begins with the student as a listener, school library programs incorporate purposeful storytime experiences that may include finger play, puppets, costumed characters, and other props that enhance the storytelling. As students move from emergent readers to fluent readers, reading aloud may remain an enjoyable component of the library program, but the focus shifts to readers' advisory and reading motivation through booktalks, reading management, and incentive programs such as Accelerated Reader or Reading Counts; young reader's choice awards; book fairs; and author visits. These programs may include the "One Book, One Community" or "Drop Everything and Read" (DEAR) programs, when the entire school community focuses on a specific reading initiative. Book celebrations such as National Library Week, literary festivals, El día de los niños/El día de los libros, Children's Day/Book Day, and author visits usually involve the entire school and provide the librarian with opportunities to coordinate reading events for multiple grade levels and disciplines. It doesn't take long for a book celebration to become an annual schoolwide event.

One way that reading beyond the curriculum is accomplished is through book clubs, reading groups, and literature circles formed because of shared reading interests, such as a Harry Potter club, a faculty discussion group, or a parent–child reading circle. These are often small, focused groups that are organized by the school librarian as a way to create and bind a community of readers. The structure of the group depends on the members, but the goals remain essentially the same. Laura J. H. Smith (2004) identifies six book club goals for young readers: improve reading, improve vocabulary, foster a love of reading, introduce worlds outside a child's comfort zone, build social skills, and build creativity.

Reading groups or literature circles organized by the school librarian for students may vary widely in format, but it is usually the students who set the pace and tone. A literature circle is "a structured reading activity" offering opportunities for discussion (Aydelott and Buck 2003). Book club meetings may include a variety of activities related to the theme of the featured book that will "enhance and enliven" the book club experience (Gelman and Krupp 2007). Judy Howitt (Castle Hills First Baptist School, San Antonio, TX) brings snacks to her "Summer Reading Club" that fit the theme of the featured book. For example, *The Cricket in Times Square* inspired "egg rolls, because the main character goes to Chinatown to ask advice for his pet cricket." Many groups choose to meet once a month and to focus on a specific book, author, series, or genre. An example is the once-a-month Harry Potter Book Club meetings held in the St. Luke's Episcopal School's Newman Library (San Antonio, TX). Club meeting activities have included playing online trivia games, acting out favorite passages, and taking turns wearing the Sorting Hat, in addition to in-depth discussions of each book in the series. In contrast, the St. Luke's parent-middle school book club gatherings held in the evenings were run more like literature circles, discussing themes and character analysis of such classics as *Beowulf, The Bacchae,* and *To Kill a Mockingbird*. A totally different kind of reading group is the Author's Birthday Book Club run by Mary Holm (formerly at San Antonio Academy, TX). Once a month the club celebrated an author's birthday by reading the author's books, playing birthday games to fit the theme of the books (for instance, pin the hat on the Cat during the Dr. Seuss party),

| Books, Books, Books |

sharing the author's life story, and ending with blowing out the candles on the author's birthday cake.

Book club meetings can occur as often as once a week, with members doing informal booktalks or book reviewing. Susan Gerding (John Cooper School, Woodlands, TX) models her Dragon Book program after the successful statewide Texas Bluebonnet Award reading program. She begins by selecting approximately 100 books for fifth graders to read and evaluate, to create a student recommended booklist consisting of five nonfiction books, five picture books, and ten fiction books. Fifth graders meet once a week for lunch and book discussion in the library. Gerding reports:

> The students look for good educational messages in picture books, engaging nonfiction, and fun and exciting fiction. When students finish a book, they mark off on a chart Y or N for inclusion on the list. We meet like this from December through March, eliminating books as we go along. I read all the books, so that I am able to support or question book choices. If there are too many books at the end, I make the final selections. Once the list is finalized, we create bookmarks to hand out to the students who will be in third through fifth grade the next year. The students keep a record of the titles they read or have been read to them on a chart in the library. In April, all students who have read five or more titles vote for their favorite, and those who have read ten or more are invited to a Dragon Book breakfast.

Book club memberships vary as greatly as the books they read. They can be coed or gender-specific, separated by different grades or intergenerational, general interest or topic-specific. Stella Gonzalez (Providence Catholic School, San Antonio, TX) runs two book clubs for her girls: middle school Page Turners, which covers grades 6–8, and the high school Page Turners, which covers grades 9–12. She says, "Students approached me because they wanted to 'read something that we want to read, something that isn't assigned'." Each group meets once a month after school in the library workroom. The reason they meet in the workroom is because the floor is tile, not carpet,which is useful because the students take turns bringing snacks and drinks. The club's Web page says "we meet and eat to discuss *our* books." There is also a continuous online discussion forum.

A factor all these book clubs have in common is a desire to share the reading experience. Rebecca Moore (The Overlake School, Redmond, WA) runs a boys-only book club. Her "Best Books for Boys" is "a secret club

| Best Books for Boys |

because I didn't want the girls to find out and be jealous—most of my activities attract only girls, and I wanted to find a way to reach out to boy readers, and I thought having a secret club would work. We're not really discussing books, though; we're putting together a list of the 100 best books for boys, which we'll publish on the library website and for which we'll set up a display in the library."

| Student Book Wiki |

Librarian Mary Martin (The Altamont School, Birmingham, AL) also uses technology to get students to share their reading interests:

> My school puts a huge emphasis on reading. Students are required to read three books a month and we have extensive lists of suggested books. So far

the rules for the wiki are that students can add any book they feel is appropriate for their grade, whether it is on the list or not. The wiki is only open to our students (in fact there are two, one for middle school and the other for upper school). For several years I have been concerned that the long lists of books we give the students weren't annotated, so students were faced with long lists of books they knew nothing about. Of course, the students traded recommendations, but got a new list each spring for summer reading with no annotations. I am hoping that students will add enough information during this year that they will be able to access it over the summer to see what the last year's class recommends.

The influence the librarian has in book selection varies from group to group, but overall the librarian is the most useful resource to narrow the list of reading options. Michelle Randall (The Episcopal School of Dallas, TX) has led a mixed student and faculty book club called *Ex Libris* for the last sixteen years. The book club meets once a month from October through April and is open to all upper school students (grades 9–12) and faculty. She explains that although she asks members to suggest books to read, 'it is usually my job to research and select three or four good options from the best-seller lists or from the new 'it' titles that seem to come along." The group then votes on the titles. She continues, "The benefits from being an *Ex Libris* member are multi-layered! Exposure to non-curricular, new titles, both fiction and nonfiction; engaging in discussions and exchanges of ideas with both peers (students of all high school ages), and with faculty on a level playing field with no grades attached; the realization that you CAN find time for pleasure reading even while in the midst of a strenuous academic homework load and athletic schedule; the reinforcement of the enrichment that reading brings every time a book is finished; and on and on!" Another benefit is obviously enthusiasm!

The librarians questioned seem to agree that creating and sustaining a reading group is worth the effort. Lori Farmer (Cornerstone Christian Schools, San Antonio, TX) admits that plenty of effort goes into preparing the meetings of her middle school book club, *Juntos*—Spanish for "coming together for a common purpose." She says that "in addition to planning the meetings and previewing all the books, I also prepare a PowerPoint for each meeting to help present the books we were choosing from and for some discussion starters for the meetings that required some effort and research, but I feel like it was time well spent."

Cheryl Werner (Oak Knoll School of the Holy Child, Summit, NJ) has figured out a way to generate enthusiasm for reading while also getting books into the students' hands. She sponsors the "Great American One-For-Two Book Swap," held in the library just in time for summer reading. Students bring in used books from home and receive a voucher that entitles them to one book for every two books that they bring in. Werner says, "Getting just one book for every two books, instead of one for one, provides more choice for all—even for the last **Book Swap** student who gets to choose." When all the students have chosen, teachers are then invited to select books for their classrooms; any left over books in good condition are donated to schools that can use them. Werner adds that "Parents look forward to this as a way to clear excess books from home and the kids love to get 'new' books." Book swaps keep enthusiasm going and feature "green living" as they put "pre-read" books in the hands of new readers. This helps to publicize the new summer reading list while giving families the opportunity to choose books for summer reading.

Sometimes an informal book group will turn into a writing group. The same students who are most enthusiastic about their reading experience are often also interested in writing. For instance, a poetry group in the library may focus on the reading or writing of poetry and can eventually evolve into an interest in performance poetry. Writing beyond the curriculum includes creative writing groups, poetry slams, and literary magazines. The school library with its ample resources is the natural setting for extracurricular reading and writing.

Creative writing groups may meet to journal together or to workshop (share and critique) material they have written independently. The intent is usually to express their ideas about writing, with attention given to the language and stylistics. If the group is process oriented, then the meetings tend to focus on inspiring the group to write and explore different writing styles. The meetings can become peer-editing workshops that encourage the students to write and to receive critiques by their peers. This allows the students to hone their writing in a comfortable setting outside of the classroom.

In an attempt to encourage young writers, Rebecca Moore (The Overlake School, Redmond, WA) organized the Middle School Writing Club, which meets once every two weeks during lunch. Beginning as a serious writing group, with students e-mailing or bringing in work for critique, it has evolved into more of a social writing club. Each meeting focuses on some aspect of good writing and a writing activity such as writing from a prompt, or writing round-robin style, and ends with sharing the results. Moore points out that not only do the students have fun, but it is a great way for them to make friends with other students "who also love books and writing, and are vocal about it."

When the group is more product oriented rather than process oriented, the club looks for opportunities to share their writing with a larger audience. The desire to see their writing in print is the natural by-product of an active writing group. The librarian sponsor may choose student work to display in the library, organize readings, establish a literary magazine, or encourage contest submissions. At the Dana Hall School, the East Asian studies teacher and the librarian collaborate on a picture book assignment for which the students write and illustrate a story set in ancient Japan. The students meet with a librarian to go over the elements of a successful picture book and techniques for interweaving illustration and text. Afterward, "we display the incredible results in one of our display cases."

Student Author Shelf

Bonnie Tollefson (Episcopal School of Dallas, TX) has a "Student Authors" shelf. She accepts original stories donated from first through fourth grades, which she catalogs, barcodes, and makes available for check out. At The Overlake School (Redmond, WA), students participate in writing and illustrating children's books for Landmark Edition's student book contest.

Literary magazines are one of the best ways to celebrate writing in a school setting. It is now much easier and cheaper to produce a high-quality student production. With a scanner, software programs like Photoshop and InDesign, and a good color printer, a forty-page magazine can be produced that includes student artwork as well as student writing. *Caught in the Pages* is the literary magazine at Annunciation Orthodox School (Houston, TX), which solicits writing from second to eighth grades. Teachers play a big part in selecting the writing in the lower school, while middle school teachers may require students to submit writing a couple of times during the school year. In contrast, the St. Luke's Episcopal School's literary magazine, *Burning Bright*, is a student-edited production with a librarian sponsor. Produced entirely in the school library, the student magazine staff encourages all students from preschool to eighth grade to submit poetry, fiction, nonfiction, and artwork. Students volunteer for committees, with the *Burning Bright* editor-in-chief participating in all committees as well as choosing the theme. The submissions are read blind, and the student editors, who are sixth, seventh, and eighth graders, fill out rubrics to determine the ranking of each piece. Students spend weeks working during lunch and after school with the school librarian, Mary Milligan, to make the final selections.

Literary Magazines

Angela Jewell (Georgetown Visitation Preparatory School, Washington, DC) is the co-advisor to the school's literary magazine, a part of the school's club/co-curricular program. All students are required to participate in a school-sponsored club, which meets approximately twenty times throughout the school year. Most of the senior members have been in the club for at least three years. Called the *Georgetowner*, the magazine is officially a literary and art magazine that includes artwork and photography as well as writing. It comes out once a year, in May. The editors are students. Any current student at Visitation can submit to the magazine. Submissions are received by e-mail and read "blind" (without any identifying information) by several editors. The students are responsible for designing and laying out the magazine, which they do in the spring, using Adobe InDesign. They use club periods to work on it, but as the final deadline approaches, more time is always required.

Susan Hodge (Flintridge Preparatory School, La Canada, CA) reports that student writing is a big focus of the library. The school newspaper (*The Flintridge Press*), literary magazine (*Folio*), and an informal writing group all meet there. For *The Flintridge Press*, the librarians primarily provide the working space and some occasional help with proofreading. The staff of *Folio,* student editors and a faculty advisor, use the same space to process magazine submissions from seventh to twelfth grades. A small informal writing group has begun meeting in one of the library's downstairs study rooms two afternoons a week. "They're just meeting to share their love of writing."

Sharing the love of reading and writing can take several forms. Those who love the printed word may also enjoy a wide variety of ways of expressing their passion for the spoken word. Performance beyond the curriculum may include participation in theater, speech, drama, storytelling, and readers' theatre. Just as the library was the natural setting for reading and writing, it is also ideal for sharing the spoken word.

The Flintridge Preparatory School Arts Club (La Canada, CA) hosts a Poetry Jam annually in the downstairs reading room of the school library for National Poetry Month. The Poetry Jam includes students' original poems as well as well- or lesser-known poets. It is held after school, and all students are invited.

A few years ago, Lee Johnson (San Antonio Christian Middle School/High School, TX) and her then high school principal, Bruce Burrowes (now retired), had a vision for a coffeehouse linked to the library. With the suggestion that it could be a joint fund-raiser, they enlisted the

Starburrowes Coffee House

help of the freshman class—although now it is done by the juniors. They had a contest to name the coffeehouse, and the winner was "Starburrowes," in honor of Mr. Burrowes, whose brainchild it was. The hallway outside the library is turned into an aromatic and inviting place where students can come to have breakfast or a snack each Friday morning from 7:00 am to noon. They play Christian music before school starts in the morning, and the aroma of freshly brewing Starbucks coffee always draws a crowd. They offer a variety of homemade baked goodies supplied by students. Some teachers bring their classes down to the coffeehouse for the last few minutes of class or send students down for a few minutes when their work is finished. Students can stop by between classes to grab a snack, and they can also come by at lunchtime. Because reading and coffee go together so well—and the library is a co-sponsor—they roll a magazine cart out from the library into the hallway to increase exposure to the wonderful periodicals and offer school newspapers for reading material. The coffeehouse provides a relaxed atmosphere in which faculty and students can get to know each other, refuel, and de-stress during the morning. They sell Starburrowes Gift Certificates to teachers for student rewards, to parents for teacher gifts, as contest prizes, and as welcoming gifts for new teachers each fall.

Alison Ernst (Northfield Mount Hermon School, Mount Hermon, MA) reports that her associate director, Pam Allan, organized "Acoustic Fridays," for which students sign up ahead of time to perform music in the library an hour before closing. Ernst says they have "had drummers and fiddlers, guitar players, a chamber orchestra and singers. Most of the time, the music was great." Next the library will begin hosting a high school movie club on Friday afternoons. Students will pick the movie from the library's collection and watch it in the library classroom, where there is a ceiling-mounted projector. Ernst says they will provide the popcorn.

Service opportunities also abound in and around libraries. Because there is always plenty of work to do in the library, student volunteers can be kept very busy. Hope Preston (Gill St. Bernard's School, Gladstone, NJ) uses fourth-grade volunteers after school to create bulletin boards, check books in, shelve fiction and picture books, help with weeding and processing, and write book reviews to post on a bulletin board. The group is called the Bookworms. Preston recruits her help in January by sending an invitation to the entire fourth grade asking for student volunteers. She gives them the responsibility for decorating the two library bulletin boards, which is generally a three-week process from planning to creation. Preston says that the students "love having the responsibility and feeling that they are doing real library work, not just make-work. The benefit to me is to tie children more closely to the library, helping them see it as a place that can have meaning outside their weekly classroom visits."

Linda Abati (Saint Mary's Hall Lower School, San Antonio, TX) runs two service projects, a Teddy Bear Drive and Book Baskets for Literacy. The library theme every October is bears, and at that time the library sponsors a

Community Service

Teddy Bear drive. This drive collects an average of 350 bears annually and presents them to the San Antonio Police Department on Teddy Roosevelt's birthday. The teddy bears are given to children who are victims of crime or witnesses in ongoing investigations. Unfortunately, according to Abati, the need is often greater than the supply, as "this is only a three-month supply for the police department." The second project, Book Baskets for Literacy, involves collecting gently used books and "unwanted baskets." Baskets filled with books, with a card attached, are taken to emergency waiting rooms, homeless shelters, and other charities. Shirley Ehman (St. George Episcopal School, San Antonio, TX) also makes book donations to local organizations serving the homeless, the families the school supports at Christmas, wounded soldiers, and a local public library that feeds needy children during the summer. "We receive so many like-new donated books that I'm always looking for anyone needing books."

St. Luke's Episcopal School has participated in donating new books to the Women's Storybook Project (WSP) of Texas. The WSP is an interfaith endeavor that helps incarcerated women reconnect with their children through literature. The mothers earn the privilege to record themselves reading a story (picture book or excerpt from a novel) as a reward for their good behavior. The tape and book are then sent to the child. According to former librarian and longtime volunteer, Nancy Wallace, "Statistics show that one out of every five children of incarcerated parents also ends up in prison. This project strives to change this statistic by developing strong relationships between mothers and their children through the powerful impact of hearing their mother's voice reading them a story."

Working in the library and collecting new and gently used books are obvious extensions of a library program. Some library service projects are not so obviously connected, but just as meaningful. The PRINTS Club—People Recognizing Injustices in Need of Thoughtful Solutions—meets weekly in the Helen Temple Cooke Library at Dana Hall School to work on issues of social justice under the supervision of an assistant librarian. The group attends the Amnesty International "Get on the Bus Day" for human rights in New York City; they manage the school's Oxfam Day events three times a year, when the Dining Center serves only rice and beans at lunch to call attention to world hunger and donates the money saved to Oxfam International; and they give presentations to the school on human rights issues like Darfur. Anne Erickson (Pembroke Hill School, Kansas City, MO) teams up with a history teacher as a freshman class sponsor. The two of them plan all the freshman class activities, including their orientation and elections. One of their major activities is Community Service Day, when approximately 100–120 freshmen are taken to five different venues in the city for a half-day of community service.

For Elizabeth Burke (Georgetown Visitation Preparatory School, Washington, DC), the library advisory board is the library's outreach to the students as well as a way for the library to sponsor student-led activities. The board is

Library Advisory Board

made up of four or five sophomores, juniors, and seniors. At the end of each school year, several freshmen who have an interest in the library, who enjoy being there and using the resources, are invited to join. The board meets about six times a year to discuss any library-related items of interest to students. Student board members requested through this board that the library extend its hours, which resulted in increased funding to support the increased staff hours; the library is open longer hours this year. The board also sponsors several book discussions throughout the year and a charity during the holiday season. They might sponsor a book drive for a local charity that ships books to a school in Africa. And they plan activities related to Banned Books Week, including a "Coming Out Party," which included cake for a few specific banned titles. The party was a huge hit, but the real hit is the opportunity for student leadership on library issues. The librarians guide the process, but the student members of the library advisory board make the recommendations. "Each year gets better than the last."

Like other faculty members, school librarians participate in coaching academic and nonacademic subjects. In Texas the Private Schools Interscholastic Association (PSIA) gives independent school students in first through eighth grades the opportunity to compete in nineteen contest categories similar to University Interscholastic League (UIL) competitions. The PSIA mission is to "inspire private, parochial, charter, and home school student

Competition Coaches

achievement through academic competition." Objective events include art and music memory, science, math, vocabulary, spelling, dictionary skills, and maps and graphs, while the subjective events include speech and drama, writing, and storytelling. The level of librarian participation varies from school to school, but when a school participates there are plenty of opportunities to coach, direct, or judge a competition at the school, district, or state level. Storytelling and dictionary skills are two events that attract librarian participation. In storytelling, participants hear a story that they later retell in their own words. Using the *Merriam-Webster Collegiate Dictionary*, students competing in dictionary skills are challenged to answer tough questions. Mary Milligan (St. Luke's Episcopal, San Antonio, TX) has coached dictionary skills for many years and has had a number of students do very well at the state competition. "This is much more than looking up a word and finding the definition. This requires a student to know how to use keywords, understanding what is being asked, and how to go about interpreting the answer. This is the heart of information literacy."

Dorcas Hand, the director of libraries at Annunciation Orthodox School, recently led a group in a history contest. The students were asked to select and explain the top ten people, places, and events in ancient history, modern world history, or American history. The final list could be presented as an essay, a PowerPoint, or a video. Despite previous training in bibliographic citation, before the final day of the contest, "It never occurred to them that they would have to cite every single image they used!" What a great catalyst for real learning of database use, historical thought, and citation skills.

Cheryl Werner (Oak Knoll School of the Holy Child, Summit, NJ) runs the Look-It-Up Club in the winter months during lunch recess time for about six to eight weeks. Students from first to sixth grades are invited to complete ten challenges. For instance, a first-grade challenge may read: "Find a book by Tomie dePaola." In second grade, they may have to look up the meaning of a word in a dictionary or find a specific book in the library's online catalog. In grades 3 through 6, the challenges increase in complexity and usually require finding the answers in a reference book or online database. An example would be: What countries border Germany? The contest is very labor-intensive for the library staff. Children must show every answer before they go on to the next challenge. The containers must remain filled with relevant challenges, because the children choose at random. Cheryl says, "This activity has gotten very chaotic at times, but long-term benefits are great."

Most often it appears that librarians choose to coach academic areas that are related to reading, writing, or research, but the interests vary from librarian to librarian. Jeanette Vilagi (Keystone School, San Antonio, TX) chose an entirely different field altogether. She is the school's Math Club director. Designed for grades 2–4, the purpose of the math club "is to provide an environment where students can have fun exploring and increasing their understanding of mathematical concepts while, at the same time, developing math skills, gaining problem solving techniques, and broadening their perspective for the pervasiveness and importance of math."

Claire Steves (San Antonio Academy, TX) had always had an interest in history, but she never expected to be the curator of a museum. Head of School John Webster asked her to have a monthly exhibit of San Antonio Academy memorabilia in the library. The school

| **School Museum** |

was founded in 1886, only fifty years after Texas gained its independence from Mexico and forty-five years after it became the twenty-eighth state. Claire and her husband Edward decided to set up other exhibits in the library's mezzanine to showcase other artifacts. Over three years, the idea snowballed into a full-fledged museum of more than fifty exhibits displaying curricular ties to history, math, science, and books. The official name of the museum is the San Antonio Academy Museum. It was established in November 2007 to celebrate San Antonio Academy's rich history and provide a living record of its relationship to individuals, families, and institutions throughout the United States. The wealth of history and artifacts collected by alumni and others connected to The Academy brings together students, teachers, and parents in greater understanding of issues related to curriculum topics. The multifaceted collection of artifacts from prehistory to the Obama presidency is open during library hours; the library staff also offers classes tying in units of study. In a hands-on exhibit loaned by the Loma Oil Company, students learn how oil is extracted from the ground; they were able to see, touch, and smell the oil and drilling equipment. A student commented, "This is cool. Can we do it again next year? Can we touch it again?" Other donors have loaned exhibits ranging from frontier Americana to World War I and II to banking, ranching, and African Americans. Parents, grandparents, and other special guests of our students visit the museum on tours and receptions; school functions can take place in the library mezzanine area. The museum's home at the school limits the collection to those artifacts that enrich some aspect of the total curriculum, and the location in the library means they cannot keep the K–8 students out of the museum. Daily they average at least twenty-five student visitors, often bringing with them parents, grandparents, or visiting friends. Besides the core mission to be a museum related to the school's history and curriculum, a goal of the museum is to offer students from other schools the same opportunity to both view Texas history from a personal history perspective and build from that personal association a passion for museums, libraries, and history.

One unusual schoolwide activity happens under the leadership of Darshell Silva (Urban Collaborative Accelerated Program, Providence, RI), who leads a group of students in transcendental meditation. Twice a day the entire school takes a meditation break. Silva says the goal is "to see if meditation will help relieve some of the stress of our urban students and create a better atmosphere here at the school. We hope it will also give them a tool they can use at home or once they leave us." And sometimes that extra activity is just being available to the school community.

Family Read Night

Chris Martinez (Our Lady of Perpetual Help, Selma, TX) has a Family Read Night once a month. She keeps the library open until at least 6:00 pm for students and their parents. Martinez saw a need for the library to be open so that parents could "spend some quality time with their child and have a quiet place away from radios, TV and other distractions from homework."

Indeed, independent school libraries each serve a community with a unique purpose and specific library needs that are central to the school's character. The uniqueness of those needs creates a variety of responses: book clubs and reading groups that range from "boys only" to wider applications that can involve students, faculty, and families; competitions, publications, museums, and community involvement are all inventive expansions on the most basic mission of the independent school library, which is to introduce students to and excite them about literature and information. The patterns that emerge from all this variety hark back to that mission again and again: the library is a vital part of the school's academic community; the librarian strives to find ways to make learning connections with the students; and the programs created fill the unique needs of the individual school. The word "independent" plays a prominent role here, allowing independent school librarians to follow their own interests and abilities, which are as varied as the schools they serve.

References

Aydelott, Jimmie, and Diana S. Buck. 2003. *Building Literature Circles*. Beavercreek, OH: Pieces of Learning.

Booksprouts.com—An Online Community of Book clubs and Reading Groups. n.d. Available at www.booksprouts.com/. Accessed July 23, 2009.

Gelman, Judy, and Vicki Levy Krupp. 2007. *The Kids' Book Club Book: Reading Ideas, Recipes, Activities, and Smart Tips for Organizing Terrific Kids' Book Clubs*. New York: Tarcher.

Hamra, Amy. 2003. *Making Literature Circles Come Alive: A Time-saving Resource*. Beavercreek, OH: Pieces of Learning.

Jacobsohn, Rachel W. 1998. *The Reading Group Handbook*. Westport, CT: Hyperion Books.

Melton, David. n.d. *Welcome to Landmark Editions! Home of Books for Students by Students*. Available at www.landmarkeditions.com/scripts/contest.asp. Accessed October 13, 2009.

Moore, Ellen, and Kira Stevens. 2004. *Good Books Lately: The One-Stop Resource for Book Groups and Other Greedy Readers*. New York: St. Martin's.

Pearl, Nancy. 2007. *Book Crush: For Kids and Teens—Recommended Reading for Every Mood, Moment and Interest*. Seattle, WA: Sasquatch Books.

Pearlman, Mickey. 1999. *What to Read: The Essential Guide for Reading Group Members and Other Book Lovers*. Brattleboro, VT: Harper Paperbacks.

PSIA—Private Schools Interscholastic Association. n.d. Available at www. psiaacademics.org/. Accessed October 14, 2009.

Smith, Laura J. H. 2004. *The Book Bunch: Developing Book Clubs for Beginning Readers*. Ft. Atkinson, WI: Upstart Books.

The Altamont School
Mary Martin, Librarian
4801 Altamont Rd.
Birmingham, AL 35222
http://www.altamontschool.org

Castle Hills First Baptist School
Judy Howitt, Librarian
2220 N.W. Military Hwy.
San Antonio, TX 78213
http://chfbs.org/

Annunciation Orthodox School
Dorcas Hand, Director of Libraries
3600 Yoakum Blvd.
Houston, TX 77006
www.aoshouston.org

Cornerstone Christian Schools
Lori Farmer, Librarian
4802 Vance Jackson
San Antonio, TX 78230
http://www.cornerstonechristianschools.com

Dana Hall School
Liz Gray, Library Director
Helen Temple Cooke Library
45 Dana Rd.
Wellesley, MA 02482
www.danahall.org

Episcopal School of Dallas
Michelle Randall, Library Department
    Chair/Upper School Librarian
Bonnie Tollefson, Lower School Librarian
4100 Merrell Rd.
Dallas, TX 75229
http://www.esdallas.org/

**Georgetown Visitation Preparatory
    School**
Elizabeth Burke, Librarian
Angela Jewell, Assistant
    Librarian/Technology Collaborator
1524 35th St. NW
Washington DC 20007
http://www.visi.org/

Gill St. Bernard's School
Hope Preston, Lower School Librarian
St. Bernard's Rd.
Gladstone NJ 07934
http://www.gsbschool.org/

Flintridge Preparatory School
Susan Hodge, Head Librarian
4543 Crown Ave.
La Canada, CA 91011
http://www.flintridgeprep.org/

The John Cooper School
Susan Gerding, Lower School Librarian
1 John Cooper Dr.
The Woodlands, TX 77381
www.johncooper.org

Keystone School
Jeanette Vilagi, Lower School Librarian
119 E. Craig Place
San Antonio, TX 78212
http://www.keystoneschool.org/

Northfield Mount Hermon School
Alison Ernst, Director of Library &
    Academic Resources
One Lamplighter Way
Mount Hermon, MA 01354
http://www.nmhschool.org/

Oak Knoll School of the Holy Child
Cheryl Werner, Library Media Specialist
Bonaventura Library
Summit, NJ 07901
http://www.oakknoll.org/

Our Lady of Perpetual Help
Mrs. Chris Martinez, Librarian
16075 N Evans Rd.
Selma, TX 78154
http://www.olph.org/school.html

The Overlake School
Rebecca Moore, Librarian
20301 NE 108th St.
Redmond, WA 98053
http://www.overlake.org/

Pembroke Hill School
Anne Erickson, Librarian
Kemper Library
400 W 51st St.
Kansas City, MO 64112
http://www.pembrokehill.org/

Providence Catholic School
Stella Gonzalez, Librarian/Textbook
    Coordinator
1215 N. Saint Mary's St.
San Antonio, TX 78215
http://www.providencehs.net/

Saint Mary's Hall
Linda Abati, Librarian, Lower School
Ruth Sagebiel, former Librarian, Lower
    School
9401 Starcrest
San Antonio, TX 78217
http://www.smhall.org/

San Antonio Academy
Claire Steves, Coordinator of Library
    Services & Director/Curator of the SAA
    Museum
Mary Holm, Former Librarian
117 East French Place
San Antonio, TX 78212
http://www.sa-academy.org/

**San Antonio Christian Middle
    School/High School**
Mrs. Lee Johnson, Librarian
19202 Redland Rd. Bldg F
San Antonio, TX 78259
http://www.sachristianschools.org/

St. George Episcopal School
Shirley Ehman, Librarian
6900 West Ave.
San Antonio, TX 78213

St. Luke's Episcopal School
Mary G. Milligan, Librarian
15 St. Luke's Lane
San Antonio, TX 78209
http://www.sles-sa.org/

**Urban Collaborative Accelerated
    Program**
Darshell Silva, Teacher Librarian
75 Carpenter St.
Providence, RI 02903
http://www.ri.net/RInet/UCAP/

Women's Storybook Project of Texas
c/o Austin Community Foundation
P.O. Box 5159
Austin, TX 78763
http://www.storybookproject.org/

Visit http://lu.com/excellence for supporting links and occasional updates
to all essays in this book.

Mary G. Milligan is the Librarian at St. Luke's Episcopal School (http://www.sles-sa.org/) in San Antonio, TX. Besides studying children's literature, she has written articles and reviews on the subject and has co-edited two groundbreaking anthologies of Latina literature: Daughters of the Fifth Sun: A Collection of Latina Fiction and Poetry *(Putnam/ Riverhead, 1995) and* ¡Floricanto Sí! A Collection of Latina Poetry *(Penguin, 1998). She has attended the TALL Texans Leadership Development Institute sponsored by the Texas Library Association (TLA). In addition, Mrs. Milligan has been appointed to the TLA Committees: Día de los niños/Día de los libros Committee (co-chair) and the Intellectual Freedom Committee, as well as the TLA Vision Task Force on Transforming Texas Libraries. She is also the Past Chair for TLA District 10 and a former member of the Texas Bluebonnet Award Program Committee. While at St. Luke's, she has founded the school's literary magazine,* Burning Bright, *run several book clubs, produced numerous readers theatre productions, organized schoolwide literary festivals, and coached various academic competitions.*

Looking Back to the Future: Traditions Reflected

Hannah Pickworth, Roland Park Country School (Bethesda, MD)

Introduction

The new edition of the *Shorter Oxford English Dictionary* defines a tradition as "the act of handing down something from generation to generation; transmission of statements, beliefs, customs, etc. especially by word of mouth or unwritten customs." By identifying the traditions of an institution, we identify its values, spirit, and people. Because libraries and librarians value reading, writing, books, and most of all readers and thinkers, affirming these values through similar traditions is not surprising. Repeating the traditions serves to enhance the beliefs of or knowledge about that institution. These time-honored practices bind together the participants and give legitimacy to the practices, values, and history of the institution as well as serving as a beacon for the future.

> By identifying the traditions of an institution, we identify its values, spirit, and people.

To gather examples for this essay, independent school librarians were asked about traditions at their schools. Their answers provided a plethora of events and programs ongoing and still developing. The consensus of the responses indicated that traditions are something shared. Whether the traditions were defined and created by several librarians (from the same or different schools), faculty, administration, parents, volunteers, or a combination of the above, all of the respondents used the word "we" or referred to creating traditions with input from others. Although most of traditions are repeated yearly, none was described as a ritual. Finally, most were extremely inclusive, although a few were grade, age, or department specific and some were seen as a type of rite of passage.

Well-established independent schools often have an archive to contain memorabilia associated with broader school traditions. Archives can be part of the library or a separate entity on campus with library-like functions. Because an increasing number of schools are considering questions related to archives, the topic is included in this essay .

Methodology

Participants in ISS (Independent School Section of AASL/ALA), AISL (Association of Independent School Librarians), and AIMS (Association of Independent Maryland Schools) and their friends responded to this informal survey about their library traditions in 2009. Although many schools identified similar traditions (e.g., book fairs, birthday books, author visits) each school put its particular stamp on its way of implementing these traditions. One of the delights of being a school librarian is belonging to a community of extremely generous professionals; librarians who answered these questions would be willing to provide more detail about their events, should the reader feel the need for additional information.

The oldest dated tradition was thirty years old, and many librarians mentioned traditions that were only a few years old. No one mentioned a tradition involving computers or electronic resources. Walter E. DeMelle of the Hotchkiss School (Lakeville, CT) put the topic of traditions in perspective:

> We need to be cautious about is attributing "traditions" to any one school or person: We "borrow" liberally from each other and, as a result, what becomes a tradition at one school may have been something that has occurred at another school for many years before. . . . (I prefer to call it being inspired by someone else's great ideas.) My first awareness of Senior bookmarks came probably fifteen years ago when Jackie Thomas started doing them at Exeter. And I know that after the AISL New England tour several years ago, many libraries started putting international time clocks behind their circulation desk a la Andover. I am sure it didn't start there, but it was where a lot of us first saw them being used in a private school library. Another example that I know others have borrowed is the READ bumper sticker idea from seeing the ones I developed in 2002, but I "borrowed" the idea from a Rhode Island bookstore and now ALA even sells them! So we should share some good ideas and traditions we see going on, but we need to be careful about attributing "ownership."

Defining and Beginning Traditions

Probably most librarians have had an experience similar to to Ellen Cullen's of Notre Dame Prep (Baltimore, MD): "At Notre Dame it seems that if you have something once it is a tradition!" Susan Weintraub of Park School (Baltimore) responded that, "Some of our traditions were begun by parents who love the library and some by librarians." Elaine Reichel from Boys Latin School (Baltimore) stated that, "We just try out new programs or ideas and if they're successful and we enjoy them, we keep them. Programs or ideas that we keep grow and develop a life of their own. That's pretty simple, but that's the way it is."

Traditional Traditions

What is a "tradition" in the library that is not also a library program to extend the curriculum? Many survey responses simply listed programs and activities most librarians think of as part and parcel of school libraries, such as birthday book programs, DEEAR (Drop Everything (Everybody) and READ) time, book fairs, author visits, and Battles of the Books, to name a few. Many of these library programs are discussed below, as well as those programs that involve a wider community than just the library.

Gift Book Programs

Gift books carry a sense of tradition in the bookplates. The books last many years on the shelves, and students ten years or more in the future will have the benefit of the same exact copy donated today. Those future donors will recognize some of the names—maybe their older cousin or their big brother's best friend. At Annunciation Orthodox School (Houston, TX), books are often donated by Chapel Buddies: kindergarten and first-grade students are paired for the year with seventh and eighth graders during chapel. This gives the older students a responsibility for leadership during chapel services, and the younger students get an older buddy, role model, and friend. The books are donated in both directions, so when those kindergarten kids reach eighth grade, they may find on the shelf a book they donated in honor of that Chapel Buddy.

Endowments That Spawn Traditions

At Episcopal School of Dallas (ESD), the school has sponsored visiting authors for thirty years. A few years ago we started an endowed fund after the library received memorial contributions honoring a beloved second-grade student who tragically died after a car accident. We have a special "logo" invitation (designed by Elizabeth's second-grade teacher) for "The Elizabeth Anne Worsham Visiting Author Presentation" that is sent to all of the lower school families, inviting them to one of the presentations. I frame the invitation each year with an original drawing or photograph of the visiting author to display in the library.

Summer Reading Lists

The basic summer reading list is pretty standard fare and a common library responsibility. Some schools are able to take the basic list and build a creative tradition around it; some of the following ideas came by word of mouth and are not attributable to a single school.

- In one school, when school opened in the fall, students each wrote a letter describing their favorite summer reading book. These letters were kept and "mailed" to younger students in the spring to help them select summer reading.

- In another school, students had a list of favorite books and a list of faculty members. The students had to try to match the book and the faculty member. The list is kept in many formats, from electronic on the school's Web page to a nicely printed booklet to be used for several years, with an addendum added each year.

- In the "MS Summer Get Caught Reading Contest," students take pictures of themselves reading somewhere in the world. Past photos have included underwater shots, students at the Great Wall of China, and students buried up to their heads in sand at the beach.

- Each year at St. John's Northwestern Military Academy (Delafield, WI), the librarian asks students, faculty, and staff to send in a review of a book they could not put down. The librarian adds their recommendations to the "Recommended Summer Reading" lists. Peer and teacher recommendations are well-received, and they help the librarian build a collection that matches students' interests.

- At Summit School (Winston-Salem, NC), the library is open one day per week in the summer to junior kindergarten children and their families for storytime. This offers the newest members of the school community a chance to become accustomed to the library and other areas of the school.

These traditions expand the impact of the standard summer reading list to inspire increased interest in students who are tired of requirements.

Book Fairs

Book fairs have been an element of school and library fund-raising since their invention. The intent of the fair is to gather the school community to celebrate books and reading, and maybe raise money as well. Book fairs are held on campus with various vendors who provide shelving and stock, or off-campus at local bookstores. Many schools have built their book fairs into a community event in some way, and those efforts generally become school traditions.

- Baylor School (Chattanooga, TN) offers sixth-graders and their parents a chance to look at and purchase titles from the summer reading list during the spring in advance of the middle school orientation. For seventh and eighth graders, the book fair is held during the academic day. The students come to the book fair during English class. They select the books they want to read for the summer and purchase them (using charge slips), and refreshments are served. The middle school literature specialist is there to talk about the books with the students.

- One unidentified school offered a pajama story hour during the book fair for the youngest children so that parents would have some time to shop for holiday "surprises" for their children.

- Annunciation Orthodox School (Houston, TX) added a Greek Spaghetti Dinner to the evening between the two days of the book fair. The school's association with Greek culture is reflected in the menu, and everyone loves Miss Nikkie's special sauce. Some 1,200 dinners were served to enthusiastic families of book buyers. In 2009 the dinner also welcomed alumni with a special tent and discounted dinner tickets. The AOS book fair is truly a community building tradition that brings together past board members, long-time Greek patrons of the school, former staff, and a high percentage of current families. It is definitely the place to be, and a no-homework night for middle school.

Support of the Curriculum

Some programs that begin as curricular projects grow into huge events in the life of the school, events that graduates remember specifically. At AOS, one such program is the third-grade States Project, a six-month research effort that culminates in the States Fair. Every third grader studies one state for the year and brings to the fair visual displays of his or her learning. The students also, and most important, bring a food associated with their state—everyone loves to come and taste the variety of foods offered. And years later, they can tell you exactly what they brought! The community comes together to celebrate the states and sing the "Fifty Nifty United States."

Fifty Nifty United States from thirteen original colonies,
Shout 'em, scout 'em,
Tell all about 'em,
One by one, til we've given a day to every state in the USA . . .

(Charles 2007)

Traditions Unique to Specific Schools

To honor each response to the question about unique traditions, the following descriptions are in the librarians' own words.

Notre Dame Prep (NDP) started celebrating Library Week in 1977. Most of those years we have celebrated during National Library Week, but we can get creative in the face of date conflicts. Anytime I send an e-mail or make an announcement, I tell the students how many days until National Library Week. The day after the week is over I tell them it is only 358 days until the next one! Any time I meet a graduate they ask me how many days until National Library Week. I make sure that I always know or can make up a number!! We fill the week with contests and special events. One year we featured Rosie the Riveters (10 wonderful women who served during World

War II) in a seventh-grade puppet show. (The girls had read biographies of women and made puppets.) The show was followed by a tea. Our contests vary from year to year. This year, NDP is celebrating the "Year of Diversity" at Notre Dame, the students enter by just submitting the title of a book they read that represented diversity. Winners will be selected at random. Prizes are creative, inexpensive and FUN—an oversized pencil, for example. (Notre Dame Prep, Towson, MD)

At ESD, we celebrate "Read Across America" during the first week of March each year, but we have renamed it "Favorite Book Week" at ESD. Each class focuses on one Dr. Seuss title which integrates with their curriculum (for example, second grade reads *The Lorax* because they do a year-long study on trees—forests, etc.) We also have different contests during the week, ideas I picked up off of the internet. One year we took photos of teachers dressed in crazy hats and glasses, holding up their favorite book so that the only part of their face showing was their eyes. This year we sponsored "in-tent reading"—we set up tents in the library, added a fake campfire, played forest sounds, gave each child a flashlight, and let them read in pairs in the tents during their library period. They loved this. (Episcopal School of Dallas, TX)

At our end of the year awards recognition assembly, the library staff presents "The Summit, NJ Annual Book Lover's Award." The student's name is inscribed on an impressive plaque which hangs in the library. In addition, the student receives a certificate that we have created and a gift card from Barnes and Noble. Method of selection—subjective!! Based on number of books student reads, interest in reading, discussing and recommending book to use and other students. It is usually an obvious choice. (Oak Knoll School, Summit, NJ)

The boys at our school love ghost stories. Since the school has a long history and many old stone buildings, cadets are always looking for ghost stories about the school. A few years ago I began to collect academy ghost stories. I send an email out to all students in mid-October (when ghosts are on their minds) and have used the stories they've sent me over the years to create a booklet and displays. There are new stories every year; many of them sent to me by younger students who (of course) heard them from older students with creative imaginations. (St. John's Northwestern Military Academy, Delafield, WI)

Each year before the winter holiday the foreign language teacher and I have a special program in the library. We alternate the Spanish Christmas tradition one year and the French Christmas tradition the next year.

- For the Spanish winter holiday program, the foreign language teacher and I read books on Los Posadas to the students. Then the first grade students go in procession from room to room to find out if there is room in the inn—and all the doors are closed on them until they arrive in the library where not only are the doors open to them but there was a

Fiesta prepared and waiting for them. During the Fiesta I also read *The Night of Los Posadas* by Tomie dePaola.

- For the French winter holiday program, the foreign language teacher and I read books on French Father Christmas. During the celebration week, as each class arrived at the library, the students lefts their shoes outside the library door. The doors were closed and while I was reading *Noel for Jeanne Marie* by Francoise, the administrative assistant played Silent Father Christmas and put candies and pennies in the students' shoes. When the story ended and it was time to leave the library, there were squeals of delight at the surprises in their shoes. (Glenelg Country School, Howard County, MD)

As Librarian, I sit on the Board of Trustees' Education Committee, a tradition which I am careful to nurture. I include a report to the Board in the packet of information that is sent out to Board members prior to their Fall and Spring meetings. It allows me to highlight program changes, problems (usually with proposed solutions), and ways the library contributes to the mission of the school. We have a beautiful library, but I am always concerned that the Trustees see the library as program as well as a comfortable and functional place. (Foxcroft School, Middleburg, VA)

Metairie Park Country Day School sponsored for years a school wide "Stump the Library" contest started by librarian Meb Norton. We invited each student and faculty member to submit one reference question. Answering these odd questions took hours of time, before the era of online reference. When high school kids come to visit it is one thing they seem to remember about the lower school library.

Volunteer Traditions

Ever since I have been here (16 years) there has been an active parent volunteer program. that has consistently been the most popular volunteer job for parents. Even though this is time consuming, the value far outweighs the negative. The volunteer program fulfills our mission "to promote life-long library users and learners." The parents (including several dads) who work in the library find this a welcoming, warm, and safe environment. It is like our own "Friends of the Library" group without a formal name, because these parents truly do become our friends. Our parent volunteers are wonderful advocates for our library program! (Episcopal School of Dallas, TX)

Chadwick School has a formal "Friends of the School Library" organization. In addition to fundraising activities, parent volunteers adopt shelves in the library and keep them in order throughout the year. This responsibility lets them drop into the library anytime, and posts their name on the shelves they manage. (Chadwick School, Palos Verdes Peninsula, CA)

Books, Libraries, and Community Service

St. Vincent Pallotti High School supports annually a charitable group that builds libraries in sub-Saharan Africa. After the students hear details about the architecture and local culture, and who will use the libraries, they begin to raise money and collect books. They hear what kinds of books are useful (no Disney books since those kids don't know Mickey Mouse), and that only books in good condition can be sent. This tradition furthers concepts of community service, social action, and cultural relativism. (St. Vincent Pallotti High School, Laurel, MD)

We have an ongoing Baltimore Reads collection program (Baltimore Reads is a nonprofit organization that collects, sorts, and distributes children's books for day care centers, afterschool programs, etc. where the need for additional books is great.) Each classroom has a collection box and kids and parents send in any and all books for kids. Many times the students will offer books to the library as well so it is a win-win opportunity. (Calvert School, Baltimore, MD)

Some libraries have used book sales or book swaps after inventory and weeding. Families can donate books to the book sale so that the selection is large and both adult's and children's materials are included. The sale is set up away from the library so that books for sale aren't confused with library items. Before any weeds can be included, all the school labels have to be pulled. The money raised can be used to support a needy library in the local community or farther away. And the remaining books at the end of the sale can be donated as well. With the current emphasis on sustainability, we may see more book swaps and used book sales as a way to promote environmental stewardship.

School History

The Library is often the place in the school with the most display space. Some libraries have ongoing exhibits of school memorabilia from the Archives, while some have only occasional collections. St. John's Northwestern Academy hosts a poetry festival in mid-February each year. As they celebrate the school's 125th anniversary, they looked into old yearbooks for student poetry to feature in this year's celebration.

St. John's Northwestern is a 7–12 military boarding school for boys, they decided to post Seniors first-year (freshman)pictures on the 8-by-10-inch bulletin board at the top of the library stairs. Some Seniors (particularly those who came to SJNMA as middle school students) had changed so much that other students did not recognize them. Younger cadets asked, "Will you do that for our class next year, Ma'am?" So we do it every year. We display each Senior's first year photo with the quotation he selected for his yearbook page. A group of Seniors are currently working on this year's display. They're having a great time. (St. John's Northwestern Military Academy, Delafield, WI)

For the past nine years we have taken a picture of every student reading a book; it's called Eyes on the Prize. It's been a subtle way to state that we think reading is important, and for students to show their favorite book. The compiled picture is used as a yearbook page, another one is laminated, and the third one is framed. The laminated pictures have been placed around the circulation desk. It makes it easy for students to search and point out each other. Especially for the younger students it's like a "Where's Waldo" activity to find their picture. The framed pictures are hung on a wall. The process of taking the pictures has improved over the years. The school is relatively new; when we began there were about 150 students. Now there are over 500. The pictures have become increasingly smaller. We are an international school with a mobile population. It visibly shows how the school has changed and it allows students to find old friends. (International School of Tianjin, China)

Each year, we have a Friends of the Library campaign which is a fund raising effort. I have worked with both a designated trustee and alum in writing the letter. I have for the past eight years highlighted some aspect of the school's history in an attempt to involve alums and build awareness of our school history and our archives. This year's letter featured "Foxcroft Goes to War, 1940–1946." It was an attempt to talk about not just surviving but thriving during hard times. It becomes an effective way to highlight the traditions of the school through the years. We include a specially designed bookmark with the letter.

Twelve years ago we began a class historians' program which has become a tradition. Each class elects as part of their class officers a class historian (often it is a pair) to work with our Archivist and me to produce a record of each class. We do an all-school scrapbook and have a digital home for our photographs on the school server. We do a class poll which we include with the scrapbook. We have also worked with faculty to produce a set of short essays providing student perceptions of an important school event. This is in response to our concern that we had lots of pictures but no narrative of what actually happened at an event. This program also helps us plug students into the history of the school and build some awareness of the importance of preservation. (Foxcroft School, Middleburg, VA)

Two weeks before Alumni Weekend in early October, and staying through Parents' Weekend at the end of the month, all of the students whose fathers and/or mothers went to Baylor have their photo along with the alumni parent(s) year book photo displayed. The kids go over this display and it is a big hit with parents and alums. Our previous circulation manager began this display about 18 years ago and our current circulation manager has kept it going and made it even better. (Baylor School, Chattanooga, TN)

Archives

The Taft Education Center (Taft School, Watertown, CT, www. taftschool. org/tec/nonap.aspx#09C09) offers a summer weeklong introductory course in school archives.

At some point in a school's history, someone realizes that the memorabilia and documentation of the school's history are being lost because no one is collecting them. The first step to making a school archive is simply to begin to collect the photos, records, and realia that offer insights into the school's earlier years. There are old uniforms, winning footballs, early curricula and report cards, photographs of various sizes with and without labels, and more. Because storage of such materials requires some expertise if the collection is expected to survive into the future, someone will be appointed as archivist. This person may be a longtime school employee, parent, or alumnus, any of whom may have no formal training but may have great knowledge of school details and people. A trained archivist will have more skills but perhaps less knowledge of the place. However it begins, the school archive will become an essential aspect of ongoing marketing, fund-raising, and student interest. The role of the archive was best described by Dorian Myers of the Kinkaid School (Houston, TX): "a service to the school to preserve the records of who we are and what we do as an educational institution." Archives are a way of honoring the past and connecting with the present and the future.

The archivist at Gilman School has formed an independent school archivist group in the Baltimore area. The group holds meetings and has attended the workshop held at the National Archives. They encourage every library to have a disaster plan for their archives—something no library should be without. (See essay 21.)

Summing up the role of the archivist, Paula Brown says, "In my first ten years I learned to listen to stories, find notes and make more to share with the evolving Development and Alumni offices for their valuable contacts and to keep the circle growing with each class that passes through and trickles back."

Archival Displays

To honor each response to the question about archives, the following descriptions are in the librarians' own words.

> Two years ago we launched our Web site (http:libraryarchives.standrews-de.org) which has become very popular with our Alum, Faculty and Staff. We send out e-mail once a week to the community with a tidbit from the archives, usually something relevant to the calendar year. We also post these on our Face book page. (Carol Ann Pala, St. Andrew's School, Middletown, DE)

The School at Church Farm (Exton, PA) has a rich history of combining an agricultural and an academic education. During the library orientation, the students learn about the design of farm buildings and how that agricultural design is unique to their school in the placement of buildings and the way light is used. Reportedly one of the windows was salvaged from a cathedral that was never completed during the Depression. Students are introduced to books as old as the school (some now in the archives) and a quilt designed by the boys with their art teacher, memorializing the aspects of school farm life.

The Asheville School creates both web and physical displays featuring what was going on at our school and historically at various times in the past: 20 years ago, 50 years ago, etc. The School also has a unit on the Jazz Age that includes the school's history as well as local history and ties in with the Senior's American Studies unit on the same theme. (Joanne Crotts, The Asheville School, NC).

Nancy Gilpin from Gilman School (Baltimore, MD) also uses the school archives to create power point displays for various events and celebrations such as the Gilman Bull Roast, dedications, and programs where alumni visit the school throughout the year.

Conclusion

Learning about traditions in our independent schools is interesting and enlightening. We all know how popular school library tours are at our professional conferences and how many questions, conversations, and relationships are built during these visits. Asking the how and the why of the programs provides a mirror to hold up to ourselves and our own library's mandate. From others we gather wonderful ideas to add to and subtract from our own meaningful traditions.

The pressures of time push us to weed traditions that don't perfectly suit anymore, while we water and fertilize others that seem to fill a current need.

Many schools initially appear to have similar traditions. When the layers are peeled away, the traditions are just enough different to be unique and affirming to that institution. A book fair is not a book fair is not a book fair. One has Greek Spaghetti and another has Pajama Storytime. This unique "tweak" provides the meaningful spark that jumps between the school and library and community. An exact copy loses a bit in the translation just like photocopies of photocopies. The copy becomes only the one-dimensional, wobbly imitation of the original program or event. In this essay, librarians have shared their best and most meaningful traditions.

> A book fair is not a book fair is not a book fair . . . [The] unique "tweak" provides the meaningful spark that jumps between the school and library and community.

Libraries don't start out to build a tradition. They start an event to celebrate reading or poetry or alumni, and the event is such a good fit because it was tailor made for one specific community. As it becomes a tradition, it gets tweaked to keep it fresh. Another school may love the idea, but must absorb it and make it their own like a chef adapting a recipe. A library tradition can continue past the librarian's tenure if it contributes to the school's ongoing ethos in a functional way; if all the energy for the tradition comes from a single librarian, it will end without that librarian to shepherd it along.

The lasting traditions enable individual students to say, "Although I am unique, I'm a part of this institution's story past, present and future" and enable the institution to say, "Although we're unique, we've built a larger community, past, present and future."

> *A library tradition can continue . . . if it contributes to the school's ongoing ethos in a functional way.*

Traditions build community. School library traditions use library themes and strengths to contribute to the greater school community: summer reading letters to younger students, book drives for disadvantaged schools, "Stump the Library" challenges. Our traditions are part of our ongoing library advocacy programs and our interactions with the admissions, development, and alumni offices. They extend our regular programs in support of the academic curriculum and build bridges between age-level divisions and the academic faculty. They bring in parents and alumni as active participants in our ongoing efforts to inspire lifelong learners. And the school archive offers a storehouse for memories of the many traditions a school and its library keep alive.

References

Charles, Ray. 2007. *"Fifty Nifty United States."* Sing365.com. Available at www.sing365.com/music/lyric.nsf/PrintLyrics?OpenForm&ParentUnid=0AE9 8363D8B3BD3B48256C24000F4F7B. Accessed November 28, 2009.

Contributors to Looking Back to the Future

Paula Brown, The School at Church Farm (Exton, PA), www.gocfs.net

Chadwick School (Palos Verdes Peninsula, CA), www.chadwickschool.org

Joanne Crotts, The Asheville School (Asheville, NC), www.ashevilleschool.org

Ellen Cullen, Notre Dame Prep (Baltimore, MD), www.notredameprep.com

Walter DeMelle, Hotchkiss School (Lakeville, CT), www.hotchkiss.org

Nancy Gilpin, Gilman School (Baltimore, MD), www.gilman.edu

Beth Gourley, International School of Tianjin (Tianjin China), www.istianjin.org

Dorcas Hand, Annunciation Orthodox School (Houston, TX), www. aoshouston.org

Judith Hay, Glenelg Country School (Glenelg MD), www.glenelg.org

Jane Jester, Summit School (Winston-Salem, NC), www.summitschool.com

Peg Koller, St. John's Northwestern Military Academy (Delafield, WI), www.sjnma.org

Steve Matthews, Foxcroft School (Middleburg, VA), www.foxcroft,org

Mary Milligan, St. Luke's Episcopal School (San Antonio, TX), www.saintlukesepiscopal.net

Dorian Myers, Kinkaid School (Houston, TX), www.kinkaid.org

Meb Norton, Metairie Country Day School (Metairie, LA), www.mpcds.com

Carol Ann Pala, St. Andrews School (Middletown, DE), www.standrews-de.org

Milly Rawlings, Baylor School (Chattanooga, TN), www.baylorschool.org

Elaine Reichel, Boys Latin (Baltimore, MD), www.boyslatinmd.com

Amy Siegel, St. Vincent Pallotti High School (Laurel, MD), www.pallottihs.org

Tina Thomas, Calvert School (Baltimore, MD), www.calvertschool.org

Bonnie Tollefson, Episcopal School of Dallas (Dallas, TX), www.esdallas.org

Joan Turk, Oak Knoll School (Summit, NJ), www.oakknoll.org

Susan Weintraub, Park School (Baltimore, MD), www.parkschool.net

---

Visit http://lu.com/excellence for supporting links and occasional updates to all essays in this book.

Hannah Pickworth has been a public, school, and university librarian and has taught children's literature at Towson University in Baltimore. She is a member of ALA, MLA, AISL, IBBY, and Beta PHi Mu. She is co-founder of the Peace Study Center, a nonprofit resource center of peace materials to encourage teachers, caregivers, parents, and all educators to include teaching peace skills to young children ages three to eight through stories, songs, books, and professional programs. Presently she is at Roland Park Country School (www.rpcs.org), a K–12 independent girls' school in Baltimore.

With thanks to all the librarians who contributed traditions to this essay. They are listed with their school contacts in the list of contributors.

Choices, Choices: Selection Issues in Independent School Libraries

Carla Bosco, Stone Ridge School of the Sacred Heart (Bethesda, MD)

In the fall of 2009, Cushing Academy, a private school in Massachusetts, eliminated its entire print collection, disposing of thousands of books, both well-worn treasures and lightly used tomes (Abel 2009). This controversial decision is a dramatic example of the dilemmas faced by many independent school librarians throughout the country during this era of revolutionary change. To paraphrase Shakespeare: To purchase print or not, that is one of many questions school librarians now wrestle with as they develop their library collections in a fast-paced, digital world.

Only a decade ago, it was expected that a school librarian would develop the library's collections by acquiring books and possibly videos, which were then neatly arranged on the shelves in the library. The world of information has shifted drastically, with an abundance of online sources, both free and subscription, which often satisfy the information/research needs of the digital generation; meanwhile, Kindles or other e-readers could become the preferred means of recreational reading in the near future. Instead of ordering DVDs, for example, the librarian might rely on a Netflix subscription to satisfy the temporary needs of a teacher, particularly for films that he or she might consider of fleeting fame. These are some of the issues facing school librarians today as they develop and improve traditional physical collections even as they attempt to anticipate the changing digital realities of the next few years. There are no easy answers. Following are suggestions for how the librarian can best select appropriate print and electronic resources to develop a high-quality independent school library.

Supporting the Independent School Curriculum: Challenges and Strategies

Regardless of format, the main emphasis should be on developing a collection that supports and enhances the school's curriculum. Whether it is officially articulated or more informally stated, every school has a certain emphasis and traditional assignments. A course of studies or curriculum map will be a helpful tool to determine the general school curriculum, although individual teachers probably design their own assignments. In the lower grades, variance between self-contained classrooms at the same grade level leads to inconsistency of service to students despite a single curriculum for that grade. Meanwhile, in the upper grades, many "subject specialists" will work with the students, meaning there will be more than one contact, sometimes even more than one teacher, per subject and grade level.

[T]he main emphasis should be on developing a collection that supports and enhances the school's curriculum.

The major difference between private schools and public schools is the independence of the teachers to develop their own curricula and assignments within the school's mission and administrative direction. Aligning the library to the academic program in this independent environment carries some potential challenges. Schools are working toward better alignment across disciplines and grade levels by means of curriculum mapping, but some teachers reject the idea of a fixed curriculum at all, citing independence as the heart of their mission. Especially in high schools, teachers may see themselves as "junior" college teachers, assuming the same academic freedoms to teach what they want. As well, teachers tend to move between subjects depending on enrollment and the larger school needs; thus in one year a teacher may teach juniors American history and then the following year teach seniors about the Holocaust. Teachers will often have "pet" interests, with one devoting time to women's studies or the Middle East. Schools experience periods of high turnover in the faculty, which can lead to conflicting pressures for the library collection. A teacher with a graduate degree in government could be followed by one who wants to teach Latin American history, thus significantly changing the school's course offerings and the needs of the library collection. Schools may also consciously change academic programs to respond to societal and community interests and demand; for example, more courses on Asian studies, Chinese language and literature, and Middle Eastern studies are now being offered. All of these factors contribute to an environment, particularly in the high school, in which developing a collection that responds to the curriculum can be very challenging. Nonetheless, schools usually have some core courses and programs or philosophy that they feature as school hallmarks year after year.

In the traditional "college preparatory" independent school, the secondary school teachers may be somewhat constrained by advanced placement, international baccalaureate, or other prestigious national programs with an established program. These programs have rigid curricula over which the individual teacher or school has no control, leaving the teacher few opportunities to take advantage of library resources. Generally, teachers of self-designed "honors" courses, especially senior seminar electives, will have more options to assign research courses and use the library's resources than the AP courses do. The history APs place great emphasis on Document Based Questioning (DBQ), which means the library should add materials with primary sources to the library's collections.

Balance this with renewed interest in so-called constructivist pedagogy, which emphasizes individual student research as a core value. In schools where this method is implemented, libraries will require more breadth and depth of holdings to support higher level research.

Of course, the savvy school librarian can develop a collection that is strong and broad enough to respond to all of these scenarios. A key ally within the school on these matters will be the dean of studies/academics, especially in the middle and high school, who can help the librarian respond to teachers and suggest ways they can coordinate projects and assignments to counterbalance some of their independence. Now that most states have adopted some standards and goals, and a core curriculum for the nation is under consideration (Common Core, Partnership), many private schools are methodically updating their curricula to be more in line with specific graduation requirements. The schools still retain the freedom to respond to community needs. Perhaps a library has a strong special collection in, for example, Holocaust studies or local history. By highlighting the particular strengths of that print collection, the school librarian can actually help shape the curriculum, suggesting various research assignments to the teachers. Once the curriculum begins to take advantage of the special collection, the librarian will work to keep the collection updated.

Developing a broad collection that has the flexibility to grow with the curriculum will definitely be helpful. Setting aside a certain percentage of the print budget for last-minute changes is a good idea. Also, by regularly selecting and ordering wide-ranging, high-quality nonfiction that does not necessarily directly support current projects, the library will have sufficient print resources to handle new requests. For example, ordering some well-reviewed books on China while they are available may well prove helpful in the next few years, when China/Chinese studies will become a focus of the curriculum.

> *Develop . . . a broad collection that has the flexibility to grow with the curriculum.*

Another helpful approach is for the school librarian to attempt to anticipate certain global and societal trends. Although it is not necessary to become a "news junkie," a general awareness of "hot topics" is helpful. Topics that became prominent in 2009 included global warming/climate change, Iran, Pakistan, and North Korea; new topics will arise over time. Inevitably, some topics are of only short-term interest, such as Obama as a presidential candidate. Subscribing to a select number of broad databases can alleviate the need to have books on every changing topic or assignment, because the e-resources are updated on a regular basis.

Digital Resources

In these changing times, libraries need to supplement print resources with database subscriptions. The sciences, especially biotechnology and genetics, now evolve so rapidly that digital resources may be the only answer. These e-resources are expensive, but can often be purchased via state or other consortia, which negotiate lower, often substantially lower, prices.

Partly due to the popularity of the Google search page, many vendors are moving from the traditional and staid database interfaces to Web "portals." These colorful, engaging pages usually have only one simplified search box. Integrated search tools are becoming more common; allowing a student to search all of a school's databases at once. Integrated searching has the advantage of minimizing the effort, but only if students are savvy searchers who use focused keywords. A vague search in an integrated search tool is like a vague search in Google: a gazillion hits in no useful order.

A drawback to databases and e-resources is the lack of control over content. Few vendors carry the full content of magazines and newspapers. For example, all stories originally issued by the AP are pulled from the record—for some newspapers, this makes up much of their content. Also, due to the ruling of the Supreme Court in *Tasini vs. New York Times*, freelance writers and columnists can request that their material be excluded from electronic reprinting, including in the subscription databases. Because these rights and agreements can change, a vendor may retain the content one month of your subscription but "pull" it the next; an article or column may simply vanish from your virtual library. Vendors make various exclusive agreements with publishers, too, that can change over time; a series may be offered by EBSCO one year and ProQuest the next. Recently a fierce controversy arose after EBSCO acquired the exclusive rights to all *TIME* products beginning in 2010, effectively cutting off Gale and others from access. Read the letters (Barnes n.d.; Brooks n.d.; Valenza n.d.) to understand the two sides of the vendor discussion, but the final result puts libraries in a difficult spot. Small libraries will be forced to choose the vendor that best fits their needs, sending patrons to other libraries for broader access. Librarians must remember that vendors only have direct control over their own proprietary content, but those same vendors hold considerable control over library access. Buyer beware: the devil will be in the details and fine print more than ever.

A similar scenario recently affected Kindle users. Because of copyright issues, Amazon could no longer offer free copies of *1984*. With the power of technology, the company simply erased any and all copies from all Kindle owners, without their knowledge, raising issues of privacy and the reality of "ownership" of such resources. The fact that the targeted book was *1984* only added to the irony (Stone 2009). Thus, librarians need to read contracts carefully to clearly understand if an e-book is truly a permanent part of their collection.

Contract limitations notwithstanding, e-books are another important and expanding option for developing a virtual collection of nonfiction/reference resources. Judicious selection of e-book collections can expand a library's coverage of specific topic areas, sometimes more easily or quickly than locating the same resources in print formats. Vendors sometimes offer discounts for ordering both a print and an electronic copy of a book. Salem Press is using free digital content as an incentive to purchase its print reference books. Other vendors have also recently launched digital options. Librarians need to understand whether they have a subscription to the digital version, as a database, or if the digital material becomes part of the library's permanent collection.

It is important for librarians to meet our digital natives on their turf.

Although librarians should always remind patrons of the excellent resources in databases and should certainly continue to add them to their virtual collections, it is equally important to recognize that the open, free Internet offers high-quality, scholarly materials that can be easily accessed with a search engine. It is important for librarians to meet our digital natives on their turf. The sciences, especially, are rich with free Internet sources, including the new National Science Digital Library and resources from NIH, NASA, and other organizations. And those are just the tip of the iceberg. The school librarian can easily add these to the library's collection, either by adding links to a special resource page on the library's Internet/intranet site, a LibGuide, or by adding a MARC record in the library's online catalog. Librarians can increase potential access to the library collection by placing links to the Web catalog on all school Web pages. Vendors of library systems (ILSs) are developing widgets to make catalog and database access easier, including external wikis or LibGuides. Very likely these vendors will also soon develop catalog applications for the iPhone or other multimedia phones. ILSs already accommodate vendor widgets for library digital subscription resources. Another approach for adding Web links to the collection is to encourage students and teachers to add their own on project wikis. These collaborative Web pages will engage the community and encourage students to develop a personal interest in adding to the library Web collection. Because some teachers may well already provide suggested Web links for various projects, this process could encourage a more centralized approach and help the librarian to see how the teacher is viewing the assignment.

Schools increasingly are creating educational technology coordinator (ETC) positions to work with faculty to better integrate technology into classroom curricula. ETCs don't have much knowledge of, or experience with, databases. They do not necessarily share a librarian's enthusiasm for evaluation of sources on the open Internet; they resemble, in many ways, digital natives who prefer the open Internet and simply don't have the years of training and experience evaluating information sources that we do. AASL's Best Websites for Teaching and Learning (www.ala.org/ala/mgrps/divs/aasl/guidelinesandstandards/ bestlist/bestwebsitestop25.cfm) begins to demonstrate that librarians are working beyond the subscription and preapproved Web site perspective to meet students where they prefer to be at the same time they teach how to evaluate resources. Our experience in concert with the technology expertise of ETC's makes a powerful team in support of the classroom curriculum (see essay 9). As librarians, we can demonstrate our own digital and technology skills by "harvesting" the best of the free Web.

In a world of tight budgets, the school librarian cannot be seen only as the custodian of a resource museum, but should instead be noted for active engagement with all sources of high-quality information. We need to use our evaluative skills to constantly determine exactly what the "best" of the Web is. Some Web sites can be found in *School Library Journal*, at the American Library Association Web site, and from database vendors themselves. *Wikipedia* was once the scourge of librarians for its unreliability; now it is almost a poster child for "buyer beware." Because *Wikipedia* results usually fall into the top five Google hits, we know students will use it. Use your

> *In a world of tight budgets, the school librarian cannot be seen only as the custodian of a resource museum, but should instead be noted for active engagement with all sources of high-quality information.*

precious real estate to focus attention on more unusual sites of value, the ones that students might not find so easily. And offer search engines other than Google (Clusty, Quintura); the search results are different, and the differences may be useful in locating new and innovative results for the same search. Librarians may encourage students to use different search engines by creating and embedding the widgets of these search engines on their pages. Librarians should also consider creating customized Google searches limited to certain URLs or subjects that will facilitate better search results—customized Google can then also be embedded directly on all library, and even all school, Web pages.

Increasingly independent school librarians are embracing other digital information resources as well. In a recent survey on the ISS (Independent School Section) listserv, respondents noted purchases of permanent e-books, audio books in MP3 format, and Kindles or other book readers (Bosco 2009).

New digital innovations can help to promote and increase access to the library's electronic resources. Many publishing companies now offer special sections for librarians with logos, icons, and search "widgets" that can be placed or "embedded" on a variety of the library, or even teacher and student, Web pages, especially within an intranet. RSS feeds and other Web 2.0 tools offer many opportunities for the librarian to bring the collection to the student, something younger generations increasingly expect. Publishers, who compete with Google and the "free Internet," are eager to help librarians highlight their products. Increasing the visibility of the library's e-collections will also enhance the role of the school librarian in the school community. Many database vendors also now offer the ability to "record" a stable URL for particular sources; these URLs can be added to the catalog or other places where they will be easily found by students. Also, many schools are now moving to "content managers," which allow librarians to add library links as "components" or add-ons to other teacher and class pages. As the lines between "collection" and "access" increasingly blur—where "access" can be somewhat confused with "marketing"—the librarian's training in search skills and source evaluation becomes even more helpful to students.

> As the lines between "collection" and "access" increasingly blur . . . the librarian's training in search skills and source evaluation becomes even more helpful to students.

Fiction

In the younger grades, greater emphasis is usually placed on developing a high-quality fiction collection. Quite simply, younger students have more free time and interest in reading for pleasure. Because exposure to a wide variety of literature is often an explicit part of a K–8 curriculum, the school librarian should attempt to add a mix of genres, from mysteries to fantasy to science fiction. Fad series like <u>Harry Potter</u> and <u>Twilight</u> offer easy promotions for reluctant readers. Even if the librarian decides not to purchase these specific works because of school philosophy, students will be hungry for similar titles.

Annual winners of the national awards are obvious choices to add to the collection. These awards are chosen for their "literary merit" rather than readability or popularity. There has been some debate in library magazines and listservs about some award decisions, wondering what is the point of an award that doesn't give readers books they *want* to read. It is important to consider the age range of your readers and the content of a book, whether it has won an award or not. Other good review sources are *School Library Journal* and *Booklist,* especially the starred reviews, and those recommended by *The Horn Book* magazine. These publications will have end-of-the-year "best of" selections, too, as do the book reviews of national newspapers like the *New York Times* and *Washington Post.* These lists are usually published in early December in time for holiday gift purchases. The ALA's children's division, Association for Library Service to Children (ALSC), also announces "best" selections at the January midwinter meetings and publishes them in February. For older readers, the independent school librarian might consider adding the winners of the Pulitzer Prize and National Book Awards.

A Sampling of Book Awards of interest to K-12 libraries

American Library Association Awards

    ALA Best Books for Young Adults

    ALA Notable Books for Children

    Batchelder Award (translations)

    Caldecott Award (illustration for children)

    Coretta Scott King Awards (appreciation of the "American Dream")

    Geisel Award (beginning readers)

    Newbery Award (literature for children)

    Printz Award (young adult)

    Pura Belpre Award (Latino author)

    Sibert Award (informational books)

Boston Globe Horn Book Awards (nonfiction, illustration, fiction) (*Boston Globe* newspaper)

Woodson Award (ethnicity in books for children) (National Council for the Social Studies)

Carnegie Medal (fiction for children) (British Library Association)

Zolotow Award (picture books) (Cooperative Children's Book Center)

Kate Greenaway Award (illustration in children's books) (British Library Association)

National Book Award (youth category) (National Book Foundation)

Because these lists and awards are announced and published at various times throughout the year, it is very helpful to stagger the spending of the book budget, so that one can quickly acquire these works if desired. In addition to these awards, publishers frequently have sales coinciding with the commencement and conclusion of the school year. The initial sales and promotions in August and September are tempting, but other equally good deals may be available in April and May. Most schools will require that all purchases end a month or so before the fiscal year ends, often June 30, for accounting and audit purposes. One thoughtful allocation of budget funds is to spend about 30 percent of the budget between the beginning of the year and October, another 30 percent between October and December, and the bulk of the remaining funds in the months of January–March, leaving a small amount to take advantage of the end-of-the year specials.

The library should reflect issues such as learning differences, character development, bullying, and friendship in the collection, especially if the school teaches the topics formally. Schools also may have units on historical fiction, mysteries, science fiction, etc.; the collection should support a broad, high-quality selection for each genre. With fiction, the issue of copyright date is fairly loose. Classics never go "out of date," but popular titles may not fare as well over the years. There is no rule to tell us when to pull older titles: *The Three Musketeers* will stay; books by Clive Cussler may only last five years. Mysteries and science fiction today are more likely to feature a diverse set of characters than those in the past, as Ursula Le Guin pointed out in a recent article in the *School Library Journal* (Perkins 2009). Some older work has plots or themes strong enough to warrant shelf space even if it does not reflect the latest views on diversity or technology.

Popular Review Tools

Booklist (American Library Association)

Choice Magazine

<u>H.W. Wilson Core Collection</u> Series

Horn Book

Library Journal

New York Times Book Review

Publishers Weekly

School Library Journal

Teacher Librarian

VOYA

Fiction should not be overlooked for secondary students. Even though the students are busy and can be easily distracted by expanding social lives, college and work plans, and technical gadgets, there is still a place for high-quality young adult fiction. Some students use reading, specifically YA literature, as a needed respite from the fast pace of their lives. Other students find that literature provides "bibliotherapy"; it helps them see how characters deal with the same issues they are facing. Literature can also provide new insight into historical and current societal dilemmas. Young adult literature is currently the fastest growing segment of the publishing industry. The edgy nature of much YA fiction may pose some challenges to some schools, particularly those affiliated with religious institutions. Reviewers may or may not detail the nature of the content (sex, language, or mature content); these books are probably more suited for the high school collection than the middle school. *VOYA, the Voice of Youth Advocates*, publishes an annual "Top Shelf Fiction for Middle School Readers" that is helpful for this age group.

Graphic novels are now popular for both nonfiction and fiction. Starting with the modern classic *Maus*, about the Holocaust, the genre has exploded. In a graphic, multimedia world, this format appeals to younger readers who may not engage with long texts anymore. Reading graphic texts requires different reading skills, skills our digital natives may acquire more easily than we immigrants. The purchase of graphic novels is often questioned by administrators, who may see them as less literary; and the genre often includes lots of violent and sexual content that administrators and librarians find problematic. Review tools for graphic literature are becoming more available and are increasingly specific about appropriate reader ages and details of potentially challenging content. The genre does include many high-quality works and can enhance the curriculum. There is a growing overlap of graphic styles into traditional prose works, both fiction and nonfiction.

The H.W. Wilson Core Collection series is helpful to assess general areas. However, it is somewhat idiosyncratic in its recommendations; for example, two Agatha Christie books were selected, neither one of the more famous ones. The reading level often underestimates the skills of many students at a "college prep" library. Wilson recently added a graphic novel component to its core collection. The Wilson collection is now available electronically as a subscription database; commercial vendors such as Baker and Taylor also offer selection lists compiled from review sources and selections can easily to added to the cart.

Weeding

As the term implies, weeding in a library is much like weeding in a garden: tedious yet absolutely necessary—and harder if ignored for a period of time. When weeds pop up on the edge of your garden, it is easy to just pull them out to keep the problem from increasing. You also have to go to the various areas of the garden periodically on weed patrol. Libraries need the same care. Early in 2009, with the demotion of Pluto to the newly designated "dwarf" status, it was clear that books on astronomy and the planets might have to be weeded. This is an example of the need for responsive, "on the spot" weeding. "On the spot" can expand quickly into a methodical examination of that area of your library garden, or it can stay limited to just the immediate issue. For instance, when examining the books on Pluto, the librarian could decide to weed all the books on astronomy and space, or even all the 500s. However, all libraries need a methodical program in place that visits all parts of the library periodically in search of dated or worn materials. Professional practice recommends that libraries write and maintain a policy delineating why and how the library is weeded. Each library should develop a plan for regular, annual weeding. A librarian might choose to do a certain Dewey range each year, or nonfiction as a whole, and then fiction, etc. Weeding should be done on a regular basis, looking for items that are in poor shape physically, out-of-date, or extra copies of a once-popular book, or even a collection that does not serve the library's philosophy or goals any more. For instance, a library might decide it no longer needs the print copies of the Opposing Viewpoints series if it is going to subscribe to the online version. In that case, older copies should be weeded for issues that are subject to frequent change in science, technique, or societal opinion: birth control and genetics are examples. A longtime teacher with "pet projects" may retire, pushing the librarian should reassess the need for that collection, or at least, to downsize the topic.

[W]eeding in a library is much like weeding in a garden: tedious yet absolutely necessary—and harder if ignored for period of time.

Other factors that are helpful in weeding are the copyright dates and circulation statistics. Most library software programs have utilities that run reports detailing usage and date of publication. There are some caveats. Don't weed too quickly. Consider the broader implications of losing a topic or individual title. The circulation reports generally do not account for different editions of the same title; *1984* as a title may circulate five times but could be reported only two or three times depending on how many copies the library has.

Trends come and go. At one school, the curriculum featured a high school course on the Holocaust; the library had built a large collection of materials to support it. When that teacher left, the books did not circulate for several years. The school is now offering the course again, and the books are circulating once more. Of course the materials needed to be updated, but if the library had weeded its collection too quickly, it would not have been able to support the new course as quickly or affordably.

Some authors fluctuate in popularity, and their works can go out of print. *Library Journal* often reports new editions of previously neglected classics. *It Can't Happen Here* by Sinclair Lewis was long out of print and only recently re-released; a library that did not weed precipitately would not have to rely on the whim of a publisher for a new release. Classic authors and titles are worth keeping unless the volume is in very poor condition. Used bookstores, whether local or online, can also be cost effective and efficient resources in this situation, allowing libraries to fill in older but still important titles.

Donna J. Baumbach and Linda L. Miller (2006) provide useful assistance in *Less Is More*, which offers information on helpful general trends and areas to consider. Its specific examples may be too obvious, as many of the books the authors suggest weeding were published in the 1970s. Unfortunately, the book also has an emphasis on more "male" subjects, such as animals and transportation. It seems geared more to middle school and younger children than to a high school collection.

The routine, systematic weeding process works hand-in-hand with an annual, or semiannual, inventory. First, the inventory process requires shelf-reading and attention to detail, which will make it easy to discover books that are in poor shape, unneeded duplicate copies, etc. Inventory will discover physically missing items, which can then be removed from the ILS system and possibly be replaced. With software, the inventory process is no longer as complicated or cumbersome as it once was. The inventory report of lost items may bring to light an entire subject, genre, or Dewey range that is missing from the collection.

For a humorous, but still helpful, look at weeding, the blog *Awful Library Books* (http://awfullibrarybooks.wordpress.com/about/) provides snapshots that visually demonstrate the need to keep the collection fresh, relevant, and up-to-date. Although geared primarily to public libraries, school librarians will still find it useful, and amusing.

Challenges

At one school the librarian was urged to discard her copy of Joseph Conrad's *The Nigger of Narcissus* because someone objected to the wording of the title. This book, from the early twentieth century, was part of an old collection that had rarely, if ever, been weeded. After investigating the literary merits of the classic, this librarian decided to keep it in the collection. She then went to the head of the school for support of her decision. Other similar cases have occurred in independent school libraries across the country. In some cases, the pressure comes from "outside," a parent or volunteer, but in other scenarios, an administrator or fellow teacher may object to an item in the collection. Approximately a third of respondents to the ISS survey reported challenges to or questions about specific purchases. Graphic novels and "mature" content are most commonly challenged.

These cases highlight the need for a clear, well-stated, and publicized library policy on challenges, which should be shared with and approved by the head of school. To prepare these documents, the librarian should consult with local and national peers for advice and suggestions. The ALA also has helpful resources on its Web site.

A strategy that may "preempt" potential challenges is to highlight the ALA's annual Banned Books Week. With posters and other publicity, the library can make the community more aware of censorship and its consequences.

Budgeting and Raising Money

There are many creative ways to raise money for a school library (see essay 17). One school offered a "birthday book" program in which parents and friends could choose from a list of desired titles and "give" that book in honor of their child; the librarian placed a bookplate in the front stating that it was given to celebrate that child's birthday. If a parent just goes to the bookstore to buy the book he or she wants to give, a library could have received, for example, twenty-five copies of one of the <u>Harry Potter</u> books, or a book on birth control for the fourth grade. Other programs may focus on themes or special events. Many libraries host book fairs to raise money. With these events, the librarian may face pressure to order books on a certain topic, for example astronomy, or to add a special collection on graphic novels, for example.

Selection Policy

This essay has examined various potentials for challenge to library materials. We recommended having a weeding policy and a challenge policy. There is another more overarching policy that is tremendously useful to school librarians: the selection policy, sometimes called a collection development policy. A selection policy opens with a statement of the library mission, which stems directly from the school's mission but focuses on the library's specific role in implementing that mission. This selection policy explains the criteria that the librarian uses to choose particular works for this library collection. Many selection policies also include a statement about intellectual freedom for students; it is important that the community also understand the importance of the freedom to read and inquire in the education of students. For more thoughts on intellectual freedom, see essay 16.

Selection Criteria

Pertinent to the curriculum

Age appropriate

Unbiased, accurate, and current content

Balanced viewpoints

Good technical quality

But how specifically does a librarian select materials? Does he or she read every book before ordering it? That would be great, but is not very realistic given that nearly 30,000 books are published annually in juvenile literature alone. Most librarians have a favorite list of review tools they read consistently. Colleagues mention great titles they have read. Perhaps there is a local group that reviews books together. There are annual compilations of best books. Whatever the tools used, the mainstays should be listed in the policy so that the community can see where and how the librarian goes about selecting books. Today, we select so much more than books; the selection policy should list review tools for nonprint materials also. There should be a gift policy that states that all donations to the library are subject to the same selection standards as purchased materials; this allows the librarian to reject the adult mystery collection from John's grandmother and the political tract from Susie's uncle running for the Senate, as well as that book on birth control for fourth grade. There also must be a weeding policy to keep the collection current and in good condition. Finally, there must be a challenge policy to delineate how materials can be questioned. A collection development policy also includes an annual analysis of strengths and weaknesses of the existing collection and a list of goals for the year's new acquisitions.

Elements of a Selection Policy

- Library Mission Statement
- Intellectual Freedom Statement
- Selection Criteria
- Review Tools
- Gift Policy
- Weeding Policy
- Challenge Policy
- Collection Development Status and Goals

These components comprise the complete selection policy and provide a methodical system for selection of new materials; acceptance or rejection of gift materials; removal of worn, dated, or surplus materials; and procedures in case of a challenge to any library materials, and offer an overview of the collection development plans for each year. This compilation should be approved by the governing board and posted publicly so that the school community can see how and why materials are chosen. That such a policy is in place, approved by the governing board, offers the library, the library staff, and the school huge protection in the case of a challenge. The selection policy can even head off a potential challenge by demonstrating to the community that you have a careful method based firmly in the school's mission.

Conclusion

In these times of fast-paced changes, the independent school librarian should view the collection as flexibly as possible. It may be print or digital, accessed at the library or remotely, or in some new format, on a Kindle or a new Mac tablet. The key is that the library is no longer simply a static warehouse of books sitting primly in the stacks. In the near future, most schools will not take such drastic action, simply eliminating thousands of books; however, it is clear that the volume and quantity of books added to the collection will be matched by the acquisition of digital titles accessed on computers, mobile devices, cell phones, and other inventions. The librarian should be aware of these developments and actively create a vibrant, dynamic multimedia collection to serve the needs of the constantly new, ever-changing, essential information hubs throughout the school, at home, and beyond.

References

Abel, David. 2009. "A Library without the Books." *The Boston Globe,* September 4. Available at www.boston.com/news/local/massachusetts/articles/2009/09/04/a_library_without_the_books/. Accessed April 11, 2009.

Awful Library Books. n.d. Available at http://awfullibrarybooks.wordpress.com/about/. Accessed April 11, 2009.

Barnes, John. n.d. *An Open Letter to the Library Community.* Gale/Cengage Learning. Available at 11 Mar. 2010. www.gale.cengage.com/fairaccess/index.htm. Accessed March 11, 2010.

Baumbach, Donna J., and Linda L. Miller. 2006. *Less Is More: A Practical Guide to Weeding School Library Collections.* Chicago: American Library Association.

Best Websites for Teaching and Learning. 2010. American Association of School Librarians. American Association of School Librarians. Available at www.ala.org/ala/mgrps/divs/aasl/guidelinesandstandards/bestlist/bestwebsitestop25.cfm. Accessed March 11, 2010.

Bosco, Carla. 2009. "Survey." *ISS Listserv,* May.

Brooks, Sam. n.d. *EBSCO's Response to Gale's Open Letter.* EBSCO, n.d. Available at www.ebscohost.com/special/temp01-2010/EP-Response-to-Gale.pdf. Accessed March 11, 2010.

Common Core State Standards Initiative. 2009. National Governors Association. November 10. Available at www.corestandards.org/. Accessed November 16, 2009.

Ivey, Bill. n.d. *Re: The Most Tweeted Remark from the 2010 NAIS Annual Conference.* Message posted to http://ised-l.blogspot.com/. Accessed March 4, 2010.

"*Partnership for 21st Century Skills.* 2004. Partnership for 21st Century Skills. Available at www.21stcenturyskills.org. Accessed November 16, 2009.

Perkins, Mitali. 2009. "Straight Talk on Race: Challenging the Stereotypes in Kids' Books." *School Library Journal* (April). Available at www.schoollibraryjournal.com/article/CA6647713.html?q=ursula+le+guin#3.%20ls%20the%20cover%20art%20true%20to%20the%20story. Accessed April 11, 2010.

Stone, Brad. 2009. "Amazon Erases Orwell Books From Kindle." *The New York Times,* July 17. Available at www.nytimes.com/2009/07/18/technology/companies/18amazon.html. Accessed April 11, 2009.

Valenza, Joyce. n.d. "EBSCOs Exclusive Content and an Open Letter from Gale Cengage; ProQuest Responds with a Few Comments." *resource shelf.* Available at www.resourceshelf.com/2010/01/22/ebscos-exclusive-content-and-an-open-letter-from-gale-cengage/. Accessed March 11, 2010.

Visit http://lu.com/excellence for supporting links and occasional updates to all essays in this book.

Carla Bosco has been the Upper School Librarian at Stone Ridge School (http://www.stoneridge.org/) of the Sacred Heart for five years. Before that, she was Assistant Director of the Virginia Wing Library at the Winsor School (Boston). She graduated from Mt. Holyoke College and received a master's in liberal arts from Harvard University in addition to her M.L.S. from Simmons College. She has also worked at the Cambridge (MA) Public Library and Lesley University (Cambridge, MA). She loves to read and follow baseball, specifically the Red Sox.

Freedom to Think and Learn: Minors' Rights in Independent School Libraries

Dorcas Hand, Annunciation Orthodox School (Houston, TX)

What is different about intellectual freedom and minors' rights issues in nonpublic schools? How do the following incidents illustrate these differences? What can librarians in these schools do to protect the intellectual freedom and privacy rights of our students? The following scenarios illustrate some of the variety of situations we may face in these broad areas of legal and ethical concerns. We in independent schools have the same responsibilities to protect the rights to information and privacy of personal information as all other libraries, but our legal status in these situations is not necessarily the same as our peers in the public school world.

Scenario 1: September 2009. President Obama announced a speech to school students. An uproar erupted: "My child should not be indoctrinated by a liberal politician on school time. I won't let him attend if you are going to show it." Many independent schools were caught unaware by the ferocity of the barrage. Some chose not to show the speech at all, some required parent permission, and some showed the speech as a matter of course.

Scenario 2: *Tales of the Early World* by Ted Hughes includes a story about how God created the vulture. God was really busy with all his creating, and tired. One night he neglected to clean up when he stopped for the day. His mother found the table in a mess and pushed all the debris into a neat pile in the middle, as mothers will do. When God came back in the morning, a vulture was sitting there. The librarian, new to this religiously affiliated school, was working to improve the worn and dated collection, especially the religion section. This collection of short stories seemed a wonderful addition, so she showed the book to the religion teacher. Soon after, the religion teacher mentioned in passing that she found the book very disturbing. What the librarian didn't know was that in church doctrine, God doesn't have a mother—even in fiction. The librarian insisted on a challenge committee, but it did little good. Despite the fact that most of the committee thought the book harmless and doubted anyone would actually read it, the book stayed in the head's office.

Scenario 3: *My Place* by Nadia Wheatley and Donna Rawlins was the 1988 Book of the Year for the Children's Book Council of Australia. In picture book format, the book mapped a single square of land in now-urban Sydney, jumping back through history in twenty-year clips to 1788. The book was cataloged as fiction rather than easy reading because its content was abstract despite the picture book format. A kindergarten student found the book. He was a precocious child who asked if he could take out the book even though it wasn't in the easy section. The answer was, "Of course." A day or so later, his father wrote to say that the book was entirely inappropriate for children because it espoused and promoted the concept of the Noble Savage, which was too political for young children. What? The librarian took it to the head, who repeated the question: What? The librarian wrote a letter to the father explaining why the book had been selected and was appropriate for the library; the father responded in stronger terms than before that the book must be removed from the shelves. The head of school backed the librarian all the way and told the father the book would be staying on the shelves.

Scenario 4: Noon, Thursday, December 6, 2007, the day before the movie *The Golden Compass* was to open. The head of school gave an hour's notice that he had decided to remove The Golden Compass series from the shelves. An e-mail about Phillip Pullman's atheistic personal views had been actively circulating for a few weeks, stirring the pot. The librarian spent a few minutes composing a response, as careful a response as time allowed. She suggested that the school should take advantage of the board-approved policy and procedure for challenged materials to demonstrate to the community that they do consider all viewpoints as they make careful decisions in these situations. She got a single word in reply: "No. An immediate response is needed," in this Christian school environment. The letter went electronically to the entire parent community and the faculty, and the phone calls and e-mails began. Shocked parents. The newspaper. Library colleagues across the city were also receiving calls from the newspaper. The librarian stayed in the library, attempting to carry on with business as usual. She didn't send any e-mails or make any phone calls. She counseled her staff to stay calm and quiet. She pulled up all the reviews and looked at Pullman's personal Web site to read his actual words in context. The Friday morning paper had the school on the front page thanks to a parent who had forwarded the letter; it was just what the press wanted on the day the movie opened. Then a phone call announced that the series would be reinstated immediately. The parent uproar and board logic turned the tide.

Scenario 5: The AP biology class was in the library researching health issues, including AIDS. The school Web filter blocked sites with references to sexually transmitted diseases. The teacher was unable to convince the school to unblock specific useful sites to accommodate the assignment.

Scenario 6: The librarian was away from the library for part of the morning, and an adult volunteer was staffing the circulation desk in the middle school library. The division head came to ask for the circulation history of a student in a disciplinary context. The adult volunteer provided him with a printout of all the titles the student had checked out since entering seventh grade.

Scenario 7: Sophomore Joey had a chronic problem with overdue books. He was otherwise a good student who spent all his free periods in the library. The librarian spoke to Joey repeatedly, sent notes to the teachers and administration, and called his parents. The problem had recurred year after year in this 7–12 school, and the librarian sought a new approach. In hopes that embarrassment would have an effect that none of the usual methods had, the librarian posted on the door of the library a list of Joey's overdue books.

A letter sent by a school in Florida about the Obama speech situation in September 2009 included these selected paragraphs:

> We very much want to engage our students about the world around them and about taking part in our democratic system. We feel that they ought to learn about our national issues and hear perspectives on those issues regardless of which party's philosophy they might endorse. As an administration, we see a big problem in our country today—that, as a nation, we are not very good right now at engaging in civil discussion and disagreement about the policies and political philosophies that are being "debated" in the public square. We very much want our school to be a place where our students learn to listen to all sides of a debate and engage in questioning, answering, and exploring, but always in a polite and civil tone. We do not want our students to become liberals. We do not want our students to become conservatives. We want them to learn how to listen respectfully, how to question respectfully, and how to come to their own opinions and votes while respecting those who may come to different conclusions. We want them to learn how to be citizens. In order to do that, they have to be exposed to different points of view. We would like them to study those points of view. . . .
>
> We want our students to learn that patriots can disagree about policy choices in a democracy while still loving their country and wanting the best for all of her people. Opting out of hearing a speech by the President or a member of the clergy from a different religion or any opinionated speaker does not serve the goal of learning about others and, eventually, yourself. We believe that our students' education is well-served by exploration and engagement about issues, not by refusing to even hear opposing views.

This letter speaks to the fact that many independent school curricula work to teach students to think for themselves. The independent school community also includes a variety of religious schools whose dogma imposes limits on the curricula. Among us is another group of schools who intentionally limit the curriculum for other reasons. We are independent schools, meaning we are not part of the public school system. We are not subject to state-mandated testing, but we are directly responsible to our individual governing boards to demonstrate the successful accomplishment of our curricular goals. And we all maintain a sense of independence as we examine issues and come to our own resolutions. We hope that our students develop that same willingness to look deeper than the surface and to hear all sides on their way to personal decisions.

Independent school librarians stand as guides into the world of information: what it is, where it is, how it can be found efficiently. Our professional ethic requires us to do our best to provide our patrons with the information they request; however, our training and professional ethics are sometimes at odds with our school administration. We librarians need to understand that private institutions can absolutely limit what happens within their own confines. In cases of censorship, we in the independent schools cannot make the same assumptions about protection of free speech that our public school and library colleagues can. However, the letter above notes that proponents of private education are also often proponents of higher academic standards that frequently include a broader awareness of all sides of issues. A common aspect of restricted speech is that schools with religious leadership can limit curriculum and library materials to those resources that support specific dogma.

As we look at the examples above, one is about political influence (1), or the fear of political influence. Two relate to religion (2 and 4) but only one of those used the actual challenge procedure. One relates to intellectual curiosity and age-appropriate considerations (3) in an unusual topic. One concerns Web filters and potential sexual content (5), and two are about the privacy of library records (6 and 7). How do our schools handle these questions, and what protections are in place for the library and the students? What elements should a library staff of an independent school have in place to best support an environment in which the students have the widest possible information set available to them?

- Look to the American Library Association's *Library Bill of Rights* and the *Code of Ethics of the American Library Association*.

- Know the state and federal laws about freedom of information and Internet filtering and whether they apply to independent schools.

- Develop and have approved by the governing board a selection policy for library materials.

- Develop and have approved by the governing board a privacy policy relating to library records.

ALA *Code of Ethics*

Independent schools hold themselves to a high standard of service. The tradition of outstanding education goes back to the early New England schools of colonial times that educated our founding fathers. Our libraries also hold themselves to that high standard of service. Although accreditation does not require our librarians to have a master's of library science, an increasing number of schools hire degreed librarians. The essay about our independent school library community (essay 4) explains in depth the advantages of belonging to the larger independent school librarian community, which includes the American Library Association. ALA is a strong resource whenever questions of intellectual freedom or minors' rights arise; it also offers librarians a concise code of professional ethics. The *Code of Ethics* (2009a) of the ALA includes these statements:

> I. We provide the highest level of service to all library users through appropriate and usefully organized resources; equitable service policies; equitable access; and accurate, unbiased, and courteous responses to all requests.

> II. We uphold the principles of intellectual freedom and resist all efforts to censor library resources.

III. We protect each library user's right to privacy and confidentiality with respect to information sought or received and resources consulted, borrowed, acquired, or transmitted.

As independent school librarians, we may work in religious institutions that limit our collections along lines of dogma or in a secular school without doctrinal restrictions, but this statement of ethics encourages us to seek the broadest information set possible within the constraints of our institution. We are the ones who can speak up when questions arise, use our professional experience and judgment to select materials that offer our students arguments on both sides of controversies, encourage students to research topics that interest them, and protect their privacy as much as possible when parents or teachers inquire.

Library Bill of Rights and the AASL Interpretation for Students

Library Bill of Rights

The American Library Association affirms that all libraries are forums for information and ideas, and that the following basic policies should guide their services.

I. Books and other library resources should be provided for the interest, information, and enlightenment of all people of the community the library serves. Materials should not be excluded because of the origin, background, or views of those contributing to their creation.

II. Libraries should provide materials and information presenting all points of view on current and historical issues. Materials should not be proscribed or removed because of partisan or doctrinal disapproval.

III. Libraries should challenge censorship in the fulfillment of their responsibility to provide information and enlightenment.

IV. Libraries should cooperate with all persons and groups concerned with resisting abridgment of free expression and free access to ideas.

V. A person's right to use a library should not be denied or abridged because of origin, age, background, or views.

VI. Libraries which make exhibit spaces and meeting rooms available to the public they serve should make such facilities available on an equitable basis, regardless of the beliefs or affiliations of individuals or groups requesting their use.

Adopted June 18, 1948, by the ALA Council; amended February 2, 1961; amended June 28, 1967; amended January 23, 1980; inclusion of "age" reaffirmed January 24, 1996. Used with permission from the American Library Association.

Our students are best protected by their constitutional right to free access to information. This right belongs to all students, no matter what school they attend; it just may not belong to them during school hours or through the school library. Our students need to be aware of and to understand their constitutional protections, especially the First Amendment. And they need to know and understand what privacy means in this world of digital information. As we teach them how to find the information they need and want, we need to also teach them how to protect their own personal information appropriately.

As students push against the limits of information available through the independent school's library, we can teach them about other libraries in the community. No library will ever have all the information in the world, even with Internet access. If a student needs further resources than the school can provide, the local public library is a great option. If the reason the information is not available happens to be school mission or church dogma, the public library will not have those restrictions and does have a mandate to support the information needs of the entire community. We should encourage our students to have active library cards for access to the databases, books, or other materials we may not be able to afford for only occasional use. The school still needs to buy those materials that directly support consistent curricular demands; the public library offers additional support for unusual requests or temporary high demand for a topic or item.

ALA's Library Bill of Rights (2009b) and its interpretations concerning intellectual freedom for minors are based on the First Amendment to the U.S. Constitution. This interpretation comes from the American Library Association document *Access to Resources and Services in the School Library Media Program: An Interpretation of the Library Bill of Rights* (2008):

> The school library media program plays a unique role in promoting intellectual freedom. It serves as a point of voluntary access to information and ideas and as a learning laboratory for students as they acquire critical thinking and problem-solving skills needed in a pluralistic society. Although the educational level and program of the school necessarily shape the resources and services of a school library media program, the principles of the Library Bill of Rights apply equally to all libraries, including school library media programs. Under these principles, all students have equitable access to library facilities, resources, and instructional programs.

Children's Internet Protection Act

The Children's Internet Protection Act (CIPA) restricts "materials harmful to minors." which include

- *visual depictions* of child pornography, as defined under Section 22 of Title 18 of the U.S. Code;

- "obscenity," as defined under Section 1460 of Title 18 of the U.S. Code; and

- material "harmful to minors," as defined in Section 1703 of Title 17 of the U.S. Code.

The CIPA definition of "age-appropriate" is very vague, and is applied by different schools in different ways. Schools and public libraries receiving federal funds are required to use "technology protection measures" to block student access to those categories of information, though that is balanced by the First Amendment protection of their right to information not in those categories. Many independent schools have opted not to receive any federal funds and can therefore make their own choices about student Internet access. Independent schools can function without any filtering if they choose, and many do, depending on the age range of the students and the administration's position on student access to information. Independent schools with multiple levels have more filtering options available and choices to make. The California Technology Assistance Program (CTAP) offers sample acceptable use policies (AUP) and other useful digital support policies for reference. There is also an "ALA and Filtering" statement. Whether or not a school filters, the library staff needs to work to teach effective search skills and safety skills related to digital information. In July 2009 the American Library Association issued *Minors and Internet Interactivity: An Interpretation of the* Library Bill of Rights; this document offers broad support to student access to digital content: "The rights of minors to retrieve, interact with, and create information posted on the Internet in schools and libraries are extensions of their First Amendment rights." Independent schools work to offer students as much access to information as their individual missions will allow, in their ongoing effort to provide a broad education that builds thoughtful citizens and community leaders of the future.

The Children's Internet Protection Act (CIPA) requires that every school receiving e-rate funding have an Internet safety policy. Most independent schools require an AUP whether they accept federal funding or not. AUPs delineate limits and guidelines for student use of digital access, including campus networks, school Web sites, school-supported research databases, and the open Internet. These AUPs, usually signed by students and parents annually, put some responsibility on the students for selecting appropriate uses and content in their 24/7 online activities if the activity may have impact on the school community. However, there will remain a tension between protecting students from inappropriate content and limiting their First Amendment rights to free access to information.

The AUP does not address directly the school's responsibility to allow free access to a range of information and opinions. Librarians need to know federal and state laws concerning students' rights to information; independent school librarians are subject to limitations imposed by the school mission. The school may limit student access to information on campus, but students can access a full range of information at their public library. Some states are very specific about student rights: California Education Code 48950 states that private secondary schools may not "make or enforce any rule subjecting any high school pupil to disciplinary sanctions solely on the basis of conduct that is speech or other communication that, when engaged in outside of the campus, is protected from governmental restriction by the First Amendment to the United States Constitution or Section 2 of Article 1 of the California Constitution" (Adams, 2008, 20). All librarians should check their state laws.

Selection Policy

Chapter 15 explains what needs to be in a selection policy, but a bigger question is why schools should have one. In publicly supported libraries, the selection policy clarifies for all constituents (library staff, library administration, patrons, and the wider community) the exact methodology used to select materials for the library, print and digital content as well as audiovisual items. The policy also dictates the method of reconsideration for any materials challenged. A strong selection policy includes a gift policy that details how gifts are accepted or refused by the library, and what weeding policy is in place to manage collection size and age.

> [T]he selection policy clarifies for all constituents . . . the exact methodology used to select materials for the library.

In our independent school world, the selection policy provides the same clarity to the community, even if we may not be provided the same legal protections as a public school.

As an aside, it is important to note that our teachers sometimes need protection when classroom readings are challenged, but the library's selection policy will not offer them direct support. School decisions about classroom challenges may be informed indirectly by our policy, because it already stands approved by the board and clearly spells out how our materials are selected. However, placing material on the library shelf for a student to find and requiring the student to read the same material in a class context are very different degrees of selection. Our policy can offer only a lesser level of protection to other challenged material in the curriculum, and our teachers must rely on the school administration to support them in the face of a challenge. However, schools have broad leeway in areas of curriculum design. When classroom challenges come, the school only needs to offer alternate materials to the specific student; there is no requirement to redesign the entire curricular unit because of a single family challenge. A library book club selection might be subject to this lesser level of support, given that all book club members are expected to read the same title.

In a recent informal survey of independent schools about their selection policies, response was entirely voluntary and probably quite spotty by locale since it did not include a demographic question. (Access to the survey was disseminated through the ISS and AISL listservs. Fifty responses were received from interested independent school librarians.) Of the schools that answered the survey, 89.8 percent do have a selection policy (Hand 2009). Robin Dearborn, a current MLIS student at San Jose State University, found two studies of independent school selection practices. In 2008, a study of forty independent schools discovered that 22 percent had unwritten and informal policies, and 65 percent had written and board-approved policies. Another study in 2009 of Texas Christian schools showed that 72 percent of these schools have no policy, preferring to defer to the school's mission and denominational orientation. The survey showed that some schools have had selection policies in place since the 1970s, whereas others are just beginning the process. The Jesuit schools cooperated in 2008 to write a single policy for all the Jesuit schools. Selection policies in international schools must reflect legal realities where they are; for example, schools in Saudi Arabia are extremely limited in the topics and images they can import even for non-Saudi students. A school anywhere might have a carefully written, fully vetted, and board-approved selection policy that is totally ignored by the head of school occasionally—or even more often. However, having the policy in place can make it much easier for the librarian or a board member aware of the policy to raise questions about the decision.

Even if the head of school can overrule your selection policy in specific cases, the policy approval process is an opportunity for the library and the administration, and even the board, to consider philosophically what the school wants. The selection policy should directly reflect the mission of the school and should also include a mission statement for the library. When the selection methodology is delineated against these missions, the school community is well-served in an ongoing way. The board approval process can be lengthy, because this document seems small in the press of other business, but even the approval process is a form of advocacy (see essay 6).

"A school can only tolerate as much intellectual freedom as the mission encourages. The school administration has to be ready to field any issues that develop from any books in the library or in classrooms" (Kelly 2009). This statement is absolutely true, but the selection policy is written to reflect exactly the particular school's mission. There is always room for disagreement over specific titles, and that disagreement can be resolved formally or informally; but the policy provides a framework for the conversation. The library selection policy should work in concert with the AUP, meaning that library selection of digital resources should keep in mind student curricular needs as well as any limitations on digital access included in the AUP. The selection policy does not absolve students of the personal responsibility they accepted when they signed the AUP.

"When the school librarian works with administration, teachers and other members of the school community to align the selection policy with the AUP, and other documents, it serves to clarify students' rights and responsibilities, , articulates common goals, values and legal obligations, builds community buy-in for intellectual freedom, and makes clear that filtering criteria should align with selection criteria."
—Abilock (2009). See enumeration 7 at www.noodletools.com/ debbie/ethical/policytemplate.html#interrelate

---

Once you have a selection policy, why should you update it? One obvious reason has to do with changes in library function: the school might grow from only a PS–5 to a PS–8 or PS–12 school. Or a school opened in the early 1980s, which only had books, now needs to manage both "realia" (globes and other 3-D models) and digital materials. The language of the selection policy and the list of review tools should reflect the totality of the library. Keep the language in the policy document open-ended enough that it covers all formats while maintaining awareness in all constituents that there is new technology coming that must be included. The policy must also remain closely tied to the school's mission, and to the library's. If you don't have a mission statement for your library, that is a great place to start. Once you have your mission clearly stated, delineating your selection methodology will be easier.

Annunciation Orthodox School Library Mission Statement

The primary function of the Library at Annunciation Orthodox School is to provide the school with a balanced collection of resources in many formats which:

- supports current learning and teaching needs at a level appropriate to student needs.
- provides current information.
- provides sufficient depth to support student research.
- provides sufficient breadth to support self-directed study.
- provides resources for recreational purposes.
- stimulates intellectual curiosity and imagination.
- develops understanding and respect for all cultural heritages.
- encourages student awareness of global concerns.
- offers professional support materials.
- offers some parent guidance materials.

Reprinted with permission from the Annunciation Orthodox School.

Now that you know you need to update your selection policy, how often should you review its contents? Annually seems a bit much. Five years is the update timetable taught in library school. However, changeover in board membership over five years means that perhaps no one on the new board will remember the old document. Resubmitting it to the board every three years makes sense; it keeps the policy fresh in their minds. If they know the policy exists and that you are working to keep it current, they'll be more likely to support its enforcement in the face of a challenge.

It is also good practice to make the entire selection policy easily available to the school community. Now that we have Web sites where policies are posted, that is an obvious option. The purpose of a selection policy is to make transparent the methods of material selection; if no one is aware that there is a consistent method, the policy is not as effective as it might be. Potential donors can be pointed to the gift policy, which states that all gifts and donations to the library will be subject to the same review requirements as purchases. Community awareness of the policy can increase trust in library selection and minimize the threat of challenges.

The weeding policy explains how you work to keep the collection current and what other reasons might cause a book to be pulled from the shelf. When the community knows that you pull books when they are falling apart, contain outdated information, or have not circulated in a long time as well as that they'll be replaced with high-quality newer titles, they know that you are not practicing censorship. This makes a selection policy a stronger protection for intellectual freedom in the specific independent school community.

Hot Button Topics and Challenges

Topics that merit negative attention vary from school to school. Jewish schools may limit anti-Israeli information, while Catholic schools (among others) will focus more on avoiding pro-choice perspectives. A "small, Christian prep school, multi-cultured environment" worries that "language and female role models" in street lit or urban fiction "sometimes mix the messages and distract from all else." One school reported an oversensitivity to diversity issues, meaning that someone counts to be sure each minority culture has the same number of books. Because many of us are multilevel schools, we are concerned with questions of leveling, labeling, and open access for all students (Hand 2009).

The informal survey found that many would-be challenges among our community are averted when a patient and prepared librarian can listen and respond with understanding to the complaint. Most patrons have no interest in the paperwork of a real challenge; they just want to be heard and respected for their opinion, and to know their child is heard and respected as well. Students who bring a book back saying it "isn't appropriate" can usually come to agree it is really of interest to older students—but sometimes they find a book that has slipped through the cracks and really doesn't belong where it is shelved.

The trickiest challenges are the internal ones, but the policy helps us there also. The librarian can insist on a full challenge procedure for such a questioned title. Even though, the book may still be removed, the broader community will be more aware of what happened. The element of secrecy is removed, and the onus taken off the librarian and the administration.

In the survey, some respondents voiced fear for their jobs in a challenge situation, a valid concern. If you already have a selection policy in place, you stand on firm ground requesting that the challenge procedure be activated. This allows a designated committee to represent the community, read the material in its entirety, and make a decision that reflects the community's concerns as well as the complainant's. This should place the responsibility on the community rather than the individual librarian or administrator. Your school will be the stronger for looking at all sides of the problem in a more public venue. This is a situation, however, in which independent school librarians must know their individual limits as they decide how firmly to stand up for challenged material. Possibly there is an alternate title that can sidestep the challenge, saving face for everyone.

The "subtle challenges" by administration are even more difficult: "You don't have these books on the shelf, do you?" Those internal and unofficial challenges cause a moral dilemma: how hard should the librarian push back? Is this book worth it? Is it strong enough in literary merit and/or content to win the day? Not every book is, even if it has solid reviews; maybe there is a title almost like it that is less incendiary. Maybe there isn't.

Many of us have notes in specific student records to indicate parent restrictions on reading. A family may request that their students never watch ANY videos, or never read any <u>Harry Potter</u> books. When classes see a video, those students might come to the library to read. That is not censorship; no student is affected beyond the specific family.

The survey inquired about any changes that resulted from challenges; the most common answer was, "Since then, I have written a selection policy." Hindsight offers strong evidence in support of selection policies in the independent school librarian's toolbox.

Self-censorship

VII. We distinguish between our personal convictions and professional duties and do not allow our personal beliefs to interfere with fair representation of the aims of our institutions or the provision of access to their information resources.

—From the *Code of Ethics of the American Library Association* (c2008)

Self-censorship is a common response, one that many librarians struggle against. We have our own views on child development and our own definitions of "age-appropriate," and those views may not mesh perfectly with the school definitions of the same terms. We wrestle with the balance between the potential popularity of materials and items whose information needs to be included to build the balanced representation of facts and issues. We also wrestle with the balance between curricular support and recreational reading that entices students to become lifelong learners and users of libraries. And finally, we wrestle with the need to provide information on edgy topics when only some of our parents want their students to have open access to those topics. When we know that some parents don't want their students to learn anything about human reproduction, we're very careful what materials we put in the library, even though we know we need to consider the rest of the students, whose parents do want them to be able to find age-appropriate information on those topics. And what exactly does "age-appropriate" mean, anyway? Everyone has an opinion. We are never certain how the administration will support us in the face of a capital fund drive that wants to solicit a large donation from a source that prefers more restrictive access to information for students.

In Lester Asheim's 1953 essay "Not Censorship but Selection," he examines the difference between selection and censorship by librarians during the selection process. He notes that the selector looks for ways to include a resource; in contrast, the censor comes from the negative perspective, looking for reasons to rationalize his or her decision to exclude the resource from the collection. According to Asheim, the censor looks for "isolated parts rather than the complete whole upon which to base a judgment." "Taken out of context and given weight completely out of keeping with their place in the overall work, single words and phrases can be used to damn a book. . . . In other words, four letters have outweighed five hundred pages. . . . [He went on to warn] librarians against rejecting a title for the collection based on anticipated external pressure and the fear of how it may affect one's job (Adams 2008, 46).

> [T]he selector looks for ways to include a resource; in contrast, the censor comes from the negative perspective, looking for reasons to rationalize his or her decision to exclude the resource from the collection.

Care is important; we only want the best materials to be available. Class management is another skill set that can come into play here: when a group is in the library and someone finds "those books," a giggle fest ensues that drives even the most liberal librarians crazy. Rather than hide the materials, we need to find ways to handle the problematic behavior. And if we know specific students are not allowed to view those books, we need to do our best to support the parents' wishes. Often books inspire problem behaviors when viewed in a group; one student starts the disruption and the others follow along. An easy solution is to limit in-house examination of those books to one reader only; the information is still available. Putting the materials on a shelf behind the circulation desk may solve the discipline problem, but the information is no longer freely available to students.

Because they may fear for their jobs in a challenge situation, some librarians are overly cautious in the selection process to be sure they buy nothing that could be objectionable. However, a strong selection policy supports the librarian's method of selection easily with a list of supporting reviews and readers. Even so, some materials may present a problem. In that situation, a librarian might first look for similar materials that are not as directly problematic, or move the challenged title to a higher level, where it may be more appropriate. You are still providing the information, but perhaps not as much of it. We are independent school librarians; the solution in each school will be different. There is no assumption in the accreditation process that we will all have the same materials, the same mission, or the same solution in the face of a challenge.

> [A] strong selection policy supports the librarian's method of selection easily with a list of supporting reviews and readers.

Literature on intellectual freedom and *Labeling and Rating Systems: An Interpretation of the* Library Bill of Rights (ALA 2009c) speak against labeling books by age or reading level. The reasoning is that students might reject books labeled "Easy" because they might look immature; but now we have literature recommending the use of picture books in middle and high school to offer simple explanations of very difficult concepts. And commonly that "E" now stands for "Everybody." Annunciation Orthodox School (Houston, TX) has a special collection in the middle school library for some of the edgier YA titles that is for eighth grade only ; the eighth-grade only designation actually gives a positive spin to books like *A Tale of Two Cities*, which is included next to Walter Dean Myers's *Fallen Angels*. With the exception of that small collection, the library encourages students to borrow from whichever area suits their needs. Maybe a lower school biography has the fast answers students need for the start of the sixth-grade history project. Maybe a middle school history book will support the fourth-grade history project. Again, we are independent schools with different needs and different solutions. Our common goal is to offer our students the broadest information set we can manage given whatever constraints we live with.

Some independent schools face a sense of entitlement from families, a sense that the high tuition they pay entitles them to force the library to include or exclude whatever topics or specific titles they choose. Again, the selection policy is a strong tool wielded with the support of the administration and the board, to bring the strongest possible collection to every student in the school. Most parents, when faced with a board-approved policy and a reasoned argument, will allow most materials to be available to most students even if they insist their own students be excluded. Many independent school parents are educated themselves and willing to talk to their own children about personal values that may differ from some members of the community and to talk about the need for diversity of thought to build our democratic society.

Confidentiality Issues

A balance point to the students' right to information is their right to confidentiality of personal information. The *Code of Ethics of the American Library Association* (2009a) makes a strong statement that librarians should maintain confidentiality concerning student library borrowing records and Internet searches. Article 3 states that "We protect each library user's right to privacy and confidentiality with respect to information sought or received and resources consulted, borrowed, acquired or transmitted." The AASL *Position Statement on the Confidentiality of Library Media Program Records* (2006) tells us that "the library community recognizes that children and youth have the same rights to privacy as adults." In *Privacy: An Interpretation of the* Library Bill of Rights (2002), privacy is defined as the right to engage in "open inquiry without having the subject of one's interest examined or scrutinized by others." Privacy and confidentiality are intertwined. A library practicing confidentiality will keep student circulation data private, despite the inconvenience that may cause the students and teachers.

The legal aspects of the confidentiality of state library records laws vary from state to state, and the exact effect of state laws on issues of library confidentiality in independent school libraries will have to be determined by local legal counsel. Another legal consideration is the Family Educational Rights and Privacy Act (FERPA), which applies specifically to schools that accept federal funds. It protects students' education records while granting their parents the right to view these records until the student turns eighteen. FERPA does not directly address library records, but "analysts within the Family Policy Compliance Office have issued guidance stating that library circulation records and similar records maintained by a library media center are 'educational records' under FERPA" (Scales 2009, 75). Basically, every library needs a written policy. Always check with the head of school to understand the legal ramifications of any internal or external request for library records. Because many independent schools accept no federal funds, FERPA may not directly affect you. However, every librarian has an ethical responsibility to protect student privacy and student library records.

The members of the American Library Association, recognizing the right to privacy of users, believe that records held in libraries which connect specific individuals with specific resources, programs or services, are confidential and not to be used for purposes other than routine record keeping.

- The library community recognizes that children and youth have the same rights to privacy as adults.
- Libraries whose record keeping systems reveal the names of users would be in violation of the confidentiality of library record laws adopted in many states.

From the AASL *Position Statement on the Confidentiality of Library Media Program Records* (2006)

Privacy policies will become increasingly essential to schools just as they have in the medical and legal worlds. We teach our students how to take care in what they post to Facebook and e-mail; we need to also teach them that their library records are their own business, and why that could matter. We must do our part to keep their personal research interests and reading records secure from the potentially prying eyes of parents and teachers, and even other students. When Jane is looking for the next book in the <u>Twilight</u> series, we shouldn't say that Susie has it. When we find the puberty books all over the table where three seventh-grade boys were just sitting, we shouldn't make a public note that those boys caused a ruckus in that section. When John has a book overdue three weeks, we shouldn't post his name with the book title to embarrass him; we may post his name as having a book to return, but we shouldn't attach the title to his name.

The question of overdue materials policies runs into confidentiality really quickly. In schools, we librarians eventually contact the parents for payment for a lost book. Parents of minor students do have the right (in most cases) to know what books their students may have lost. Their teachers do not. This would seem an unnecessary level of constraint most of the time, but deciding when to begin confidentiality on a case by case basis doesn't make much sense. A simple approach is to create no more patron records than necessary, and to keep even fewer. Write a privacy policy that spells out who may access library patron records and under what circumstances, as well as for how long circulation records will be retained. Train your staff, volunteer and paid, professional and clerical, about confidentiality and its importance. Teach the students to respect the confidentiality of their own library information, and the other students'. Use your ILS function to purge circulation history regularly, as stated in your privacy policy. (Adams 2008, 82).

Conclusion

Independent school librarians can support student information needs most successfully when they

- know and apply the *Library Bill of Rights* and its school interpretation;

- have a strong selection policy approved by the school's governing board every three years;

- work closely with the school administration to offer students the broadest possible information set within any school specific restrictions;

- remain aware of state and federal laws concerning student privacy rights and other legal aspects of library management, and consult the school's legal counsel when questions arise; and

- develop and maintain a written privacy policy for board approval that concerns library records, and consistently apply the provisions of the policy.

Our associations encourage us to be knowledgeable about our legal and ethical responsibilities. The accreditation process pushes us to stay current in our policies and collection development methods. Ongoing advocacy efforts help us to keep our school communities aware of the strengths of our libraries, and of why libraries are so essential to the overall academic success of their students. Intellectual freedom and rights to confidentiality, as well as education of students concerning their rights, are important aspects of our larger impact on the school community and on the final product of that community, which is well-educated graduates who are ready for the next step in their development, whatever age they are.

References

Abilock, Debbie. 2009. E-mail to author, July 23.

Acceptable Use Sample Policies. 2009. California Technology Assistance Project (CTAP). California Department of Education. August 28. Available at www.myctap.org/index.php/cybersafety-home/70-acceptable-use-sample-policies. Accessed November 16, 2009.

Adams, Helen R. 2008. *Ensuring Intellectual Freedom and Access to Information in the School Library Media Program.* Westport, CT: Libraries Unlimited.

American Association of School Librarians. 2006. *Position Statement on the Confidentiality of Library Media Program Records.* American Library Association. September 27. Available at www.ala.org/ala/aboutala/offices/oif/statementspols/otherpolicies/policyconfidentiality.cfm. Accessed November 12, 2009.

American Library Association. 2002. *Privacy: An Interpretation of the Library Bill of Rights.* American Library Association. June 19. Available at www.ala.org/ala/aboutala/offices/oif/statementspols/statementsif/interpretations/privacy.cfm. Accessed March 7, 2010.

———. 2003a. *Libraries and the Internet Toolkit: Checklist for Creating an Internet Use Policy.* American Library Association. December 1. Available at www.ala.org/ala/aboutala/offices/oif/iftoolkits/litoolkit/checklistcreating.cfm. Accessed November 11, 2009.

———. 2003b. *Libraries and the Internet Toolkit: Tips and Guidance for Managing and Communicating about the Internet.* American Library Association. December 1. Available at www.ala.org/ala/aboutala/offices/oif/iftoolkits/litoolkit/default.cfm. Accessed March 4, 2009.

———. 2005. *Libraries and the Internet Toolkit: ALA and Filtering.* American Library Association. May 10. Available at www.ala.org/ala/aboutala/offices/oif/iftoolkits/litoolkit/alafiltering.cfm. Accessed November 11, 2009.

———. 2008. *Access to Resources and Services in the School Library Media Program: An Interpretation of the* Library Bill of Rights. American Library Association. July 2. Available at www.ala.org/ala/aboutala/offices/oif/statementspols/statementsif/interpretations/accessresources.cfm. Accessed November 10, 2009.

———. 2009a [c2008]. *Code of Ethics of the American Library Association.* American Library Association. January 22. Available at www.ala.org/

ala/aboutala/offices/oif/statementspols/codeofethics/codeethics.cfm. Accessed November 10, 2009.

————. 2009b. *Library Bill of Rights.* American Library Association. March 4. Available at www.ala.org/ala/aboutala/offices/oif/statementspols/statementsif/library billrights.cfm. Accessed November 10, 2009.

————. 2009c. *Labeling and Rating: An Interpretation of the* Library Bill of Rights. American Library Association. July 15. Available at www.ala.org/ala/aboutala/offices/oif/statementspols/statementsif/interpretations/labelingrating.cfm. Accessed November 16, 2009.

Bassett, Patrick. 2009. "Controversy over the President's Speech to Students." Message to ISED listserv, September 4.

CTAP 4 Cybersafety Project. 2009. CTAP Region 4. March 10. Available at www.ctap4.net/projects/cybersafety.html. Accessed November 16, 2009.

Dearborn, Robin. 2009. "Selection Policy: An Overview." Unpublished paper, San Jose State University, California, May 13.

The Golden Compass. 2007. Film. By Phillip Pullman. Dir. Chris Weitz. New Line Cinema.

Hand, Dorcas. 2009. "Intellectual Freedom in Independent Schools." *SurveyMonkey* file.

Hughes, Ted. 1990. *Tales of the Early World.* Illus. Andrew Davidson. n.p.: Faber & Faber.

Kelly, Mark (head of school, Annunciation Orthodox School). 2009. Interview with author, June,

Rawlins, Donna, and Nadia Wheatley. 1987. *My Place.* N.p.: Collins Dove. (U.S. publisher Kane/Miller, 1994).

Scales, Pat. 2009. *Protecting Intellectual Freedom in Your School Library: Scenarios from the Front Lines* Chicago: American Library Association.

Visit http://lu.com/excellence for supporting links and occasional updates to all essays in this book.

Dorcas Hand grew up the daughter of independent school teachers; she has attended or been librarian of seven independent schools ranging from Florida to Massachusetts and then Texas. Her library career has included three schools and two public libraries, as well as a tour as editor of SLJ's Adult Books for Young Adults. *She has been active in ALA/AASL/ISS and TLA/TASL (Texas) since 1978. 2009–2010 is her twentieth year as Director of Libraries at Annunciation Orthodox School in Houston, TX (www.aoshouston.org).*

What Does It Cost? Budget and Funding

Sarah Knetzer Davis, Viewpoint School (Calabasas, CA)

Picture this—a huge, light-filled library building with fabulous shelving, an extensive collection of print resources, the latest technology, and attractive, colorful seating for your young patrons. Could this be paradise? It could—if that building and program plan suit the individual school, and that school can afford to maintain the building, the collection, and the requisite staff year after year. Without that ongoing commitment of money, this huge, light-filled library building will not be well-used by students and will quickly lose its luster.

An ideal world might give independent school librarians access to an endless supply of funds to support student and teacher needs with no need to justify expenditures AND a library that is well-used by the entire campus community. But in reality, the process of planning a budget and then adhering to it pushes the librarian to analyze in depth the needs and wants of the library program for a specific school. People who come into a large sum of money have been known to not spend it wisely; knowing that a budget is finite requires careful use of existing funding. So, how does a librarian go about the process of planning and managing a budget?

Independent schools inherently and historically value the importance of the library's role as the heart of the academic community. Yet according to Joyce Kasman Valenza, we "face a major change in the economic rationale for libraries." She writes that "for the first time in history we are moving from a time of information scarcity to one of information abundance. Can we define why libraries are necessary when information is ubiquitous, more scalable, far more convenient, and often "free" online?" (Valenza and Johnson 2009).

Not all administrations understand the potential impact of the library on the academic program. In addition, not all independent schools benefit from similar economic demographics. Therefore, there are disparities even in the "private school" world. And at this writing, the U.S. economy has made it impossible for many librarians to rely on their usual sources of funding. Therefore, assessing your library's financial needs and creating a budget is imperative.

Whether you are new to your school or are a veteran librarian, it is vital that you understand your school's budgeting process, regularly assess your library's expenditures, and seek out additional funding when you come up short. How can independent school

273

librarians develop the funding resources necessary to establish and retain the library's position as the heart of the campus learning community?

The Budgeting Process

You are the chief executive officer of your media center.
—Franklin and Stephens (2007, 159)

Most school librarians did not enter the profession to crunch numbers. Perhaps you are a bibliophile. Perhaps you enjoy helping patrons find information. Or are you an educator at heart, and wanted to give librarianship a try? If any of these descriptions fits you, there is a good chance you were never taught to create or balance a budget. Much of what we do as independent school librarians is learned on the job.

A well-devised budget accomplishes more than simply allocating your funds on paper. According to *Library 101* (Franklin and Stephens 2007, 160), budgets "define your vision" for the library and help identify goals for your program. A budget "forces you to look at how you plan to spend your funds," and helps to communicate your intentions to your supervisors. By assessing and projecting your library expenses and funding requirements, you establish priorities, keep track of your spending, and justify your requests to administrators who might not understand your library's day-to-day needs.

Who establishes your budget? If you are starting a new job, it is important to determine your school's budget cycle. When are budgets due, and how far in advance do you have to project? Are you able to spend funds at your discretion throughout the school year? Are you required to get approval for your expenditures? Who makes the final decision about how much funding the library will receive?

A recent analysis of thirty independent school libraries (taken from an informal AISL and ISS listserv survey) demonstrated that independent school librarians generally prepare their own library budgets, submit the budget to the school administration, and are then permitted to allocate the funds to the appropriate library expenditures. This can differ from school to school, so it is important to determine the chain of command at your institution. Once that has been established, you should commit to communicating with your administrators on a regular basis to best advocate for your program. These school leaders might have an impact on the library budget:

- head of school
- business manager, director of finance, chief financial officer
- board of trustees
- budget committee
- dean of academics
- director of technology
- library advisory committee

Once you have established which administrator directly oversees the library budget, you should ask if you are required to spend all of your funds each year or if you are permitted to roll over funds to the next year. You do not want your budget reduced due to unspent funds, nor do you want to overspend and be seen as an irresponsible bookkeeper, but you might want to accumulate funds over time to support a pet project. You should also request information on any procedures for requesting funds for special projects, and if the school has policies about accepting funding from donations and other sources.

In "setting up shop" back at your office, you should

- review a copy of the current library budget and the previous year's expenditures;

- mark on your calendar if there are times when you expect a large expenditure, such as a database renewal or periodicals renewal;

- request a monthly printout of your expenditures and the status of your budget from your school's business office;

- keep a binder with copies of your invoices organized by date, or by type of expenditure, or keep the same information on a spreadsheet; and

- consolidate the billing procedures for larger items at the beginning or end of the school year (such as all of your database renewals), to ensure that remaining funds can be freely spent on other items.

The independent school environment offers librarians the unique opportunity to buy a wide variety of library resources, and usually at any point throughout the school year. Therefore, it is important to map out the year to ensure that your budget is not overspent. This, along with regular meetings with the appropriate administrator, should ensure that you have a full understanding of your school's budgeting process.

Assessing the Year

In September it might seem like the year will go on forever, but before you know it you'll wonder where the time went! Do not wait until the end of the year to gather evidence of your successes. As you go, analyze your usage statistics and review your spending. Take note of any changes that might affect your budget in the future.

In order to be treated like the "chief executive officer" of your library, it is important to demonstrate "chief executive" qualities. Just as teachers are expected to turn in assessments of what they have taught and learned, librarians should be expected to assess what they have provided to their patrons throughout the school year. This can easily be accomplished by compiling a year-end library report that demonstrates how your funds were put to use. By highlighting your accomplishments you will justify your expenses, and your school will better understand your spending needs. Your year-end report might include highlights from the year, your goals for the following year, the number of books circulated in your library, the number of "hits" on your databases, etc.

It is helpful to provide documentation; for instance, a recent report from the "Unquiet Library" (Creekview High School) used copious numbers of color photos showing students using library resources. What a great way to showcase your efforts! Go beyond a simple report of circulation statistics and offer your administrators a colorful portfolio of library brochures and handouts, letters from thankful students and teachers, etc.

Ideally, you will share your year-end report with your top administrators, your department head, and your business manager. Meeting in person is effective, especially if you have any special requests for the next year.

What Do I Budget For?

There is a good chance that every school librarian looks back at an item he or she purchased and thinks, "I bought *that*?" At the time, it seemed like a necessary expenditure. Maybe you had heard about that resource in library school. Perhaps it was a vital source at a previous job. Could a teacher have requested the item, only to leave the school the following year? Or maybe a sales representative or an article touted the item as the "next best thing." Regardless, all librarians have tales to tell about meaningful purchases that were not fully put to use.

Is there a way to guarantee that a library resource will be used? No, but there are ways to assess whether or not a resource is the right fit for your school. Before allocating money to a new resource, check the selection policy and the library mission statement. If you discover as the new librarian that there is no selection policy in place, set about writing one—and meanwhile, use your best understanding of the school's mission and curriculum to guide your purchase selections. The selection policy, which is based on the library's mission, will provide a clear vision of what you are trying to achieve, in the same way your school is guided by its mission statement. This is your opportunity to demonstrate that your library has a plan. (See essays 15 and 16.)

With this plan in mind, you should then evaluate the collection needs of the library by involving administration, faculty, students, and parents. This process of need evaluation will be an annual event. Sometimes it is a bigger and more comprehensive evaluation, but each school year you should meet with department heads, teachers, and students and ask for their input. This encourages collaboration and will ensure that the faculty and student body are aware of the library program. Your policy for selecting resources should ultimately be connected to student learning and achievement, and therefore should reflect their suggestions. (Toor and Weisburg 2007, 144).

Once your policy is in place, ask yourself the following questions when making purchasing decisions:

- Do I have adequate funding for this resource, especially if I need to renew it from year to year?

- Have I fully assessed the value of this resource to my campus community of teachers, staff, parents, and students?

- Is the resource up-to-date? Will it be out of date by the time I purchase it and make it available?

- Is the resource available online, in a format that is updated frequently?

- Will the resource be widely used by members of the campus community? If it is an item specifically for one department, can that department share in the cost?

- Is the resource available at another local community or academic library? If so, can students and faculty access the offsite resources easily?

In addition to yearly renewals and general collection updates, you will also want to consider library enhancements that might involve special budget requests:

- Funding for special sets of books, DVDs, or unique databases
- Funding for supplies and furniture, or other library enhancements
- Funding for technology and audiovisual equipment
- Funding for new and future upgrades, such as automation, building upgrades, etc.
- Materials and equipment rotations (such as new print encyclopedias every five years, new LCD projectors every three years, etc.)
- Funding for special events (such as visiting authors, book clubs, reading promotion, etc.)

Advocating for Additional Resources

We always hear about tight budgets, but education has lots of money; you just need to find it.

—Franklin and Stephens (2007, 164)

Many independent school libraries are more than adequately funded, yet recent economic woes have required librarians to seek creative ways to supplement their budgets. Quality books and scholarly databases are expensive, and you might find that you have to tirelessly advocate and defend the need for these purchases.

Once you have assessed your collection needs, prepare documentation for your administrators. This could include results from a library needs assessment that directly connects library resources to another academic department. You might also include results from a survey of your area independent schools that show the amount of funding their libraries receive. You can also refer to professional studies that have been completed such as the School Library Spending Survey in *School Library Journal,* or surveys from the American Association of School Librarians.

Once your goals for increasing your library budget have been communicated, you might find that your school simply cannot increase the library budget. With your administration's approval, consider creating a network of resources for additional funding.

Fund-raising for the Independent School Library

School library budgets fall into several categories, and your school may or may not ask the library to budget for the following:

Staffing

Librarians

Paraprofessionals

Professional development and memberships

Collections

Print materials (books)

Online database subscriptions

Magazine subscriptions

DVDs and other media, such as audiobooks

Special collections (archives, alumni collection, memorial collection, etc.)

Supplies

Library supplies (book processing supplies, magazine covers, etc.)

General office supplies

Copy and printer paper

Technology

Computers for students

Computers for library staff

Audiovisual equipment and repair

Copy machines and paper

Daily Operations

Automation and cataloging fees

Maintenance and contract services

Library Programs

Book clubs

Special events

Reading incentive, bookmarks, summer reading incentive, etc.

Visiting authors

Whether or not your budget falls short of your expectations, why should you expend the energy to seek funds from other sources? Extra funds that are raised to increase operations budgets often allow the librarians to go above and beyond the regular library program. Want to check out a new database, but you did not budget for an additional item? Gift funds allow "wiggle room" for trying new resources. In addition, gift funds often do not expire from year to year as do fiscal budgets, thereby allowing librarians the opportunity to plan for future projects.

In addition, parents of students in independent school want to be involved in their children's education. They want to support the school community through fund-raising and volunteer activities. Fund-raising for the library provides the perfect outlet for families who otherwise may not have the opportunity to make an impact on campus.

Chadwick School in Palos Verdes, California, has a unique program—a Friends of the Library (FOL) parent group. FOL groups are very common in public libraries; however, not many schools have adopted this model. Some schools are already saturated with parent groups, and some schools prefer that all fund-raising be managed by the development office. However, if your school allows for the establishment of an FOL group, it can serve both as a parent advisory board and a resource for additional funds.

The Chadwick FOL's primary function is to create opportunities to raise funds and promote the joy of reading. Therefore, yearly events include a major book fair, a parent booktalk program, several visiting author programs, and other fund-raising efforts at schoolwide events.

The Chadwick School FOL was created by a dedicated librarian and a few committed parents. Over the last fifteen years it has evolved into a highly sophisticated organization, with formal bylaws, monthly meetings, subcommittees, and official board positions. The board meets monthly, and at least once a year there is a long-range planning meeting to discuss future FOL programs.

One of the main sources of FOL funding is parent membership. At the beginning of the school year, Chadwick families are given the opportunity to become members of the FOL for $25. Many families see this as an easy opportunity to support library programs; therefore there is usually a significant response. The book fair is also quite lucrative, as well as Chadwick's birthday book program and Family Day fund-raising. The librarians pick new books that have already been purchased for the library and display them at events that attract parents. Bookplates honoring the donors are placed in the books. All in all, the Chadwick library gets $7,000–$10,000 a year from FOL fund-raising.

Whether you establish an FOL or other parent advocacy group, or simply foster a few good volunteers, many schools and librarians raise funds to optimize their library services. Not all fund-raising programs will be lucrative, and many will seem to take more work than they are worth. You will have to decide if the time invested was worth the effort, but the opportunity to promote your program and collection is worth any amount of money!

A recent list of fund-raising ideas on the Association of Independent School Libraries (AISL) listserv included:

- **Birthday Book or "Adopt-a-Book" program.** New books are purchased, or selected from reserved books in honor of the student.

- **Campus book fairs** through Scholastic or through a local bookfair company.

- **In-store book fairs at the local bookstore.** Independent bookstores and major retailers often offer in-store book fairs. The stores do much of the work so that the librarians or volunteers can focus on marketing the fair and creating in-store social events for the school community.

- **Fairs around holiday times, which generate greater funds.** Some libraries also do book fair events to promote summer reading. Several librarians reported that these book fairs were not as lucrative as they had hoped.

- **Fund-raising at Family Day, Open House, graduation, or other schoolwide events.** Librarians or parent volunteers display new library books in areas where parents gather. Families are given the opportunity to donate these books in honor of loved ones.

- **Student fund-raisers, such as pizza sales or bake sales.**

- **A magazine subscription fund-raiser** through companies such as QSP.com (www.qsp.com/Magazines.aspx)

- **A used book fair.** Collect gently used books, DVDs, and CDs throughout the year. Have volunteers sort and price items and set up tables. Sell any items that are not purchased at deeply discounted rates in order to clear out remaining stock.

- **A "Wish List,"** with a card attached that lets parents donate a book from the list in honor of their student, family members, etc.

- **Research grants or funds acquired through district, state, and federal programs**. Seek support from local civic organizations and create connections with community businesses and bookstores.

- **Working with the school's director of development** to create an endowment fund specifically for the library collection and programs. An article in *Knowledge Quest* (Medeiros 2004) provides details and links on how to support an endowment fund.

Conclusion

Raising funds is a community effort that needs to build over time. Do not take on these efforts alone—make friends with the parents, teachers, and administrators who sit on school committees. Collaborate with your school's development professionals to take advantage of their expertise. Strong library budgets are generally the result of ongoing advocacy by the library staff, advocacy that makes sure all the shareholders know the value of library services in dollars and student achievement. (See essay 6.)

Just as your library collection takes years to grow, so does creating a solid funding base. Successful budgeting and library advocacy will emanate from your ability to think on your feet and take some risks—which is something any independent school librarian should be well-qualified to do!

References

Cahoy, Ellysa Stern, and Susan G. Williamson. 2005. *Studying the Independent School Library*. American Association of School Librarians. Available at www.ala.org/ala/mgrps/divs/aasl/aaslpubsandjournals/slmrb/slmrcontents/volume11/ALA_print_layout_1_520109_520109.cfm. Accessed November 24, 2009.

Davis, Sarah Knetzer. 2009. *Budget Survey* [distributed by e-mail in April 2009]. AISL (Association of Independent School Librarians).

Farmer, Leslie J., and Marilyn Shontz. 2009. "School Library Journal's Spending Survey." *School Library Journal* (April 1). Available at www.schoollibraryjournal.com/article/CA6648082.html. Accessed November 21, 2009.

Franklin, Paricia, and Claire G. Stephens. 2007. *Library 101: A Handbook for the School Library Media Specialist*. Westport CT: Libraries Unlimited.

Hamilton, Buffy. 2009. *Creekview High School Media Center Annual Report*. May 29. Available at http://theunquietlibrary.wikispaces.com/file/view/Creekview+ High+School+Media+Center+Annual+Report+2008-09.pdf. Accessed November 21, 2009.

Medeiros, Trish. 2004. "Beyond the Budget: Endowments as Alternate Sources of Funding." *KnowledgeQuest* (September–October). Available at http://aasl.org/ ala/mgrps/divs/aasl/aaslpubsandjournals/knowledgequest/kqwebarchives/v33/3 31mederios.cfm. Accessed March 11, 2010.

Toor, Ruth, and Hilda K. Weisburg. 2007. *New on the Job: A School Library Media Specialist's Guide to Success*. Chicago: American Library Association.

Valenza, Joyce Kasman, and Doug Johnson. 2009. "Things That Keep Us Up at Night." *School Library Journal* (October 1). Available at www.school libraryjournal.com/article/CA6699357.html. Accessed November 26, 2009.

Sarah Knetzer Davis is the Director of Libraries at Viewpoint School in Calabasas, California (www. viewpoint.org). She received her master's in library service degree from Rutgers University and has worked in both public library settings and independent schools for the past twelve years. Her dedication to building connections with other librarians was evident at the start of her career, which found her driving over two hours from the Idyllwild Arts Academy each time there was a meeting of the Southern California Independent School Library Exchange (ISLE). When she is not over-seeing the Viewpoint Libraries or writing extensive questions on the AISL listserv, Knetzer Davis can be found chasing (and reading to) her two daughters, ages two and five.

Role of the Library in Admissions and Institutional Advancement

Catherine Greene, Miami Country Day School (Miami, FL)

Introduction

When this topic was first suggested to me, the teamwork that exists among the library, the admissions office, and the institutional advancement committee came immediately to mind. The library's role at my school was clearly valued; in fact, school admissions offices often ask school librarians to be members of their admission committees. They recognize that the librarian offers a unique view of candidates by providing additional, evaluative feedback reflecting a student's potential outside the classroom: "Kids are being raised in a culture of high expectation" (Robbins 2006). Because librarians work with all students, they have a comprehensive view of the skill sets that students must have to effectively handle their workload. They are excellent advocates in encouraging the competencies set forth by Tony Wagner in *The Global Achievement Gap* (2008), which emphasizes critical thinking and problem solving. Curriculum mapping (a more comprehensive method to accomplish scope and sequence with alignment) and ongoing faculty discussions of information literacy skills ensure continued focus on these needed attributes. Conducting library tours for potential students and families also offers an opportunity to converse with students to learn if the applicants like to read and what their favorite Web sites are, allowing the librarian-interviewer to see their enthusiasm for learning, etc.

Like the admissions office, the institutional advancement office (IAO), sometimes called the development office, traditionally collaborates with the school's library because the library can contribute hugely to the academic image of a school. The IAO is usually responsible for fund-raising beyond the core budget, including money for scholarships that can foster a more diverse student community and for marketing of the school "brand" through use of pertinent school strengths, events, and traditions. An independent school relies on a ready pool of applicant families who can appreciate the rigorous academic program and most of whom can pay the tuition. IAO and admissions work together to advertise the school image in such a way as to attract the pool of applicants and to differentiate the school from other similar schools. That every independent school is unique is a concept woven through this entire book; because every independent school is unique, each school's structure for institutional advancement is different.

> [B]ecause every independent school is unique, each school's structure for institutional advancement is different.

The IAO may be involved in grant writing, school publications, alumni contact and support, and other aspects of the school that contribute to the external image seen by the larger community, which includes current parents, prospective parents, alumni, and the community at large. Because a successful admissions program relies on a great school reputation, the institutional advancement and admissions offices are closely tied. In some schools, an institutional advancement committee supports the IA program, whether there is an actual IAO or not, by keeping the administration and director of institutional advancement aware of campus events and new programs; members would include a representative of the parent association as well as other department heads and administrators. The librarian often sits on this committee to keep the group abreast of major library news, which enables them to capitalize on this information and foster further teamwork with the alumni office and the parent association.

When the initial signs of a potential recession began in 2007, schools did not expect changes in academic or departmental relationships. The recession deepened and continued; economists predicted that its effect will reverberate for years. Job losses, foreclosures, bankruptcies, and heightened stress in all types of job situations grew. As of the fall of 2009, these events continue to affect our work and to have a negative, domino effect on many plans and projects.

At regional and local meetings of consortia in Florida, it is clear that school staffing levels have shrunk, and the remaining staff works longer hours on reduced budgets with increased responsibilities. The recession isn't just affecting librarians; private schools face serious cutbacks as endowments shrink and fewer families can afford tuition. With a smaller pool of new applicants, admissions offices have refocused on retention of current students, some of whom may now need scholarships. The IAO focus on outside funding is more intense in a climate where foundation funding and parent gifts are less available. Campus libraries are seeking new ways to provide superior services within budgetary and staffing constraints. In 2009 many private schools contended with serious financial and enrollment challenges.

> [E]ven when money is tight, the library must offer a big bang for the buck.

Crises provide an opportunity for creativity and innovation, often with positive results; but clearly, roles have changed. It isn't that departments are less collaborative, but that schedules and focus have changed. Libraries are charged to develop aggressive marketing strategies in compliance with long-range planning: as the IAO looks for funding, the school needs a strong library program to show potential donors the strength of its commitment to education—even when money is tight, the library must offer a big bang for the buck. In addition, libraries remain a showpiece of admissions tours: Where else can prospective families observe a range of students actively engaged in study, see displays of student projects and/or art, and get an overview of the kinds of library materials available for the students? Within the school, the importance of the library to the ongoing curriculum remains high: when teachers assign research, they insist on a balance between books and technology. This is exactly where librarians are invaluable, teaching research skills, explaining specialized databases, and helping students with reference work. They also assist teachers with related coursework by obtaining materials, purchasing needed resources, and researching current developments in specific subjects.

Libraries may also now be asked to find ways to fund their extras—author programs or additional databases—outside of budget monies. This pressure comes at the same time schools prefer that all fund-raising happen under the aegis of the IAO, to minimize requests to the same potential donors. Yes, libraries may now be between the proverbial rock and a hard place. They need to become financially innovative to provide additional services; this is a new piece of the librarian's job description that is time consuming and demands difficult decisions. The economic crisis of 2009 provoked these changes, but there is a silver lining to this cloud: we are now wonderfully positioned to reexamine traditional methods and adapt them to new perspectives and strategies.

> *[W]e are now wonderfully positioned to reexamine traditional methods and adapt them to new perspectives and strategies.*

Standards

FCIS standards for accreditation, issued in summer 2009, reflect a trend to more general guidelines and less specific language. When accreditation required minimum numbers of books and other materials, schools sought to provide more. However, modern resources are difficult to count: is access to EBSCOHost (for example) one database or several—and how many journals are included in EBSCOHost for which the school now does not need a print subscription?

Checklist for the Evaluation Visit

5.1 Library Media Center

5.1.1 The library/media center has adequate facilities (centralized or decentralized) and technological resources to support the school's philosophy, mission, and programs.

5.1.2 The library/media center has a definite and appropriate budget to meet the needs of the educational program.

5.1.3 The library/media center is adequately staffed, including a trained library media specialist. (See also professional requirements in 3.5.4.)

5.1.4 Adequate records are kept, including catalogues, inventory of print and electronic resources, and acquisitions.

5.1.5 The library/media center has adequate print and electronic resources to support the educational program.

3.5.4 Instructional staff members shall spend the major part of the day teaching in the field(s) in which they are academically prepared. If the academic preparation is out of field, a minimum of 12 semester hours and/or in-service equivalents must be obtained in the field in which the individual is teaching.

From the Florida Council of Independent Schools (FCIS) Accreditation Standards (2009), www.fcis.org/page.cfm?p=234.

Certainly stronger accreditation standards would make libraries more viable and indicate the school's supportive role in its library, which would benefit admissions and assist in fund-raising. Reviewing standards of several states may aid in strengthening a library's viability (www.sldirectory.com/libsf/resf/evaluate.html), as will reference to the *Standards for the 21st Century Learner* issued by the American Association of School Librarians (http://aasl.org/ala/mgrps/divs/aasl/guidelinesandstandards/learningstandards/standards.cfm). These standards can provide excellent guidelines that point to various levels of excellence. The Texas standards are leveled from "passing" to "outstanding," which offers a school a goal-setting measure. If a school meets the Outstanding level, it can add this to promotional materials (www.tsl.state.tx.us/ld/pubs/schlibsurvey/index.html). In general, independent school libraries can use the accreditation process to strengthen themselves; essay 20 offers further suggestions.

When money is tight, construction plans are often delayed. However, librarians should continue to stress the importance and value of a state-of-the-art library to the overall school image. The library makes an essential contribution to the curriculum specifically and to the academic community generally, a riveting selling point when seeking funding and enrollment.

Bridging the Gap

Our present economy has accelerated the urgency to show increased value for services and products. This must be shown in tandem with continued progress, current philosophies, and expected outcomes. This is fair—particularly for parents who are striving to provide a private school experience for children during difficult financial times.

A review of school library professional literature emphasizes the priority that schools place on teaching twenty-first-century skills. When these forward-looking skills are taught at all levels, the library eases the transition from lower to middle school and middle to upper school by maintaining consistent procedures and services; students know what to expect as they advance. Libraries, in collaboration with other departments, emphasize the twenty-first-century skill set each level needs by contributing to the excellent education that enables their student graduates to move to the best schools at whatever the next level may be—middle school, high school, or college. In addition, the success of the Universal PreK movement has changed the kindergarten curriculum; younger students are better prepared and ahead of those who haven't had pre-K. Georgetown University professor William Gormley found that "children who had been in PreK for a year had a 52% increase in letter-word recognition and a 27% edge in spelling over children the same age who were just entering PreK" (Wilson 2008). Jenny Dorl, a kindergarten teacher at Charter Oak Academy in West Hartford, Connecticut, feels that pre-K experience leads to more balanced kindergarten classrooms (Wilson 2008). Parents are so enthusiastic about these programs that some private schools already have active programs for three-year-olds.

Any time a school extends its range of grades, whether at the bottom, or at the top with a new level or "gap year" program, admissions and libraries are affected. If your school decides to add a pre-K—or an IB program—the library will immediately add materials that support the new programs. Boards of trustees have already decided they want the program, both from a mission perspective and a financial one; the library's contribution to the program, beyond the obvious academic support, is to team with admissions and development in presenting this to parents. Libraries are in a pivotal position to provide new programs and influence acquisition of innovative materials.

When a student enters middle school, he or she enters a new world. Everything is different: higher expectations, more responsibilities, heavier work load, more independence, choices, and activities. It can be overwhelming. Miami Country Day has successfully initiated a transitional program for future sixth graders, which begins at mid-year for fifth graders. In these programs, students use the main campus library, mingle with middle and upper school students, and attend special classes on reference and research skills. They become immersed in learning how to use references (print and electronic), and how to find specific sources, and more important, they absorb the ambience of the library while observing older students studying and working on assignments. Their confidence level rises as their initial feelings of confusion or intimidation are erased. New sixth graders who have had this experience report that adapting to middle school was easier, and they say they felt more at ease having gone through the library program. This transitional effort offers the IAO and admissions department an excellent marketing point, an example of a school working hard to maximize student success. It's an excellent example of great teamwork.

By ninth grade, students are more focused on their ultimate goal: graduation and college acceptance. APs, honor classes, academic societies, and visits to colleges consume their time. This is an opportunity for libraries to initiate pilot programs of new, electronic learning tools; add to database selections; and assist students with portfolios, videographies, and writing samples. Some enterprising librarians offer "free" reference requests for recent graduates for the first six months of their freshman year in college. Although this may be construed as another way to bridge the gap between high school and college, it also signals a continued commitment to easing a graduate's transition into college life. Parents appreciate this touchstone, too. The library then collaborates with the alumni office as new graduates acclimate themselves to their new academic life. (See essay 12.)

Library Advocacy

The library can be a central resource for every class, a place visited in person or virtually—and it is available every day. It is a location proudly featured as a destination of every school tour so that all visitors can see what a vibrant program the library offers. Getting to that point requires an ongoing program of advocacy that shows teachers how the library makes their job easier, showing them that library resources—print and digital, subscription based and open Internet—for their curriculum are easy to use. Support of library programs contributes to the successful accomplishment of the school's mission. While many teachers and administrators look to the library as a requirement to their own success, the IAO can use this enthusiasm in fund-raising. Admissions can also dovetail this enthusiasm to sell prospective parents on the value of this library in this school. It is most important that admissions, the parents association, and the IAO/Committee be well briefed on library services and all innovative projects currently underway. The library needs to be viewed as one of the busiest places on campus—as it is.

Enter Stephen Abram, "one of the world's leading library visionaries" (2007, back cover), who is known for his positive, no-nonsense approach to promoting libraries and librarians. Advocacy is one of his major themes, as reflected in his writings and speeches. His encouraging advice and statements are pertinent for current and future generations of librarians. The recession and its resulting immediate and long-range effects dictate that libraries need to be out front with a commanding role as their own advocates. Abram states that "we must become better advocates for libraries."

One of the characteristics of leadership and advocacy is the ability to inspire. You need charisma, enthusiasm, and an unshakable belief in your mission. You need competence and vision. Unless these traits are seen as coming from librarians themselves, all the committees, groups, and meetings will lack the spark of true advocacy. Persistence and focus are the linchpins of advocacy. For a broader discussion of advocacy, see essay 6.

Roles change and shift, but the threads of advocacy should remain intertwined in the library sector and among major departments of private schools.

We need to assume responsibility in creating and nurturing advocacy programs directed toward the admissions and institutional advancement offices. Roles change and shift, but the threads of advocacy should remain intertwined in the library sector and among major departments of private schools. Such teamwork is advantageous to all.

Guidelines for Libraries, Admissions, and Institutional Advancement

These suggestions have broad implications for our school academic programs, admissions efforts, and institutional advancement generally.

1. **Think globally—in education, business, marketing, finance, etc.:** A global perspective must permeate our thinking as we educate twenty-first-century students. Today's digital natives demand immediacy; thus, new products and systems must be developed to provide credible facts. Today, being connected assumes instant knowledge transferred globally.

2. **Promote information access:** The field of education must shed aspects of limited thinking to swiftly adapt to new concepts of learning and teaching. Advocate creativity, empowerment, and potential as a priority for our students. They will be working in a global arena where innovation and information will partner with flexible thinking and collaboration. (See essay 9.)

3. **Give students an interdisciplinary approach** to learning that opens doors to the new concepts and the creative questioning processes they will need.

4. **Read** "Can You Hear Me Now? School Marketing and the Social Web" by Louie Jackson in the winter 2009 issue of *Independent School*, the magazine of the National Association of Independent Schools.

5. **Provide balance:** Whether it is traditional practices vs. today's trends, or books vs. computers, students need more than ever to be taught how to balance perspectives, decisions, and judgments. As their world accelerates and their future responsibilities broaden into global actions, our students need librarians and teachers to impart the wisdom of balance—particularly in their reasoning, as they come to see that decisions affecting the United States have immediate global ramifications. Balance includes the acknowledgment of ethics and morality; global citizenship will require students to know how to find information and establish the validity of that information as well as to understand how the information supports or denies a political position or ethical dilemma. Independent schools have the daunting opportunity and obligation to instill in our students a sense of right and wrong in a world where gray is common, and to build in these students the tools with which to analyze the facts.

6. **Adapt to prioritizing the role of knowledge management** in a world where technology changes at warp speed, new products abound, and the arena is collaborative and global. Develop international ties, join global organizations and societies, while simultaneously developing new perspectives for words like "reading," "text," and "research." Associate these terms with animation, videography, voice in–voice out, images, streaming video, etc. But remember, it's still information, albeit in multiple forms, and that's where librarians excel. In whatever form information will be disseminated in the future, librarians already possess the needed mindset of knowledge management. We've gone from papyrus to computers, and we're still filling user's information needs. However the future dictates information access, librarians will be its facilitators.

7. **Remain a lifelong learner:** This reflects the independent school philosophy and defines the lasting role of librarians as facilitators of learning—in all its forms.

8. **Be cognizant of brain research** that continues to illuminate for schools how younger generations learn, how they perceive ideas and process facts. This dictates how librarians adjust their own learning perspective to fulfill inquiries in the current knowledge environment.

9. **Keep looking ahead:** It's an exciting ride! Sidelines are for sissies. Take the risk, embrace new technologies, and lead the way. Give wisdom and balance to our students by demonstrating that libraries hold the keys in a knowledge-seeking world.

Thinking Futuristically

We know that libraries, technology, and learning methods will be drastically different in the future. Roles will change, and forward-thinking individuals will revel in this opportunistic environment. We're fortunate that we can participate in this.

To stay abreast of new developments, librarians need to cultivate more partnerships, particularly with museums as libraries evolve into cultural meeting places. This changes our marketing focus to prioritize our services and link our expertise to all facets of our school community. Visionary library services sustain the knowledge environment.

Library design trends stress flexibility in assessing changing space requirements based on services, technology, and user demand. Interactive learning, project-based assignments, and collaborative outcomes dictate group study areas with media access. (See essays 10 and 19.) In addition to its intellectual role, perceiving the library as a community space gives the IAO a perfect forum for marketing the school. Think outside the box. Maybe the best location for the admissions office is in (or next to) the library; that way, admissions staff will see every day how vibrant a place the library is and how many students enter the library doors.

Conclusion

> [T]he library's management of information for students and faculty keeps it at the epicenter of academic activity and an icon of community standards for academic integrity.

Independent school libraries will continue to work collaboratively with admissions and institutional advancement. As we've seen, roles shift and change according to economic times and technological advances—but the library's management of information for students and faculty keeps it at the epicenter of academic activity and an icon of community standards for academic integrity. The core mission, however, remains rooted in teamwork, and the key ingredient is the ability to be flexible in a changing, global society. We're in it together, and students remain our joint priority. That's a great privilege.

References

Abram, Stephen. 2007. *Out Front With Stephen Abram: A Guide for Information Leaders*. Chicago: American Library Association.

Bloch, R. Howard, and Carla Hesse. 1995. *Future Libraries*. Berkeley: University of California Press.

Dempsey, Kathy. 2009. *The Accidental Library Marketer*. Medford, NJ: Information Today.

Florida Council of Independent Schools. 2009. *Accreditation Standards—Checklist for Evaluation.* Available at www.fcis.org/page.cfm?p=234. Accessed October 19, 2009.

Freeman, Geoffrey T. 2005. "The Library as Place: Changes in Learning Patterns, Collections, Technology, and Use." In *CLIR Reports.* Council on Library and Information Resources. Available at www.clir.org/pubs/reports/pub129/freeman.html. Accessed November 21, 2009.

Jackson, Louie. 2009. *Can You Hear Me Now? School Marketing and the Social Web.* National Association of Independent Schools (NAIS). Winter. Available at www.nais.org/publications/ismagazinearticle.cfm?Itemnumber=151413&sn.Item Number=145956. Accessed November 21, 2009.

Robbins, A. 2006. *The Overachievers: The Secret Lives of Driven Kids.* New York: Hyperion.

Wagner, Tony. 2008. *The Global Achievement Gap.* New York: Basic Books.

Walser, Nancy. 2008. "Teaching 21st Century Skills." *Harvard Education Letter* 24, no. 5: n.p.

Wilson, David McKay. 2008. "When Worlds Collide." *Harvard Education Letter* 24, no. 6 (November–December): n.p.

Visit http://lu.com/excellence for supporting links and occasional updates to all essays in this book.

Catherine Greene has been a professional librarian for over twenty-five years, working in medical, law, business, and school libraries. Presently she is Director of Library Services at Miami Country Day School (http://www.miamicountryday.org/) in Miami, FL. She is a member of Beta Phi Mu.

If You Build It: School Library Facilities

Walter DeMelle, Hotchkiss School (Lakeville, CT)

We all feel confident that we know what a library is—yet no two libraries are alike. When planning a new library facility or a substantial renovation of an existing one, it is important to keep that point in mind. Because many feel they already know what a library is, heads of school, even most architects, are unaware of the special planning required to develop a library building program. They have no idea how many problems can result from a lack of extensive discussions with the library staff. As a result, many school boards or administrators simply direct their architect to build a library. Librarians

> *We all feel confident that we know what a library is—yet no two libraries are alike.*

are seldom consulted by either their head of school or the architect as plans are developed to build a new library facility. Many people do not understand how complex the operation of a library is, or how much planning is required to create appropriate spaces. Consultants may ask what someone would do if building his or her own house. All agree that they would instruct the architect in whatever details reflect personal needs and idiosyncrasies. A tall person might want raised counters in the kitchen; a dual-career couple may need two home offices. Schools embarking on a library project should remember that there is no such thing as an "off-the-rack" library. You will need to define your own needs and idiosyncrasies—as well as the particular spirit or ethos of your school—so that architects can plan a facility that reflects your school.

The librarian is the most knowledgeable person in the school about how the library functions and how it can be used, but often architects and administrators ignore the librarian when making decisions about a new facility. In order to not relinquish that power, the librarian must take an aggressive role in educating people about how a library facility should be planned. Whenever the librarian gets a hint that someone in the school has begun to think about the library facility, it is immediately time to meet with the head of school and suggest the formation of a working group to discuss the library program and the facility. Even if the possibility of a new or renovated library seems to be several years in the future, the time to start the planning and the group is "the sooner the better"; the group should be facilitated or led by the librarian and should begin meeting to help create a building program.

Start as early as you can with discussions, investigation, and decision making. There can never be too much time to develop the details and definitions for the library building program, because it is the tool that defines for the architects what will be required to create the best library for this school. The library building program is an essential element for the planning of any new library or significant renovation project. The document serves as a blueprint for the architects and designers as they work to develop the scope and form of spaces to house the school's library.

> *[T]he library building program . . . is the tool that defines for the architects what will be required to create the best library for this school.*

There is also no such thing as too much team; the librarian cannot write the building program without substantial input from the community. This planning group writing the document should consist of representatives from major constituent groups at the school. The library director and representatives of the staff (whether on the payroll or volunteer) are key sources of expertise. Open lines of communication with the head of school are essential; if the head cannot sit on the committee, a key associate should. The business manager should be part of the planning, along with someone representing the plant management and custodial staff. Include representatives of the faculty and the student body also. Depending on the specific situation of a school community, you might consider including parents or alumni representatives. The chief development/fund-raising office must be included to be kept fully aware of all of the needs of a program—and the rationale behind those needs (see essay 18). Without that understanding, fund-raisers cannot explain the project clearly to potential donors, making it significantly more difficult to raise the funds required to cover the costs. Who actually will make the decisions? The head, the board, a wealthy alum? Be sure this person or group is included every step of the way. It makes no sense to work through the process of planning if the final decision lies with a major donor, an influential trustee, or a head who operates independently of the planning committee. Finally, include voices of those who are not necessarily current devotees of the library. If critics can be part of the planning, they become strong advocates for the project because they feel their viewpoints have been considered. From the beginning, the librarian and the head should mutually understand that the task of the library planning committee will be to fully inform themselves about the needs of the library in the school and how those needs can best be addressed. Then it is the task of the committee to educate the decision-makers about its recommendations as described in the building program document.

> *It makes no sense to work through the process of planning if the final decision lies with a major donor, an influential trustee, or a head who operates independently of the planning committee.*

The new head of a Massachusetts boarding school asked me to meet with his librarians and faculty to provide a "snapshot" impression of the library and its program. This head knew that some significant renovation would likely be necessary to the existing library. For two days, I met on campus with a variety of groups—library personnel, students, faculty members, administrators —and observed the library in action for several hours at different times of the day so that I could raise issues for further discussion, allowing the school community to find the appropriate solutions.

Because consultants do not have awareness of internal political issues or areas of possible conflict, they frequently can bring otherwise sensitive matters into the arena. In this particular case, as a result of the consultant visit, the school created a planning committee that met for two years; the committee recommended that the school build a new library in a central place convenient to classrooms and dormitories where the library could serve as the academic core of the campus. No one on that planning committee went into the discussions intending to make such a recommendation. This school, which thought it simply wanted to reorganize the library and upgrade its furnishings, wound up committing itself to building a new library and creating a new academic center. The school's willingness to engage in a process that examined the issues surrounding the library facility and its functions allowed them to reach a surprising conclusion that ultimately benefited the school enormously. Ten years later the library continues to be seen as one of the most significant buildings on the campus.

In her first months as library director at a suburban girls' school, a librarian colleague was asked by the head of school to meet with architects to discuss the requirements for a new library. With little time on the job and no significant input from others on the faculty or the student body, this librarian had to tell the architects what she felt they should accommodate when drawing up preliminary plans for a new facility. Decisions about overall size of the facility, complexity in terms of its technology and design requirements, and projections about cost, were all made based on a ninety-minute interview between an architect and a librarian new to her job. Fortunately, that project was put on hold. Five years later the same librarian learned that the project was again going forward. However, she also learned that the architect planned simply to dust off the sketches based on those old, brief interviews, so she took a proactive approach and intervened. Sensing her voice might not be influential enough, the librarian asked the school to appoint a library planning consultant to work with her and a committee of students, administrators, and faculty to create a revised program document. The end result of this process was construction of what has been recognized as one of the finest independent school libraries built in the late 1990s.

My interest in library facilities began in 1970 when I was first hired as the library director of a leading New England boarding school to update and renovate the library, which had been built in the model of a gentlemen's library/reading room only eighteen years earlier. Everyone at the school expected the upgrade would require some paint, perhaps some new furnishings, and a few other touches required by the ideas of this young new professional; no one understood that the library was already outdated when it was built. At the first library planning committee meeting, the chairman of the committee produced a large cardboard template of the present library's floor plans and several cutouts of library furnishings. His agenda for that meeting was to sit around the table with committee members and together design the renovation of the library. Even forty years later I run across situations in which

The first task of a library planning committee is to define the role of the library within the particular school.

people want to start moving the furniture before they have considered all they want to achieve. The planning process might eventually involve paper cutouts, but first should come some definition of philosophy, purpose, and program.

The first task of library planning is to define the role of the library within the particular school. There is no "one" answer or cookie-cutter library. We all think we know what a library is, but descriptions of the "ideal" library vary tremendously. For example, you can visit four independent girls' school libraries serving grades pre-K to 12 in Manhattan. Each library serves similar populations, and each was built within a few years. All four libraries are markedly different from one another, each evoking the spirit of the school they serve. Nearby in Connecticut there is a girls' boarding school that serves the same population, pre-K–12, and its library presents an entirely different ambience and design from those in Manhattan. The task of a library planning committee is to articulate for the architects what the unique qualities and needs of their own school are.

The library program and philosophy are based on the library mission statement, which is rooted in the school's mission statement. When planning a new library, the committee must know the school's mission and the library's. If the school seeks to promote independent thought or lifelong learning, the library should do so as well. Such a commitment, for example, would have strong implications for the size and breadth of the collection, requiring more space than a library intended to support only the academic program. A boarding school must have resources available for the faculty children living on the campus and for the staff and adults for whom the library supports lifelong habits of reading and inquiry. A boarding school library may also open to the local community; the presence of adults of all ages is clear evidence of learning as a lifelong endeavor. No example is more powerful than an adult campus member standing in the stacks perusing the choices or waiting behind a student at the circulation desk to check out library items. Likewise, if the school acknowledges different learning styles and the necessity of developing its programs to support these modalities, then it becomes even more likely the library will develop substantial collections in visual, audio, and digital resources, in addition to the more traditional print materials. These resources require additional (and sometimes different) space for the materials along with the equipment needed to use them and more sophisticated equipment and information delivery systems. These spaces need to be described in the library building program.

> *No example [of lifelong learning] is more powerful than an adult campus member standing in the stacks perusing the choices or waiting behind a student at the circulation desk to check out library items.*

When defining the role of the library within the institution, the planning committee must assess current practices. A few years ago I worked with a library in a regional high school serving a large population of students in various educational programs ranging from college prep to vocational and technical to English as a second language, to basic skills for the developmentally challenged. The existing library facility was quite modest and barely met the needs of its college prep program. The planning group, however, did not at first consider that a large-percentage of students in the school were not being served at all. Students for whom English was a second language did not have materials in their native languages; those in auto mechanics or food preparation or childcare programs did not have suitable materials to serve their interests. There was nothing for beginning readers in basic studies. While defining the role of the library, the planning group must address the needs of those not using the current library in addition to improving services and facilities for those who are.

Pauline Anderson is librarian emerita at Choate Rosemary Hall in Connecticut and consultant for hundreds of school libraries. In *School Library Media Facilities* (1990), Pauline emphasizes that above all, *form follows function*. This truth continues to be the mantra for the library planning process. Yes, there are book stacks and study tables and lounge chairs and a circulation desk. But what happens at these places, and how do actions in one place relate to those in another? Just as a cook carefully plans a kitchen so that the sink and the chopping block, the refrigerator and the stove, the work space and the cooking utensils, are planned in careful relation to each other, the spaces and component parts of a library should be planned in terms of how the library functions.

[A]bove all, form follows function.

The planning committee examines in detail every aspect of library functionality and describes for the architect the relationship between its parts. The person on duty at the circulation desk needs to have visual access to the entire library; the desk needs to be near the entrance to facilitate and oversee checkout; the copy machine needs to be near staff who can provide patron assistance; a multipurpose classroom should be near the entrance so that people going to it don't interfere with the work of others in the library. One of the great challenges in contemporary libraries is to provide sufficient instructional space so that librarians can teach students and faculty how to access and evaluate resources. This instruction necessitates a carefully planned classroom to teach information literacy using print, visual, and digital resources. We know that group-based or collaborative learning is highly effective. Therefore, in addition to single-user study carrels or desks, a library should provide small sound-proofed rooms where groups can work together. Every library must be able to accommodate the legitimate needs of different user groups simultaneously. For example, while one teacher might be working with a group on a project, another class might be divided into several small groups working independently. At the same time, some will be there to work individually and require a quiet place. A class of younger students might be in the library for story hour or an author visit. The effective planning process includes the needs of all populations served.

Every library must be able to accommodate the legitimate needs of different user groups simultaneously.

Architects and others do not understand intuitively the various functions of an effective school library program; therefore the planning committee defines these differing programmatic needs. Different styles of teaching and learning require different spatial solutions. The committee describes these needs. Pre-K and kindergarten students require quite different spaces than those used by second and third-graders; students (and teachers) seeking a place to be alone in a focused environment need spaces for that, as do those working collaboratively in groups or on a project. A library serving lower, middle, and upper school students requires quite different strategies and spaces to provide services that meet the unique needs of these groups all within the same space and often at the same time. Legitimate, simultaneous, competing uses that require quite different environments are characteristic of how school libraries function. The planning committee defines these differences for the architect. Through this planning process, the committee educates itself, and through the written program informs the architect and the final decision makers.

Legitimate, simultaneous, competing uses that require quite different environments are characteristic of how school libraries function.

There are several approaches that can be beneficial in educating the planning group. You can begin with a general discussion of the important elements that members of the group think go into an effective library. Ask what positive experiences in libraries people have had. What qualities describe spaces conducive to these positive experiences? Consider ways to achieve these as plans develop for a new facility. In this discussion, consider any library that people value for any reason. Inevitably people will mention large chain bookstores and the qualities that make them effective and attractive; these qualities should be articulated. What do people DISLIKE about libraries they know? From each of these examples will spring some common ground of understanding—appreciation or dislike—which can help inform the group's conversations and provide a framework for further examination.

Engaging in this first step generally helps the group begin to identify points of agreement and areas where they disagree. Some will place considerable value on distraction-free reading rooms where one can hear a pin drop; others lobby for places for group study or collaborative work, a place of busy-ness and activity. Some seek the comfort and relaxed atmosphere of libraries that provide lounge furniture and popular reading materials, which offer respite from an intense schedule or a lot of school work, while others see a library as a formal and serene workplace similar to the grand reading rooms of the large universities or the Library of Congress. Often during these discussions someone will reminisce about the comfort of an overstuffed chair positioned in the sunlight of a large bay window. Inevitably people recall the basement stacks, which offered quiet sanctuary in a university library. Whatever qualities people recall as positive elements of a library they have known, they provide the group opportunity to reflect on the appropriate balance of comfort and formality, silence and interaction.

A second approach to developing common understanding and vocabulary, not limited to examples of your own space, is for members of the group to visit several other libraries, at least one of them as a shared-group experience. These "field trips" can provide examples of different solutions to questions similar to the ones you will consider, examples that can open the world of possibility for your local situation. On one of my consulting efforts, the library committee was resistant to most of the "new" ideas presented. When nothing seemed to help the committee members understand why their eighteenth-century-like reading room was not suitable for a contemporary library, I decided to break the box where their thinking was trapped. I loaded the group into a school van and took them to visit the library of a competitor school. This new facility featured a great variety of study and work spaces, well-organized stacks and easily accessible collections, and a staff work area planned for efficient support operations that also offered the staff the opportunity to both work and supervise from a central vantage point. The library had group studies, seminar rooms for small classes, and a viewing room suitable for projection and large group instruction. Seats varied from soft lounge chairs to adjustable task chairs and more traditional wooden desk chairs at individual carrels. The library had the grace and understated elegance valued by my colleagues, along with strikingly modern elements of design and furnishings. Lighting, wall coverings, and changes in carpet color all contributed to how effectively the library functioned. Through this shared afternoon

[The] "field trip" open[s] eyes to new possibilities, to differing solutions to similar problems.

excursion, members of that group learned a new language and returned to our own planning meetings with very different points of view. The "field trip" opened eyes to new possibilities, to differing solutions to similar problems. The group began to see that some of the features they had identified as important elements for a library can be realized in different ways. Visiting several libraries—especially those with similar constituencies —can demonstrate the value of paying attention to details in color, texture, ambience, and light and to the preference for variety in experiences the building can offer.

Examples of field trip questions might be:

- Should there be a computer lab in the library?
- Do you need a professional collection for faculty?
- Should there be parenting resources for families?
- Do you need recorded books for commuting teachers or students with reading challenges?
- How does the library store different kinds of material?

Before you plan a group's visit, develop a list to consider so the group looks at how spaces and qualities you have discussed are handled in the visited facility. If the group is wrestling with certain questions, assign each committee member one question to investigate at each site. They'll be able to compare the various solutions and extract elements that may be useful in the new space not yet designed.

If the group already knows specific elements they would like to incorporate in the new library (spaces for story hour, work areas for volunteers, age-appropriate furnishings, special shelving for videocassettes or CDs), plan to focus special attention on how the visited libraries include them. If you have a specific facility issue in your library—a dark basement space, a third floor space in need of renovation, a desire for lots of natural light—which the group wants to treat differently in the new space, look for good (or bad) examples you can show your architect at the beginning of the design process for your space. And, of course, take photographs. Through scrapbooks or digital presentations the group can demonstrate and explain to the architect, administration and trustees, and other interested parties the elements they value and can explain their importance for the library being planned. As the design/development stage progresses, use these visual diaries to illustrate important points.

A thoughtfully educated planning group, armed with shared vocabulary and the experience of visiting libraries other than the one at their own school, is a powerful part of the planning process. I once observed members of a planning committee argue passionately against a last minute decision to eliminate an internal circular stairway from within a two-story structure in a very tight multistory urban building under construction. The decision to eliminate it was made by the head of school based on cost overruns for the whole building project. However, the persuasive comments by the library planning group demonstrated their understanding of the need for this stairway as essential to provide internal circulation within the two-story library. With their arguments they demonstrated a clear understanding of the stairwell as functionally necessary for internal circulation connecting the two parts of the library, which served the two

A thoughtfully educated planning group, armed with shared vocabulary and the experience of visiting libraries other than the one at their own school, is a powerful part of the planning process.

divisions of the school. It was not merely a design element or grandiose architectural gesture, it would enhance interaction and the flow between grade levels that the committee (and school) sought to achieve. The committee members argued compellingly, and the head reversed her decision. To this day, the stairwell serves a key function in supporting the interaction among the two floors and the two parts of the school. And, the portrait of that head stands at the entrance of this wonderful library, later named in her honor.

At some point in the process, the planning group should harvest ideas from students. Although students' perspective often lacks a 'big picture' view, their thoughts will provide important keys to understanding what a successful library needs to be. A few years ago I visited the library of a prestigious international school and found considerable upset among the students. They were angry at their new librarian. Talking to her at the end of the day, she explained to me that soon after she began working in this school she realized the library needed more places for students to study. At times some of them were sitting on the floor or on adjacent porches. In front of the large window overlooking the spectacular landscape above which the school was situated, there was a large upholstered couch. Seeing that space as an opportunity to provide more desktops, the librarian replaced the couch with two study tables for four. She had eight seats where previously there were three. Unfortunately, she had seriously miscalculated the value of that couch to the school community. Not only had the couch been in front of a window overlooking a magnificent view everyone valued, the students saw it as "the only comfortable seat in the school where we could relax." By not soliciting the support of the student community, a small change made with good intentions became a big problem for the librarian.

In recent years, schools have been considering the appropriate balance between traditional printed books and digital resources. Some administrations and boards wonder if a library of books may any longer be a necessity—or even desirable—in this digital age. Could the book be in its waning years as a source of information? Will digitized resources available via the Internet provide everything one would want to know? One board chair wrote me that by providing each student and faculty member with a laptop, his school had supplanted the need altogether for a library. Any library planning group must focus considerable attention on this issue, as methods of providing access to information are changing continuously. For a deeper consideration of this issue, read essay 8. For me, the short answer is that digital resources cannot do everything and never will. They can certainly provide enormous quantities of important information—increasingly the only source for some kinds of content—but all information will never be digitized, simply for economic reasons and by virtue of the fact that those who control most information resources have some profit motive. Throughout the history of libraries, new information resources have been touted as the next best and only thing, and we have repeatedly learned that is not the case. In fact, libraries must facilitate access to information of all types made available with these new technologies, as well as whatever resources exist only in books or manuscripts.

[D]igital resources cannot do everything and never will.

In this complex environment with different forms of information and most content not even in the building, the library is the nexus for instruction, the place where students learn essential information literacy skills that enable them to manage the enormous amount of content that exists. Just as the many instructional centers of the Science, Industry and Business Branch of the New York Public Library and all public and university libraries are booked solid by patron groups seeking to learn how to access information, our independent school libraries cannot be built or renovated today without instructional classrooms and teaching spaces for the library curriculum. We need to provide spaces where small groups can work on cross-disciplinary projects. These collaborative spaces must be within the library facility close to library instructional support and with ready access to print and digital resources that are either on-site or can be accessed remotely. The planning committee will have to learn as much as possible about the collaborative nature of much research today and the reality that academic disciplines are no longer separate but interrelated and overlapping. Students need facilities that offer easy access to resources that reflect the overlap of information needs, staff support of those information needs, and tools that facilitate final production requirements, which may include, for example, digital projection of scanned primary sources. Many academic libraries are developing facilities incorporating Information Commons. In the context of planning facilities, the Information Commons approach reflects the vital role library facilities can and must play in our schools. For details on the Information Commons movement, see essay 10.

Combined with the need to provide access to information in all formats, from our own collections and those of other libraries, our libraries provide a place for people to gather, interact, and share information. Librarians assist students (and teachers) in learning how to evaluate information resources and how to select those most authoritative and appropriate for their assignments or research. Early in the discussion about the future of libraries in an electronic age, Librarian of Congress James H. Billington, himself an eminent historian, provided a cogent reminder:

> Libraries as places will also be needed in the future because human mediation will be needed in locations where both the new technologically dispensed information and the old knowledge repositories of books are present in the same place. There will need to be human mediation in a shared communal setting, where electronically dispensed information is linked with a storehouse of human memory, with human judgment, and with the miscellaneous humanity of the community itself. The role of libraries as well as librarians becomes more, not less, important. (Billington 1996)

Similarly, a blue ribbon task force charged with planning the "library of the twenty-first century" for Dartmouth College concluded in its report calling for the expansion of its prestigious Baker Library with the addition of the new Berry Library:

> [T]he (Berry and Baker) Libraries remain necessary as resource and study areas for students who need materials and equipment that are available only in a physical center, as well as for those who are seeking quiet study areas in which to do their work. Of equal importance is the new role of the library staff as full participants in the educational process; users will come to the libraries to receive instruction on new interfaces and searching possibilities. The libraries will become a significant instructional area that also must provide equipment and space for its trained users to become independent researchers of the available formats. ("Report of the Task Force" 1998)

The online resource *DesignShare* (the Web site that accompanies the book the *Language of School Design*) interviewed two leaders in school library thought in 2006. They were asked to share their vision for the future of school libraries. Both focused on the need for school libraries to grow beyond their 1960s model of a room full of books into something much more, a "value-added" interpretation of the library.

Rolf Erikson, facilities consultant and coauthor of *Designing a School Library Media Center for the Future*, commented that he hoped

- More and more school administrators will recognize the growing body of research that demonstrates the positive effect of school libraries and school librarians on student reading abilities and academic achievement;

- Architects and school facility planners will recognize that their end product will benefit from working with experienced school librarians who have expertise in school library facility design, and they will bring someone with that unique expertise and perspective to the design process; [and]

- Recognizing that there are no good reasons to design school libraries that are based on an outdated model, that are too much like school libraries from the 1960s, everyone involved in the planning of new school libraries will work together to achieve innovative design. (Erikson and Markuson 2001)

Doug Johnson, library director, frequent keynoter, author, and expert on facilities and program for school libraries, responded:

All libraries will need to redefine their "value-added" qualities. The reality is that information seekers no longer need to visit a physical library to meet their basic information needs. Growing affluence means that many readers can and will purchase information rather than borrow it. The "Net Gen" prefers the visual and the virtual.

I see three primary things libraries can do:

1. Become the high touch environments in a high tech world. (Think Barnes & Noble)

2. Offer our services in a virtual environment. (Think online banking)

3. Become uber information experts. (Think a highly competent, highly personalized travel agent (Johnson and Erikson 2006)

Planning Committee Considerations: Getting Specific

Thirty years of consulting for many independent schools in some aspect of their planning phase for a new or renovated library offer many perspectives on questions of school library design and contribute to the following list of points, which are considerations in any library planning process. Every school library project is different, and every planning committee has different constraints and charges, but reviewing and discussing the following points can help a committee better understand local issues and develop more creative solutions to any anticipated problem areas. In every case, the process of engaging these considerations with the planning committee has a positive impact on the final design.

> *[E]very school library project is different, and every planning committee has different constraints and charges.*

1. Define your target audience: Who are the library users? Who are the underserved groups or nonusers you want to attract? In schools with several divisions (e.g., elementary, middle, upper; pre-K through 8) are the needs different among the different groups? Do you have a responsibility to local parents or residents? If you are a residential school, what service should you provide resident faculty and their families? Do you have a responsibility to be the "public" library of the residential community, as well as the school library? (Answer: Yes, YOU DO.)

2. Let function drive the form and the design: Architects do not understand how libraries function or how librarians do what they do; often administrators do not, either. Throughout the planning process, remain aware of how the user and staff need to function. Although libraries are often places of great significance and celebration in a school community, they cannot be dominated by expensive or extensive architectural signature elements at the cost of the building's spaces required to serve the functions of the users. By working closely with the architect and designers, the library committee can be certain that how the place works for the users and the staff is not secondary to the aesthetic or design elements the architect (or donors) want. This can be a challenge unless the planners pay close attention to the functional aspects of library use.

3. Choose variety in furnishings: Architects and interior designers think of libraries as vast public spaces (think airport terminals). They tend to select a uniform look throughout, one or two items replicated dozens or more times. A reading room will have all the same tables and chairs; a comfortable seat is selected to be uniform throughout the building; carpets are always the same color. What about the warm, comfortable, welcoming atmosphere planning groups often say they want? Or the fact that our students and teachers represent all sizes and shapes of the human form? Each time we enter the library, we bring different personal comfort needs. At times we want hard, upright chairs to keep us awake and focused; at other times, we seek a soft seat in which to curl up to read or study. We may want an adjustable task chair to work at a computer screen, or a chair with arms to support a laptop or a notebook. Just as one would not select six of the same chairs for a living room, planners should be urged to select several styles of all types of chairs to put in a library. These selections offer more variety of choice to users and a more visually interesting interior; they also offer more manageable long-term maintenance and replacement costs.

4. Consider having one library in one location: Avoid the temptation to have satellite libraries or different collections, by either format or topic, scattered across the campus. Certainly, separate libraries for separate divisions of a school, as in K–6 and 7–12, can be appropriate, but consider the impact of separate division libraries and resolve in advance matters of potential duplication of service or collections; consider ways to mitigate the impact of those duplications and separations on the whole school. Avoid having different libraries for different types of materials. Several decades ago, with the development of more curriculum-related materials in various formats, many schools developed separate music and film libraries. As a result, these schools often had one library for print, one for its film collections, and another—often with expensive listening stations—for recorded music. Not only did this raise issues of duplicate staffing and services; it also created barriers to use. When information is segregated by format, it is that much more frustrating for students to locate and use it. Now that we know more about "multiple intelligences," learning differences, and engaging the whole child, libraries can best support how students acquire information by collecting in one place resources of all types. The next step in this integration is to catalog all materials using the same system, so that all materials on one topic are in proximity. Students can browse the

When information is segregated by format, it is that much more frustrating for students to locate and use it.

shelves and "trip" across wonderful materials they might not have thought to seek. A class studying *Hamlet*, for example, can locate in the stacks copies of the text in books along with biographical and critical studies, and various performances of the play can be heard on CDs or viewed on DVDs, both formats cataloged and packaged to sit on the shelves beside the books. In other words, this integrated arrangement provides the one-stop shopping that our digital generation expects. For a student audience in particular, employing this integrated approach to shelving and cataloging invites more use of a wider variety of materials and significantly increases efficiency in space and shelving costs.

Departmental and classroom collections separate from the main library do not make sense, either. Current research about effective educational teaching calls for more interdisciplinary approaches, a fact that argues against satellite collections by topic. Financially, with such collections there will be duplication, which adds unnecessary cost. Without cataloging the satellite collections and monitoring circulation, users of the main library will remain unaware of the perfect resource that is hiding in the satellite or has disappeared into a teacher's bottom drawer or a student's backpack. Current integrated library systems (ILS) easily keep catalog records for items that will be circulated annually to specific classrooms; now these items will show up in a patron search. Arguments against satellite libraries include expense in materials budget, staff support, and student time spent locating the items in different buildings.

5. Take into consideration how students learn and how teachers teach: Start with your graduation requirements, and rephrase them in library terms. Do you anticipate changes in pedagogy or curriculum? Do you see trends in elementary schools that feed your admissions, or in colleges and universities that accept your graduates? Might these trends affect your curriculum? What are the different modalities now understood, which could be better served with different spaces or environments? How might Gardner's Multiple Intelligences, increased numbers of ADHD and other learning challenges, and increases in enrollment numbers affect library use and function? An example of something frequently overlooked in planning school libraries is the increasing requirement of student collaboration in project completion. We expect them to work in groups to prepare a project, a presentation that could be in the form of a written document, a Web page, a digitally projected report, a panel discussion or a student-led class session. In planning we need to make certain we get a facility in which all of these kinds of collaborations can occur . . . simultaneously.

6. What difference does it make to be a boarding school library?: Residential schools should focus on the significant role the library can and should play as a resource for recreational materials (e.g., popular fiction, sports books, magazines, entertainment or documentary films on DVD, CDs or access to digital downloads). If we wish our users to become lifelong learners, then we need to curry the habit of using tools for learning in all parts of their lives. Just as we have a responsibility to provide them with academic support, we need to offer access to materials that will enrich their leisure-time experiences, providing moments for relaxation or opening them to new worlds and different ways of thinking. In a boarding school community, the library is the campus living room or family room, a place open to all for relaxation and escape.

7. Avoid defining spaces with fixed elements when possible: A library is a dynamic space that is regularly changing to accommodate new information resources or ways of learning and teaching; even new buildings elsewhere on campus can change student travel paths. The interior design and layout of a library should evoke a school's own personality. While design elements (large atriums, fireplaces, monumental staircases, sunken rooms, pillars and columns and balconies) are often appealing, especially to architects and donors, avoid letting them force you into inflexible uses for space. Built-ins are a source of construction economies, but their inflexibility can also cause difficulty over time as operational needs and functions change. The easiest way to create an environment for a particular style or function is through furniture arrangement and layout; the most expensive in both the short term and the long is to build a wall or fixed physical barrier. When planning how the library is to function, consider the possibility of designing space or furniture for multiple functions. Nothing is certain in libraries, except that needs will change.

> *Nothing is certain in libraries, except that needs will change.*

8. "Function reforms form perpetually": The design/development phase of library planning requires that we operate with the mantra *"form follows function,"* but Stuart Brand's (1994) advice, "Function reforms form perpetually," cannot be overlooked. There is nothing at all boring about information delivery and access. It is constantly undergoing development, invention, and change. In a relatively short period of time, we have gone from computers housed in spaces the size of large rooms to a computer smaller than the palm of the hand; our sound systems can be worn on our ears; our movie screens have become handheld items. What once required significant space and infrastructure (recall the large listening station tables with multiple oversized earphones plugged into a central console), is now portable or even transmitted wirelessly. Where we once had many different types of classroom configuration, we can now have adjustable seats, modest light control, and an efficiently designed storage cabinet at the circulation desk for managing circulation of portable equipment.

> *"[F]orm follows function" [and] "function reforms form perpetually."*

This rapid and constant change illustrates that before we build designated spaces in our new libraries, we need to make certain that we retain sufficient flexibility for those spaces to take on other uses as *"function reforms form,"* continuously.

9. Work closely with the architect on design elements: As the planning committee considers the components of the library in its design, consider as well the aesthetic the building should reflect. Construction or renovation of an existing facility offers a unique opportunity to present a building that reflects how a school values architectural design. Maybe the exterior wants to reflect architectural elements from neighboring buildings on campus. The interior may want historic or archival references in a modern space to demonstrate through the space that the school has its feet on the ground but looks to the future of information. Look at images of other libraries you have visited (or take trips!) with the architect. Spend lots of time looking at the possibilities and developing the language the building will illustrate. Give careful consideration to every element of design to make certain it is consistent with the purpose of the building, its historical roots if they are significant, the school's mission, and the feeling you desire people to have when they enter the space. You must balance the architect's need to let the artist out with the school's need for a functional space that is artistically pleasing to inhabit. All architects are basically artists and want to express their talent in the spaces to which they give form and shape. But the artistry cannot become an end in itself. Libraries are vital. They are LIVING and constantly changing spaces. For that reason, library buildings should not be constrained to a particular architecture or period, but should reflect the energy, adaptability, and liveliness of the school itself and its ever-changing population.

> *You must balance the architect's need to let the artist out with the school's need for a functional space that is artistically pleasing to inhabit.*

10. Describe in detail what you care about: The building program should include comments about everything about which you care. If it matters to you, write it down in the program. Assume nothing, right down to the smallest detail. No one knows *how* you work unless you tell them. If it suffices to say that the custodial staff needs a closet for cleaning equipment, let it go at that. But if that includes a need for a large sink to clean mops, or special storage for chemicals you want to keep under lock and key, then you should write that detail into the document.

> *If it matters to you, write it down in the [library building] program.*

Focus especially on service areas like the staff work areas, the offices for the librarians, and the circulation desk, because the architect will have no idea how this particular library staff works. While architects understand that they need to conform to various building codes, and should be responsible for details to comply with local ordinances and the Americans with Disabilities Act (ADA) requirements, they may not understand that you generally have staff meetings in the librarian's office, so you need room for a conference table there. Perhaps your staff works through meal hours, so a small kitchenette in a quiet staff-only space is desirable. Schools with a lot of media production need spaces for special equipment, and those spaces need to have easy access to library staff assistance. The details of how your program and services and staff operate must be considered in terms of any and all space requirements.

11. Share what you know and what you like: The best way to communicate with architects and designers what you are thinking or envisioning is to show them examples of what you have experienced or seen that works (or does NOT work). Get product information about anything you feel meets a need or catches your attention. Turn over the chair that you like and write down its manufacturer and model information. Urge committee members to photograph any piece of furniture or equipment or space they see that they think is a good (or bad) one. Certainly there are many opportunities in the library, architecture, and interior design literature to see exciting and successful library spaces. As the committee educates itself by visiting examples of all sorts of libraries, they should record images and take notes along the way. These can be used to demonstrate to trustees, architects, and others some of the examples that have inspired or informed your thinking. Photographs and documentation of why something works well can be extremely effective in illustrating a point with administrators, architects, and donors. Each library is different because it reflects the institution of which it is a part. Rarely does anyone want to replicate some other space, but almost always the images help articulate the goals sought. Nothing does it better.

Each library is different because it reflects the institution of which it is a part.

12. Remember being "green": As we confront greater awareness of scarce resources, it makes sense to consider "green building" design for every project. Most schools understand the need to approach every new project with environmental integrity and that they should attempt to meet at least minimal standards of Leadership in Energy and Environmental Design (LEED) certification. The United States Green Building Council is continuously developing these LEED standards, which are third-party evaluation standards designed to encourage implementation of "practical and measurable green building design, construction, operations and maintenance solutions." Because of the constant changes in the standards and evolving understanding among architects and planners of what makes a project truly green, the library committee should work with the architect to consider LEED certification issues every step of the way. In every decision on every detail, remember to step toward being "green." It may not always be easy, but it is essential.

13. Prepare to compromise (or, know your bottom line): The librarian and the planning committee WILL have to compromise during the course of the project. Emphasize the extended planning and programming phase so that all the stakeholders are fully informed about the reasons behind every recommendation and decision. The resulting design should be the outcome of planning. However, in any project a variety of factors can come into play to require changes in execution of even the most carefully developed plan. Cost overruns or material shortages can necessitate cuts or changes; items may no longer be available on which quotes were prepared or plans made; value engineering may require doing something differently or delaying it to a "next phase." Whatever the reason, the well-prepared librarian and the planning committee should have a strong sense of priorities that will allow them to add valuable insight to the change decision. No one should be appointed to a planning committee who is not able to compromise.

Conclusion

The need to plan a new library facility can arise very abruptly, as evidenced by this comment from a librarian facing the daunting request for an immediate set of suggestions:

> Late on Wednesday this week, I learned that our trustees are going forth with an expansion of our upper school's facilities, and that a new library is likely to be a part of the project. Defying all reason, they want a preliminary verbal plan by next Wednesday.

But when the librarian can offer cogent thoughts about a viable building program, the results can be extremely rewarding, as this note indicates:

> Hello Walter,
>
> We returned to a spectacular new library—so transformed that everyone has been distracted from the many elements not yet in place. The books are here

and mostly shelved, but today three teams were still at work: electricians, woodworkers, and [the] installer. We completely lack soft seating and computers. Nevertheless, we're very happy and can hardly wait to be back in business.

I'll send pictures, but you really have to come and see for yourself!

The process of writing a library building program is exciting as the librarian and school dream beyond the existing box to specify details that can make the library more inviting, useful and functional. The same process can also be challenging as the librarian works with administration and architects to understand what exists and which improvements would add the most to the specific school environment. "Everyone feels confident he or she knows what a library is—yet, no two libraries are alike." The process of examining a current facility and projecting what renovation or new construction will maximize library effectiveness for a specific school environment emphasizes that each school environment is definitionally different, and that each resulting library will be instructed by the individual school mission, location, and community. The process that describes the new library to the architect requires care, research, and creativity as well as understanding of the questions and possible answers as interpreted in physical spaces. When all is said and done and the new library has opened, the school community will be thrilled to receive a letter that ends, "I'll send pictures, but you really have to come and see for yourself!"

References

American Association of School Librarians. 1988. *Information Power: Guidelines for School Library Media Programs*. Chicago: American Library Association.

———. 1995. *Building Blocks for Library Space: Functional Guidelines*. Chicago: American Library Association.

———. 1998. *Information Power: Building Partnerships for Learning (1998)*. Chicago: American Library Association.

Anderson, Pauline H. 1985. *Library Media Leadership in Academic Secondary Schools*. Hamden, CT: Library Professional Publications.

———. 1990. *Planning School Library Media Facilities*. Hamden, CT: Library Professional Publications.

Baule, Steven M. 1999. *Facilities Planning for School Library Media and Technology Centers*. Worthington, OH: Linworth Publishing.

Bazillion, Richard J., and Connie Braun. 1995. *Academic Libraries as High-tech Gateways: A Guide to Design and Space Decisions*. Chicago: American Library Association.

Billington, James H. 1996. "On My Mind." *American Libraries* (June–July): 39.

Brand, Stuart. 1994. *How Buildings Learn: What Happens After They're Built.* New York: Viking.

Brown, Carol R. 1995. *Planning Library Interiors: The Selection of Furnishings for the 21st Century.* Phoenix, AZ: Oryx Press.

———. 2002. *Interior Design for Libraries.* Chicago: American Library Association.

Cirillo, Susan E., and Robert E. Danford, eds. 1996. *Library Buildings, Equipment, and the ADA: Compliance Issues and Solutions.* Chicago: American Library Association.

Dahlgren, Anders C. 1996. *Planning the Small Library Facility.* 2nd ed. Chicago: American Library Association.

Darnton, Robert F. 2009. *The Case for Books: Past, Present, and Future.* New York: PublicAffairs.

DesignShare: Design for the Future of Learning. 2009. Language of School Design. available at www.designshare.com/index.php/about. Accessed November 21, 2009.

Erikson, Rolf, and Carolyn Markuson. 2001. *Designing a School Library Media Center for the Future.* Chicago: American Library Association.

Feinberg, Sandra, Joan F. Kuchner, and Sari Feldman. 1998. *Learning Environments for Young Children: Rethinking Library Spaces and Services.* Chicago: American Library Association.

Foote, Steven M. 2004. "Changes in Library Design: An Architect's Perspective" *Portal: Libraries and the Academy* 4, no. 1: 41–59.

Fraley, Ruth A., and Carol Lee Anderson. 1990. *Library Space Planning: A How-to-do-It Manual for Assessing, Allocating, and Reorganizing Collections.* New York: Neal Schuman.

Gorman, Michael. 2003. *The Enduring Library: Technology, Tradition and the Quest for Balance.* Chicago: American Library Association.

Harrington, Drew. 2001. "Six Trends in Library Design." *Library Journal* 126, no. 20 (December 1): 12–14.

Holt, Raymond M. 1989. *Planning Library Buildings and Facilities: From Concept to Completion.* Metuchen, NJ: Scarecrow Press.

Johnson, Doug. 1998. "Some Design Considerations When Building or Remodeling a Media Center." *ERIC.* January 1. Education Resource Information Center. Available at www.eric.ed.gov/. Accessed September 26, 2009.

Johnson, Doug, and Rolf Erikson.2006. "Imagining the Future of the School Library: An Interview." *DesignShare* (November). Available at www.designshare. com/index.php/articles/school-library-future. Accessed November 21, 2009.

Klasing, Jane P. 1996. *Designing & Renovating School Library Media Centers.* Chicago: American Library Association.

LaGuardia, Cheryl, ed. 1998. *Recreating the Academic Library: Breaking Virtual Ground.* New York: Neal-Schuman.

Leighton, Philip D., and David C. Weber. 1999. *Planning Academic and Research Library Buildings.* 3rd ed. Chicago: American Library Association.

Martin, Ron G., ed. 1992. *Libraries for the Future: Planning Buildings That Work: Papers from the LAMA Library Buildings Preconference, June 27–28, 1991.* Chicago: American Library Association.

McCarthy, Richard C. 1999. *Designing Better Libraries: Selecting and Working with Building Professionals.* 2nd ed. Fort Atkinson, WI: Highsmith Press.

"Report of the Task Force on the Library of the 21st Century: The Berry and Baker Libraries." 1998. *Berry/Baker Library Building Project.* Dartmouth University. Winter. Available at www.dartmouth.edu/ ~library/BerryBaker/task.html#exec. Accessed November 21, 2009.

Sannwald, William W. 2001. *Checklist of Building Design Considerations.* 4th ed. Chicago: American Library Association.

Shirato, Linda, ed. 2001. *New Learning Environments: Papers and Session Materials Presented at the Twenty-Sixth National LOEX Library Instruction Conference Held in Ypsilanti, Michigan, 4 to 6 June 1998.* Ann Arbor, MI: Pierian Press.

Taney, Kimberly Bolan. 2003. *Teen Spaces: The Step-by-Step Library Makeover.* Chicago: American Library Association.

Truett, Carol. 1994. "A Survey of School and Public Children's Library Facilities: What Librarians Like, Dislike, and Most Want to Change about their Libraries." *School Library Media Quarterly* 22, no. 2: 91–97.

Whelan, Debra Lau. 2008. "Café Society: Do School Libraries Need a Double Shot of Espresso?" *School Library Journal* 54, no. 1: 36–41.

Each year the April issue of *American Libraries* and a December issue of *Library Journal* are devoted to reports on library buildings and architecture. These are excellent for visual "inspiration," as well as being a resource about regional projects of interest.

Related Web Documents

ALA Library Fact Sheet 11: Building Libraries and Library Additions: A Selected Annotated Bibliography. American Library Association, June 2009. Available at www.ala.org/library/fact11.cfm. Accessed September 26, 2009.

American School & University. Penton Media. Available at asumag.com/. Accessed September 26, 2009. Since 1928, *American School & University* has been the information source for education facilities and business professionals—serving the nation's K–12 and higher education administrators responsible for the planning, design, construction, retrofit, operations, maintenance, and management of education facilities.

Buildings and Equipment Section: Library Buildings. American Library Association, Library Leadership and Management Association. Available at www.ala.org/ala/mgrps/divs/llama/committees/bes/index.cfm. Accessed September 26, 2009.

Johnson, Doug. "Some Design Considerations When Building or Remodeling a Media Center." In *Doug Johnson: Writing, Speaking and Consulting on School Technology and Library Issues.* Available at www.doug-johnson.com/dougwri/some-design-considerations.html. Accessed September 26, 2009.

Library and Media Center Design—K–12: Resource List. National Clearinghouse for Educational Facilities: Resource List. Available at www.edfacilities.org/rl/libraries.cfm. Accessed September 26, 2009. NCEF's resource list of links, books, and journal articles on the design and planning of K–12 school libraries, including sample city and state guidelines, and resources on technology requirements.

Planning and Building Libraries. The University of British Columbia. School of Library, Archival and Information Studies. Available at www.slais.ubc.ca/RESOURCES/architecture/index.htm. Accessed September 26, 2009. This site has been created for architects, librarians, design consultants, and students interested in planning and building libraries. It contains information on architects, planning, programming, standards, interiors, lighting, automation, barrier-free design, security, health, and notable libraries.

"School Designs." *American School & University.* Penton Media, Inc. Available at www.schooldesigns.com/. Accessed September 26, 2009. Launched in 1999 as a virtual gallery of *American School & University* magazine's Architectural Portfolio and Educational Interiors Showcase issues, SchoolDesigns.com has become the online destination for everyone interested in the latest education facility ideas and information.

School Library. National Institute of Building Sciences. Available at www.wbdg.org/design/school_library.php. Accessed September 26, 2009.

Standards for Libraries in Higher Education. American Library Association, Association of College and Research Libraries, June 2004. Available at www.ala.org/ala/mgrps/divs/acrl/standards/standardslibraries.cfm. Accessed September 26, 2009).

Whole Building Design Center. National Institute of Building Sciences. Available at www.wbdg.org/design/. Accessed September 26, 2009.

Visit http://lu.com/excellence for supporting links and occasional updates to all essays in this book.

Walter DeMelle has been the Director of the Edsel Ford Library at The Hotchkiss School (www.hotchkiss.org) since 1970. He has consulted with more than thirty independent school libraries on facilities planning and programming. He is a member of the American Library Association, the American Association of School Librarians (AASL), and the Independent School Section. Walter is also a member of the Association of Independent School Librarians and the 2006 recipient of its "Marky" award for distinctive service to the profession and to that organization.

Navel Gazing, or How to Survive the Accreditation Process

Laura Pearle, Hackley School (Tarrytown, NY)

Introduction

Independent schools are evaluated on a regular basis by one of a number of regional accrediting agencies. Although at present there is no national accrediting agency, the National Association of Independent Schools has approved *NAIS Guidelines of Professional Practice for Librarians*, which we can use to guide our administration and our own practice as we face the accreditation process.

State, Regional, and International Independent School Accrediting Associations That Are Members of the NAIS Commission on Accreditation

Association of Colorado Independent Schools (ACIS)

Association of Independent Maryland Schools (AIMS)

California Association of Independent Schools (CAIS/CA)

Canadian Educational Standards Institute (CESI)

Connecticut Association of Independent Schools (CAIS/CT)

Council of International Schools (CIS)

Florida Council of Independent Schools (FCIS)

Hawaii Association of Independent Schools (HAIS)

New Jersey Association of Independent Schools (NJAIS)

New York State Association of Independent Schools (NYSAIS)

Pennsylvania Association of Independent Schools (PAIS)

Virginia Association of Independent Schools (VAIS)

Association of Independent Schools in New England (AISNE)

Independent Schools Association of the Central States (ISACS)

Independent Schools Association of the Southwest (ISAS)

New England Association of Schools and Colleges (NEASC)

Pacific Northwest Association of Independent Schools (PNAIS)

Southern Association of Independent Schools (SAIS)

Southwestern Association of Episcopal Schools (SAES)

Taken from the NAIS Web site.

"Evaluation for accreditation" is a useful process that allows schools to see themselves as they are at that moment. Because all aspects of the school are examined, the recommendations and commendations of the accrediting agency are valuable guides to assessing current practice and pedagogy and to planning for future growth. The independent school library benefits from this process in a number of ways. First, it allows the library staff to get a sense of how the library is perceived within the school community. Second, it allows the school community to learn more about the library. Third, in combination with the assessment of the academic program, the library can plan for curricular and academic challenges. In addition to this, the library staff can do a mock self-evaluation at each important juncture in the life of the library (e.g., adding or subtracting staff or a division, or after renovating a facility) to ensure that the community is getting the library service that it deserves.

The Process

Ideally, a school will spend a year working on its self-study, a process prompted and guided by each accrediting agency's manual, which outlines and highlights areas the school should examine. After the self-study is completed, a committee of outsiders, chosen by the agency, visits and spends some time getting to know the school and its various constituencies. The committee generally comprises faculty, administrators, and staff of other member schools and the educational community. Members of the visiting committee visit classes, the library, and other facilities. In addition to meeting with representatives of specific constituent groups (i.e., parents, teachers, and students), the committee members usually meet with individual administrators and groups of administrators such as department chairs. At the end of the visit, the committee prepares a report describing its experience at the school, assessing how well the school's own self-study comports with the committee's observation. This report, sent back to the school, generally forms the basis for schoolwide discussion and strategic planning for the future.

The self-study manuals vary in format: some accrediting agencies require a narrative response, providing questions as a guide for appropriate areas of inquiry; others employ a more structured approach and ask for more definitive answers to specific questions. The former approach seems to be winning favor as more agencies are opting to convert from the question/response method to the narrative method, which allows more considered input from the institution.

Regional Accrediting Associations Serving Public and Private Schools in the U.S. and American Schools Abroad (Not NAIS)

> Middle States Association of Colleges and Schools (MSACS), Commission on Secondary Schools and Commission on Elementary Schools
>
> New England Association of Schools and Colleges (NEASC)
>
> North Central Association of Colleges and Schools (NCACS)
>
> Northwest Association of Accredited Schools (NAAS)
>
> Southern Association of Colleges and Schools (SACS)
>
> Western Association of Schools and Colleges (WASC)

Taken from the NAIS Web site.

Preparing the Self-Study Section

Generally, the self-study effort is coordinated by a school's internal steering committee, which provides guidelines on how the school should respond to the questions. The steering committee will then assign subcommittees to complete the internal report with respect to various aspects of the school. One such subcommittee will focus on the library. In addition to members of the library staff, it should include other members of the school community. As the professional librarian, you must not only take part in the subcommittee, but also carefully review the library section of the proposed report. If the library section is not included within the main academic program, it is advisable for the librarian to bring that to the attention of the person coordinating the self-study at your school. Explain how important the library program is to the overall health of the school. Even though they do not play a role in the creation of the current self-study, you should be sure to take a good look at previous evaluations, both the internal self-study and the report by the visiting committee (for example, you are on a ten-year schedule, with a five-year interim "check up"; read both). Make note of particular issues that were mentioned then and that are still problematic. Pay close attention to the questions asked and the language being used. The choice of words sometimes is an indication of the weight attached to the library program by the accrediting agency and, ultimately, by the school.

At the 2001 American Association of School Librarians (AASL) conference in Indianapolis, the Independent Schools Section (ISS) hosted a session on accreditation, at which the language used in the evaluation instruments was discussed. The first was the use of the terms "school library media specialist" and "school library media center." It was generally felt that many independent school librarians are not comfortable using these terms as identifiers for themselves or their libraries. In a passionate discussion on the Association of Independent School Librarians listserv, Sue Berlin, librarian at Hawken School in Ohio, declared, "Frankly, I think the term 'media specialist' is pretentious, unnecessary, and confusing and was probably 'invented' by some misguided individual who thought it sounded more 'professional.' If Librarians and Libraries are not professional enough, I don't know what is!" (Berlin 2001). And in 2010 AASL decided to make "school librarian" our official title; simplest is best, after all.

Another term discussed at the same ISS session was "support" to describe the library program. "Support" may have far-reaching implications for how the library is viewed within the educational institution. "Support," according to the *Oxford American Dictionary*, means "bear all or part of the weight of . . . give assistance to . . . enable to function or act." Yet to schools, "support" frequently means "appendage." Barbara Weathers of Duchesne Academy (Houston) eloquently argued that we should change "support" to "enhance"—a reminder to schools that the library program is critical to student achievement and cannot be cut when finances are low, or additional space is needed, without harming the entire academic program (Weathers 2001).

A third discussion centered on the use of the term "certified" to describe a school library professional. Because independent school librarians are not required to be state certified, the use of the term "certified" in any accreditation document is irrelevant. Independent school librarians should, however, be expected to have a master's of library science or a master's of library and information science and to continually engage in professional development.

Standards vs. Criteria

Many of the NAIS-related accrediting agencies divide the accreditation process into two areas: standards to be met and the criteria with which to meet them. As a rule, the standards for libraries are good. They indicate that there is a basic understanding of the role of the library in a school. However, there remains a need to educate schools and accrediting agencies on the specific criteria of that role. Sample criteria appear in figure 20.1.

Following are some exemplary standards:

- "The library collection adequately reflects and supports the philosophy and mission of the school." (CAISCA 2002)

- "The school shall provide adequate program support, including, when appropriate: library/media and computer services, guidance services, special needs support, and health services." (ISACS 2002)

- "The school has a plan for library and related technological resources which is integrated with the curriculum and which provides students with age appropriate experiences in research and reading." (Bennett 2001)

- "The library/learning/media center, or its equivalent if it does not exist as a single facility, is so organized, supplied, and staffed as to provide for the program of the school and the needs of the students and the professional staff" (NYSAIS 2009)

- "Are library skills embedded in the classroom courses or are they taught during scheduled library time?" (Matthews 2009)

One outcome of the discussions at the November 2001 Independent School Section session was the recommendation of a series of assessment criteria that addressed this problem. They are offered here as a guide to those wanting to create a self-evaluation response in line with best practice.

Mission

- Describe the primary mission of the library and show how the specific purpose and objectives of the school are served.

Desired Results for Student Learning

- Students demonstrate the ability to identify their information needs and show competence and independence in solving information problems.

- Describe how the library and related technology materials are integrated into the curriculum. How is the plan for library and related technological resources formulated? How often is it reviewed? By whom?

- Describe the ways in which the library both leads and supports the educational endeavors of the school; how are the resources and services of the library integrated into the life and program of the school?

- Describe how students are encouraged to take advantage of the resources of the library and how they are instructed in the library's proper use. To what extent is the school using new technologies to augment or replace traditional library management tools and techniques?

Access

- The library program is available to the school community throughout the academic day and beyond.

Staffing

- The library program is staffed by a librarian with an MLS from an ALA-accredited institution.

- Describe the way in which library and technology staff interact with other segments of the school community—administration, faculty, students, and the extended school community.

- If volunteers are used, explain the ways in which they are recruited, trained, assigned tasks and supervised.

Facilities

- The library facility provides an inviting environment that is conducive to student learning.

- The library facility is of sufficient size and flexibility to accommodate a variety of functions simultaneously.

- Learning materials and technology, including A/V and digital resources, are maintained in a manner that makes them accessible to the school community. They are properly catalogued, housed, and periodically reviewed for currency.

Resources

- The library program provides print, nonprint, and electronic materials that directly strengthen school goals and curriculum reflecting a diversity of learning styles, levels of skill, and cultural differences.

- A written collection development policy is used to continually evaluate the quality, depth, and breadth of the collection. This policy shall include procedures for responding to challenged materials, the receipt of gifts of library materials or technology and deaccessioning materials.

- The budget of the school shall include sufficient funds to provide and maintain library services and equipment to strengthen the curriculum.

- The school community is encouraged to offer input into the types, quality, and format of the information resources provided.

Figure 20.1. Proposed Assessment Criteria.

Another positive sign is that some agencies have recognized the importance of libraries in schools and have taken steps to ensure that the accreditation process reflects this. A white paper prepared for the New England Association of Schools and Colleges states:

> These compelling findings establish a strong rationale for evaluating school library media programs in terms of teaching and learning in the accreditation process. . . . Implicit in the placement of the school library media program in the accreditation process is the expectation that school library media programs will have a place in the teaching and learning in every school accredited. . . . To that end, school library media programs are integral to the process of educating our young people because, "Student achievement is the bottom line." (AASL, quoted in Gordon 2002)

Unfortunately, however, when new administrators are appointed, they frequently have little or no knowledge of what comprises an exemplary library program. When visiting accreditation committees are formed, librarians are seldom included without specific request by the school. Without a librarian on the committee, there is rarely anyone who understands the relevant issues, including what makes an "exemplary program," or who can effectively evaluate one of the most important parts of the academic program. This lack of understanding of what constitutes an exemplary library program is a prime reason that the current evaluative instruments often contain outdated or inaccurate criteria.

Additional Resources

If outside resources are used to meet standards, those resources are listed and a description of how they are used is provided. Where are the school archives (historical records, corporate documents) located? Is maintenance of these records a responsibility of the library staff? Describe any specific cooperative programs or projects in which the library participates (Pearle 2001).

Many agencies require a minimum number of books per student. One such outdated criterion (from 2000) reads:

> The Library/Media Center must provide:
>
> 8.1.8.1 A minimum of 1,500 acceptable and usable books or twelve books per student (not including textbooks), whichever is greater. These books must be age appropriate, selected from one or more of the standard library lists, properly distributed over different subject areas and uniformly marked according to cataloging principles. There must be a definite and appropriate annual budget within the school budget for print materials, electronic resources and subscription services. Once the minimum number of books per student has been achieved, the required annual budget expenditure of $15 per student in elementary school and $20 per student in secondary school may be used for the purchase of print materials and/or electronic materials.

By merely prescribing numbers, criteria such as this acknowledge the need for professional librarians, but do not address the quality of the service necessary for a well-functioning library. Collection development, including weeding those 1970s science books, is critical to providing exemplary library service. The above also ignores the value of reading for pleasure, and prescribing "standard library lists" does not allow for the innovation in curriculum and materials that is usually found in an independent school.

There is hope: in 2002, one agency included a requirement that the collection be renewed at a minimum rate of 5 percent (SACS 2002). A collection of 50,000 items (such as exists at some of the larger schools) would require that institution purchase 2,500 items annually. Assuming an average cost of $25 for a hardbound book (fiction, nonfiction, or reference), the budget for this item alone would have to be $62,500, which does not include the additional costs of processing. In 2009, that requirement is nowhere to be found in the SACS accreditation materials (SACS CASI 2009).

Exemplary criteria should place more emphasis on how the library program enhances the school's academic program through the use of its resources and its instructional activities. Some agencies have not incorporated this thinking into their process, but a few accreditation agencies have created excellent criteria.

It is important to look at both the standards and the criteria by which your accreditation process will be governed before preparing your section of the accreditation self-study report.

The Self-Study Subcommittee

Pay close attention to the composition of the subcommittee assigned to writing the library section. Ideally this will include "outsiders" (that is, faculty members) so as to help you get a good sense of how the adult community views the library. You should seek to have at least one newly hired member of the faculty on this subcommittee to minimize bias and bring a fresh perspective. You should also have at least one, more experienced, frequent user, who can help to highlight the more positive aspects of the program. Finally, if possible recruit a few students to add their valuable perspective on the role of the library in their school.

Surveys

Surveys offer a gauge to measure the view of the library within the school community. The surveys should be as general as possible, and responses should be anonymous. (See figures 20.2 and 20.3.) This will free people to speak their minds and prevent the possibility of highlighting personal agendas. It may even be helpful for the library staff to withdraw completely from this process, asking another faculty member and/or students to create the survey, collect and analyze the results, and then report back to you.

Teacher Survey

1. Have you used the library in the past year?

2. How do you use the library: research projects? orientation for students? bibliographies of resources? showing videos?

3. What resources do you use most: references? videos? Internet? databases? print (fiction and nonfiction)?

4. Are you aware of what the library has to support and enhance your curriculum?

5. How accessible are: the resources? the library? the librarian? (1 = VERY, 2, 3, 4, 5 = NOT AT ALL)

6. What do you feel are the strengths and weaknesses of the collection?

7. Has the technology lab changed your use of the library? If yes, how?

Suggestions/comments:

Figure 20.2. Teacher Survey.

Student Survey

Please let us know a little bit about you: _____

Grade: _____

Most recent visit to the library: _____

1. How satisfied are you with the following aspects of the library's environment: hours? temperature? lighting? noise level? comfort of study area? availability of group study area? (I = LEAST, 2, 3, 4, 5 = MOST)

2. How effective do you feel you are at using the library for RESEARCH purposes? (I = LEAST, 5 = MOST)

3. How often do you use the library for RESEARCH?

4. How effective do you feel you are at using the library computers? (I = LEAST, 5 = MOST)

5. How often do you use the computers in the library?

6. How satisfied are you with the following regulations in the library?: limit of books to be lent? noise level? time on using the computers? no eating/drinking policy? due date? (I = LEAST, 5 = MOST)

7. Which of the following resources are most important to you in general (circle): books? handouts/guides? computerized book catalog? magazines/newspapers? Internet access? library hours? librarian/ reference staff? other?

Comments/additional suggestions

Figure 20.3. Student Survey.

Next Step

Using the responses from the surveys and the questions/standards provided by the accrediting agency, start writing your section. Be as long-winded and blunt as you want to be: mention all the good things, the bad things, the wish-list things, etc. Then put the document away for a while. When you come back to it, re-read and weed out all the extremely inflammatory and extremely positive statements. The goal is to produce a section that is well-balanced, one that recognizes and celebrates the good things while acknowledging that there is room for growth and change. If there is any one particular problem to be stressed, do not be afraid to do so, but do it gently. For example, if there is a real need to renovate the space, point out why this is problematic for the program; if your budget has not kept pace with inflation, prepare an example of why an increase is necessary (for example, purchasing a database or updating a specific section to reflect current curricular offerings).

Make your points as clearly as possible, and always remember that there is a good chance that the people reading your section will only have their home library as a benchmark, possibly will not have any idea what an exemplary program is (not that they do not come from a school that has one, but they do not have the background to know what one would be or how to identify one), and probably will not understand "library talk." It is a good idea to have a neutral nonlibrarian look over the section to ensure that anyone can understand the points you are trying to make; you want to be as clear and precise as possible.

If you have not yet created a mission statement for your library, now is a good time to formulate one. The Independent School Section meeting in Indianapolis in 2001 created the following mission statement. It may be useful in formulating an appropriate statement for your school.

> The school library media program is an integral primary resource for literacy, information, and curriculum support. Through the coordination efforts of a librarian with an MLS, the program provides media service, print and electronic resources to enhance classroom instruction and other school activities in order that the school community may become effective, independent users of ideas and information as well as lifelong readers and learners. (Pearle 2001)

This is also a good time to review and rework any library policies, because yours may be outdated and fail to take into account new technologies. As schools move from print and film through video to current digital and on to future media, it is important to make sure that your policies are compatible. (See essay 16.) Your board of trustees should approve any policy changes, and this presents an ideal opportunity to educate them about the current state of librarianship in general and your school's library in specific.

Most schools will have the internal accreditation steering committee read and re-read your response. They may have questions, some based on a lack of knowledge about libraries and some based on reading other sections. Be prepared to discuss your concerns, anticipate, and collect facts, figures, and/or documentation to back up your position. This may prevent attempts to remove items that are important to you. It is a good strategy to ask for the opportunity to review the committee's edits to ensure they have not changed the objectives of your report.

When the Accreditation Committee Arrives

Your library should look as warm and inviting as possible. If at all possible, try to have at least one member of the committee observe the library "in action," not just during scheduled classes, but before and after school as well as at times when there are "drop in" students.

Prepare for the Visitors

1. Create a library portfolio that includes:
   - Library policies and a development plan
   - Facts and figures about stock and use of the library, e.g., total number of books, other resources, number of fiction items, books per head, spending per pupil, shelf life of stock, loan statistics, etc.
   - Details of [information technology] taught or training given to pupils in the library
   - Cooperation and use of library by other departments (examples of work done by pupils using the library resources)
   - Photos of events and displays
   - Details of improvements to the library since the previous evaluation and aims for the future; accessibility to the library and organization of stock; additional use of the library; financial reports
2. Update your displays.
3. Check notice boards, etc.

From a posting on the British school librarian elist, School Librarians Network, SLN.

When speaking with the committee, be honest but do not gripe. For example, if additional space for library resources is not an option, mention that you could use additional space but that you know that is not a priority for the school at this time. Remember, the committee is there to help you, but not to fight your particular battles.

Although some of the above may seem self-evident, it is often not obvious to the accreditation agencies. Some visiting committees make no requests for library policies; others do not care about the history or progression of the library program. Including this information either in the self-study report or in a stand-alone package indicates how important it is to the health of the academic program. Also be sure to include examples of any and all publications the library might produce, such as bookmarks, study guides, summer reading lists, and letters to parents. Many of us have school library Web sites; be sure to promote yours (and if you can find usage statistics for both the site and online resources, include those). Do you produce an annual report? That is a "must have" for the ancillary materials.

Interpreting the Visiting Committee's Report

Once the committee has submitted its report, ask for a copy. Do not just read the library section, read the entire document (at the very least, read the sections devoted to the academic program and support services). The reason is simple: if you are going to take your program into the next decade, this report will give you a basic blueprint for any changes needed. In addition to specific recommendations for the library, the committee's suggestions might indicate that more coordination with other departments is necessary or perhaps that the school needs to renovate the physical space. Getting involved with these projects during the early stages allows the library's voice to be heard and issues to be discussed.

Look at the specific library recommendations. If they are concrete (more staffing, bigger budget, improved technology), it is fairly easy to approach your administration with quantitative information to achieve these goals. However, some recommendations are more ephemeral (for example, more integration into the curriculum or better marketing of library programs/services). For these, the key is to quantify the possible steps and outcome. In the case of the former, make lists of classes in which you are already welcome as well as what skills need to be learned by specific grade levels; talk to those teachers and see if they would be willing to turn existing collaborative efforts into improved, skill-based projects. Take the skills lists to the administration and explain how you could enhance the curriculum in different subjects with specific projects or by instituting defined library/information skills classes (these work best in lower and middle school environments, where many libraries have fixed schedules). If the issue is one of marketing, look at what you are doing now (newsletters, in-service sessions, e-mail to faculty/department members) and then explore ways to improve on them (bulletin boards, for example, or a library Web site).

The key thing to remember here is that the school must respond directly to the specific recommendations made by the visiting committee. In some cases, the response may be that, based on the school's stated mission, this is not feasible or necessary. In all cases, some sort of response needs to be formulated, and the librarian should attempt to be part of that process. If your administration chooses to respond without requesting your input, make every effort to see the response as it pertains to the library so that you know what you need to work on over the next few years as you carry your program forward.

The Future of Independent School Library Accreditation

With apologies to the Watergate Commission, "what do administrators learn about school libraries and when do they learn it?" This question becomes increasingly important at the point of an evaluation for an accreditation process, because many people setting the criteria and performing the accreditation evaluations are not librarians, nor does their training include anything about the role of the library in the educational program. For example, the New York State School Administrator and Supervisor (SAS) certification program contains little discussion of libraries. Todd Flomberg, who received his SAS certificate in 2000, commented. "Very little attention was paid to library staffing and services. I can remember in one public policy course there was a day spent on budget making and line items... In another class we did talk briefly, and I do mean briefly, about Internet Protocol and the school's need to monitor student behavior on the web." Flomberg went on to say,

> My administrative course work did not give me much training in this area as you can see, but I would not be uncomfortable evaluating a school's library services if I were on a visiting team one day. It would not be my first choice... but I think I could do a decent job. I have seen the [one school] library program rise like a phoenix out the ashes [and] the [another school] library seems pretty solid and is integrated well into the curriculum. I think that I would have a decent idea of what to look for, plus I would do some HW about it before I went in to make observations (i.e. what should I be looking for).

Nine years later, Alona Scott, director of Middle School at Hackley School, commented that in her many professional development and postgraduate courses (including some through the Klingenstein Foundation of Columbia University), she has not encountered any discussion about the role of the library, programming, or the evaluation of either; rather, the focus has been on more general, schoolwide issues. Like Flomberg, she feels that her previous experiences and training would enable her to be an effective member of an accreditation team assigned to a school's library.

Even the "new" (as of 2006) AdvancED standards, which claim that "The combined strengths of NCA CASI, SACS CASI, and NSSE under AdvancED create a powerful organization built on and committed to *advancing excellence in education worldwide*" do not mention the library as part of their commitment to "education quality" (AdvancED 2009). It is clear that we need to be more proactive and self-advocate within our schools and in the outside world of administrator training and development.

Conclusion

Most accreditation agencies do not include library issues in their professional development programs. And by the very nature of being "independent," some administrators and accreditation agencies do not believe that a set of standards can be formulated.

It is therefore increasingly important that we educate administrators and accrediting agencies about what constitutes exemplary library programs. Spending time with teachers and administrators in your school and modeling the type of professional quality that today's students deserve are important strategies. Another possible method of educating the larger community is to serve on accreditation committees, which will enable you to see the process from the other side as well as give you the opportunity to teach the other members of the committee how to assess a library program.

Use your personal learning network to determine how you can best self-assess your program. Advocate for the inclusion of another librarian on the evaluation for accreditation committee. Promote *NAIS Guidelines of Professional Practice for Librarians* and model best practices for your community.

References

AdvancED. 2006–2010. *About Us.* Advance Education, Inc. Available at www. advanc-ed.org/about_us/. Accessed March 11, 2010.

Barker, Sarah. 2001. "Re: [sln] Inspection." *SLN.* November. Available at http:// groups.yahoo.com/group/sln/messages. Accessed August 5, 2009.

Bennett, William. 2001. E-mail to author, July 16.

Berlin, Susan. 2001. E-mail to Association of Independent School Librarians, December 12.

CAISCA. 2002. *The Self-Study K–12 Document.* California Association of Independent Schools. August 19. Available at http://caisca.org/publications/ 2_proappis.pdf. Accessed August 5, 2009.

Flomberg, Todd. 2002. E-mail to author, August 7.

Gordon, Dr. Carol A. 2002. *The Place of the School Library Media Program in the Accreditation Process of the New England Association of Schools and Colleges: A position paper of the New England Educational Media Association.* Boston: New England Educational Media Association.

ISACS. 2002. *Accreditation Manual, 12th Edition.* Independent Schools Association of the Central States. August 19. Available at http://isacs.org/accreditation/ links/default.asp. Accessed August 5, 2009.

Matthews, Karen. 2009. E-mail to Dorcas Hand, May 13.

NAAS. 2002. *2002 Annual Report.* Northwest Association of Accredited Schools. November 21. Available at www.northwestaccreditation.org/publications/selfstudy.html. Accessed August 5, 2009.

NAIS. 2009. *Accreditation.* National Association of Independent Schools. Available at http://nais.org/about/index.cfm?itemnumber=145844&sn.ItemNumber=1482 &tn.ItemNumber=10241. Accessed August 5, 2009.

NYSAIS. 2009. "The Library, the Learning Center or Media Center." In *Manual for Evaluation and Accreditation,* 26–27. Schenectady: New York State Association of Independent Schools.

Pearle, Laura. 2001. "How to Evaluate Independent School Library Programs." Lecture Presented to American Association of School Librarians. Indianapolis, November 18.

Professional Children's School. 2001. *Student and Faculty Survey.* New York: Professional Children's School.

SACS. 2002. *Accreditation Standards 2000.* Southern Association of Colleges and Schools. No longer available.

SACS CASI. 2009. *Overview of the AdvancED Standards and Accreditation Process for Schools.* Southern Association of Colleges and Schools Council on Accreditation and School Improvement. Advanced-Ed. Available at www. advanc-ed.org/accreditation/school_accreditation/accreditation_process/. Accessed August 5, 2009.

Weathers, Barbara. 2001. "How to Evaluate Independent School Library Programs." Group discussion at American Association of School Librarians meeting, Indianapolis, November 16.

Visit http://lu.com/excellence for supporting links and occasional updates to all essays in this book.

Laura Pearle began her library career with a three-year stint as a student library aide at Emma Willard School, followed by a sixteen-year hiatus while she explored the varied worlds of college, off-Broadway theater, investment banking, and executive recruiting, among others. Since returning to independent school libraries in 1996, she has focused on the evaluating accreditation process, investigating the K–20 skills curriculum and developing her personal learning network. Her writings have appeared in such journals as Independent School *and* Knowledge Quest, *as well as the Association of Teachers in Independent School quarterly. Laura is currently Head Librarian at the Hackley School in Tarrytown, NY (http://www.hackleyschool.org/).*

Don't Lose It All: Disaster Planning

Cynthia Grady, Sidwell Friends School (Washington, DC)

Introduction

Since 9/11/2001, most schools have revised and improved their emergency drill and disaster plans. We practice the usual fire drills, but no matter where our schools are located, many of us have drills for disasters most unlikely to hit us: earthquakes, tornados, and hurricanes, as well as biological weapons and bomb threats. We have distance learning plans in case of flu or other pandemic health crises. We've developed relationships with businesses in the area, in case the students and staff need to be evacuated to another site. We have emergency water and food supplies. So why do we need a separate disaster response plan for the school library?

The plans and procedures mentioned above are in place to protect the personal and physical safety of the students and staff inhabiting the schools. A library disaster plan will minimize harm done to the library collection in the event of a disaster, and it will help preserve the physical safety of the library materials, so that when normal school routines resume, teachers and students will have access to a functioning library.

Defining a Disaster

Most of the literature on disaster planning for libraries describes recovery and response to natural disasters such as flood, fire, and insect infestation. This essay also discusses those events. But not all disasters are natural disasters.

During the summer of 2006, the Sidwell Friends middle school building was scheduled to be renovated. While planning the move, the librarian requested that the administration use a professional library moving company to pack up the library rather than use the moving company that was contracted for the rest of the school. The request was not granted. The entire contents of the middle school, including the library, was packed and taken to a storage facility for the summer. This company had moved parts of the Library of Congress, so the library was hopeful everything would be fine.

Construction crews worked around the clock in June, July, and August, and school was scheduled to reopen the week following Labor Day. The previous June, the principal had encouraged faculty to take home for the summer any "September" things they would need in case of construction delays. The librarian dutifully did so. She boxed her prior year's lesson plan book, a clean lesson plan book, and the beginning-of-year activities. The faculty was informed that library classes would not begin the first week of school as usual because library staff needed that first week of school to unpack and shelve the 10,000-book library collection.

The weekend of September 9 arrived, and the administration was granted the necessary permits to enter the building. The renovation was not finished, but faculty were allowed to move back in. School would begin on time.

The library boxes were delivered. The delivery seemed incomplete, but no one panicked. The library staff unpacked books as planned during the first week of school. To their horror, they discovered 6,000 books, nearly *all* of the nonfiction and reference books, were missing, as well as several hundred works of fiction (the Cs, the H–Is, and Ps). The library staff was told the books would arrive soon.

Four weeks passed. During this time, the librarian discovered all kinds of other things missing: all of the library and office supplies (the school stamp, book jackets, pockets, magazine covers, storage bins, and date due slips); teaching supplies; file cabinets; the rolodex; and all five rolling book carts. The only things that made it through the move besides most of the fiction were a few filmstrip projectors kept on hand for the science teachers to use in a light projection experiment and a few other obsolete odds and ends that staff had simply run out of time to discard properly.

That fourth week of school they were told that the books were gone permanently, as well as many, many other items that didn't survive the move. The science department's telescope. The music department's musical instruments. The props and costumes from the drama department. All of the Chinese studies program materials. Every single art supply. Some teachers lost twenty years' worth of files and lessons. The entire contents of an eighteen-wheel moving van was taken to the landfill. Dumped. And it wasn't dumped that weekend before school began. It had been dumped back in June, and the school was finding out about it in October.

Once the librarians finally knew things were officially beyond recovery, they could begin to plan to replace the collection. There was no written disaster plan at the time, so advice was the first step. The first thing the librarian did in the recovery process was contact library directors whom she knew had experienced *natural* disasters in their libraries. These were primarily university librarians, and they were very helpful in the beginning stages. They gave practical advice, student and faculty-oriented tips, as well as information and advice regarding the insurance claim.

Planning

Volumes of excellent books and Web sites have been written on how and why to have a disaster response plan for libraries. But few are written with K–12 school libraries in mind. School library collections are relatively small, and except for a school's archives and some signed books from alumni or visiting authors, they are generally replaceable collections.

Building Facilities Information

Meet with your facilities manager to learn and document

- where water shut-off valves are located;
- where the building has structural weaknesses;
- the soundness of library shelving;
- how to minimize fire hazards in library and its storerooms;
- contact information for building utilities (gas, electricity, plumbing, telephone, elevators); and
- contact information for emergency responders (fire department, medical/ambulance, police or other law enforcement, city emergency management, county emergency management, state emergency services, health departments, and Red Cross).

The school librarian has responsibility for the library and its collection, but only administrators can work with insurance adjusters, contractors, or other emergency personnel. In university settings, the librarian has broader autonomy.

An effective disaster response plan should include preparatory plans for prevention, response, and recovery from different kinds of disasters that could affect the library collection. Planning is crucial to recovering successfully from a library disaster, and for those who are superstitious, planning will prevent the disaster from occurring at all.

Prevention

Much of prevention involves having the right information at your fingertips. Take the time when life is normal to collect all of these details in a notebook and in digital copy for each of your staff and your administrators. If you discover pieces of information missing or issues that can be prepared, go to work to fix them BEFORE a problem occurs. See figure 21.1.

Library Staff Disaster Preparation

Meet with library staff to

- Flesh out records in the online library catalog. Be certain vendors are identified and the purchase prices of materials are noted.

- Determine the value of the collection. *This is critical to an accurate insurance assessment after a disaster.*

- Create a vendor list for services in your area. You will need vendor information for water recovery, freeze drying books, mold management, insect infestation management, and fire and smoke damage.

- Determine and document priorities for recovery of materials by format, usage, subject, and rarity of items. Identify items that are irreplaceable and tied to the school's identity.

- Assemble a library disaster response kit to be kept in the library at all times. Evaluate and revise it annually.

IT/Library Disaster Preparation

Meet with IT staff to

- Make certain the library online catalog is backed up daily and stored off-site or on a separate server, disk, etc.

- Prioritize recovery of library computers and other technology equipment.

Administration and Library Disaster Preparation

Meet with specific administrators to

- Review current insurance coverage and make a plan to review and update it annually.

- Name a disaster response team with assigned responsibilities. Ideally, this team will include library staff, at least one administrator, facilities personnel, one IT person, and parent association officers.

Figure 21.1. Library Disaster Preparation.

Insurance

To the extent possible and prudent, the school librarian should discuss with the administration the library insurance coverage. What the Sidwell librarian learned from the moving disaster was that administrators become even busier than usual during any kind of emergency. The librarian must deal with the material loss, but the claim process may go more smoothly if the librarian is already aware of coverage and procedures. Generally speaking, an insurance policy should cover the *replacement cost* of one-third of the collection. Most insurance policies are not large enough to fund the replacement of an entire library. However, if the library or archive contains special collections or rare books of high value, consider adding a separate rider for these materials. The sidebar lists some questions that would be helpful to discuss with regard to insurance coverage:

Insurance Questions

- How frequently is the insurance plan reviewed and revised? This should be done every three years if not annually to include inventory, computer additions, and inflation.

- What natural disasters are covered in the policy, and are there any special and separate clauses or riders about the library and its materials?

    Are water/mold, fire/smoke covered?

    Is insect infestation included?

    Are biological agents covered?

    Are theft, vandalism, and bomb explosions included?

- What about any other disasters that are accidents or otherwise not natural?

- Are the library computers covered? A computer rider generally covers replacement of the physical objects (monitors, diskettes, etc.) but not the cost of reconstructing data.

- What are the insurance restrictions on staff and volunteers when entering a disaster area?

- Is there a "contingency fund?" Contingency funds cover unexpected, uncovered expenses as well as the insurance deductible.

Replacement costs for library materials are approximate, but should be determined ahead of time, taking into account the time (labor) it takes to order, receive, catalog, and process a book (or CD, DVD/video, etc.) to make it shelf ready. Work with human resources to determine an hourly rate for the librarian and then use this figure to determine the labor cost. Depending on your institution and location, you would be adding anywhere from $15.00 to $150.00 per item to the purchase price to calculate its *replacement cost*. See figure 21.2.

When reporting an emergency, it is important to provide the details of the problem and to stay on the line until you are certain the responders have accurate information:

- What is the emergency?

- When did it begin? Is it still occurring or has it ended?

- Where did the event occur?

- Give your name, location, and telephone number(s).

Do not enter the affected area until your facilities manager or other administrator has ensured it is safe to do so.

Minimizing Water Damage

Shield library materials from the source of water:

- Cover library materials with plastic sheeting (found in the disaster kit) if water is coming from above.

- Create a barrier to keep water away from materials if flooding is from below.

- Move undamaged materials to another location and cover them with sheeting if they are in jeopardy from water damage or high relative humidity.

- Place wastepaper baskets and buckets under ceiling leaks.

Stabilizing the Environment

Quick response is essential to prevent mold growth, which causes irreversible damage to materials. Materials are vulnerable to mold after forty-eight hours. Work with facilities staff to stabilize a wet environment.

- Keep the temperature below 65 degrees, lower if possible:

    Turn down the heat or crank up the air conditioning.

    Open windows if outside is colder than inside.

- If materials are not archival papers that need a specific climate control setting, keep relative humidity below 50 percent:

    Run dehumidifiers.

    Run fans to keep air circulating.

    Remove water-soaked materials such as books, carpeting, and ceiling tiles.

    Remove water using wet-vacuums, mops, and squeegees.

- Monitor the temperature and relative humidity for at least seventy-two hours.

A note about climate control: If your school is undergoing renovation and the library will be stored in an off-site warehouse, make certain the storage facility is climate controlled. A library collection can be damaged or lost completely in a poorly controlled storage facility.

Figure 21.2. Response and Recovery.

Assessing the Scope of the Disaster

- Assess damage to collections, the building, and technology resources.
- Document with photos and videos, and note the type of disaster, the extent of the damage, the areas affected, and the types of materials damaged.
- Establish whether the off-site server is backed up and functional.

Salvaging the Collection

Your approach to salvaging the collection should reflect the priorities that you established during the planning phase. It is important, however, to take into account the accessibility of materials and the extent of the damage.

- Identify and gather emergency supplies from the disaster kit.
- Organize your response team.
- Contact designated parent association officers.
- Wear appropriate safety protection when entering the disaster area.

Water Issues with Books

Flood or Severe Water Leak

- Wet library materials should be cared for immediately. Use caution in handling all wet items.

Handling Precautions for Books

- Do not open volumes, or close those that have fallen open.
- Do not separate covers from text blocks.
- Do not press water out of wet books—the paper is too fragile when wet.

Packing Books to Be Frozen

- Wrap each volume (or every other) in freezer or waxed paper (coated side in). Wrap a single sheet around, open at the fore-edge. Wrapping keeps frozen books from sticking together and keeps dyes from bleeding from one book cover to another. These can then be placed in individual freezer bags, although they are not necessary.
- Pack books spine down in boxes or crates lined with plastic trash bags. Full boxes are desirable to prevent further distortion. If boxes will not be put in freezers immediately, however, do not fill them completely (wet books will continue to swell).

- Do not close wet books that have fallen open. Pack them as is on top of a layer of packed books with waxed paper beneath.

- If your bar codes are attached to the outside of the books, and if your catalog is working, check books out to a "Book Repair" patron to keep track of them. In addition, label each box with the library's name and number each box. Create a list of each box's contents to keep while books are being dried. Note the call number range, number of volumes, and whether materials are wet or damp.

- Call freezer vendors as soon as possible for the transfer of wet materials.

Related Issues

- If water is leaking from above, cover materials with plastic sheeting. Place wastepaper baskets under leaks. If entire rows of materials are bulging with water damage, wait for assistance from others before trying to relocate them.

- Library materials that are not yet in a flooded area should be moved away from the water source and covered with sheeting.

CDs and Computers
Salvage and Recovery Procedures for Compact Disks (CDs)

- Compact disks that are damaged by mud or sewage should be washed in soapy water at room temperature and then rinsed in distilled water. They can be air dried or gently wiped with a soft, lint-free cloth in straight lines from the center to the outer edge.

- If the CDs are damaged by fresh water, they just need to be rinsed in distilled water and dried as mentioned above.

Computers

- All computer damage should be referred to IT personnel. If the librarian is responsible for computer technology, equipment recovery should be prioritized in the planning phase and recovered or salvaged accordingly.

Figure 21.2. Response and Recovery (*cont.*).

Insects and Other Pests

Pests can become a problem in a library at any time, but especially if there is a break in the building during a disaster through which insects, mice, bats, and other small animals can enter the institution. Insects in particular like a moist environment, with the relative humidity between 60 and 80 percent.

Pests that may nest in a library include cockroaches, silverfish, book mites, and termites. These pests eat book bindings and adhesives as well as seeking shelter within the stacks. Termites will eat into the book covers and damage library materials as well as the structure of the school building. These issues become more pressing after a disaster, which is why it is imperative to monitor a flooded environment for pests in addition to mold growth.

Fire and Smoke Emergency

Libraries should be equipped with smoke detectors, zoned sprinklers, and at least one fire extinguisher. In the prevention plan, the librarian has assessed the library's fire safety with the building facilities manager. Generally speaking, though, if a fire does break out, all staff should exit the building and call fire and police departments according to your school emergency plan.

Items that survive the fire, but are not damaged by water, will be charred, melted, or otherwise distorted, and covered in ash. Decide which items are to be salvaged and which should be replaced. HEPA vacuums will be effective in removing dry soot. Smoke odor, however, is nearly impossible to eliminate. "Records which survived the 1906 San Francisco fire and are today in the National Archives still smell strongly of smoke—over 90 years later" (Trinkley n.d.).

Resuming Normal Operations

Once the Sidwell library knew the scope of the loss, they began the recovery process. They printed out shelf lists by section and began a hand inventory. Somehow, they had retained a few books from each Dewey section. On the advice of the more experienced library directors, the librarian began calling publishers' sales representatives. All of their names (which were lost with the rolodex) were found on the publishers' Web sites. Many nonfiction books in series for middle schoolers are still sold exclusively through the publisher rather than distributors such as Baker & Taylor. In this situation, contacting the reps was definitely the right thing to do.

Thomson Gale responded immediately. They automatically considered this a "natural" disaster and offered to replace all exact titles at a 50 percent discount. Any like-replacements, they offered at 30 percent off. And since the librarian had such an enormous order, she paid no shipping costs. The librarian decided to order noncirculating reference titles first. That way, as the replacement collection grew, all titles would be available to all students. She ordered everything she could from Thomson Gale over the next few weeks. Hundreds of books were delivered within weeks.

Once the books began rolling in, the librarian trained a few key parents to do the processing. Sidwell had always had parent volunteers, but this needed a large-scale assembly line of people working. One parent took on the job of organizing work sessions and training a large crew of volunteers. After library staff printed bar code and spine labels and added a "truck replacement" note to each record, the crew of parent volunteers attached the bar codes and spine labels, stamped, pocketed, and covered books for almost the entire year. Not all publishers responded as Thomson Gale did. The librarian reordered missing and like books through other sales reps as needed, but the Thomson Gale experience was never replicated.

In the early stages, getting the library open with any materials at all for teaching was a challenge. Perhaps you are thinking that information needs could have been filled by using the many databases that Sidwell subscribed to? No. At the time of the renovation, the school had also renovated the technology plan. All previously owned computers were discarded or given away at the end of the prior school year, and new computers had been purchased over the summer. They were not installed and ready for student use, however, until early December. There were no library books and no research databases for students at all for the first trimester of school. Life was very interesting as the library entered the recovery phase.

Working with Faculty

After the disaster has been cleaned up and library operations have been restored, it is important to keep the faculty informed as more materials become available. They need to be reminded that things are not going to be the same as they were before the disaster—nor will they be for a very long time. Depending on the size and depth of the loss, the librarian will need to do the following:

- Solicit from each department (or faculty member) a list of planned projects that involve library research. Use this list along with priority checklists to begin planning the repurchasing of materials.

- Let teachers know immediately what materials are available, if any, for a particular research assignment. Emphasize that teachers will have to rethink and adapt that project, eliminate it, or change its order in the calendar year until the materials become available. *Teachers will not want to do this, nor will they remember to* —you must repeat, repeat, and repeat this step.

- If the loss is of books only, and online materials are intact, work with faculty to adapt their assignments to include more online source information. This is not an ideal solution, but it is a reasonably quick, albeit temporary, fix.

- Inform the local public library of the loss. That library may be able to help supplement the school library collection on a long-term basis as you begin rebuilding the collection.

- Encourage your faculty members to use their own public library cards (and obtain an educator's library card for themselves) to supplement their teaching materials and help you meet student needs. They may not want to do this either, but it is a good way to remind everyone that libraries exist in a community to serve a community.

• Enlist the help of your parent association. Once you begin repurchasing materials you will want those materials catalogued and on the shelves as quickly as possible. Use one or a few key parents in book processing and have them train a whole crew of parents to work weekly for as long as you need them. Make sure the parent group is organized to report to one specific head parent, not the library staff. Under normal parent volunteer circumstances, this kind of hierarchy is not usually needed or even preferred, but during a disaster recovery, the librarian must be able to rely on one lead parent to handle the rest of the volunteers, so that he or she can spend energy and time with vendors, sales reps, faculty, students, and library staff.

Working with Students

Teachers will be concerned with nonfiction materials for student research needs, but students will be concerned with their pleasure reading in addition to their homework needs. Sometimes, of course, these two overlap—in the case of required quiet reading for homework and daily or weekly silent reading in homeroom classes. The librarian may need to limit the number of items a student may check out at a given time, if that has not been a practice before, or reduce that limit if the school already imposes one, until the library has fully recovered.

This is a good time, if it hasn't been done already, to have the local public librarian come in to meet with classes or take a field trip to the local public library to get library cards for all students who do not yet have one.

Like the faculty, students, too, will "forget" that their books have been destroyed. Booktalking what remains of the collection during the course of the recovery will help remind students that there are still books for them. In fact, it might be the best time for them to discover an old gem that they otherwise would not have read.

Conclusion

A disaster recovery plan is at best an outline of what to do during and immediately following an emergency, but it does not specify how to organize a recovery effort beyond the technicalities of physical recovery from immediate damage. Nor does it tell you what the recovery process will look and feel like in your particular institution with your particular school culture.

A loss of thousands of books will take years of hard work to recover. At the time of this writing, it has been three years since Sidwell's "moving" disaster, and the library is still recovering the loss. Well meaning but ill-informed community members will want to donate materials right away. Be wary of this. This is not the time to have people unload the books their children have outgrown. In fact, this is the last thing a librarian needs—unless a systematic plan and qualified staff for receiving donated materials are already in place. Refer to your library's selection and gift policies before taking this on, and only do so if you have a qualified library employee or regular parent volunteer to tend to it. (See essay 15.)

Contents of a Basic Disaster Kit

Plastic sheeting (4 ml)

Freezer paper

Duct tape

Masking tape

Caution tape

Paper towels

Latex gloves

Large sponges, squeegee

Flashlight and battery

Disposable camera

Paper, pens

Waterproof markers

Humidistat

Library disaster plan

The same well-meaning people will ask, "Isn't everything you need online? Do we need to repurchase books? Might this be the best time to rethink the library, its mission, and its direction?" First and foremost, librarians know that everything students need is not online. (See essay 8 for details of this discussion.) It is true that libraries in the twenty-first century have undergone change, as well as delivery methods for information. We know more about how children learn. But the time to develop a new strategic plan for a school and its library is NOT during an emergency. The mission of a school and its library require and deserve calm, reflective thought with the community as its focus, not its possessions or lack thereof.

Copies of the library disaster plan should be stored in the library's disaster kit, in library offices, and at the homes of library staff, in case the school or library is inaccessible during a disaster. The plan should be updated annually to account for changes in personnel, hardware, software, and the building. A disaster plan will not guarantee full recovery from a disaster, but it may minimize the impact afterward.

References

Kahn, Miriam B. 2003. *Disaster Response and Planning for Libraries*. 2nd ed. Chicago: ALA.

Lyrasis. n.d. "Disaster Resources." In *Lyrasis: Advancing Libraries Together*. Lyrasis. Available at www.lyrasis.org/. Accessed June 16, 2009.

New York University. 2007. *Disaster Planning and Preparedness.* New York University Libraries. November–December. Available at http://library.nyu.edu/ preservation/disaster/planningpreparedness.html. Accessed June 16, 2009.

Trinkley, Michael. n.d. "Protecting Your Institution from Wildfires: Planning Not to Burn and Learning to Recover." *CoOl: Conservation Online.* Stanford University. Available at http://c00-palimpsest.stanford.edu/byauth/trinkley/ wildfire.html. Accessed June 22, 2009.

University Libraries. 2008. *Disaster Plan.* University of Maryland. July 31. Available at www.umd.edu/TSD/. Accessed June 16, 2009.

Wellheiser, Johanna, Jude Scott, and John Barton. 2002. *An Ounce of Prevention: Integrated Disaster Planning for Archives, Libraries, and Record Centres.* 2nd ed. Lanham, MD: Scarecrow.

Helpful Organizations

American Association of Museums
1575 Eye Street NW, Suite 400
Washington, DC 20005
202-289-1818
www.aam-us.org

Conservation Center for Art and Historical Artifacts (CCAHA)
264 South 23rd Street
Philadelphia, PA 19103
215-545-0613
www.ccaha.org

Institute of Museum and Library Services (IMLS)
1800 M Street NW, 9th floor
Washington, DC 20036-5802
202-653-4657
www.imls.gov

Northeast Document Conservation Center (NEDCC)
100 Brickstone Square
Andover, MA 01810-1494
978-470-1010
www.nedcc.org

Society of American Archivists
17 North State Street, Suite 1425
Chicago, IL 60602-3315
312-606-0722
www.archivists.org

Visit http://lu.com/excellence for supporting links and occasional updates to all essays in this book.

Cynthia Grady has worked in libraries for ten years and before that was a classroom teacher. She has taught students in kindergarten and graduate school and many grades in between. She currently works at Sidwell Friends School in Washington, DC (www. sidwell.edu; www.sidwell.edu/libraries/index.aspx).

Appendix A:
NAIS Guidelines of Professional Practice for Librarians*

At the heart of the independent school library program is a professionally trained librarian who:

1. As a member of the faculty, partners with teaching colleagues to integrate information, technology, and research skills into the curriculum.

2. Motivates and guides students to appreciate literature and reading.

3. Teaches information-seeking, critical analysis of sources, citation methods, synthesis, and the ethical use of information, and is thus a strong resource to students, teachers, and the school.

4. Provides intellectual, physical, and virtual access to print and digital learning materials that are efficiently organized and conveniently stored according to accepted standards.

5. Evaluates continually the currency, quality, depth, and breadth of the collection.

6. Understands the school's curriculum so that he or she can develop a collection that coordinates with long-term teaching goals as well as current and emerging needs.

7. Maintains a facility that is active, inviting, and conducive to student and faculty learning.

8. Utilizes a variety of interactive tools to provide services, information, and tutorials to the learning community.

9. Encourages both formal and informal input from the school community into the types, quality, and format of the information resources provided.

10. Partners with the school administration to provide knowledge, vision, and leadership to plan for change and the future success of the library program and thus guarantees that the library facilities, collection, and staffing will continue to meet the needs of the school over time.

11. Assesses the effectiveness of the library media program on an ongoing, regular basis.

*Approved by NAIS in 2008. Reprinted with permission from the National Association of Independent Schools.

12. Leads the school community in support of the principles of intellectual freedom, free inquiry, and equal access to information.

13. Offers professional growth opportunities (e.g., workshops, reading groups) for faculty on topics of current and emerging importance.

14. Maintains a personal commitment to professional growth by remaining current in the fields of library and information science, education, and emerging technologies.

Appendix B:
Librarian's Performance Assessment

NAME: _____ TITLE: _____

DATE: _____ EVALUATOR: _____ TITLE: _____

Definition of Rating:

M/E SS—Meets/Exceeds School Standards   **UNS**—Unsatisfactory
NMI — Needs Minor Improvement   **N/A** —Not Applicable

(The school standards include the regulations listed in the faculty contract and in the faculty handbook.)

Open to Growth	M/E SS	NMI	UNS	N/A
1. As a member of the faculty, partners with teaching colleagues to integrate information, technology, and research skills into the curriculum.				
2. Understands the school's curriculum so that he or she can develop a collection that coordinates with long-term teaching goals as well as current and emerging needs.				
3. Partners with the school administration to provide knowledge, vision, and leadership to plan for change and the future success of the library program and thus guarantees that the library facilities, collection, and staffing will continue to meet the needs of the school over time.				
4. Maintains a personal commitment to professional growth by remaining current in the fields of library and information science, education, and emerging technologies.				

Comments on Open to Growth:

_____

_____

Professionally and Intellectually Competent

Administrative Competencies	M/E SS	NMI	UNS	N/A
1. Assesses the effectiveness of the library media program on an ongoing, regular basis.				
2. Meetings/events are well prepared.				
3. Maintains administrative authority in positive manner.				
4. Maintains nourishing relationship with stakeholders.				
5. Demonstrates a thorough knowledge of administrative area				
6. Communicates effectively with students, faculty and other community members.				

Comments on Administrative Competencies:

_____

_____

Professional Competencies	M/E SS	NMI	UNS	N/A
1. Teaches information-seeking, critical analysis of sources, citation methods, synthesis, and the ethical use of information, and is thus a strong resource to students, teachers, and the school.				
2. Provides intellectual, physical, and virtual access to print and digital learning materials.				
3. Evaluates continually the currency, quality, depth, and breadth of the collection.				
4. Uses a variety of interactive tools to provide services, information, and tutorials to the learning community				

5. Encourages both formal and informal input from the school community into the types, quality, and format of the information resources provided.				

Comments on Professional Competencies:

_____

_____

Committed to Doing Justice	M/E SS	NMI	UNS	N/A
1. Leads the school community in support of the principles of intellectual freedom, free inquiry, and equal access to information.				
2. Provides a clear and accurate evaluation of people supervised on a regular and predictable basis.				
3. Provides clear and just expectations for students.				
4. Supports the school's commitment to a diverse student body.				
5. Models behavior which demonstrates respect for others in interpersonal relationships with peers and students.				
6. Supports the school's commitment to Christian service.				

Comments on Doing Justice:

_____

_____

Pursues Leadership Growth	M/ SS	NMI	UNS	N/A
1. Maintains membership in and reads research in appropriate professional organizations/journals.				
2. Effectively takes the lead in organizing or helping to organize faculty and/or student activities				
3. Seeks the advice of administrators, faculty and staff prior to decision-making.				
4. Shares concerns directly with involved parties.				
5. Takes initiative and anticipates difficulties & problems.				

Comments on Pursues Leadership Growth:

Loving	M/E SS	NMI	UNS	N/A
1. Treats students in a loving and professional manner.				
2. Treats colleagues in a loving and professional manner.				
3. Treats parents in a loving and professional manner.				
4. Actively serves on school committees and/or co-curriculars.				
5. Provides encouragement and praise for students and faculty				
6. Motivates and guides students to appreciate literature and reading.				
7. Maintains a facility that is active, inviting, and conducive to student and faculty learning.				

	M/E SS	NMI	UNS	N/A
8. Offers professional growth opportunities (e.g. workshops, reading groups) for faculty on topics of current and emerging importance.				

Comments on Loving:

_____

_____

Religious	M/E SS	NMI	UNS	N/A
1. Shows a positive attitude towards Bellarmine's mission.				
2. Contributes to the schools' ministry program				
3. Seeks to understand Ignatian vision of the school.				
4. Seeks to participate in religious life of the school.				

Comments on Religious:

_____

_____

Strengths

_____

_____

_____

Areas for Growth

_____

_____

_____

Librarian's Signature   **Date**

Administrative Supervisor's Signature   **Date**

Index